FROM LORD TO PATRON

FROM LORD
TO PATRON

Lordship in
late medieval England

J. M. W. BEAN

Manchester University Press

Published by Manchester University Press
Oxford Road, Manchester M13 9PL, UK

British Library cataloguing in publication data
Bean, J. M. W. (John Malcolm William), 1928–
    From lord to patron : lordship in late medieval England.
    1. England. Feudalism, 1154–1216.
    I. Title
    321.3'0942

ISBN 0 7190 2855 8 hardback

Typeset in Sabon
by Koinonia Limited, Manchester
Printed in Great Britain
by Billings of Worcester

CONTENTS

PREFACE

Some features of this book require an explanation. Like my previous two books, it forms part of a larger investigation into the landed society of late medieval England in all its social and economic aspects. It was originally my intention to devote no more than an article or two to the theme developed in the present work. But it became clear that a book was required. I also became convinced that previous studies of 'bastard feudalism' had been too brief and summary, sometimes simplistic, especially in their treatment of indentures of retinue. For this reason I attempt in this work to give the documents relating to the relationships of lord and man in late medieval England the same degree of detailed examination as has been taken for granted for generations in the study of their Anglo-Norman predecessors.

The result, however, is that the first three chapters, especially the second and third, may seem excessively technical, overdetailed, even dull, to some readers. But the issues so elaborated were important to contemporary lords and their followers. It is my conviction that the time has come when all the available evidence in this should receive a thorough examination. In the case of the details supplied regarding indentures of retinue some readers may feel the need for biographical detail that would bring the individuals concerned more to life. I certainly hope that the details supplied will be of use to those scholars who are interested in the political activities of the nobility and gentry of late medieval England. But the purpose of the present study is the delineation and analysis of the forms of relationship between lord and man in this period and an assessment of their importance.

It is a pleasure to acknowledge the assistance I have received in my research and writing. County archivists have been helpful in supplying photographs of documents in their custody. I benefited greatly from comments made by those who read the typescript for the publishers. Some of the research was carried out during my tenure of a Fellowship of the American Council of Learned Societies during the academic year 1976–77. Some of the costs of research and writing have been paid for by the Dunning Fund of the Department of History of Columbia University.

J. M. W. B.

ABBREVIATIONS

Note: Abbreviations have been employed in the case of all those secondary and printed original authorities cited outside a single section of a chapter.

Arch.Ael.   *Archaeologia Aeliana.*

Baldwin, 'Household administration'   J. F. Baldwin, 'The household administration of Henry Lacy and Thomas of Lancaster', *English Historical Review*, xlii (1927).

Bean, *Decline of Feudalism*   J. M. W. Bean, *The Decline of English Feudalism, 1215-1540* (Manchester, 1968).

Bean, *Percy Estates*   J. M. W. Bean, *The Estates of the Percy Family, 1416-1537* (Oxford, 1958).

Beauchamp Cart.   *The Beauchamp Cartulary Charters, 1100-1268*, ed. E. Mason (Publications of the Pipe Roll Society, lxxxi [New Series, xliii], London, 1980).

Berkeley Charters   *Descriptive Catalogue of the Charters and Muniments in the possession of the Rt. Hon. Lord Fitzhardinge at Berkeley Castle*, ed. I. H. Jeayes (Bristol, 1892).

BIHR   *Bulletin of the Institute of Historical Research.*

BL   The British Library.

Black Book   A. R. Myers, *The Household of Edward IV. The Black Book and the Ordinance of 1478* (Manchester, 1959).

Bodley   The Bodleian Library, University of Oxford.

BPR   *The Register of the Black Prince* (4 vols., London, 1930-3).

Brand, 'Oldcotes v. d'Arcy'   P. A. Brand, 'Oldcotes v. d'Arcy', in *Medieval Records Edited in Memory of C. A. F. Meekings*, ed. R. F. Hunnisett and J. B. Post (London, 1978).

CAD   *Catalogue of Ancient Deeds* (6 vols., London, 1890-1913).

Cal Inq. Misc.   *Calendar of Miscellaneous Inquisitions* (London, 1916–, in progress).

Cameron, 'Livery and retaining'   A. Cameron, 'The giving of livery and retaining in Henry VII's reign'. *Renaissance and Modern Studies*, xviii (1974).

Carpenter, 'Beauchamp affinity'   M. C. Carpenter, 'The Beauchamp affinity: a study of bastard feudalism at work'. *English Historical Review*, xcv (1980).

CCR   *Calendar of Close Rolls.*

Chesh. RO Cheshire County Record Office, Chester.

Comp. Peer.   *The Complete Peerage,* ed. G. E. Cockayne, new edn, (London, 1910–59).

Cooper, *Land, Men and Beliefs*   J. P. Cooper, *Land, Men and Beliefs: Studies in Early Modern History,* ed. G. E. Aylmer and J. S. Morrill (London, 1983).

CPR   *Calendar of Patent Rolls.*

Cumb. Westm. RO Cumberland and Westmorland Joint County Record Office, Carlisle.

Denholm-Young, *Seignorial Administration*   N. Denholm-Young, *Seignorial Administration in England* (Oxford, 1937).

Denton, *England in the Fifteenth Century*   W. Denton, *England in the Fifteenth Century* (London, 1888).

Devon RO Devon County Record Office.

DKR   *Thirty-Sixth Report of the Deputy Keeper of Public Records* (London, 1875), Appendix ii (*Calendar of Recognizance Rolls of the palatinate of Chester*).

Dugdale, *Baronage*   Sir William Dugdale, *The Baronage of England* (2 vols., London, 1675-76).

Dunham, *Hastings' Retainers*   W. H. Dunham, *Lord Hastings' Indentured Retainers, 1461-1483: The Lawfulness of Livery and Retaining under the Yorkists and Tudors* (Transactions of the Connecticut Academy of Arts and Sciences, xxxix (New Haven, Conn., 1955]).

East Sussex RO East Sussex County Record Office, Lewes.

Econ. H.R.   *Economic History Review.*

EHR   *English Historical Review.*

Fifteenth-century England   *Fifteenth-century England, 1399–1509,* ed. S. B. Chrimes, C. D. Ross and R. A. Griffiths (Manchester, 1972).

Fortescue, *Governance*   Sir John Fortescue, *The Governance of England,* ed. C. Plummer (Oxford, 1885).

Fowler, *Henry of Grosmont*   K. H. Fower, *The King's Lieutenant: Henry of Grosmont, first duke of Lancaster, 1310–1361* (London, 1961).

Guillaume le Maréchal   *Histoire de Guillaume le Maréchal,* ed. P. Meyer (4 vols., Paris, 1891–1901).

Hatton's Book of Seals   *Sir Christopher Hatton's Book of Seals,* ed. L. C. Loyd and D. M. Stenton (Oxford, 1950).

Hewitt, *Organization of War*   H. J. Hewitt, *The Organization of War under Edward III, 1338–62* (Manchester, 1966).

HMC   *Reports of the Historical Manuscripts Commission.*

Holmes, *Higher Nobility*   G. A. Holmes, *The Estates of the Higher Nobility in XIVth century England* (Cambridge, 1957).

JGRA   *John of Gaunt's Register, 1372–6,* ed. S. Armitage-Smith (2 vols; Camden Society, 3rd series, xx–xxi: London, 1911).

JGRB   *John of Gaunt's Register, 1379–83,* ed. E. C. Lodge and R. Somerville (2 vols., Camden Society, 3rd Series, lvi–vii, London, 1937).

Jones, 'Mohaut–Bracebridge indenture'   M. Jones, 'An indenture between Robert, lord Mohaut, and Sir John de Bracebridge for life service in peace and war, 1310', _Journal of the Society of Archivists,_ iv (1970–73).

Lancs. RO   Lancashire County Record Office, Preston.

Lewis, 'Indentured retinues'   N. B. Lewis, 'The organisation of indentured retinues in fourteenth-century England', _Transactions of the Royal Historical Society,_ Fourth Series, xxvii (1943), reprinted in _Essays in Medieval History,_ ed. R. W. Southern (London, New York, 1968).

Lewis, 'Gaunt indentures'   'Indentures of retinue with John of Gaunt, Duke of Lancaster, enrolled in Chancery, 1367–1399', ed. N. B. Lewis (Camden Society Miscellany, xxii, London, 1964).

Lewis, 'Decayed and non-feudalism'   P. S. Lewis, 'Decayed and non-feudalism in late medieval France', _Bulletin of the Institute of Historical Research,_ xxxvii (1964), reprinted in his _Essays in Later Medieval French History_ (London, 1985).

Longleat MS.   The Muniments of the Marquess of Bath at Longleat House, Wiltshire.

Lyon, _Fief to Indenture_   Bryce, D. Lyon, _From Fief to Indenture_ (Cambridge, Mass., 1957).

McFarlane, _Nobility_   K. B. McFarlane, _The Nobility of Later England_ (Oxford, 1973).

Maddicott, _Thomas of Lancaster_   J. R. Maddicott, _Thomas of Lancaster, 1307–1322: A Study in the Reign of Edward II_ (Oxford, 1970).

McFarlane, _Collected Essays_   K. B. McFarlane, _England in the Fifteenth Century: Collected Essays_ (London, 1981).

Morgan, _Medieval Cheshire_   P. Morgan, _War and Society in Medieval Cheshire, 1277–1403_ (Publications of the Chetham Society, Third Series, xxxiv, Manchester, 1987).

NCH   _A Northumberland County History_ (15 vols.: Newcastle-on-Tyne, 1893-1940).

Nicolas, _Agincourt_   Sir Harris Nicolas, _History of the Battle of Agincourt and of the Expedition of Henry the Fifth into France in 1415; to which is added, The Roll of the Men of Arms in the English Army_ (London, 1832).

Norfolk RO   Norfolk County Record Office, Norwich.

Northants, RO   Northamptonshire County Record Office, Northampton.

Northumb. RO   Northumberland County Record Office, Newcastle upon Tyne.

Ormond Deeds   _Calendar of Ormond Deeds (1172–1603),_ ed. E. Curtis (6 vols., Dublin, 1932–43).

Paris, _Chronica_   Matthew Paris, _Chronica Majora,_ ed. H. R. Luard (Rolls Series, 7 vols., London, 1872–83).

Paston Letters   _The Paston Letters,_ ed. J. Gairdner (new complete library edition, 6 vols., London, 1904).

Paston Letters and Papers   _Paston Letters and Papers,_ ed. N. Davis (Parts I and II, Oxford, 1971–76).

Perc. Chart.   _The Percy Chartulary,_ ed. M. T. Martin (Publications of the Surtees Society, cvii, London, Durham, 1911).

Phillips, *Aymer de Valence* J. R. S. Phillips, *Aymer de Valence, Earl of Pembroke, 1307–1324,* (Oxford, 1972).

Plucknett, *Legislation* T. F. T. Pluckett, *The Legislation of Edward I* (Oxford, 1949).

Plucknett, *Common Law* T. F. T. Plucknett, *A Concise History of the Common Law* (5th edn., London, 1959).

Plumpton Corr. *The Plumpton Correspondence,* ed. T. Stapleton (Publications of the Camden Society, Old Series, iv, London, 1839).

Prestwich, *War, Politics and Finance* M. C. Prestwich, *War, Politics and Finance under Edward I* (London, 1972).

PRO Public Record Office.

    C54 Chancery, Close Rolls.

    C66 Chancery, Patent Rolls.

    C146 Chancery, Ancient Deeds (Series C).

    DL25 Duchy of Lancaster, Ancient Deeds (Series L).

    DL26 Duchy of Lancaster, Ancient Deeds (Series LL).

    DL27 Duchy of Lancaster, Ancient Deeds (Series LS).

    E13 Exchequer, Plea Rolls.

    E40 Exchequer, Ancient Deeds (Series A).

    E101 Exchequer, King's Remembrancer, Various Accounts.

    E159 Exchequer, King's Remembrancer, Memoranda Rolls.

    E210 Exchequer, Ancient Deeds (Series E).

    E326 Exchequer, Ancient Deeds (Series EE).

    E368 Exchequer, Lord Treasurer's Remembrancer, Memoranda Rolls.

    CP40 Court of Common Pleas, Plea Rolls.

    Just.1 Justices Itinerant, Assize Rolls.

    KB26 *Curia Regis* Rolls.

    KB27 Court of King's Bench, *Coram Rege* Rolls.

Rawcliffe, *Staffords* C. Rawcliffe, *The Staffords, Earls of Stafford and Dukes of Buckingham, 1394–1521* (Cambridge, 1978).

Richardson and Sayles, *Governance* H. G. Richardson and G. O. Sayles, *The Governance of Medieval England* (Edinburgh, 1963).

Roskell, *Parliaments and Politics* J. S. Roskell, *Parliaments and Politics in Late Medieval England* (3 vols., London, 1981).

Rot. Parl. Rotuli Parliamentorum (Record Commission).

Saul, *Gloucestershire Gentry* N. Saul, *Knights and Esquires: The Gloucestershire Gentry in the Fourteenth Century* (Oxford, 1981).

Scott, *Stricklands* D. Scott, *The Stricklands of Sizergh Castle* (Kendal, 1908).

Somerville, *Duchy* R. Somerville, *History of the Duchy of Lancaster,* vol. i, 1285–1603, (London, 1953).

Stonor Letters The Stonor Letters and Papers, 1290–1483, ed. C. L. Kingsford (Publications of the Camden Society, Third Series, xxxix–xxx, 2 vols., London, 1919).

Storey, 'Liveries and Commissions of the Peace' R. L. Storey, 'Liveries and

Commissions of the Peace, 1388–90', in *The Reign of Richard II: Essays in Honour of May McKisack*, ed. F. R. H. Du Boulay and C. M. Barron (London, 1971).

Tout, *Chapters*   T. F. Tout, *Chapters in the Administrative History of Medieval England* (6 vols., Manchester, 1920–33, reprinted 1967).

Trans. Cumb. Westm. AAS   Transactions of the Cumberland and Westmorland Archaeological and Antiquarian Society.

TRHS   Transations of the Royal Historical Society.

Walter of Henley   D. Oschinsky, *Walter of Henley and other Treatises on Estate Management and Accounting* (Oxford, 1971).

War and Government   War and Government in the Middle Ages, ed. J. Gillingham and J. C. Holt (Woodbridge, Suff., 1984).

Warkworth, *Chronicle*   John Warkworth, *A Chronicle of the First Thirteen Years of the Reigh of King Edward the Fourth*, ed J. O. Halliwell (Publications of the Camden Society, First Series, x, London, 1839).

Waugh, 'Tenure to contract'   Scott L. Waugh, 'Tenure to contract: lordship and clientage in thirteenth-century England', *English Historical Review*, ci (1986).

Westm. Chron.   The Westminster Chronicle, 1381–1394, ed. and trans. L. C. Hector and B. F. Harvey (Oxford, 1982).

Wormald, *Lords and Men*   J. Wormald, *Lords and Men in Scotland: Bonds of Manrent, 1442–1603* (Edinburgh, 1985).

YBRS   Year Books, 20–35 Ed. I and 11–20 Ed. III, ed. A. J. Horwood and L. O. Pike (20 vols., Rolls Series).

YBSS   Year Book Series for the Reign of Edward II, Publications of the Selden Society (London, 1903–, in progress).

YBVE   Les Reports del Cases en Ley (London, 1678–80).

INTRODUCTION

Feudalism and 'bastard feudalism'

The present generation of historians of medieval Europe has, as one of its major tasks, the reassessment of the concepts of feudalism it has inherited from its predecessors. The growth of archival research, extending into the records of landowning families as well as those of central government, has exposed fundamental weaknesses in the ideas and definitions formed by historians of the nineteenth century who created most of the traditions in this area of medieval historical studies. Nor is this surprising. To a substantial extent their knowledge was based on sources that were available to the antiquarians of the seventeenth century; and it was these who originally created a picture of a society which their successors in the eighteenth century labelled as 'the feudal system' and which those of the nineteenth century converted into the 'feudalism' we study today.

In the development of these historical interpretations the inheritance of the historian of medieval England differs from those of his continental counterparts, especially those of France. On the continent the interaction between the political and social forces unleashed by the collapse of the Roman Empire and the efforts by rulers, both those of local territories and those who exercised a wider hegemony, to impose control has led historians to use the word 'feudalism' and its cognates in ways that do not distinguish between the ties that connected the nobility with one another and with their kings and those which bound the tillers of the soil to the lords immediately above them. This point of view has commended itself to those historians who accept, or find attractive, the Marxist conception of historical development, since its view of the 'feudal' stage stresses similar elements and relationships.

In the case of England, though there are those who emulate their continental colleagues, it is both possible and necessary to distinguish between the manorial system – the relationships between the lords of manors and their dependent peasantry – and the structure of a landowning hierarchy that owed military service to the king who stood at its head. The contrast with the continent is due to the different historical development of early England. The elements as well as the foundations of the manorial society were already there before the Normans conquered England. To be sure, outside the Church, the kingdom of England which was created in the five centuries or so following the Anglo-Saxon invasions was ruled by a warrior caste below its kings; but the relationships of this society were not organised along the firm tenurial lines that developed after the Norman Conquest. And a century after 1066 the appearance of a common law that was an instrument of royal authority and hinged on the protection of interests in the occupation and inheritance of land meant that the rights of feudal lord and feudal tenant were defined by royal judges and legal commentators. Over the past generation there has been much debate about the origin as of feudal institutions in England; but on the existence of a hierarchy of feudal tenures below the King by the end of the twelfth century there has to be agreement. This tenurial structure has, as it were, formed the hard core of English historians' understanding of the structure of land-owning society in medieval England. Many may have doubts about erecting this into a 'feudal system', let alone into an all-embracing 'feudalism', if only because there are so many aspects of English medieval society inadequately covered by such concepts. Even so, most of the land in England was held of the king by his tenants-in chief who had to swear oaths of homage and fealty and owed a specified obligation of military service when the king called out his host. The descending ladder of tenurial relationships which led down from the earls and barons and great church-men to the level of the manorial lord and even some of his peasant tenants, gave the lord at every level a body of rights over those who held of him that was a replica of those the king exercised over his tenants-in-chief. While some of these were activated only under special circumstances – an emergency in which the lord needed financial help or the age of an heir when an inheritance passed from one generation to another – the king's right to the military service of his tenants-in-chief was always there, ready to be activated by the king's command.

Conceptions of any system inevitably carry with them assumptions that it must decline. The historians of medieval Europe all share in common the view that the right of kings to call upon their leading subjects for milit-ary duty was increasingly less important as a source of their kingdoms' military resources from the thirteenth century onwards. But in the delineation of these changes English historians have achieved a degree of precision lacking among their continental counterparts. The close definitions that they have been able to employ in the description of a body of tenurial rights and obligations over the whole of the kingdom of England has meant that they have looked for the replacement of one 'system' by another.

For several generations English historians have operated with the concept of 'bastard feudalism'.[1] The classic study remains that of the late K. B. McFarlane, published in 1945.[2] This gave new meaning to a term employed in 1885 by the Victorian historian Charles Plummer.[3] On that occasion he had used the epithet 'bastard' in the sense of 'misbegotten, debased'. He did this in a depiction of late medieval English society which sought to explain its lawlessness and its failure to fulfil the promise inherent in the creation of parliamentary institutions by the beginning of the fourteenth century. Instead, McFarlane turned to another meaning contained in *The New Oxford English Dictionary* – 'having the appearance of, somewhat resembling'. In his view the relationship between lord and man in the fourteenth and fifteenth centuries had a superficial similarity with that of traditional feudalism but was different in its basic character.[4] 'Its quintessence was payment for service. The idea of lordship was retained, but because it was divorced from tenure it was a lordship which had undergone a scarcely visible process of transubstantiation, leaving all but a few of its accidents unchanged.' McFarlane went on to relate the emergence of this 'bastard feudalism' directly to the decline of the feudal system of military service and its replacement by a contract system under which the king's subjects were mobilised for war service in return for wages.[5] From the time of Edward III's campaigns in France in the 1340s onwards it was the practice of the kings of England to make written contracts with leading commanders, which specified the number of men each would bring in campaign and the conditions of their remuneration and service. In their turn these commanders subcontracted, delegating the actual work of recruitment to those who served as officers under them. Although the military prowess of lesser men could and sometimes did earn them a direct relationship with the crown, in the society of the day it was inevitable that most commanders would be leading nobles who then made subcontracts with their social inferiors, knights and squires, who in their turn recruited members of the lower orders as archers and other infantry. In general, runs the argument, the king made contracts for brief periods, often a single campaign. But the contracts made by his commanders, and even by those with whom they subcontracted, were often for life.

The combination of learning and lucidity displayed in McFarlane's

interpretation is part of the explanation for its dominance in the study of
late medieval English politics and society since 1945.[6] But this also owes
something to the word 'bastard'. More than a whiff of Plummer's views
remains in historians' minds, if only because contemporary lawlessness and
the contribution to it made by the leading nobility were demonstrably present, especially during the Wars of the Roses. Plummer, in fact, was maintaining a tradition which Bishop Stubbs had endowed with his immense
authority, viewing the late fourteenth and fifteenth centuries as a morally
offensive interlude in constitutional progress: and the epithet in 'bastard
feudalism' was employed with all its Victorian overtones.

Research on English military institutions over the next few generations
stressed the difference between those of the fourteenth century onwards
and those introduced after the Norman Conquest. The main outlines of
the contract system of military service were sketched; and the long conflict
with France, the so-called Hundred Years' War, was shown to be a palpably powerful influence in English politics and society, especially in making
the contract system part of the way of life of many nobility and gentry.
One element in 'bastard feudalism' stressed by Plummer and others had
been the 'overmighty subject' whose territorial power enabled him to
attempt to rival, sometimes defeat, the Crown in local affairs, while joining
with others of like strength and ambitions to dominate the central government. It was from the ranks of the 'overmighty subjects' that the king chose
his leading commanders in time of war. The contract system thus appeared
as one reason for the strength of such nobles, because the methods they
used to provide contingents for the king's wars could also be employed to
build up private armies in time of peace. At the same time emphasis on
the role of the contract system had the merit of linking late medieval
developments with those of the two centuries that followed the Norman
Conquest. There was an obvious connection, it seemed, between the
deficiencies of the feudal host as a fighting force – notably the limitation
to forty days' service – and the use of mercenaries by Richard and John.
Rooted in royal policies in these two reigns was a practice that was defined
kingdom-wide in the middle years of the reign of Henry III – the quota
system under which a tenant-in-chief sent only a small fraction of the
number of knights he owed the king, paying scutage on his remaining fees.
This could only appear as some sort of link betwen the feudal and the
contract systems, since its premises were the inadequacies of feudal arrangements and the Crown's need to find its armies outside these. Indeed, the
known chronology of events supported such an interpretation, since the
contract system appeared only a generation or so later in the Welsh wars

of Edward I. Although all these arguments were not spelled out in McFarlane's exposition, historians' awareness of them helps to explain their ready acceptance of his definition of 'bastard feudalism'. Within a few years T. F. T. Plucknett in his discussion of the statute of *Quia Emptores* (1290) in his Ford Lectures on *The Legislation of Edward I* stressed its abolition of subinfeudation as a factor in the origins of 'bastard feudalism'.[7]

Once the classic definition has been achieved, work on this subject tended to develop at two levels. At one of these a great deal more information about the contract system in the late thirteenth and fourteenth centuries was collected.[8] At the other level historians working within the framework of the McFarlane interpretation produced results that enlarged its dimensions in ways that raised important questions. It was demonstrated that lawlessness on the part of bands of retainers recruited by great lords was not the sole preserve of the late fourteenth and fifteenth centuries. In 1957 G. A. Holmes showed that the reign of Edward II was 'the first age of turbulant bastard feudalism'.[9] This, and later more detailed work on this reign by J. R. Maddicott[10] and J. R. S. Phillips,[11] indicate that the sort of relationships between lord and man comprised in 'bastard feudalism' must have been fully developed well before the beginning of Edward III's war with France. Indeed, indentures of retinue remarkably similar to those of the next century have been discovered in the latter half of the thirteenth century. In 1972 M. C. Prestwich[12] concluded his analysis of households and retinues in the wars of Edward I by stating that 'The way in which the cavalry was organised in retinues shows that the so-called "bastard feudalism" of the later middle ages was already well-established in the reign of Edward I.'

How far back, then, into earlier centuries of medieval England must we now push our concepts of 'bastard feudalism'? Issues raised by the work of other historians suggest fundamental weaknesses in the basic assumptions underlying the classic interpretation of 'bastard feudalism'. In 1955 W. H. Dunham opened up several problems in his analysis of the indentures of retinue of a Yorkist peer and courtier, William, lord Hastings. He stressed the absence in these documents of a financial relationship between lord and man, arguing[13] that there occurred in the reign of Edward IV the 'final substitution of what medieval men called good lordship – aid, favor, support, and preferment – for the fee'. But can we be certain that this phenomenon belonged only to the latter half of the fifteenth century? Dunham at one point stressed that 'the character of lordship in Yorkist England resembled the Old English institution more than it did the intervening Norman–Angevin feudal tenancy'.[14] At the other end of the chronological spectrum

H. G. Richardson and G. O. Sayles,[15] building on a study published by J. O. Prestwich[16] in 1954,[16] have argued vigorously against the notion that a contract system of military service emerged only in the thirteenth century. On their side is the demonstrable fact that William the Conqueror and his sons found the feudal resources of England inadequate as a supply of men for their wars and hired mercenaries, at times on a quite remarkable scale, the Anglo-Norman methods of government being dominated by the need to raise money for this purpose. Richardson and Sayles rightly stress that the employment of mercenaries must have involved contractual relationships. Their arguments are certainly strengthened by the discovery in recent years of a number of written contracts made before 1300, the earliest belonging to 1270.[17]

It is important to place the results of this research in its proper perspective. As soon as we admit the existence of written contracts before 1300, we have to remember that our knowledge of the existence of these is a very recent development; and we thus encounter the possibility that the quantity of information at our disposal is simply a reflection of the luck of survival. It is unwise to assume that there were not many more written contracts than we know of in the late thirteenth-century; and we must also consider the possibility that some at least were made in the first half of that century or even earlier. Nor does an accurate reading of the Statute of *Quia Emptores* permit us to accept the existence of a direct connection between the effects of this statute and the emergence of 'bastard feudalism'. The statute's abolition cf subinfeudation applied only to grants of land in fee simple; after 1290 it remained legal for a lord to grant a man a portion of land to be held of him for life and there was no legal constraint forcing the creation of money fees.[18]

Furthermore, even without the conclusions of these scholars and the questions and doubts they raise, it is possible to detect fundamental weaknesses in the classic interpretation of 'bastard feudalism'. In the first place, the foundations of our knowledge of the social phenomena comprised in this term (as distinct from the contract system of military service) lie in a body of indentures made by great lords with knights or squires for the lives of these men. But there was no necessary reason why a commander who had contracted with the king should then make agreements for life with the men he recruited. The classic view leaves us to assume that he needed to maintain a nucleus of knights and squires to whom he could turn for his subcontractors in recruiting and his officers on campaign whenever the king's decision to take the field made this necessary.[19] 'If this was so, an ancillary advantage would certainly have been the assurance that knights and squires of the highest quality of leadership would b~ manently available. And an additional inducement would hav~ power and influence in time of peace promised by the existen body of permanent dependents, strengthened as this would ~ ~ord chose for this purpose knights and squires tied to him by traditions of family loyalty or dwelling in areas where he himself was territorially powerful. But such arguments provide an explanation for life-contracts that lies totally outside the arrangements and needs of the contract system of military service. In the light of all these considerations, it is difficult to avolid the conclusion that there has never been a thorough analysis of the relationship between the contract system and 'bastard feudalism', despite the importance given it in the classic interpretation.[20]

In the second place, McFarlane[21] and others in their discussions of 'bastard feudalism' have observed the existence, side by side with the retaining of men for life by indenture of retinue, the practice of granting annuities, or pensions, as rewards for past services and as inducements to perform similar services in the future. McFarlane himself stressed the importance of this practice, stating that, because annuities generally issued from the revenues of particular manors, 'There thus came into existence between a great lord and those who actually cultivated his estates a class of pensioners resembling the mesne tenants of the old feudalism.'[22] If the contract system of military service played a crucial role in creating 'bastard feudalism', its relationship with annuities for past and future services needs to be examined,[23] especially since the services involved in the grant of an annuity might not be military at all. An effort in this direction has, in fact, recently been made by Professor Scott L. Waugh. In effect, he sees the indenture of retinue developing out of the practice of granting annuities. He argues that the breakdown of relationships based on the tenure of land by the beginning of the thirteenth century led to the emergence of the practice of paying for services by means of annual payments of money, a process facilitated by the development of a jurisdiction over such contractual obligations on the part of the royal courts.[24]

Although no historian can be entirely free from the inheritance of preconceptions and conclusions he has inherited from his predecessors, the state of our present knowledge of 'bastard feudalism' suggests that in any further investigation an effort should be made to strip away the assumptions of earlier historiography and proceed from an awareness that the concept of 'bastard feudalism' arose at a time when historians had much less evidence at their disposal than is currently available and were proceeding from premises that have long since been rejected or seriously revised. Together the classic interpretation of 'bastard feudalism' and the additions, to, and criticisms of, it that have appeared since 1945 inevitably form the framework of the present study. But its theme is the development of the relationship between lord and man within the ranks of landowning society in late medieval England. The term 'bastard feudalism' occasionally has to make its appearance in the discussions that follow; but this is because from time to time it is necessary to refer to current views that bear on the interpretation of particular evidence.

Notes

1 For discussion of similar phenomena in France see Lewis, 'Decayed and non-feudalism'.

2 Reprinted in McFarlane, *Collected Essays*, pp. 23–43. McFarlane's discussion, as he himself stressed, was indebted to a paper by N. B. Lewis which had been delivered the previous year ('The organisation of indentured retinues in fourteenth-century England', *TRHS*, 4th Ser., xxv (1947), [reprinted in *Essays in Medieval History*, ed. R.W. Southern (London, New York, 1968), pp. 200–12]. But this had a much narrower focus than McFarlane's study and, because of this, has not had the same sort of impact. McFarlane himself had employed the concept of 'bastard feudalism' two years earlier in his study of the relationships of lords and commons in parliament and parliamentary elections ('Parliament and "bastard feudalism"', *TRHS*, 4th Ser., xxvi (1944), reprinted *Essays*, ed. Southern, pp. 240–69).

3 Fortescue, *Governance*, Introd., pp., 15–16.

4 McFarlane, *Collected Essays*, p. 24.

5 *Ibid.*

6 A tendency to drop the inverted commas is a telling illustration of this.

7 Plucknett, *Legislation*, pp. 107–8. His views were echoed by F. M. Powicke, *The Thirteenth Century* (Oxford, 1953), pp. 379–80; and by Holmes, *Higher Nobility*, p. 83.

8 See especially the list of indentures in Jones, 'Mohaut–Bracebridge indenture'.

9 Holmes, *Higher Nobility*, p.82.

10 Maddicott, *Thomas of Lancaster*, pp.. 40–46.

11 Phillips, *Aymer de Valence*, pp. 253–68.

12 Prestwich, *War, Politics and Finance*, p. 66.

13 Dunham, *Hastings' Retainers*, p. 9.

14 *Ibid.*, p. 52. See also *ibid.*, p. 10.

15 J. O. Prestwich, 'War and finance in the Anglo-Norman state', *TRHS*, 5th ser., iv (1954).

16 Richardson and Sayles, *Governance*, p. 463.

17 Listed in Jones, 'Mohaut–Bracebridge indenture', pp. 391–4.

18 Bean, *Decline of Feudalism*, pp. 306–9.

19 E.g., Lewis, 'Indentured retinues', pp. 203–5, esp. p. 205: 'it was the members

of the indentured retinues, retained to serve their lords for life in peace and war, who mitigated the instability of the contract army by providing a force always ready and under contract to save whatever it was required'.

20 The issue is touched on in a later version of McFarlane's views which appears in his posthumously published sixth Ford lecture (McFarlane, *Nobility*, p. 104). See also his remarks in McFarlane, *Collected Essays*, pp. 45–6, 52–3.

21 E.g., *ibid.*, pp. 29–30.

22 *Ibid.*, p. 29.

23 This issue is touched on in Bean, *Decline of Feudalism*, pp. 306–7, and in Lewis, 'Gaunt indentures', p. 81.

24 Waugh, 'Tenure to contract'.

I

The forms of relationship between lord and man

Any discussion of the relationship between lord and man in late medieval England must, like all previous inquiries into 'bastard feudalism' be based primarily on the surviving indentures of retinue, the written agreements laying down the terms of service and reward. So large do these bulk in the sources available that their language – the employment of the term 're-tained'[1] in its Latin or French forms – has given rise to the word 'retainer'[2] which has long been used as a general description of a lord's following, as distinct from the more limited meaning of the term from which it is derived. In the more general sense the word is encountered outside the period of 'bastard feudalism'. Yet at the outset it is necessary to be cautious over the general use of this term and to be aware of its vagueness and ambiguity. Even a cursory reading of McFarlane's seminal study, or of any of the discussions of 'bastard feudalism' that have appeared since it, shows that not every 'retainer' was tied to his lord by an indenture of retinue. Some simply received annuities; and there were those who merely wore their lord's livery and received his pay without the relationship being defined in an indenture. It is thus desirable to define the forms of relationship with as much clarity as possible. Three forms are to be found in existing authorities – one an agreement made in the form of an indenture of retinue, one the grant of an annuity, and the third the wearing of livery. In one respect these should not be regarded as mutually exclusive, since a retainer also wore his lord's livery. At the same time there is another form of relationship which requires discussion. In a substantial number of indentures of retinue the man retained is described as a 'bachelor'; and this term is also encountered in the letters patent, or charters, granting annuities and in documents relating to estate administration. Because of the kinds of contexts in which we see this term, it makes sense to investigate its meaning and examine the connection between it and the other forms of the relationship between lord and man.

The purpose of such a structural approach is to provide definitions of contemporary terminology that might in due course assist in a close analysis of the complex of relationships that has been labelled 'bastard feudalism'. Yet there are also grounds for caution in following even this approach. Any understanding we reach of the various forms of relationship should not blind us to the continuing imperfections of our knowledge. The historian of the relationships between lord and man in late medieval England should not be under the illusion that his evidence exists in the quantity available to those who study feudal relationships in the two centuries following the Norman Conquest or provide as solid a basis for investigation. To be sure, recent scholarship suggests that the historians of this generation can no longer approach their evidence with the confidence of J. H. Round or Sir Frank Stenton.[3] Even so, there are many more deeds and charters dealing with feudal landholding in the twelfth century alone than there are indentures of retinue from the late thirteenth to the fifteenth century; and these can be evaluated within the context of the developing law of real property. The historian of 'bastard feudalism' can eke out his knowledge from the texts of parliamentary legislation, from the financial records of great lords and a few collections of family correspondence. But there are many great families for which no financial records have survived, or very few, and only three families – the Pastons, the Stonors and the Plumptons – belonging to the gentry as distinct from the parliamentary nobility, have left substantial bodies of private correspondence. Above all, the assistance we gain from such additional sources of information is often fraught with problems of interpretation. The historian of feudal institutions in any period is ultimately the beneficiary of the lawyers of past centuries. The deeds and charters that tell us about feudal institutions in the late eleventh and twelfth centuries have survived through the generations since they were written because they were deeds of title. But there was no essential need for families or their legal advisers or administrators to preserve indentures of retinue or any other similar documents beyond the settlement of a lord's or a retainer's affairs after his death. Occasionally family pride or antiquarian interest might lead to survival – for example, in the form of a copy entered in a family cartulary[4] – but in terms of our documentation as a whole such survivals are comparative rarities. In fact, almost all the surviving indentures of retinue we owe to three circumstances. First, the seizure of the throne by Henry of Lancaster in 1399 which brought into the hands of the Crown the estates of the duchy of Lancaster, the largest noble inheritance in late medieval England. Its archives have stayed, in consequence, in the hands of the Crown down to the present day and, while only a portion of these relating to the period before 1399 now exists, it does include registers of John of Gaunt for the years 1372–76 and 1379–83 which contain indentures of retinue for life he made with many knights and squires.[5] Second, good fortune has preserved a total of sixty-nine life indentures made with his followers by William, lord Hastings (d. 1483). Third, the patent rolls of the royal chancery contain a number of confirmations of life-indentures made by the Crown after the death or forfeiture of the magnate who had made them.[6] This practice arose from a rule of law dating back to the mid-thirteenth century under which a tenant-in-chief could not alienate without royal licence; and this in turn led to legislation in 1327 under which alienations of land held in chief without licence could be permitted to stand provided a pardon was sued.[7] Strictly speaking, a grant of a retainer's fee or annuity involving payment out of landed revenues of lands held in chief fell within the terms of this rule of law. It is fair to assume that more often than not a lord did not bother to sue out a license before such a grant was made; but his death leaving an heir within age and thus subject to royal wardship or his forfeiture through treason would put the recipient's financial interest at risk.

In view of the sparsity and inadequacies of our evidence, we cannot be absolutely sure that every relationship between lord and man in late medieval England took the form of an indenture of retinue, an annuity, or the wearing of livery. And, indeed, there are occasional glimpses into other forms of relationship.[8] In 1252 William de Wydendon demised his lands to Sir Philip Basset for seven years in return for an undertaking that Sir Philip would keep him in his service and provide him with food and clothing as one of his squires.[9] In 1333 Richard, son of Sir Henry Trafford, entered the service of a Lancashire gentleman, William Botiller of Warrington, in return for the giving of counsel and the receipt of robes:[10] a bond of 33 marks was to be forfeited to Richard if he was dismissed without cause.[11] In 1470 several individuals in Cumberland entered into a bond of £40 to serve a local gentleman, Thomas Sandforth, against all men except the king for life, undertaking also never to serve John Salkeld, another local gentleman.[12] The use of bonds for such purposes is especially interesting because recent scholarship has shown that 'bastard feudalism' in late medieval Scotland involved this form of relationship.[13] But it is unwise to do more than note the existence of these bonds for a similar purpose in England.[14] There are remarkably few of them; and each may well reflect special circumstances. The agreement between Trafford and

Botiller may simply involve an arrangement under which a young man (possibly a younger son) sought a career in the service of a leading local family and had enough influence to secure good terms for himself. Thomas Sandforth's agreement with his followers was an attempt to secure support amongst local landowners in local feuds,[15] one of which was between him and John Salkeld: those who made this agreement with him were not members of the gentry class, a fact that might have made the indenture of retinue seem inappropriate.[16] And a member of the Cumberland gentry was probably aware of the practice involved over the Border.

(i) Annuities and indentures of retinue

Even a cursory examination of the indentures of retinue that have survived from the late thirteenth century onwards, shows that they were complex documents and that important changes can be observed in them over a period of two centuries or so.[17] But for the purpose of delineating their nature and basic structure it is possible to define certain characeristics that remained constant. There were in fact two copies of every indenture, one retained by the lord and the other by the man retained.[18] These were written on a single piece of parchment and were then separated by means of an indented cut – that is, one with jagged, or tooth-like edges that would help, if ever the two copies were compared, to establish authenticity. They were finally sealed interchangeably, the lord attaching his seal to the retainers's copy, the latter attaching his to his lord's. In law the effect of this transaction was an enforceable agreement between the two parties, the two copies constituting a single deed.[19]

The indenture of retinue set out the terms of an agreement of service on the part of the retainer and of remuneration on that of the lord. The services it specified could be intended to last for the life of the retainer and, if so, they were generally for peace as well as war. But they could be for a more limited period, in most such cases for a campaign or for a portion of a year. The financial benefits accruing to the retainer could take the form of an annual fee or wages or both. In addition, he might be promised benefits in kind – for example, food in his lord's hall and saddles, shoes and provender for his horses. This complex of benefits was not invariably available through both peace and war. A retainer might, for example, receive only benefits in money; and these might be provided only in time of war. Even a glance at any selection of surviving indentures makes it abundantly clear that the details of the bargain set out in any indenture depended ultimately on the lord's need to recruit the individual knight or squire involved.

The grant of an annuity differed totally from an indenture of retinue. It was made in most cases in the form of a charter or letters patent,[20] there being only one document under the lord's seal, any copy kept by the lord or his administration being for purposes of record only. More important, while an indenture of retinue specified in detail the services the retainer was to perform, the grant of an annuity was invariably for services that received no other description than words such as 'performed in the past and to be performed in the future'.[21]

In short, the indenture of retinue involved a specific and limited contract, whereas the grant of an annuity was open-ended in terms of any obligations imposed on the recipient. And on this point the courts of common law had already evolved a firm body of doctrine before the close of the thirteen century. In 1301 William de Doilly failed in an action of annuity in the court of Common Pleas to recover five robes worth 20 shillings each, which he claimed under an agreement made with William de Cressy on 19 September 1294. The defendant succeeded in his plea that his retainer had refused the request, made ten days later, that he go on service in Gascony and had, in fact, gone with another lord.[22] In 1307 a writ of annuity was brought against a defendant who had withheld payment because of the plaintiff's refusal to do service, apparently as pleader in a court case. The defendant lost because the deed granting the annuity 'witnesses the cause to be as well as the service done as service to be done'.[23]

There is evidence to show that the basic doctrine was maintained and followed through the fourteenth and early fifteenth centuries. In 1312 John of York brought a writ of annuity against John de Swinburne claiming that the latter had granted him an annual rent of twenty shillings and a robe every year out of his chamber for life and that arrears of £16 and sixteen robes were due to him. But the deed he tendered stated that in consideration of the annual payment John of York had bound himself to be Swinburne's attorney. The defendant countered that the arrears were not due since on an occasion he specified the plaintiff had refused to act in this capacity and the payment to him had then been terminated. The judges accepted that, if the facts alleged by the defendant were true, the arrears were not payable. The court's views were clearly in accord with those of 1301 and 1307, indicating that a lord would not be bound in law to pay an annual fee or anything in kind under the terms of an indenture if the conditions of service imposed thereby were broken by the man.[24] In contrast, there was a case which Sir Nicholas Kingston brought against Sir Alan Plokenet before the justices of assize at Gloucester in August 1320, claiming that he had been disseised of an annual 'rent' of two robes assigned out of one of Plokenet's manors in the county, the robes being payable for Plokenet's lifetime. Kingston tendered a deed in evidence and Plokenet did not appear. Accordingly the court gave Kingston authority to distrain for the amount he claimed as arrears.[25]

It would require a thorough search of all the extant rolls of the Court of Common Pleas and the assize rolls (many of which have not survived) to determine how often the recipients of fees under indentures of retinue who were denied payment took their lords to court. As it is, only one case in these specific (as distinct from similar) terms after 1301 is known. A few years after 1403 Ralph son of Ralph Brit brought a writ of novel disseisin[26] in the county of Dorset against Sir Ivo FitzWarin claiming that he had been unjustly disseised of lands, tenements and a rent he had been granted for life by FitzWarin, in return for an undertaking, defined in an indenture, to serve his lord in peace and war as a squire. The indenture apparently included a clause under which the lands, tenements and rent remained in the grantee's hands for life unless he was physically unfit to perform his duties or he continued to be physically fit but FitzWarin did not perform his part of their bargain. On 4 October 1403 FitzWarin required his man to ride with him to his manor of Blounderton in Wiltshire and was met with a refusal. The plaintiff lost his case, the jurors bringing in a verdict that supported FitzWarin's story, rejecting in particular the plaintiff's defence of illness.[27]

Both these cases, however, involve the action of novel disseisin as distinct from that of annuity. In the case of the latter action the extant Year Books and abridgements contain a few entries that throw some light on the application of the doctrine first stated in 1307.[28] In a case of 1347 an annuity of 20 shillings and a robe had been granted in return for past counsel and future service.[29] The grantor requested the annuitant to go with him to a certain place where homage was to be taken and there give counsel. But the court held that the required counsel might be given wherever the annuitant happened to be and he was not required to travel anywhere. In a case of 1358 it was held that an annuity granted to a lawyer 'for his good counsel to be performed (in the future) and performed (in the past)' (*pro bono consilio impendendo suo et impenso*) did not oblige him to travel at the grantor's request and, as eleven years earlier, his counsel might be given wherever he happened to be.[30] Both the details of a case of 1367 and the court's discussion (which referred to the case of 1358) confirm that the Court of Common Pleas applied strict construction to the actual language of a grant of annuity.[31] The plaintiff was a physician who had received such a grant in terms similar to those discussed in 1358. The

case was adjourned and there is no indication in the surviving accounts
that it went to a jury. But there is enough in the discussion we have to
show that the court was unwilling to adjust the basic doctrine relating to
annuities or its position in 1358 so as to take into account the special
functions of a physician.

Both indentures of retinue and charters, or letters patent, granting
annuities could contain clauses that gave additional protection to the interest
in a fee or annuity thereby created. A clause might be inserted in which
the lord, or grantor, provided a warranty on behalf of himself and his
heirs.[32] He might also grant the right, in event of non-payment, to distrain
the manor, lands or tenements from which the fee or annuity issued, the
extent of arrears that would justify distraint being carefully defined (generally a month after a payment was due). Not every indenture or grant of
annuity contained such clauses. And clauses of distraint are more frequently
encountered in the surviving documents than ones of warranty. This is not
surprising. Only if it was especially necessary or desirable would a lord
put obstacles in the way of his heirs maintaining control over the revenues
of his inheritance. And a clause of warranty was of limited practical benefit
to the recipient of a fee or annuity. If put to use, it would be fraught with
the hazard of litigation in the Court of Common Pleas; and, in any case,
the doctrines relating to warranties were far from clear.[33] It is difficult not
to feel that a clause of warranty merely mirrored the status and esteem a
knight or squire enjoyed in his lord's eyes, rather than a positive guarantee
of his rights. A clause of distraint, however, was a much more real benefit
since the deprived payee did not need to go to any court to assert his right;
and the onus of defending non-payment was placed on the grantor who
would have to be the one to resort to litigation. Moreover, distraint did
not preclude the simultaneous, or later, recourse to a writ of annuity.[34]

Any discussion of the nature of the legal rights and interests conveyed
in indentures of retinue and grants of annuity assumes, of course, that lords
and men paid all due regard to legal niceties. Quite obviously these legal
issues are only part of a more complex situation. It may certainly be argued
that there is an air of unreality in the delineation of the technicalities of
clauses of warranty and distraint. If a powerful lord saw fit to cease payment, would the deprived man go readily to litigation over a warranty,
and, more important, would he risk the physical consequences of exercising
his right of distraint? In the latter case the threat of retribution would have
been a powerful deterrent. Nor can we be absolutely confident that every
lord and every man were fully aware of all the legal issues pertaining to
indentures and grants of annuity. To be sure, this must have been so in

the case of the Crown and its administrators and the great earls; but, as we have seen, much lesser lords employed indentures of retinue and granted annuities. Even so, three arguments suggest that there are serious grounds for believing that the technical differences between indentures of retinue and grants of annuities deserve serious attention. First, lords and men did occasionally resort to litigation. Second, the diplomatic technicalities provide a possible tool of analysis when we come to study the development of the indenture of retinue over a period of over two centuries. Indeed, in this connection it is necessary to inquire whether every indenture conformed with the lawyer's doctrines. Third, and above all, there is the fact that the greatest lords at least knew that, when they granted an annuity, they were conferring a benefit that was absolute in law for the life of the recipient and that not even his open disobedience or disloyalty could justify the termination of payment, a fact that did not apply to an indenture of retinue.

(ii) Livery

Livery is at once the most well known and the most amorphous of the links between lord and man encountered in late medieval England. Our knowledge of this practice is anchored in the phrase 'livery and maintenance' which has, since the late nineteenth century, defined the consequences of 'bastard feudalism' for the preservation of law and order. But, while the existence of 'livery' is palpably demonstrable, it is very difficult to delineate its features in precise terms. The word refers to the practice under which a man wore a distinctive uniform, provided by his lord, that differentiated him from the followers of other lords. But, once beyond this simple definition, we move into an area where evidence is sparse. There is contemporary comment, notably in parliamentary petitions and legislation and in private correspondence, especially that of the Paston family. But we lack what would have been the main source for an elucidation of 'livery'. Grants of livery in the case of a great noble were made from the household office known as the wardrobe. Very few documents relating to baronial households in the middle ages have survived; and, when they do exist, they are generally concerned with the disbursement of revenues for the maintenance of the household or provide a record of daily expenditure for this purpose.[35] The source of grants of livery, however, lay within the inner workings of the household. Only one complete wardrobe account has survived – that of Thomas of Lancaster in 1313–14.[36] A great lord's wardrobe kept lists of those to whom liveries were given. But we have only two of these – one

for Elizabeth de Burgh, countess of Ulster, in 1343–44.[37] and one for
Edward Courtenay, earl of Devon, in 1384–85.[38]

The most definite feature of 'livery' that appears from the available
sources is this origin within the lord's household. To be sure, the receivers'
accounts of great lords occasionally contain mentions of the purchase of
cloth for liveries.[39] But these are comparatively rare and generally relate to
special circumstances. One other definite feature is the fact that all household servants wore their lord's livery, this being regarded as a *sine qua
non* of the relationship between the lord and a household servant. When
a lord hired a household official or servant by means of an indenture or
other formal instrument, it generally contained an undertaking that the
man would receive the robe, or robes, appropriate to his station. Moreover,
in all the efforts made by the Crown in the course of the fourteenth and
fifteenth centuries to control the evils caused by livery, it never sought to
erode the principle that household officials and servants should be so clothed.

Yet this very programme of reform and control on the part of the Crown
points to the fact that grants of livery were not confined to members of
the household. In analysing this phenomenon it is important to avoid
importing later notions of the household into the discussion. It is natural
enough for the modern historian to assume that the household comprised
simply those officials and servants whose regular, in most cases daily, presence there was necessary for the provision of the necessities of life for the
lord and his family. But throughout the middle ages contemporaries viewed
the household in a much looser way. Indeed, they used the term *familia*,
a word that denotes not the functioning of a household economy but a
group of dependents, spreading outwards from the lord's nearest kin. The
lord was in a very real sense a 'bread-giver', the word itself being derived
from the Anglo-Saxon word *hlaford* which had that meaning, since he provided for all those dependent on him whether or not they were his kin.
The fact that these notions and the assumptions embedded in them went
back to primitive times that have left no written record did not lessen their
consequences in the late middle ages. It was natural enough for lords to
assume that, when they attracted followers, these were brought within a
relationship which differed only in degree from that of the day-to-day
household attendant who provided for the needs of physical maintenance
and comfort.

It is difficult to delineate the role of livery within this situation because
we are dealing with a body of accepted custom, rather than carefully
defined rules. And this point is especially emphasised by the existence of
a serious gap in what knowledge we have. A few of the comparatively

small number of extant indentures of retinue from the late thirteenth and fourteenth centuries contain clauses referring to the benefits associated with livery. But, few as these are, such clauses then disappear. This can only have happened because it was thought superfluous to mention benefits that were part and parcel of accepted notions of relationships within a lord's following. Even so, it is possible to detect two trends at work. First, it is quite clear that livery was granted to several classes of dependent who held offices or derived financial benefits from the lord but were not in day-to-day attendance on the needs of him, his wife and children. In 1343–44 the livery roll of Elizabeth de Burgh included ten of her manorial bailiffs and two reeves.[40] These must have been a fraction of the lower manorial officials of so wealthy a landowner: presumably they were so honoured because of the importance of the manors they administered. In the case of the earl of Devon in 1384–85 the livery roll lists[41], after the knights and squires, two canons, one prebendary, four parsons, four 'damoiselles' and then goes on to list the men of law. These include four sergeants of the Court of Common Pleas and three of the earl's stewards. Another entry *vallets* (yeomen)[42] – includes two of the earl's manorial bailiffs. The categories employed by this livery roll – knights, squires, men of the church, men of law, yeomen, pages and minstrels – are what we would expect in a noble household organised on a hierarchical basis. But, as in the case of Elizabeth de Burgh, bailiffs were far from being a necessary feature of household administration. And this can equally be said of sergeants-at-law and estate stewards. Nor did the spiritual needs of the lord's entourage require a total of seven clergy, some of them beneficed. Thus, even more than that of Elizabeth de Burgh, the livery roll of the earl of Devon demonstrates that a wider following than household servants enjoyed the benefits of the lord's livery.

What precise form did livery take within these households? If we can rely on the descriptions of noble households in *The Black Book* of Edward IV, livery embraced its own internal hierarchy. A robe for a knight cost 10 shillings as did a squire's, a yeoman's 8 shillings and a groom's 6s 8d.[43] Apparently the differences lay in the quality of the cloth provided, as distinct from its quantity; and this is confirmed by the livery roll of the earl of Devon a century earlier which assigned the same amount of cloth to all these categories. But variations must have existed between households. In that of Thomas, earl of Lancaster, in 1313–14 a total of 391 furs was bought for overtunics, 208 for the liveries of barons, knights and clerks and 123 lambs' furs for squires, all for winter wear.[44] Somewhat smaller amounts were bought for summer robes. Thus in this household at the beginning of the fourteenth century the robes of barons, knights, squires and clerks were trimmed with fur, unlike those of lesser servants and followers, the quality of the fur descending with rank. Nor could this have been the only noble household to use furs as part of its system of livery. Elizabeth de Burgh in 1343–44 granted furred liveries to the knights, squires, clerks and ladies of her household. But there is no indication of this practice in the livery roll of the earl of Devon half a century later.[45] It may well be that it belonged only to the households of nobles of exceptional wealth and importance. Support for this suggestion is provided by *The Black Book* of Edward IV which indicates that robes for summer as well as winter were provided by a duke, but makes no mention of this practice in the case of the households of a marquis, an earl or a baron.[46]

In the case of the households of both Elizabeth de Burgh and the earl of Devon it is possible to be certain in the case of a number of categories – the men of law and the estate officials especially – that the recipients of livery were not permanent members of the household. But information on this point is lacking for the knights and squires. In the case of the earl of Devon there were eight knights[47] and forty-three squires. This seems large for the permanent household of a magnate who was one of the least wealthy of the kingdom's earls, a fact that leads to the conclusion that some of these knights and squires must have been outside the permanent organisation of the household. Support for this comes from *The Black Book* of Edward IV, according to which, in the household of a duke summer and winter robes were given to six household knights and sixty squires and others 'within and without' (*infra et extra*)[48] and in that of an earl to thirty 'gentlemen' (*generosi*),[49] presumably a category that might include either knights or squires. Some of those in receipt of livery from the earl of Devon may have been indentured retainers; but it is equally possible that they were simply knights or squires who were given his livery as a mark of attachment to the earl's affinity. At any rate, *The Black Book* explicitly refers to such grants 'outside' (*extra*) the household of a duke or earl. Certainly the practice of giving liveries to indentured retainers is documented by a series of parliamentary statutes, the ordinance of 1390 being aimed at the contol of this practice and the statute of 1468 at its prohibition.[50] But, in the light of our discussion of the legal aspects of indentures and annuities, it is desirable to secure more precision. Did annuitants, as distinct from indentured retainers, receive livery? On this point there can be no definite conclusion. On a number of occasions in our sources those wearing a lord's livery include his 'feed men'. For example, in 1465 the duke of Norfolk wrote to John Paston, the youngest,[51] as 'one of our servants of household', to attend him in London for the ceremony in which, since he was now of age, the duke would receive livery of his inheritance. Paston was also commanded 'that ye do warn our feed men and servants, such as be nigh to you, that they be there then in our livery'. The same phrase – 'feed men' – is used to describe the followers attending the earl of Northumberland on the occasion of Henry VII's first visit to York.[52] It is unwise to construe this term too strictly and assume that it means only indentured retainers. First, annuitants would themselves be anxious to be present on such important ceremonial occasions as this to demonstrate their loyalty to their lord and the point of doing so would be lost if they did not wear livery. Second, there is good warrant for the view that the words 'fee' and 'annuity' were often interchangeable[53], since the latter is used on many occasions to describe the payment to a retainer. 'Feed men', in fact, would appear to be a general description of those who, as distinct from officials and servants of the household and those involved in the administration of the lord's landed interests, were in receipt of any annual payments from him. In any case, there are references through the thirteenth century to grants of annuities that also involved the provision of robes once or twice a year. And the practice of incorporating both an annuity and robes in a single grant continued well into the next century: in 1339 John, son of Sir William Tracy, gave a man one robe of his livery (*de secta mea*) and 20 shillings a year for life 'for the service he has performed for me'.[54] Just as the practice of mentioning livery in indentures of retinue seems to have vanished after the middle of the fourteenth century, so also it may have disappeared from charters or letters patent granting annuities. Indeed, it is very difficult to believe that a knight or squire who was being rewarded for past or future services would not expect to wear his lord's livery.

At the same time livery was not necessarily connected with membership of the lord's household or administration or with indentures of retinue or annuities. Contemporaries could treat it as something quite separate from any sort of fee: a Year Book case of 1337 refers to a man who granted to another either twenty shillings or a robe a year for life.[55] In 1462 John Paston, junior, wrote to his father of a rival of the family who sought 'to give jackets of his livery to divers persons which be waged by other men'.[56] There is nothing in this passage to suggest that the recipients were in receipt of any sort of wage from the grantor. Livery was a visible sign that a man belonged to his lord's affinity; but there was a flexibility embedded in this basic characteristic that converted livery into a means of extending a lord's influence beyond the circles of his household members, the administrative staff of his estates, his indentured retainers and his annuitants. And the grant of a lord's livery might in itself be sufficient inducement to join a lord's following because it was a public indication that the recipients enjoyed his support and protection.

At the same time there could be flexibility in the form that a grant of livery took, since it did not necessarily have to be a robe. By the end of the fourteenth century badges or other tokens were in use besides robes. The practice of giving out caps was singled out as a form of livery in a parliamentary statute of 1377.[57] Richard II in 1387 gave out badges of silver and gilt to gentry from whom he took oaths of loyalty. And shortly after his accession the new king Henry IV purchased silver collars for his knightly retinue as duke of Lancaster.[58] Collars of such quality were used for their knights by his successors on the throne through the fifteenth century.[59] Livery without a robe, however, did not have to take the form of such a precious gift. And even robes were not cheap gifts, the cost ranging from £2 in the case of a knight to 18s in the case of a yeoman.[60] In time of war or riot they could be lost or damaged or even interfere with the use of weapons. And robes were hardly suitable in terms of either cost or status for distribution *en masse* to whole groups of men from the ranks of the peasantry. For these reasons it is tempting to suggest that such reduced forms of livery may well have existed before the late fourteenth century.[61] At the same time they did not replace robes entirely. In its models of households of a duke, an earl or a viscount *The Black Book* of the household of Edward IV assumes that robes are given to knights and those of gentlemany status;[62] and in 1412–13 knights and squires in Staffordshire and Shropshire were giving out liveries of cloth.[63] Nevertheless, in times of emergency, when a lord wished to recruit a group of men speedily, caps, signs, or other emblems were a means of demonstrating at minimum cost the mutual attachment and loyalty between him and these followers.

(iii) The 'bachelor'

The sources relating to the relationships of lord and man in late medieval England frequently mention the word 'bachelor' in contexts that suggest it denoted the follower of a great lord.[64] In 1267 pardons issued by the Crown to those who had rebelled under the leadership of the earl of Gloucester employed the word to describe some of these.[65] It is encountered in a similar sense in the course of the Scottish wars of Edward I. On two occasions the author of the *Song of Caerlaverock* speaks of 'bachelors' in the sense of a lord's followers.[66] On several other occasions the word was employed by a magnate in the same sense.[67] Much fuller documentation can be traced throughout the fourteenth century. Thomas of Lancaster granted a manor for life 'to our dear and well-loved bachelor'.[68] Hugh Turplington was described as one of the 'bachelors' of Hugh Despenser the younger.[69] In 1346 Henry, duke of Lancaster, granted an annuity to Richard Shelton his 'well-loved bachelor'.[70] In 1330 Sir Henry Ferrers of Groby who held an annuity from the household revenues of Henry, earl of Lancaster, had been described in the same way.[71] Humphrey, the last Bohun earl of Hereford, made grants of annuities for life to three 'bachelors'.[72]

The largest body of such information exists in the case of the Black Prince and John of Gaunt. The four surviving registers of the administration of the Black Prince's estates contain the names of seventy-two knights who are described on one occasion at least as 'bachelors'.[73] In the register of John of Gaunt which belongs to the years 1372–76 the total of such names is twenty-one[73] and in that of 1379–83 it is twenty-seven.[74] It must be said that the chancery clerks of the Black Prince and Gaunt exercised some license in attaching the term to the name of an individual, since its use on one occasion does not guarantee its presence on future occasions. Nevertheless, the evidence of these registers leaves a powerful impression of the importance of the 'bachelor' in the followings of these magnates of royal blood. Quite frequently a 'bachelor' was a leading official in the administration of the estates. Again and again, 'bachelors' were employed on special missions, sometimes involving estate administration, sometimes to deal with particular matters of urgency,[75] some often to raise men for their lord's campaigns[76] and even occasionally as emissaries overseas.[77] References to 'bachelors' continue well into the fifteenth century. Shortly after he gained the crown Henry IV described Sir John Pelham as his 'bachelor'.[78] In the collection that William Worcester compiled from the archives of his master Sir John Fastolf the word is used of one of the ranks in the household of John, duke of Bedford, the Regent of the Lancastrian kingdom of France.[79]

What is especially noticeable is the association between the 'bachelor' and indentures of retinue. In a large number of those made with knights by John of Gaunt, for example, retainers were promised the privileges of a 'bachelor' in peace or war or sometimes both.[80] Nor was Gaunt the only magnate to offer this benefit in the late fourteenth century. We encounter it in indentures made by Roger Mortimer, earl of March, Thomas Mowbray, earl marshal of Nottingham, and Thomas Beauchamp, earl of Warwick.[81] Some indentures survive from the fourteenth century in which retainers of special wealth or importance are permitted to bring their own 'bachelors' with them when in attendance on their lord.[82]

In the light of these details it is impossible to avoid the impression that the functions of the 'bachelor' were an integral part of the relationships between lord and man. But what precisely did the word mean? In late medieval England (it was also current in France) the word and its cognates contained more than one strand of meaning. It was occasionally used to describe a large body of the knightly class of the realm. It was in this sense that it was employed by the Burton annalist when he described the *Communitas bachelerie Anglie*[83] and the demands this group made in 1259. A century or so later the Chandos Herald described the Black Prince's expedition of 1355 which led to the victory at Poitiers the following year as 'the flower of chivalry and right noble bachelry [*bachelrie*].[84] The great council summoned by the government of Richard II's minority on hearing of the French invasion of Flanders in 1382 contained 'a great number of the more sufficient bachelors of the realm'.[85] At the deposition of Richard II in 1399 proctors met with him on behalf of the 'bachelors and commons' of the north and south of the kingdom.[86] It was with the same sort of meaning that the English knights at the Brackley tournament in 1249 had called themselves 'bachelors'.[87]

In other contexts the word 'bachelor' could denote a youthful member of the knightly class. There are many examples of this in the courtly literature, both Latin and vernacular, of the twelfth and thirteenth centuries. Indeed, here we see the root of the present meaning, since in these sources the young 'bachelor' was assumed to be unmarried. Certainly the indications are that in the twelfth century the concepts of youthfulness and unmarried status went together, the one depending on the other.[88] According to the social conventions then the married knight could not be a 'bachelor'. But is is equally clear that the word in this context was changing it meaning by the middle of the thirteenth century. The future Edward I, although married for several years and already possessed of estates that made him the wealthiest landowner in the kingdom below the king his father,[89] could be described as a 'bachelor' in 1260.[90] When Chaucer used the word in the late fourteenth century, the emphasis was definitely on youth rather than knighthood, or on an aspiration towards knightly status.[91]

The last meaning we encounter belongs within the area of the relationships between lord and man. When the word was applied to a king's knight, it denoted a member of his household. In 1200–1 King John wrote to the seneschals of Poitou and Normandy commanding that they seize the lands that had been given to 'bachelors' of his household (*de familia nostra*) who had not done fealty and homage for them.[92] In 1216 he described as his 'bachelor' a knight who was to be paid an annual fee out of his chamber until provided with land.[93] This notion of the 'bachelor' as a household knight lasted through into the fifteenth century. The household of John, duke of Bedford, as Regent of France,[94] of which 'bachelors' were part was, of course, virtually royal. But as late as 1471–72 *The Black Book* of the household of Edward IV described as one of its important categories, 'banerets, or bachelor knights, to be carvers and cupbearers in this court of like degree for the king's person, sitting in the hall at one of the meats with a person of like service . . . They are called knights of the chamber.'[95] In the next section the compiler comments on,

> Knights of the Household, xii. bachelors sufficient and most valiant men of that order of every country, and more in number if it please the king. Whereof iiii. to be continually abiding and attending upon the king's person in court, besides the carvers abovesaid, for to serve the king of his basin, or such other service as they may do the king in absence of the carvers, sitting in the king's chamber and hall, with persons of like service.[96]

In order to understand the role of the 'bachelor' in the relationships between lord and man in late medieval England it is necessary to choose which of these strands of meaning is the proper one when the word is encountered in indentures of retinue and documents of magnates' estate administration. Three preliminary conclusions are helpful in finding an answer. First, the 'bachelor' had already taken knighthood. The clearest illustration of this is in the career of Sir John Darcy, a retainer of Aymer de Valence, earl of Pembroke. In an agreement he made with his lord in November 1309 it was stipulated that he would become one of his lord's 'bachelors' only when he had assumed knighthood.[97] Two or three generations later in the registers of the Black Prince and John of Gaunt the word 'bachelor' is never found in association with the rank of squire.[98] But at the same time there are several indentures of retinue in these registers in which a knight is given the privileges of a 'bachelor' in either peace or war, or sometimes both. Second, it is quite apparent that the terms 'knight' and 'bachelor' are not interchangeable. The royal pardons issued to the followers of the earl of Gloucester in 1267 quite explicitly refer to some individuals as 'knights' and others as 'bachelors'.[99] In his agreement with John Darcy the earl of Pembroke promised to increase the land or rent with which his retainer was to be enfeoffed on his taking knighthood and the latter undertook in his turn to become one of the earl's 'bachelors'. But in another indenture, made six months later, even though it was in return for a larger grant, Darcy simply bound himself to take up knighthood.[100] In the registers of John of Gaunt the same document can refer to one knight simply as such but to another as 'bachelor'.[101] Third, there is abundant evidence that the word 'bachelor' in late medieval indentures of retinue or analogous documents does not necessarily indicate a young knight, or a youth aspiring to knighthood. To be sure, there is a number of occasions when we encounter the word without any other details or information about the circumstances of the transaction between the 'bachelor' and his lord, or the privileges provided by the indenture of retinue. In these cases there is nothing *per se* to rule out a youthful situation. An impression of the 'bachelor''s age and social circumstances can, in fact, only be achieved through a prosopographical approach which discovers fuller details of his career and, in particular, his age. This is most easily achieved in the case of the registers of the Black Prince and John of Gaunt. An examination of these shows that the 'bachelors' in the retinues of both these magnates were gentry of weight, who often held leading positions in estate administration and were employed on other important business.[102] In the case of the Black Prince the most striking illustration of this is Sir William Shareshull, described as the prince's 'bachelor' at times when he was a judge of the Court of Common Pleas and when Chief Justice of the Court of King's Bench.[103] The 'bachelors' of John of Gaunt included, for example, Sir William Hawley[104] and Sir Thomas Hungerford,[105] his chief stewards north and south of the Trent respectively; and the latter was Speaker of the Commons in the parliament of January 1377.[106] Any notion that the 'bachelors' of John of Gaunt were necessarily youthful cannot be reconciled with a number of entries in his registers where both father and son were so described.[107] To be sure, we must exercise caution in reading conclusions from the registers of the Black Prince and John of Gaunt back into the previous century or earlier periods. But there is strong support for the view that these arguments apply at least to the beginning of the thirteenth century. In the verse history of William Marshal we learn how, when in 1205 the Marshall refused to fight against Philip Augustus on the grounds that the French king was his lord in Normandy, King John sought the advice of his 'bachelors' after failing to secure the support and encouragement of his barons.[108] In such a crisis he would hardly have turned to the inexperienced, let alone the youthful. The whole tone of this incident suggests that the king's relationships with his 'bachelors' was very much like that of the Black Prince with his, when in the words of the Chandos Herald, on his deathbed he 'made all his men come who had served him in his life and still gladly served him', these including his 'bachelors'.[109] Both this language and the conduct of King John a century and a half earlier imply a degree of trust that cannot be reconciled with youthful status. It is, of course, necessary to explain how the word could be used by John of Gaunt of a mature knight but also of a youth in the writings of Chaucer, a member of his affinity. The explanation lies in the fact that centuries before young men served in lord's households to start their careers and only married when they had achieved the necessary resources, a practice that eventually gave rise to each of the meanings we encounter. By the thirteenth century it was the context that determined which meaning applied.

How, then, do we elucidate the term 'bachelor' when we see it in the documents relating to the relationship of lord and man in late medieval England? It is best to proceed from the area of most solid knowledge. A reference to the 'bachelor' in the occasional indenture of retinue or other document issued by a lord may tell us what the word does not denote – for example, in the indentures between John Darcy and the earl of Pembroke or mandates issued by the Black Prince or John of Gaunt in the administration of their estates. But, in order to discover what a great lord precisely had in mind when he called a knight his 'bachelor', it is necessary, in the absence of a deliberate definition, to find documents that supply surrounding details that enable us to supply an answer. The largest collection of evidence in the case of a single magnate is the surviving indentures of retinue made by John of Gaunt.[110]

Six of the indentures of retinue with knights entered in his register of 1372–76 mention the word, promising the privileges of a 'bachelor' when the retainer was in attendance on his lord, sometimes confining these benefits to peace or war, occasionally giving them in both.[111] In the register of 1379–83 the total mentioning the word in the same sort of contexts is twelve.[112] In the case of those of Gaunt's indentures that survive in the form of confirmations made by Richard II and Henry IV the total is ten.[113] It is especially interesting that in this last category there are three which describe the knight concerned as a 'bachelor' mentioning his status at the opening of the indenture.[114] Unfortunately we possess information of this quantity in the case of no other magnate.

In the case of John of Gaunt the grounds for seeing a connection between the 'bachelor' and the household are especially strong. On 13 March 1373 the duke ordered his receiver-general to pay household wages owed to his 'bachelor', Sir Walter Blount.[115] On 6 November 1379 his receiver in Yorkshire was ordered to pay from his issues the annuities due to 'all our bachelors, squires and other officers dwelling within our household'.[116] On 9 September 1381 Sir William Frank was described as a 'bachelor of the duke's chamber'.[117] Such information can only support the view that the 'bachelor' was a household knight. But can we dig deeper to uncover the precise function of the 'bachelor' within the household? Because the answer must lie within the household it is useful to inquire into two areas where Gaunt's indentures of retinue impinge on its functioning – the benefit described as *bouche de court* and the payment of wages when summoned to service within the duke's retinue. The term *bouche de court* meant food and drink.[118] It is provided in time of peace in fourteen knights' indentures in the register of 1372–76[119] and in twelve in that of 1379–83.[120] But in none of these is there anything to suggest that the knights concerned were 'bachelors'. At first sight the investigation of wages is more useful. In the register of 1372–76 there are four indentures conferring on a knight wages in time of peace 'as other bachelors of his condition' (with slight variations in language);[121] and in that of 1379–83 the equivalent figure is three.[122] In contrast there are also indentures providing wages that do not contain any references to 'bachelors' – seventeen in the register of 1372–76,[123] and eight in that of 1379–83.[124] On the basis of these details it is certainly difficult to discern any correlation between the use of the term 'bachelor' and the provision of either wages or *bouche de court*.[125] It might, of course, be argued that equivalent details for time of war should also be taken into account. But wages might then be determined by the terms of a contract with the king, a circumstance which the language of Gaunt's later indentures often takes into account. And in the one case among Gaunt's surviving indentures in which wages are provided in time of peace but not in war there is no mention at all of the 'bachelor'. In any event it is important to note that the provision of *bouche de court* or wages, or both, can be found more often than not in the surviving squires' indentures.

At this point it is helpful to place the knights' indentures entered in these registers in the wider context of all the references to the 'bachelors' of John of Gaunt. An investigation along these lines yields interesting results. On 3 January 1373 Sir Richard Burley entered into an indenture of retinue in which he was promised *inter alia* wages in peace and war as other 'bachelors';[126] but he was referred to as a 'bachelor' on 1 August 1372.[127] On 26 March 1373 Sir Roger Curzon in another indenture was promised wages in peace and war 'as other members of his rank'[128] The indenture contains no mention of him as a 'bachelor'; but he had been so described in November 1372.[129] Similarly, Sir Walter Blount received wages in peace and war 'as other bachelors of his conition' in an indenture of 18 May 1373;[130] but he had been called a 'bachelor' in August 1372.[131] Equally compelling is the fact that of those so mentioned in the register of 1379–83, six were not named in the list of Gaunt's indentured retinue entered at the beginning of this volume.[132]

From these details there emerges the conclusion that a knight's status as 'bachelor' did not depend on an indenture of retinue. In one sense, indeed, we have now to divide the surviving indentures of John of Gaunt and his knights into two categories. On the one hand, there were those made with knights who were already 'bachelors'. On the other hand, there were those indentures made with knights who did not enjoy this status. However, such knights could acquire the privileges of a 'bachelor' in peace or in war, or even both, when performing their duties of attendance and service. A careful examination of the language of the indentures shows that not all knights were treated equally in these respects. For example, in the register of 1372–76 out of a total of thirty knights' indentures, twenty-three made no mention of the privileges of a 'bachelor' in time of peace;[133] and in that of 1379–83, out of a total of thirteen, the equivalent figure is none.[134]

In the light of this body of information and argument, two conclusions are possible about the 'bachelor' in the retinue of John of Gaunt. First, he was a household knight who received wages and *bouche de court* during his periods of attendance. Second, his was an especially privileged position, since the terms of indentures of retinue suggest that other knights were anxious to be treated in the same way as the 'bachelors' when in attendance on their lord. Some support is given to these conclusions by the evidence of fragments of the rolls of attendance that were kept in Gaunt's household.[135] Each of these fragments covers a month or so, listing a number of knights – in three cases eight, in one thirteen and in another fifteen. Most of those listed were present for the greater part of the months concerned; and a marginal note indicates they were paid at the daily rate of one shilling a day. It is worth comparing these totals with the information in *The Black Book* of the household of Edward IV which gives the figure of six for the total of household knights in its model of a ducal household.[136] It may well be that some of those attending were not 'bachelors'; but it is equally possible that Gaunt maintained a larger number of them than other dukes.

Such conclusions serve to raise further questions. It is quite clear that the 'bachelors' received daily wages and *bouche de court* during their periods of attendance in the household. But did they receive annual fees as well? The difficulty in answering this question is the same as runs through the whole of our discussion of the 'bachelor' – the absence of records of the household administration. If such fees were paid, they would have come from the treasurer of the household whose records have not survived. *A priori*, to be sure, it would seem unlikely that knights who were so valued by the lord as to be brought into a close relationship with him as his 'bachelors' would not receive more than their wages and keep. Certainly *The Black Book* of the household of Edward IV assumes that the household knights of a duke would be paid annual fees.[137] Perhaps, some clues on this point are provided by an indenture between Gaunt's brother the Black Prince and Sir Edmund Manchester.[138] This may indicate that in the case of the Black Prince there was an intermediate stage linking the life-indenture with those for limited durations. This indenture gives Manchester the status and privileges of a 'bachelor' in time of peace and also an annual fee paid from the prince's wardrobe. If the 'bachelors' of Gaunt's household received similar treatment, they each brought with them a squire and a chamberlain. But, if this was the case and the 'bachelor' received an annual fee as well as daily wages and keep, were all these benefits guaranteed to him in any sort of indenture, or other form of grant? What we know about the administration of Gaunt makes it seem unlikely that the same standards were not applied within his household as through his estates and the collection and administration of his revenues from them. It is thus reasonable to assume that there were written agreements between Gaunt and his 'bachelors' and that these took the form of indentures. It is not difficult to explain the failure of such indentures to survive.[139] They were part of the records of the household. Unlike those we encounter in indentures of retinue, the annual fees paid to 'bachelors' were not paid from the revenues of receivers or manorial officials and for that reason copies did not have to be entered in the registers of the central administration. Unfortunately, there is neither information nor clue on one aspect of the 'bachelor''s relationship with his lord – the tenure of his appointment. But there is good reason to believe that he served during his lord's pleasure. It is difficult to believe that the word had entirely dropped its connotations of apprenticeship. There is, in fact, an element of paradox built into the 'bachelor''s relationship with his lord. On the one hand, the 'bachelor' was an important person. On the other hand, he was being placed in a position to prove his worth to his lord. It is worth noting that the Black Prince did not make an indenture with Sir Edmund Manchester for the retainer's life.

These arguments lead to an important issue – the relationship between the 'bachelors' and the retinue as a whole. There is abundant evidence that the 'bachelor' was a person of superior knightly status who occupied a position of special trust within the immediate entourage of his lord. Why, then, did he have to bother to enter into an indenture of retinue? The answer is twofold. First, the prospect of further reward from his lord was built into his relationship with him as his 'bachelor'. If he performed well, the time would come when his lord would decide to give him financial rewards in excess of his perquisites as 'bachelor'. If the suggestion that the appointment of a 'bachelor' was probationary was implied, the ambition to gain lifetime relationship would also be present. In these circumstances the natural stage of reward for the knight concerned would be a grant of landed revenues (or even lands for life), especially since this would give him a security that according to the doctrines of the common law was missing in the case of an annual fee out of househld revenues. But such a grant required a document that gave proof of the creation of such a legal estate and at the same time imposed a clear obligation on officials whose responsibilities lay entirely outside the household. Second, the prospect of additional reward apart, the time would almost certainly come in late medieval England when a lord would want his 'bachelor' to go with him on the king's wars or, in the case of John of Gaunt, his own efforts to conquer a kingdom. In this situation the need for additional payment, the knight's desire for a share in the profits of booty and ransoms and the involvement of financial dealings with the Crown all led to the creation of relationships outside the household and thus to an indenture of retinue.

From this discussion there emerges a picture of a hierarchy within the knights of the retinue of John of Gaunt. The language of the indentures of retinue made with those who were already 'bachelors' suggest that they retained this status. From their standpoint, of course, the indentures gave them benefits during attendance in the household that they already enjoyed as 'bachelors'. Yet, when members of both groups were serving in the household, they must have been distinguishable from one another. In practice, therefore, there were in the household of John of Gaunt regular 'bachelors' and those who were 'stand-ins' in that status. The differences between these two groups were real. First, the indentures of retinue made with those who were already 'bachelors' contain nothing to suggest that the fees they received from household revenues were terminated so that their financial benefits must have been superior to those of ordinary indentured retainers. Second, as far as the obligation of attendance in the household was concerned, that of the 'bachelor' was a regular one, whereas the non-'bachelor' knight attended in response to an *ad hoc* summons. In practice, appearances from this group must have been somewhat occasional and sporadic and confined to times of crisis or emergency. When indentures of retinue promised the rewards of 'bachelor' status to ordinary knights, it was more a matter of contingent promise than intended execution. In some measure, indeed, the intention must have been psychological – to make the knight feel part of a real entourage and to offer the hope of occasional contact with a great lord.

Because of the absence of household records, this discussion of the 'bachelor' has had to be an essay in reconstruction; and it is based almost completely on indentures of retinue made by John of Gaunt and the surviving records of his estate administration. Even so, there is no reason to believe that these conclusions cannot be applied to other magnates. Minor variations may have occurred. But this picture of the 'bachelor' and his relationship with his lord fits what we know of the organisation of the household and retinue of the Black Prince; and there is nothing in the surviving indentures of other magnates to conflict with it.

The relationships between lord and man in late medieval England thus form a far from simple picture. The term 'bastard feudalism' has, indeed, served to mask from the historian's view the existence of several different relationships. It is palpably unwise to generalise on the basis of a structural approach alone. But from this perspective it is difficult to discern any 'feudal' or 'quasi-feudal' elements, especially in the sense of a substitution of a money fee for a grant of land. To be sure, there were characteristics in common between the man who wore his lord's livery, the indentured retainer and the 'bachelor'. All wore the lord's livery; but this was neither 'feudal' nor 'quasi-feudal'. What is important from the standpoint of an understanding of these forms of relationship is that both 'livery' and the 'bachelor' had their origins within the household. At the same time the 'bachelor' could be an indentured retainer; and the latter's functions involved him in service in the household in time of peace. However, an annuity granted in return for services performed in the past and to be performed in the future was a quite different phenomenon. To be sure, we must never lose sight of the fact that service in the entourage of a great lord was undertaken in the hope of reward. The 'bachelor' or indentured retainer might look forward to an office in his lord's household or estate administration – the constableship of a castle, for example – or, best of all, an annuity for life. The comparative wealth of information we have about the entourage of John of Gaunt enables us to chart with some precision the fashioning of careers along these lines in a number of cases. The most fortunate of Gaunt's knights could end up with an annual income from household wages, retainer's fees and an annuity, or annuities, for life markedly higher than that of his landed inheritance.

Vewed in purely structural terms, a great lord's relationship with his knights and squires has the appearance of widening circles of affinity. In a perfect model of the relationships with his entourage he would be closest of all to his 'bachelors', then next with his indentured retainers, the knights followed by the squires, and finally with those he might recruit from time to time in return for livery and wages. But, though this picture of concentric circles of affinity contains a substantial measure of truth and is helpful in the exposition of these relationships, it has two weaknesses that must constantly be borne in mind. First, it does not include the fact that a 'bachelor' could be simultaneously an indentured retainer. Second, it does not take into account the annuitant, whose role points at one and the same time to both the value and the insufficiency of a purely structural approach to the relationships between lord and man in late medieval England. On the one hand, there is the fundamental difference in law between the annuitant and others in the lord's affinity. Over the 'bachelor', the indentured retainer and the simple wearer of his livery the lord had a real control: in the event of disloyalty or defective service, the payment of fee or wages could be terminated and, in any event, such followers were constantly in search of further reward from him But a man who had been granted an annuity for past as well as future services for life had a freehold in the eyes of the common law. On the other hand, an annuity could be enjoyed by a 'bachelor' or an indentured retainer. And, in practice, it is more than likely that, whatever their legal rights, many annuitants who proved unfaithful found themselves deprived.

Notes

1 The Latin word is 'retentus'. When indentures in the vernacular appear in the fifteenth century, the language is generally 'beleft and witholden'. In the late thirteenth and fourteenth centuries indentures of retinue were almost always in French, the words used being *demore et retenu* or similar language.

2 See *The Oxford English Dictionary*: 'A dependent follower of some person of rank or position; one attached to a house, or owing it service.' The examples of usage cited all assume that the retainer is not continually resident in the household.

3 An examination of the *Cartae Baronum*, in particular, suggests that those who submitted returns there may not have attached as great importance to them as historians have assumed. The discrepancies of approach between individual returns, not to say the apparent eccentricities of some, deserve more serious attention.

4 See, e.g. below, pp. 64, 98.

5 In addition, there are indentures of service (in approximately the same form as for knights and squires) for priests, clerks and menial servants, e.g., *JGRA*, i, 321–2, 327, 335, 346; ii, 1; and *JGRB*, i, 15–6, 23.

6 The indentures of John of Gaunt printed by Professor N. B. Lewis from confir-

mations enrolled on the Patent rolls (Lewis, 'Gaunt indentures') fall into an analogous category, since most of them belong to the period when the Lancastrian inheritance was in the hands of Richard II following the death of John of Gaunt.

7   Bean, *Decline of Feudalism*, pp. 66–79, 99–101.

8   Phillips, *Aymer de Valence* (p. 255), treats as an indenture of retinue an agreement for mutual assistance between Hugh Despenser the younger and John de Ber-
mingham, earl of Louth, made in 1321 (Bodley MS. Dugdale, 18, f. 39v). But this
is misleading. The text reads: *qe chescun des ditz counte et monsieur Hugh demorra
avecque altre encontre totes gentz qe porrunt vovre et morrir, sauve la foie, l'onour
et le profit nostre dit seigneur le Roi.* Although Despenser was the more powerful
of the two, the form and tone are those of an agreement between equals. The document is similar to other agreements between equals (for which see McFarlane, *Collected Essays*, p. 46) and is also analogous to the French *alliance* (for which see P.
S. Lewis, 'Decayed and non-feudalism'). It is, of course, possible that there were
other similar agreements in so disturbed a period as the reign of Edward II. If so,
the absence of any financial consideration would be bound to reduce the chances
of survival.

9   PRO, E. 40/391 (*CAD*, i, A. 391).

10   *de son conseil et ses robes*, receiving a robe yearly with other servants.

11   PRO, C146/3295 (*CAD*, iii, 350–1).

12   Cumb. Westm. RO, AS 65 (Lowther deeds).

13   See Wormald, *Lords and Men*, pp. 34-75.

14   Indentures of retinue for life were also employed in Scotland, at least in the
Border country (*HMC*, Fourteenth Report, App. III [Duke of Roxburgh] pp. 9–10.

15   Se also below, pp. 111–12.

16   Cf., however, the Clifford indenture, discussed below, p. 94.

17   See Chs. II–III, *passim*.

18   See Plucknett, *Common Law*, 612–13.

19   e.g., *YBSS*, 5 Ed. II (1312), p. 3: 'For, since the writing is indented, even though
one clause charge you and the other charge us, yet it is all one deed.' For evidence
that this statement by counsel was accepted by the court, see *ibid.*, p. 7.

20   For an indenture used to grant a manor for life in return for past and future
services, see *Hatton's Book of Seals*, p. 318 (no. 457).

21   Almost invariably the phrase is *pro servitio suo impenso et impendendo*.

22   PRO, CP40/139/rot. 147, also discussed below, p. 73.

23   *YBRS*, 35 Ed. I, pp. 402–4.

24   *YBSS*, 5 Ed. II, pp. 1–9. There are four Year Book accounts of this case; and
in these the defendant's name is given as John of Cardiff. The details in the above
discussion are taken from the text of the Common Pleas record.

25   Saul, *Gloucestershire Gentry*, pp. 96–7, 265–6. Saul rightly comments that the
Statute of Westminster II of 1285 had extended the assize to include annual payments from one fixed place. Presumably, therefore, Kingston's robes fell within the
category of 'necessaries' mentioned by the statute. But why did he choose the pro-
cedure of novel disseisin rathe than a writ of annuity? The likely answer is that the

presence of the justices of assize nearby in Gloucester made novel disseisin the more convenient and speedy means of securing his rights, since the manor from which the robes were assigned was in the shire.

26 BL, Addit. R., 74138, cited in McFarlane, *Nobility,* pp. 105–6.

27 Like Kingston in 1320, Brit apparently took the opportunity, presented by the presence of justices of assize in the neighbourhood.

28 The doctrine only held, of course, if the deed of grant contained no further limitation of the words 'for his service performed in the past and to be performed in the future'. An annuity could be extinguished when the deed contained a provision that, if the annuitant did not remain in the grantor's service, the grant would be null and void (*YBRS, 11 Ed. II,* pp. 68–9). But there is no evidence that the annuities discussed in the pages that follow were of this kind.

29 *YBVE,* 21 Ed. III, Hil. (pl. 20, p. 7).

30 Anthony Fitz Herbert, *La Graunde Abridgement,* (ed. 1565), *Annuitie,* 30 (Trin., 32 Ed. III).

31 *YBVE,* 41 Ed. III, Hil., pl. 14 (pp. 6–7) and Mich., pl. 3, (pp. 19–20). See also Sir Robert Brook, *La Graunde Abridgement* (ed. 1586), f. 41 (*Annuitie,* 19).

32 On warranty see Plucknett, *Common Law,* 611–12.

33 See, e.g., *YBVE,* 2 Hen. IV, Mich., pl. 13 (Brooke, *La Graunde Abridgement, Annuitie,* 16), where it was agreed that an annuity granted by one man to another and his heirs, with warranty by him and his heirs, was extinguished by his death. In this case, however, the grantee's heir brought the writ against the grantor's heir.

34 See F. A. Enever, *History of the Law of Distress for Rent and Damage Feasant* (London, 1931), pp. 180 and 191–92.

35 For comments on household records see McFarlane, *Nobility,* pp. 109–12.

36 Printed and discussed in Baldwin, 'Household administration'.

37 PRO, E 101/92/23.

38 BL, Addit. R., 64320.

39 E.g., in the case of Henry Lacy, earl of Lincoln the account of the receiver of his household in 1304–5 (PRO, DL29/1/2/m. 15) and that of the constable of Bolingbroke castle in 1295–96 (ibid., /1/1/m. 10).

40 PRO, E 101/92/23.

41 BL, Add. R., 64320.

42 For the translation of *vallet* as 'yeoman' see Denholm-Young, *Collected Papers,* p. 200, n. 4.

43 *Black Book,* pp. 96, 99, 102.

44 For these various kinds of furs, see E. M. Veale, *The English Fur Trade in the Later Middle Ages* (Oxford, 1966), pp. 11–15.

45 These details do not support the statement by Denholm-Young, *Seignorial Administration,* p. 25, that bailiffs and constables had robes trimmed with lambskin.

46 *Black Book,* pp. 96, 99, 102, 104.

47 This includes Sir Peter Courtenay but not the earl himself, although he is listed.

48 *Black Book,* p. 96.

49 *Ibid.,* p. 99.

50 See below, Ch. VI, *passim.*

51 *Paston Papers*, ii, 430 (no. 784); *Paston Letters*, iv, 200–1.

52 Cited in Bean, *Percy Estates*, p. 134.

53 See e.g., *ibid.*, p. 95; PRO, DL 29/16/202.

54 PRO, E 40/11263. For thirteenth-century examples, see, e.g., *ibid.*, E13/10/m. 3, –/18/m. 60.

55 *YBRS, 11 Ed. III,* pp. 66–9; Brooke, *Abridgement, Annuitie,* 27.

56 *Paston Papers*, i, 393 (no. 233); *Paston Letters*, iv, 41.

57 See below, p. 202. For bitter contemporary comment on Richard II's giving out of badges, see the poem on his deposition in *Political Poems and Songs relating to English History, composed during the Period from the accession of Edward III to that of Richard III*, ed. T. Wright (Rolls Ser., London, 1859), i, xcii–iii, 379–81.

58 *Westm. Chron.*, pp. 186–7; PRO, DL28/4/1/f. 13v.

59 E.g., K. B. McFarlane, *Hans Memling*, ed. E. Wind with the assistance of G. L. Harriss (Oxford, 1971), p. 4. Richard, duke of York also gave collars (*ibid.*, n. 19).

60 *Black Book*, p. 96.

61 Cf. Hewitt, *Organization of War*, p. 39, for details of whole uniforms purchased at the beginning of the French wars of Edward III. But a royal campaign was a different matter from a magnate's household.

62 *Black Book*, pp. 96, 99, 102. The equivalent entry for a baron, however, was *Pro liberacione pannorum xxx hominum per annum in vestura* (*ibid.*, p. 104).

63 See below, p. 209.

64 The discussion on this topic that follows is a substantially amended version of arguments developed in my article '"Bachelor" and "retainer"', *Medievalia et Humanistica*, New Ser., iii (1972), 117–31.

65 *CPR, 1266–72*, pp. 145–7.

66 *The Roll of the Princes, Barons and Knights who attended King Edward I to the Seige of Caelaverock in 1300,* ed. T. Wright (London, 1864), pp. 24 and 27. Cf. *ibid.*, pp. 5 and 28, where 'bachelors' denotes a body of knights. For its use in the sense of knightly followers see Winner and Waster, *A Good Short Debate between Winner and Waster,* ed. I. Gollancz (London, 1921), line 328.

67 *Calendar of Documents relating to Scotland*, ii, 255 (no. 995), 307 (no. 1205), 324 (no. 1274), 346 (no. 1346), 372 (no. 1418) and 48 (no. 1789).

68 Holmes, *Higher Nobility*, p. 73.

69 E. B. Fryde, 'The deposits of Hugh Despenser the Younger with Italian Bankers', *Econ. H. R.*, 2nd. Ser., ii (1951), 352, 360–1.

70 Holmes, *Higher Nobility*, p. 66.

71 PRO, DL 40, 1/11/f. 4.

72 Holmes, *Higher Nobility*, p. 70; *CPR, 1370–4*, p. 325. For a grant to a 'bachelor' by Roger, earl of March (d. 1398) see *CPR, 1399–1401*, p. 196.

73 *BPR*, i–iv, *passim.* A list of fourteen (Tout, *Chapters*, v, pp. 387–9) is badly defective. Not all the seventy-two named in the registers, of course, could have enjoyed the status of 'bachelor' at the same time.

74 *JGRA, passim.*

75 *JGRA, JGRB, passim;* Tout, *Chapters,* v, 387–9.

76 *Ibid.*

77 *JGRB,* ii, 285 (no. 905).

78 *Hatton's Book of Seals,* p. 340 (no. 492). For a grant to a 'bachelor' by the prince of Wales in 1401 see *CPR, 1413–6,* p. 91.

79 *Letters and Papers Illustrative of the Wars of the English in France* (Rolls Series: London, 1861–64), ed. J. Stevenson, ii (2), 453.

80 See App. III(a), *passim.*

81 See below, pp. 89–90.

82 See, e.g. App. III(a), no. 4.

83 The discussion of this incident by T. F. Tout, 'The "Communitas Bachelerie Angliae"', *EHR,* xvii (1902), 89–95, is now superseded by E. F. Jacob, *Studies in the Period of Baronial Reform and Rebellion, 1258–1267,* (Oxford Studies in Social and Legal History, ed. P. Vinogradoff [Oxford,1925]), pp. 126–43.

84 *Life of the Black Prince by the Herald of Sir John Chandos,* ed. M. K. Pope and E. C. Lodge (Oxford, 1910), p. 18. For similar language, see also *ibid.,* p. 91.

85 *Rot. Parl.,* iii, 144b.

86 *Ibid.,* iii, 434a.

87 Matthew Paris, *Chronica,* v, 83. A different interpretation is presented by A. Tomkinson, 'Retinues at the Tournament of Dunstable, 1309', *EHR,* lxxiv (1959), 86, who suggests that the 'bachelors' on this occasion may have been 'a social grouping distinct from any division for combat'. Paris's language, however, argues against this view. He states that one side consisted of 'multi de militibus universitatis regni, qui se volunt bachelarious appellari'. *Bachelarios* should be taken in conjunction with *universitatis regni.* They obviously thought of themselves as representing the knighthood of England, combating aliens who formed the opposing side. This interpretation certainly fits with Paris's comment in the same passage on the ill-repute occasioned by the conduct of the earl of Goucester, who fought against his fellow-countrymen.

88 See G. Duby, *The Chivalrous Society,* trans. C. Postan (London, Berkeley and Los Angeles, 1977), pp. 112-22.

89 Denholm-Young, *Seignorial Administration,* pp. 8–9.

90 N. Denholm-Young, *Collected Papers* (Cardiff, 1969), p. 130, n. 2.

91 Geoffrey Chaucer, *Complete Works,* ed. W. W. Skeat (6 vols, Oxford, 1894), i. pp. 132, 155 ('The Romant of the Rose', ii, pp. 918, 1469); iv, p. 3 ('The Prologue to the Canterbury Tales', l. 80). For the whole range of meanings in late medieval English writings see the *Middle English Dictionary,* ed. H. Kurath (Ann Arbor, London, 1956), i, p. 599.

92 *Rotuli Chartarum* (Record Commission), pp. 59a and 102b.

93 *Rotuli litterarum patentium* (Record Commission), i, 190b–1a.

94 *Letters and Papers. . . Wars of the English in France,* ii (2), 453.

95 *Black Book,* p. 106.

96 *Ibid.,* p. 108. In its table of contents this compilation puts this category under

the heading *De militibus curialibus* (*ibid.*, p. 77). The editor is correct in stating (*ibid.*, p. 270) that the word 'bachelor' is not used here in the seventeenth century sense of knights of the lowest but most ancient order (*ibid,.* p. 270). But his view that they were 'young knights' is hardly supported by *The Black Book*'s statement that they were 'sufficient and most valiant men of that order of every country'.

97 PRO, E40/11547, abstracted in Phillips, *Aymer de Valence*, p. 309.

98 *BPR*, *passim*; *JGRA*, *passim*; *JGRB*, *passim*.

99 *CPR*, *1266–72*, pp. 145–7.

100 PRO, E40/6404, (*CAD*, iv, A.6404), abstracted in Phillips, *Aymer de Valence*, p. 309.

101 *JGRA*, ii, 78 (no. 1043), 132 (no. 1179); *JGRB*, i, 29 (no. 64).

102 Tout, *Chapters*, v, 387–9; *BPR*, i–4, *passim*; *JGRA*, i–ii, *passim*; *JGRB*, i–ii, *passim*.

103 B. H. Putnam, *The Place in Legal History of Sir William Shareshull* (Cambridge, 1950), pp. 7, 38, 162-3.

104 *JGRB*, i, 35 (no. 41), 271 (no. 433), 280 (no. 601).

105 *JGRA*, i, 114–5 (no. 269), 154 (nos. 360, 362); *ibid.*, 213 (no. 1396).

106 For an account of his career see Roskell, *Parliaments and Politics*, ii, pp. 15–43.

107 See, e.g., *JGRB*, ii, 6–13 (Hungerford, d'Ipre, Roucliffe).

108 *Guillaume le Maréchal*, ii, 110. Cf. S. Painter, *William Marshal* (Baltimore, 1933), pp. 142–3.

109 *Life of the Black Prince by the Herald of Sir John Chandos*, ed. M. K. Pope and E. C. Lodge (Oxford, 1910), p. 128.

110 Listed in App. III(a).

111 *Ibid.*, nos. 6, 7, 14, 15, 19, 27.

112 *Ibid.*, nos. 35–46.

113 *Ibid.*, nos. 48–56. These figures do not include the indenture made with John Neville, lord of Raby in 1370 (*ibid.*, no. 4). This gives him the right of attendance of his own 'bachelor' when he served in the household in time of peace.

114 App. III(a), nos. 54–6.

115 *JGRA*, ii, 132–3 (no. 1179).

116 *JGRB*, i, 32 (no. 72).

117 *Ibid.*, ii, 20 (no. 40).

118 T. Blount, *Nomo-Lexicon: A Law Dictionary* (London, 1670), *sub* 'Bouch of Court'; *Calendar of Charter Rolls*, p. 196, cited in Denholm-Young, *Seignorial Administration*, p. 167, no. 2; Nicolas, *Agincourt*, App., p. 11. In the record of a case relating to a retainer's loss of his benefits in 1403 (discussed below, pp. 149–50) the Latin equivalent is *cibaria*.

119 App. III(a), nos. 6, 7, 9, 14, 15, 18, 21, 26, 28, 29, 31–4.

120 *Ibid.*, nos. 35–46.

121 *Ibid.*, nos. 14, 19, 27, 30.

122 *Ibid.*, nos. 41, 43, 44.

123 *Ibid.*, nos. 6–8, 12, 17, 18, 20, 22–5, 28, 29, 31–3.

124   *Ibid.,* nos. 35–40, 42, 45.

125   Sir John d'Ipre the son received wages and *bouche de court* whenever he was sent for in time of peace, and in war a fee of £20 a year together with *bouche de court* or wages (*JGRB,* ii, 24 [no. 49]). But we cannot be certain that the 'ot' (or) was absolutely disjunctive. For discussion of such language see below, pp. 111–3.

126   App. III(a;, no. 19.

127   *JGRA,* ii, 78 (no. 1042).

128   App. III(a), no. 24.

129   *Ibid., JGRA,* ii, 87 (no. 1074).

130   App. III(a), no. 27.

131   *JRGA,* ii, 78 (no. 1042).

132   Sir William Atherton (*JGRB,* i, 46–7 [no. 116]), Sir John Fitz William (*ibid.,* ii, 359 [no. 1140]), Sir Nicholas Harrington (*ibid.,* ii, 260 [no. 805]), Sir Thomas Hesulden (*ibid.,* i, 189 [no. 577]), Sir Adam Houghton (*ibid.,* i, 74 [no. 222]), Sir John Orwell (*ibid.,* ii, 260 [no. 805]).

133   App. III(a), nos. 5, 8, 9, 10–13, 16–18, 20–6, 28, 29, 31–4.

134   *Ibid.,* nos. 35–40, 42, 45, 46.

135   East Sussex RO, Glynde 3469/5, 7, 10, 11, 12. These household rolls were at some time broken up to provide bindings for volumes (*The Glynde Place Archives. A Catalogue,* ed. R. P. Dell [Lewes, 1964], p. 260). Precise dating is an impossible task in most cases, since the years are missing; and the nature of the 'bachelor''s status means that one cannot rely on the dates of the indentures of retinue made by a number of those listed (cf. *ibid.*). It is, however, clear that, while the majority of the rolls probably belong to the early 1390s, at least one (no. 5) may be a decade or so earlier since it includes Sir Richard Burley. It is interesting to note that these rolls contain details on a daily basis of the horses kept in the duke's stables. It would thus appear that Gaunt followed a practice at least very similar to that of the royal household and that of the duke of Clarence in the late fifteenth century, a record kept in the office of the stable being used to check in the case of at least some of those daily wages (*Black Book,* p. 23, no. 4).

136   *Ibid.,* p. 96.

137   *Ibid.,* p. 95. The fee was ten marks. This was also listed for the four knights assigned to the household of a marquis (*ibid.,* p. 97).

138   See below, pp. 59–60.

139   Copies of such indentures may, however, have survived in the case of Aymer de Valence, earl of Pembroke (PRO, A. 11547, summarised in Phillips, *Aymer de Valence,* p. 309); and Stephen, lord Segrave (*Berkeley Charters,* p. 156 [no. 490]).

II

The beginnings of the indenture of retinue

In any study of the relationships between lord and man in late medieval England the development of the indenture of retinue deserves separate treatment. Throughout this period the basis, character and meaning of livery remained unchanged; and from the late thirteenth to the fifteenth century annuities granted in return for past and future services were subject to basically the same legal rules. But in the case of indentures of retinue it is easy to discern lines of development over the late medieval period as a whole and to impose a chronology on the interpretation of these. In particular, even to the most casual inspection, the indentures of the late fifteenth century appear markedly different from those of the fourteenth century. It is, therefore, both useful and necessary to examine the development of the indenture of retinue within a chronological framework.[1] The advantage of this approach is, of course, that it makes it easier to investigate the effects of both English political crises and the wars waged by the English Crown in Scotland and in France.[2]

As the terminal date of the first stage of this investigation 1360 has been chosen. The quantity of indentures that have survived increases quite markedly a few years after this year because of the survival of a comparatively large number of those made by John of Gaunt. It is thus especially desirable to treat the period of the beginnings of the indenture of retinue as ending in 1360 in order to avoid the possibility that the sheer bulk of surviving Lancastrian indentures might distort conclusions about the earlier materials. An equally important advantage of concluding the first stage of the investigation in 1360 is that this year marked the end of the first stage of the major conflict between England and France conventionally known as the Hundred Years' War. It is thus possible to give some attention to the effects of a war of aggression abroad on the development of the indenture.

The years down to 1360 can be divided into three sections, each coinciding with a well-defined period that also comprises a group of surviving indentures. The first covers the reign of Edward I, within which special attention can be given to the effects of the king's wars of conquest in Wales and Scotland. The second section covers the period between the accession of Edward II in 1307 and the *coup* achieved by the young Edward III in 1330, terminating a period of tension within the kingdom which had at times exploded into civil war. The materials for this period permit some assessment of the influence of baronial ambition on the development of the indenture of retinue. With the third section, 1330 to 1360, we revert to a situation, like that of Edward I's reign, in which the dominating influence in English politics was that of foreign war. Once his campaigns in France had begun, Edward III needed at times to exploit the resources of his kingdom, including the services of his nobility and gentry, on a scale that exceeded the efforts made by his grandfather in the last decade of his reign.

Throughout this discussion attention is primarily given to the indenture for the retainer's life. The justification for this must lie in the basic needs of the relationship between lord and man. Both sides wanted as lasting a relationship as possible, the lord in order to be able always to rely on his retainer's loyalty and assistance, the man in order to able to guarantee for himself as long as possible the fruits of his lord's favour. To be sure, on the lord's side financial constraints might dissuade him from making a great many indentures for life: even the most wealthy magnate would have to count the cost of imposing on his landed revenues a burden that was permanent as long as the retainer survived. Even so, the life-indenture by its very nature provides the clearest definition of what both lord and man sought from their mutual relationship. Occasionally attention must be given to indentures made for single campaigns, or other limited periods; but the life-indenture serves as a yardstick by which these must be judged by the historian.

(i)   1272-1307

If we use the term life-indenture in its precise technical meaning – that is, a deed in the form of a indenture sealed interchangeably between lord and man, six such documents are available before 1307,[3] all after 1307. Two belong to 1278, being made by the same lord. The rest come from the last decade of Edward I's reign. The two groups differ in the character of the contracts that were made. Those of 1278 were not concerned with war, whereas those of 1297-1307 all mirror the needs of the king's wars in some degree.

In form the two documents of 1278 are quite different from the later ones. Technically it is correct to call them indentures, since both are indented deeds; but the legal features embodied in them are more complicated. On 13 March 1278 William de Swinburne granted to William de Kellawe a rent of twenty shillings a year for life in return for his services performed in the past and to be performed in the future.[4] Kellawe promised to be faithful to Swinburne and his heirs, to stand by them and assist them with his counsel or help whenever they were present. On 19 May in the same year John de Insula made an agreement with Swinburne but in a rather different form, since it was a bond.[5] The clause dealing with the retainer's annuity also occurred in a different position in the deed. It began with Kellawe's promise to be faithful to Swinburne and his heirs for his life. The language employed echoed that of the earlier indenture, except that there was, in addition, an undertaking to protect Swinburne and his heirs against all men save the retainer's chief lords. Kellawe stated that he was bound to his chief lords before the making of the agreement with Swinburne. But he undertook that he would 'not stand with nor give aid and counsel' to them against Swinburne. He took an oath on relics to act faithfully and without fraud in all these matters because Swinburne had given him a rent of 20s a year for his good service performed in the future. Whereas Kellawe's rent apparently issued from the revenues of the manor of Halton, Insula's was to be paid out of Swinburne's chamber there.

These two indentures present several remarkable features. It is obvious that the practice of making agreements of service in return for annual payments of money was known in the late 1270s to a Northumbrian squire, dwelling in Tyndale,[6] an area virtually in the 'no man's land' between England and Scotland. The fact, however, that the annual payments to both retainers are called 'rents' may indicate some uncertainty about the use of the term 'fee' in this context. In describing this as given in return for past and future services the indentures ignore the legal distinction between a retainer's fee and an annuity; but this may be due to the date, 1278 being over a decade earlier than the first appearance of a doctrine on this point in the courts of common law. It is especially interesting that, in these two agreements, even though they were separated by a mere two months, the lord was agreeing to terms couched somewhat differently and, indeed, there were distinct differences in drafting. In one case there was a simple commitment to remain faithful and give counsel and support: in the other there

were qualifications added to this that give us a glimpse into the local rival-
ries, perhaps feuds, of the Border country. There is a strong hint that the
links created by feudal tenures had been strengthened by the lords concerned by means of bonds; but in agreeing not to assist his chief lords
against Swinburne Insula was making a commitment that cut across these
strengthened feudal connections. There is no mention of peace or war or
of any other benefits for the retainers concerned or even of any followings
they were expected to bring with them when they gave assistance to Swinburne. To be sure, the distinction between peace and war might well have
seemed artificial in the conditions of the Border country. Swinburne was
a ordinary squire, dwelling in a poor, largely pastoral area that was often
damaged by Border raiding. It is likely that two annual payments totalling
forty shillings were a burden for him. In these circumstances additional
benefits for his retainers would hardly have been feasible. Both of Swinburne's indentures are, therefore, important as survivals of conditions in
a outlying part of the kingdom; and, in so far as they throw light on tendencies that belonged to the kingdom as a whole, their importance lies in
the demonstration that a country squire who had limited financial means
and was distant from the centre of affairs knew of retaining by indenture.

Of the life-indentures that have survived from the last decade of Edward
I's reign, three belong to 1297. One has been known since 1937 when Mr
Denholm-Young printed it from Sir William Dugdale's transcript: it was
made on 9 June 1297 between the earl marshal and John, lord Segrave.[7]
The two others come from the same summer. One, made on 15 July
between Sir John Grey of Rotherfield, and Robert de Tothale, has
hitherto remained unnoticed by historians.[8] The other was between Sir John
Bluet and William Martel, dated 10 August.[9] From the close of the reign
(15 February 1307) comes a life-indenture between Humphrey de Bohun,
earl of Hereford and Essex, and Sir Bartholomew de Enfield.[10] Because of
the paucity of such survivals in this period, it is useful to examine them in
connection with another indenture of retinue which is not for life. It belongs
to 1297 – dated 2 July and made between Aymer de Valence and Thomas,
lord Berkeley.[11] It is, indeed, unwise in the case of this indenture to place
much emphasis on the absence of a mention of service for life: its terms
applied to both peace and war and even a cursory inspection reveals an
open-ended aspect that tempts one to describe it as a 'quasi-life' indenture.

In the case of the four life-indentures and the one 'quasi- life' indenture
that belong to the years 1297–1307 we encounter a basic similarity of
form. Despite differences in the opening formulae,[12] all are indentures
sealed interchangeably. There are two other features they all share in com-

mon. One is their apparent emergence from the Scottish and French wars
of the last decade of Edward I's reign. John, lord Segrave, entered into the
service of the earl marshal on 9 June 1297 at the point when his lord was
in conflict with the king over the consequences of his war policies for the
community of the realm. The indenture itself made specific reference to
the possibility of war in England, Wales or Scotland and of royal demands
for military service in Gascony, France or any other land beyond the sea
of Greece. Robert de Tothale promised to serve Grey in person with the
king's army across the sea, or whenever his lord might wish, except to
the Holy Land. The connection between the expected service and the king's
wars is especially noticeable in the stipulation that it would be lawful for
Grey to resume the payment for his man's service if he was not admitted
to the king's army or did not cross the sea, provided that Tothale did not
incur bodily harm in his lord's service. William Martel promised Sir Johm
Bluet that he would serve him loyally as a yeoman[13] 'in the war now
between the king of England and the king of France and also in England
if any war arise, which God prevent, and in Wales and in all lands on this
side and on that side of the sea in his own person.' The indenture between
the Bohun earl and Sir Bartholomew Enfield was made at Lochmaben in
the Scottish lordship of Annandale which the earl had been granted on the
forfeiture of Robert Bruce.[14] Its date – 15 February 1307 – was less than
a year after Bruce's seizure of the Scottish throne; and by giving Enfield
lands in the lordship it gave him a vested interest in its successful defence.
The 'quasi-life' indentures between Valence and Berkeley referred to service
in Engand, Wales and Scotland. It is true that the references to war service
in all these indentures were not confined to Scotland or France. But in
1297 it would not have been wise to exclude the possibility of service in
England or Wales: rebellion within the kingdom was a real possibility and
within the past three years there had been a Welsh rising. Nor is it surprising that the indentures of the earl marshal and the Bohun earl made provision for circumstances in which the lord went on crusade, since the need
for yet another effort to win back the Holy Land was never far from the
consciences of the nobility of Christendom. But it is no coincidence that
four of these indentures, including the 'quasi-life,' belong to the summer
of 1297, while that made by the Bohun earl was made within a recently
acquired Scottish lordship.

The second common feature lies in the methods of providing a reward
for the retainer's services. In each case there was a specific grant of land
or money. The earl mashal enfeoffed lord Segrave with a manor, together
with the advowson of its church, it being stipulated that this be restored

to the earl if Segrave was constrained from performing his service by
the king or took service with another lord. Grey granted Robert Tothale
6 marks' annual rent to be taken from Elias de Yapham in the village of
Yapham, Tothale performing the customary services to the lord of the fee.
Sir John Bluet granted his man 60s a year to be paid from his manor of
Llangstone in the lordship of Caerleon. Both the Grey and Bluet indentures
gave the recipient the right of distraint in the event of payment falling into
arrears. The Bohun earl granted Sir Bartholomew Enfield land worth forty
marks a year in Annandale, this grant taking the form of the earl's lands
in two places in the lordship, the earl undertaking to make up the value
elsewhere in Annandale if these lands fell short. Special care was taken to
ensure that Enfield retained this grant only as long as the requisite service
was performed, the earl's right to resume in the event of non-performance
being stated explicitly, sickness or injury being permitted as exceptions.
Aymer de Valence granted lord Berkeley £50 a year; but this indenture,
unlike the others, did not specify the source from which payment was to
be made.

But there are also marked differences between these documents. None
of them handles the mutual obligations of lord and man in the same way;
there are variations both in language and in the order in which matters
are dealt with. The indentures of the earl marshal, the Bohun earl and
Aymer de Valence articulate a distinction between the conditions of peace
and war which is missing in the other two. Most important of all is the
existence of conditions and details in the indentures of the three great lords
which are much less pronounced, or even missing altogether, in those of
the other two. The indenture made by Sir John Grey of Rotherfield is a
comparatively bare and simple document. It moves from the definition of
Robert de Tothale's service in war, specifying geographical location, to
financial compensation in the form of an annual rent, then to the circumstances that might annul the agreement. Sir John Bluet, in contrast with
Grey, promised his man two robes of livery a year from his chamber, at
Christmas for the winter and at Pentecost for the summer. During the
period of Martel's service he undertook to provide food and drink for him
and two grooms (*garsuns*), with hay, oats and shoes for two horses. In
addition, in time of war Martel was to receive a war horse with its armour
(*un graunt chevall de armes*).

It is tempting to describe the approach and details of Bluet's indenture
with Martel as a sort of intermediate stage between, on the one hand, that
of lord Grey and, on the other hand, those of the two earls and Aymer de
Valence. These three were leading magnates. And the terms of their inden-

tures reflect a situation in which their retainers, when in actual performance of their service, whether in peace or in war, became part of a great household; and, since it was as lords themselves that the knights concerned joined these lords, they secured conditions of service for their own followers as well as themselves. When summoned by the earl marshal in time of peace, lord Segrave was to bring fifteen knights with him, five of them members of his own household *(bachelors)*, each apparently with his squire.[15] Segrave and his five 'bachelors' were to have two robes a year of the earl's livery. In addition while in the earl's household this following was to be maintained at the earl's expense, the knights and squires receiving food and drink, the grooms *(garsons)* wages, and the horses provender. The indenture between the Bohun earl and Sir Barthlomew Enfield in this area of benefits reflected the difference in social status and political importance between the latter and lord Segrave. Enfield's following comprised, in addition to himself, a chamberlain and three grooms, the grooms receiving wages, the chamberlain food and drink in hall, while four horses were to have hay and oats. As befitted his importance, lord Berkeley was to bring a larger following than Enfield to his lord's household, though not in the scale of lord Segrave. He was to be accompanied by four knights, he and they receiving robes.[16] Food and drink were to be provided for Berkeley and his knights, his two squires, the knights' squires and the two household yeomen required to convey the baggage of Berkeley and his knights. From the indentures of these magnates there thus emerges a picture of a great household composed, in part at least, of some smaller households, absorbed within the greater one when their lords attended their lords.

In time of war these benefits were raised upwards. Segrave brought the same five 'bachelors', with ten troopers in addition, and the number of horses was raised to twenty. In addition to the manor he held, he was to receive a fee of £80 a year, together with wages for his men and horses at the rate of forty shillings a day.[17] The earl undertook to provide mounts for Segrave and his banneret, the horses being valued to provide for the contingency of their being lost during service. If the war occurred in Gascony, France, Flanders or elsewhere this side of the sea of Greece, apart from England, Wales or Scotland, a minimum of sixteen horses was specified, the earl promising to pay the costs of transportation overseas. Although the indenture is somewhat imprecise on this point, it would appear that the additional money fee and wages in time of war took the place of maintenance in the household which was provided for Segrave and his men in time of peace. The reason for this probably lay in another provision: if the earl did not go on the king's service overseas but the king wanted service from him, Segrave promised to go if requested by his lord. In this stipulation of the indenture we have an echo of the earls' resistance to overseas service which was endemic in the late thirteenth century and especially strong in the summer of 1297. No such provision or replacement of maintenance in the household occurred in the indenture between the Bohun earl and Sir Bartholomew Enfield. Such benefits were simply increased in time of war, wages being provided for seven grooms and hay and oats for eight horses, the chamberlain continuing to eat in hall. In addition, sufficient war equipment was to be provided for Enfield's following. It is interesting to note that this portion of the indenture dealt also with service during tournaments, providing on such occasions the same benefits as in time of war.

In its provisions for time of war the Valence indenture is much more complicated, partly because it dealt with the possibility that lord Berkeley's son Sir Maurice might become a banneret, this necessitating revisions in the size of the Berkeley contingent. Benefits were provided in time of war in both cash and kind. Lord Berkeley was to have wages as a banneret at four shillings a day, each of his knights taking two shillings and each squire with a barbed horse one shilling. If the war took place other than in England, Wales or Scotland, these payments were increased by an annual fee of 100 marks paid to lord Berkeley, the undertaking that Valence would provide wages and *bouche de court* being repeated. As in the earl marshal's indenture, the contingent's horses were to be valued, Valence being responsible for the costs of transportation overseas. The relationship between Aymer de Valence and lord Berkeley seems to have been closer and more personal than that between the earl marshal and lord Segrave. Berkeley and his son were to have accommodation in their lord's own dwelling for themselves and their knights,[18] it being specifically stated that this was to make it possible for them to be at his command night and day.

It is obvious that serious risks are involved in drawing conclusions about the precise relationships between lord and man in this period when the amount of solid documentation is so slight. We can, however, be certain that there were other life-indentures in these years. Some of the provisions of two of them are set out in the records of the court of common pleas relating to disputes that later occurred over the non-payment of the fees concerned.[19] On 19 September 1294 William de Cressy made a life-indenture with William de Doylly,[20] in which *inter alia* he promised the latter a robe worth twenty shillings a year for life in return for service in the Gascon campaign of that year.[21] And on 16 July 1297 Robert de Tony promised Adam de la Forde £5 a year, together with a robe and a saddle, for life, presumably, in the light of the date, for services that involved participation in the king's wars.[22]

The dominant feature of all save one of the surviving indentures of these years is the way they involved the retainer in a body of household arrangements. William Martel, lord Segrave and lord Berkeley attended their lords in person in time of peace and, with their followings, were fed out of their lord's resources while they remained in attendance. These three also received robes of their lord's livery (as did William de Doylly and Adam de la Forde in the case of the two indentures for which we have only partial information). The benefits provided Sir Bartholomew Enfield and his men by the Bohun earl were remarkably similar, this retainer being a 'bachelor'. It is tempting to state that such arrangements created an 'extended household' during the periods when these retainers and their followers were in attendance. But the details and tone of the actual documents suggest that this is terminology which neither lord nor man would have appreciated: the epithet 'extended' is superfluous. At any one time the household was no more or less than the body of those in attendance on their lord, whether in peace or in war. The one indenture which does not fit perfectly into this picture is that between the earl marshal and lord Segrave, since the retainer and his following were not treated as part of the lord's household in time of war. But this can easily be explained in terms of the political conditions of 1297 which made it all too likely that circumstances would arise in which the earl found it expedient to send his retainer on the king's service when he himself refused to go.

(ii)   1307–30

The reign of Edward II and the first few years of his son's form a period from which a total of eleven life-indentures have survived.[23] Like their predecessors of Edward I's reign, these share several features in common, and there are others that can be seen in a substantial proportion of them. The heart of the discussion of this group of documents must lie in those made by the earls of Lancaster, five out of the eleven – four in the case of earl Thomas (d. 1322) and one in that of his brother Henry. Of the other six indentures all except two relate to single lords.

There are difficulties in examining the indentures of Thomas, earl of Lancaster. Only one is an original half of an indenture, the other three being known from transcripts made by seventeenth-century antiquarians – two by Sir William Dugdale and one by Roger Dodsworth in which there may be omissions. However, the one original is also the most important of these indentures since it was especially lavish in its terms and was made with the retainer who was an importnt landowner in his own right and received a personal summons in time of parliament. The date of this indenture,[24] made with William, lord Latimer – 15 May 1319 – places it within the most troubled period of Edward II's reign, when the collapse of the English war effort in Scotland following the defeat at Bannockburn required the launching of a counter-offensive: the king's need for Lancaster's participation in this, following as it did the earl's stance of rebellious aloofness, put him in a position of special power in the realm. Both the fact that Lancaster retained so powerful a landowner as Latimer and the actual terms of the indenture attest to this. Latimer was retained for life in peace and in war in return for the manor of Sedgebrook in Lincolnshire, together with a total of £86 10s 8d in rents issuing from three other manors and the right to distrain in the event of non-payment. In setting out the services due from Latimer the indenture gave precedence to those during war. He was to serve the earl in England, Scotland, Ireland and Wales against all man save the king with forty men-at-arms. As in all such indentures, it was specified that these be properly armed and mounted; but Latimer and ten of those who were knights were to receive robes and saddles from the earl. Latimer himself was to be mounted at the earl's expense; and he was to receive compensation for any horses lost during his service in war. In return, in addition to his lifetime grant and rents, he was to be paid at the rate of £1,000 a year 'for the maintenance of his household' (*pur son hostel tenir*) and his other costs.[25] The extent of his services in time of peace was rather less precisely defined. He was to join the earl when summoned by letter to parliament and on other occsions. His knights were to wear the earl's robes; but neither their number nor that of the men accompanying them was laid down, the indenture simply requiring a reasonable and proper complement.[26] The indenture went on to mention Latimer's obligation to counsel his lord or go at his command, calling Latimer a 'bachelor' in this context.

At first signt it is puzzling to find so little precision in the case of peace, as distinct from war, especially in comparison with the indentures of the previous reign and the size of the benefits bestowed on Latimer. But three considerations may explain this. First, it may well have been thought at one and the same time superfluous and presumptuous to impose absolutely precise terms on so great a person as Latimer. And the mention of his being a 'bachelor' may have seemed enough. Second, the information we have indicates that this was not the first such agreement made between the earl and Latimer. At one point the language of the indenture indicates that it had a predecessor.[27]. And a note (in Latin) on the dorse refers to a renewal. Third, the emphasis given to the needs of service in war suggests that because of the Scottish expedition of 1319 there was re-negotiation of Latimer's contract of service between him and Lancaster. In fact, the indenture's date – 15 May – fell within the York parliament at which this campaign was planned. In this situation primacy would have been given to service in war; and there may well have been an assumption that loose ends in the definition of peacetime service could be left to the good sense of both sides in the light of details in the previous indenture.

In contrast, the three other life-indentures of Thomas of Lancaster all belong to 1317 – 21 June in the case of Sir Adam Swillington,[28] 24 July in the case of Sir Hugh Menill,[29] and 29 December in the case of Sir John Eure.[30] Because these were lesser men, their benefits in return for serving Lancaster for life in peace and war were on a lower scale than Latimer's. All three were paid annual money fees from the earl's lands – £40 for Swillington, ten marks for Menill and forty marks for Eure. As in the case of Latimer's their indentures gave precedence to service in war. Swillington and Eure were to bring continents of ten men-at-arms each, each of which had to include three knights. Service in war was also limited to England, Scotland, Ireland and Wales, against all men save the king. The retainer was responsible for the horses and armour of his contingent;[31] but he himself and three of his knights were to receive robes and saddles from the earl. He was to have *bouche de court* for himself and his men-at-arms, food and supplies for his horses and wages for as many grooms as horses. Menill whose contingent was only three men had benefits scaled down appropriately. In time of peace Swillington and Eure were to come when summoned by letter in time of parliament or on other occasions, they and their knights receiving robes from the earl and dining in hall,[32] the same allowances for horses and grooms being available as in war. Both these indentures go on to specify conditions that were to obtain when the retainer was summoned to give counsel or appeared accompanied by only one knight.[33] Menill's indenture, however, contains no details of benefits in time of peace apart from provender for four hourse and as many grooms. But, like his more important fellows, he had to come to the earl in time of parliament or when summoned on other occasions.

The indenture which earl Thomas's brother and successor, Henry, made with Sir Philip Darcy on 1 October 1327 is remarkably similar to those of Swillinton and Eure.[34] The retainer's annual fee for life was forty marks issuing from two manors. War was again limited to England, Scotland, Ireland and Wales against all men save the king. Darcy's contingent was smaller than those of Swillington and Eure.[35] But the same distinction was made between parliament and other occasions, on the one hand, and, on the other hand, those occasions when Darcy came to give counsel to his lord.[36] Perhaps the most striking difference between this indenture and its Lancastrian predecessors lie in its closing clauses. If Darcy defaulted or in any way refused to perform the required services the earl had the right to seize and retain the annual rent. And Darcy took an oath on the Gospels in the presence of named witnesses to perform all the services specified in the indenture.

Two of the surviving indentures of Aymer de Valence, earl of Pembroke. from this period were made with the same man – John Darcy 'the nephew'. On 29 November 1309 he undertook to serve as the earl's yeoman for life.[37] In peace and in war he was to receive his keep (*bouche de court*) together with robes. In time of war he was also to receive his mount and armour. The indenture emphasised his duty to attend his lord's person, although he was explicitly given freedom to choose another lord at tournaments in peacetime when the earl did not himself attend. In return for these services he was given one hundred shillings in tail in rent. The indenture also contained arrangements based upon the assumption that a yeoman had further ambitions in his lord's service. Pembroke promised to enfeoff Darcy of thirteen and a half marks of land and rent when he became a knight, Darcy on his side undertaking to serve the earl as one of his 'bachelors' on both sides of the sea and in the Holy Land. By the date of the second indenture[38] – 10 April 1310 – it was possible, or desirable, for the earl to treat Darcy's ambitions more seriously. He now promised to enfeoff him in tail of the fords of the river Trent in Gainsborough and Dunham, until he was found lands and rents worth twenty marks a year elsewhere; the value of Darcy's fee was thus increased by 50 per cent. In return, Darcy promised to take knighthood by the following 3 May (roughly three weeks later) and to serve the earl for life in peace and war in England and abroad and in the Holy Land. A third Pembroke indenture is badly damaged and, in particular, the name of the retainer is missing.[39] But enough has survived to show that its terms were markedly different from those of the other two.

Only two of the other life-indentures of this period relate to members of the higher nobility; but, because they deal with the same retainer, they must be discussed together. On 30 August 1316 Hugh Despenser the younger entered into an agreement with Sir Peter Uvedale.[40] It began with terms that strongly resemble those of the earls of Lancaster. Service was to be for life in peace and war, the latter being limited to England, Scotland

and Wales, Sir Peter undertaking to bring ten men-at-arms. There was no
explicit definition of the retainer's following in time of peace. But in war
he and his men-at-arms were provided with their keep (*bouche de court*).
In other respects, however, the terms were different from the Lancastrian
ones. To the explicit reservation of his fealty to the king Sir Peter added
that to his father, Sir John Uvedale. More important, there was no payment
of fee or wages of any kind by lord Hugh. Financial obligations were all
on the side of the retainer. In default of his service, or in the event of his
being opposed to lord Hugh, he undertook to pay the sum of £400 in
which he was bound by letter of obligation under his seal. The explanation
for this is to be found in the closing clauses of the indenture which reveal
that it was part of the arrangement involved in a marriage settlement. Sir
Peter promised that, if he married lord Hugh's sister, the lady de Hastings,
he would pay a sum of 400 marks by the following feast of the Purification.
The whole document obviously formed part of bargaining under which
lord Hugh and Sir Peter had jointly been trying to better themselves, the
lord by securing an ally, the retainer by making an advantageous marriage.[41]
This would bring him a widow's dower. More important, it would give
him a close family relationship with the Despensers, father and son, who
were already influential at the royal court: lord Hugh the younger was
about to be catapulted into great territorial power through his wife's succession to one-third of the great Clare inheritance as a result of her brother's
death at Bannockburn. A covenant by Hugh with which the indenture ends
– that he would assist Sir Peter to the utmost, saving the estate of the king
and of his father – suggests that success in this enterprise was not certain.

Apparently Sir Peter Uvedale's hopes from the Despensers achieved
nothing. On 12 March 1318 he made an agreement with Humphrey Bohun,
earl of Hereford and Essex.[42] Its existence and its date, belonging as it does
to a point when the Despensers' fortunes were even more clearly on the
rise than eighteen months earlier, can only mean that the agreement with
lord Hugh Despenser the younger was no longer in force. Compared with
the indenture with the latter, that with the Bohun earl is conventional,
though somewhat different from those of the earls of Lancaster. Precedence
was given to peace, not war. Sir Peter promised to remain in the earl's
service, taking robes and saddles like his other 'bachelors', together with
his keep (*bouche de court*), provender for four horses and wages for four
grooms, whenever summoned to his side by the earl. In time of war and
for any tournament such wages and provender were doubled.[43] The indenture is more terse in its terms than the Lancastrian ones,[44] making no
explicit mention of Sir Peter's benefits in time of war; but this may well

be because of an assumption that the benefits of a 'bachelor' carried over into wartime. The indenture shows that Sir Peter continued to be a knight who was bent on making his career, since he took service as a 'bachelor' and the term may have had a more literal meaning than was usual: the closing clause of the indenture – the stipulation that the earl provide his mount during his first year of service – suggests that Sir Peter was without solid resources.

The remaining three life-indentures involve lords at a much lower level of status and wealth. Both Robert, lord Mohaut, and Ralph, lord Fitz-william, were barons, in terms of landed wealth little different from many gentry but with a degree of importance and influence attested by their personal summons in time of parliament. On 30 August 1310 lord Mohaut entered into an indenture with Sir John Bracebridge.[45] It began with the statement that he had granted Bracebridge an annual rent of £10 for life from his manor of Walton-on-Trent in Derbyshire, specifying by name the tenants from whom the rent was to be received, assigning a precise sum to each, and giving his retainer power of distraint. In return Sir John promised his loyal service in peace and war in all places where it was needed and in all lands save the Holy Land. Lord Mohaut was to provide his mount and robes and all his reasonable costs. As in other indentures recompense for horses lost on service was promised; but in this case specific reference was made to the kinds of horses. The indenture closed with Mohaut's undertaking that, if Bracebridge was disturbed in his possession of the rent he had been given, he would be paid the sum of £100, this to be levied by the king's steward or marshal. Two features of this document require specific comment. One is the remarkable treatment of the annual rent: in all the surviving indentures of late medieval England the involvement of royal officials in giving security to the retainer is quite unique. One explanation for this may be lord Mohaut's lack of confidence in the administration of his estates, especially since the base of his territorial power and wealth lay in Cheshire and the surrounding Welsh marches and, indeed, his duties as steward of Chester must have kept him in this area. He could not have enjoyed the administrative resources of the earl of Lancaster or other leading magnates. Indeed, in awarness of this, Sir John Bracebridge may have requested what amounts to a penalty clause administered by the Crown. A second interesting feature is the way in which the retainer's benefits are treated. On the one hand, the language is less explicit than in other contemporary indentures, containing no reference to *bouche de court* or wages while in attendance on the lord. The explanation for this may well lie, in part at least, in the absence of a substantial household organisation. On the other hand, there is a pronounced precision in dealing with horses to an extent not encountered elsewhere. Here an explanation has to be even more speculative. It may well be that such precise enumeration was superfluous when a contingent consisted of a stated number of knights and other men-at-arms with their respective grooms. The accepted usages of war would provide acceptable rules; but Sir John Bracebridge was apparently accompanied only by his yeoman.

The indenture which Ralph, lord Fitzwilliam made with Sir Nicholas Hastings on 21 August 1311 was only slightly less different from those of leading magnates.[46] Sir Nicholas agreed to stay in the service of his lord 'for term of their two lives'. In time of war he promised to come to him on reasonable warning with two yeomen and ten grooms. In time of peace the contingent was reduced to only four grooms but the same number of yeomen. On his side the lord promised to provide the retainer with his mount, two robes and a saddle as befitted a knight, with reasonable compensation for any 'great horse of war' lost in his service. Lastly, he undertook to pay the reasonable costs of Sir Nicholas in travelling from any place in Yorkshire from the moment he left and also the wages of his men in both peace and war. Two features of this document are especially interesting. First, once again, the language of the great lords relating to household benefits is missing. We can only speculate that, like lord Mohaut, lord Fitzwilliam was not making commitments on the sure grond of an organised household. Second, there is the absence of an annual fee. Sir Nicholas Hastings only secured financial rewards in two ways – directly in the form of his keep and travelling costs and indirectly in the form of his men's wages so that he himself did not have to pay these while they were with him on his lord's service.

The indenture made by Hamo Massy of Cheshire with Philip Sammlesbury in 1312 is interesting partly because lord was a member of the gentry class.[47] In it he granted Sammlesbury an annual rent in return for his service in peace and war. In some respects the indenture is reminiscent of those made by William de Swinburne in 1278.[48] Unlike them it refers to service in peace and war; but it did not contain the detailed clauses we find in the surviving indentures of earls and barons.

In interpreting this body of documentation as a whole and placing it in the context of wider developments we are on somewhat firmer ground than in studying the comparatively few indentures that have survived before 1307. In the case of the family that produced the greatest number of survivals from 1307 to 1330 – that of the earls of Lancaster – it is quite clear that the earls and their administrators were dealing with basic formulae for defining the relationships between them and their followers.[49] And, whatever the differences, it is equally clear that the surviving indentures of most other lords shared features in common with the Lancastrian ones. Moreover, indentures were made by lords whose wealth was well below that of the kingdom's earls. All these considerations suggest that in England by the opening of the fourteenth century the relationship between lord and man was formulated quite frequently in indentures of retinue.

This conclusion is supported by much more than the body of surviving indentures. The information we have about the size of the retinue maintained by Thomas of Lancaster demonstrates that he must have made many more indentures of retinue than the mere four that have survived.[48] And the language employed by royal clerks who made lists of his muniments after his death in 1322 leaves no doubt that they were thinking in terms of indentures of retinue. One lists the 'names of the earls, barons, knights and squires of the retinue (*retenaunce*)';[49] and another lists lands and rents granted 'to divers men for their lives for their service in time of peace and war'.[50] In the case of the earl of Pembroke the evidence is more circumstantial, undoubtedly because he died a loyal subject so that his muniments did not find their way into the archives of the Crown. But there is a great deal of information to suggest a substantial following.[51] Although not all may have been indentured for life, the number of known followers is such as to justify the assumption that a substantial proportion must have been in this category. A list of the muniments of another magnate of this period – Bartholomew, lord Badlesmere – mentions indentures of retinue for life that he had made with four named retainers.[52]

If, then, the life-indenture was an accepted form of stating and binding the relationship between lord and man, what main features in such a document would a contemporary lord, knight or squire expect to find? The forms of language varied; and, indeed, that between lord Mohaut and Sir John Bracebridge used the older term 'chirograph' (*chirographum*) instead of indenture. In general contemporaries would expect an annual fee with more substantial benefits in time of war. But this could not always have been the case: there is no annual fee in the indenture between lord Fitzwilliam and Sir Nicholas Hastings. The one feature common to the terms of most of the surviving life-indentures of these years is the attention given to the maintenance of the retainer and his following when in attendance on the lord. In peace and war the retainer formed part of his lord's household.[53] The terms in which this situation was defined ranged from the precise language of the great earl's indenture to the vague statements of lesser lords. But even in the case of the former there could be imprecision. This is especially noticeable in the case of the provision of robes. Only in the case of William, lord Latimer do we encounter an explicit statement that two a year are to be provided. Nevertheless, the remaining four of Lancaster's surviving life-indentures use the plural 'robes'. And, quite apart from evidence that other magnates gave out two a year, Lancaster's wardrobe accounts for 1313–14 indicate that this was the practice for all his knights and squires.[54] The failure to mention this detail in some indentures can only be explained in terms of the basic character of the retinue: it, and the indenture with it, were rooted within the body of household usage that often made absolute precision in defining all the interests of the retainer seem unnecessary. It may well be that those cases of precision we do encounter resulted from insistence on the part of the retainer or a particular desire, because of his importance to the lord, to treat him with care.

At the same time two aspects of the relationships embedded within the household did receive close attention. The indentures take account of the status and importance of the individual retainer. Under Thomas of Lancaster in time of war Sir Adam Swillington and Sir John Eure were bannerets; their lesser colleague, Sir Hugh Menill was a 'bachelor', as was Sir Peter Uvedale in the case of the earl of Hereford and Essex. And the exalted status of Sir Adam Swillington and Sir John Eure under Thomas of Lancaster and of Sir Philip Darcy under his brother earl Henry, was mirrored in the provision of wine and candles for the knight's chambers. The other feature is that, just as the indentures paid careful attention to the obligations and benefits of the retainer as a member of his lord's household, so also it took into account the relationship between him and his own following. On this the Lancastrian indentures are especially explicit: the earl's knightly retainers, the knights and other men-at-arms within their own followings – *ses gentils gentz*, in the words of the Swillington and Eure indentures – ate in hall as part of their *bouche de court*. In contrast with this treatment their grooms were paid wages.

(iii) 1330–60

The collection of life-indentures from the years between Edward III's seizure of personal power in 1330 and his treaty with the French Crown in 1360 is dominated by those of two magnates – three in the case of Henry, lord Percy, and a much larger group in the case of the Black Prince. This is not simple accident. Within these years affairs in England were conducted against a background of war – first in Scotland, then in France; and these were leading generals, lord Percy on the Scottish border and the Black

Prince in his father's wars in France. The surviving indentures of lord Percy belong to the beginning of the period, those of the Black Prince towards the end.

The life-indentures of Henry, lord Percy bear a strong resemblance to those of the earls of Lancaster. The first was made on 1 August 1328 with Ralph, lord Neville, the head of another ambitious but less powerful northern family.[55] Neville was retained in peace and in war 'for the whole of their two lives' with twenty men-at-arms of whom five were to be knights. In return he obtained an annual fee of £100, to be taken from two of Percy's Yorkshire manors. In addition, he was to be given robes and saddles for himself, his five knights as well as 'his other companions', presumably the other men-at-arms. In time of war, he and his *gentiils gentz* (again, presumably his knights and men-at-arms) were to eat in hall with six yeomen (*vallets de mestier*) and to take provender and supplies for fifty-nine horses and wages for fifty-three grooms. Neville himself was to have his mount provided by lord Percy, being responsible for the arms, horses and equipment of his own men. He and they were to serve lord Percy against all others, saving their allegiance to the king. There was the usual clause about recompense for horses lost in the lord's service in war. A separate body of clauses then dealt with occasions when Neville was summoned to assist in a tournament. He was then to come with four knights who were also to bring with them *gentiz gentz come affierent* (that is, such well-born attendants as seemed fitting). On such occasions the benefits available were proportionately the same as those in war – dining in hall with five serving-men, provender and supplies for thirty-seven horses and thirty-two grooms. When summoned for attendance at parliament or any other occasions, the size of the knightly following was not specified, the words *come affiert* (as seems fitting) being used only; but there were to be nine horses and three serving-men, with the usual provender and supplies and also wages for six grooms. Neville promised that, if prevented by illness from obeying his lord's command in person, he would send the appropriate contingent under a 'sufficient captain'. Lastly, he was promised his costs in making reasonable journeys coming to and returning from his lord. On 22 January 1332 another indenture was made between Percy and Neville's heir.[56] There was only one difference between it and its predecessor: in place of the annual fee of one hundred pounds the new lord Neville secured a grant for life of Percy's manor of Newburn.[57]

There can be little doubt that Percy's engagement of Neville formed part of his activities in the Scottish wars. The earlier indenture belonged to the point when he was prosecuting his rights as one of the 'disinherited' who had lost family holdings in Scotland; and the second was drawn up at the point at which he was planning to assist Edward Balliol to seize the Scottish throne.[58] The aftermath of these events, and their absorption within the wider Anglo-French conflict, provide the background to another indenture made by lord Percy which possesses remarkable interest.

On 1 September 1337 he engaged the services of William, son of John de Roddam, a member of a Northumberland gentry family.[59] The indenture was for both peace and war, the retainer to be accompanied when summoned by a 'sufficient companion'. In time of war he was to receive for himself and his companion robes 'like other yeomen', fodder and supplies for six horses and wages for six grooms, with recompense for any horses lost. The features of interest presented by this indenture are twofold. First, its duration was not for life or a campaign or a portion of a year: it was to last until the coming of age of John, son and heir of John de Roddam. Second, there was no annual fee: instead, the retainer obtained the wardship of the lands of John, son and heir of John de Roddam, until he came of age. Apparently this was his nephew. The absence of any indication that William de Roddam would then continue to be retained by other means suggests that the heir's father had been so retained before his death and that lord Percy intended, when the heir came of age, that he should take his father's place. At any rate, in these respects this indenture is unique among all the survivals from late medieval England.

The surviving indentures of the Black Prince are embedded in the efforts he made to maintain a nucleus of commanders for his campaigning in his father's wars in France. Those prior to 1361 are to be found as copies entered in the registers of his estate administration. We cannot be sure that all such documents were registered,[60] or that the other main records of the prince's administration – the recognizance rolls of Chester, the palatine county's equivalent of the royal patent rolls – included copies of all those involving payments from his lands in Cheshire.

Two of these indentures belong to the same knight – Sir John Sully. On 27 January 1353 he was retained for life with one esquire, receiving a fee of £40 a year by the hands of the prince's receiver-general.[61] On 10 March of the same year this indenture was cancelled, another being executed which provided that the annual fee was to be paid out of the annual issues of the prince's manors in Devon.[62] Sully was retained in peace and war with one squire. In time of peace they were to eat in hall:[63] five horses were to be supplied with provender and supplies and four grooms were to be paid wages by the prince. In time of war the number of horses was raised to ten and that of grooms to nine, the same conditions applying; but Sully himself was to be provided with his mount by the prince. In both peace and war the treatment he received was that of a 'bachelor' of the prince's chamber. It is interesting to note that the indenture of 10 March differed from its predecessor in that it stated that Sully was retained as one of the prince's special retinue (*especiale retenue*). This may suggest that there were gradations within the ranks of the prince's 'bachelors': indeed, the term 'bachelor of the prince's chamber' in the second indenture may be a substitution for 'special retinue'.

A third life-indenture was with Sir Baldwin Freville. He was retained for life in return for an annual fee of £40 out of specified estates.[64] But it did not contain the customary phraseology about 'peace as well as war'. It did state that, when the prince went to war, Freville was to receive benefits in proportion to the number of men he brought on the same conditions as applied to others of his condition.

In the case of the Black Prince it is possible to place his life-indentures of the years 1330 to 1361 in a wider context. This is provided by documents from three sources. First, there are indentures of retinue of limited duration entered in his surviving registers. Second, there is some information in the Cheshire recognizance rolls. Third, there are confirmations (enrolled both on the royal patent rolls and on the Cheshire recognizance rolls) made by the Black Prince's son and heir Richard II after he ascended the throne in 1377. Some of these documents relate to the years after 1361; but it is convenient to treat them at this stage. It is reasonable to assume that the Black Prince's attitude towards the making of indentures with his retainers did not change after 1361; and the indentures that have survived for other magnates after that year, including those of his younger brother John of Gaunt, belong to a different generation.

One way to place the life-indentures in a wider perspective is to investigate the role of the Prince's 'bachelors'.[65] The indenture of Sir John Sully indicates that such knights could also be retained for life. Even so, a substantial proportion did not achieve the position of an indentured retainer. But, if they did not, their special status as 'bachelors' did receive recognition and they obtained some form of special treatment. The case of Sir Edmund Manchester is especially instructive.[66] In an indenture of 3 May 1351 he was retained in peace and war in return for a fee of twenty marks a year, to be paid out of the prince's wardrobe, it being specifically stated that this was to be paid quarterly as long as he remained with the prince. In all respects except the mention of life service these terms resembled those of a life-indenture. Manchester was to serve the prince with a squire and to go with him wherever he went on either side of the sea. He was to have the same privileges with his squire as other 'bachelors', eating in hall and taking victuals or wages when they did. His chamberlain was to enjoy the same privileges as those of other 'bachelors', eating in hall or receiving wages of twopence a day. In war he was to have six grooms at the prince's wages with four hourses supplied with necessities by the prince. He was to provide his mount, receiving suitable compensation in the event of loss. The prince undertook to provide sufficient shipment for him, his men and horses across the sea and for the return voyage. This, to be sure, is the only indenture of its kind surviving in the materials relating to the Black Prince; but there is nothing in it or elsewhere to suggest it was the only one of its kind. However the absence of additional documentation prevents us from being certain about its provenance. Since there was no stated term and the retainer's fee was to be paid out of the wardrobe, this may well have been the type of indenture that was made in the case of 'bachelors'.[67] But the fact that it was the only one of its kind entered in the surviving registers also may mean that it was a special arrangement.

It is also clear from the surviving documentation that the Black Prince did not always employ an indenture when he wanted to enter into a life relationship with a knight or squire. On 28 January 1348 he granted 100 marks a year for life to Sir Henry de Eam from one of his Devon manors, with the right of distraint.[68] The letter patent in which this was done described how, when he received the order of knighthood from the prince, Eam had promised 'of his own free will to attend to our service for term of his life' in peace and in war against all men save his lord, the Duke of Brabant, when the latter was fighting in defence of his own lands. The prince stated that the grant of the annual fee was to bind Eam more closely to his service and help him in the maintenance of his estate and the further-ance of his career.[69] There was no reference to any separate indenture. It may, of course, be argued that this was a special case, since Eam was not a native Englishman. But on 31 July 1352 the prince granted letters patent announcing that he had retained his 'bachelor' Sir William Daubigny for life in peace and in war.[70] Daubigny received fifty marks a year for life from borough farms in Cornwall, with the right of distraint, in order that he might better maintain his estate. In this document also there is no refer-ence to a separate indenture. Nor was this an isolated case of a native English retainer receiving such treatment. On 1 March 1356 the prince issued an order to his chamberlain of Chester to have letters patent made out in the form of a grant of £10 a year for life to his yeoman William Greenway whom the prince had retained to stay with him in peace and in war.[71] In a similar order to the same official on the same day he announced that he had retained his 'bachelor' Sir Richard Massy for life with two squires in time of war and one in time of peace in return for fifty marks a year.[72] The chamberlain was ordered to make out the necessary letters patent and to pay the fee. It is quite likely that in all these cases the grant of an annual fee for life was accompanied by a separate indenture of retinue. Yet there is another – Sir Aubrey de Vere on 1 October 1367 – where the retainer was retained for life in peace and war and at the same time granted an annuity for his past and future services. There was no mention of the contingent he would bring to the prince's service and no commitment to pay additional remuneration when on active service. To be sure it is possible to suggest that that was an exceptional arrangement: de Vere's importance as a retainer is indicated both by the size of his fee – 100 marks – and by the fact that he was the brother of an earl.[73]

These examples, however, do not exhaust the variety of the Black Prince's retaining practices. Perhaps the most remarkable of these is first encountered in letters under the prince's privy seal enrolled on the Chester recognizance rolls and issued in November 1367.[74] In these he granted four[75] of his knights annuities of £40 each for life 'in return for which annuity we wish that (he) be bound to serve us as well in time of peace as in war for the whole time for which he shall have been summoned by us, that is, in time of war with two sufficient squires without taking any other fee for himself or the two said squires'.[76]

It is reasonable to suggest that all those retainers in whose cases there were apparently no indentures may have made some sort of oral engagement, presumably before witnesses; but it was not thought necessary to mention this in the prince's letters patent. It is equally interesting to note that in these cases the annual fee was the only form of payment involved: there was no mention of any additional fee or wages or benefits of other kinds in time of war. Indeed, in the case of the four knights of 1367 there was a specific exclusion of a wartime fee. We cannot totally exclude the possibility that wartime benefits were taken for granted, being left to the body of custom that operated between the prince and his following in time of war. If so, it would have been necessary to insert the exclusion of a wartime fee in the letters patent granted to the four knights of 1367. But a strict construction of the language employed in all those cases where an indenture apparently was not employed, and the contrast with the deliberately explicit references in the indentures of retinue of others, suggest that at least some of these retainers were content with annual fees alone. In some of these cases, notably the four knights of 1367, these fees, it must be said, were large, giving the knights concerned annual incomes from the revenues of the Black Prince that must have exceeded the incomes they and other knights received from their own estates.

In any event it is clear that the retaining practices of the Black Prince involved a range of usages. In some measure, it must be said, some retainers would have been content with substantial annual fees alone simply because service under so great a lord as the Black Prince was its own reward, since it opened up several avenues to personal gain – further advancement in his service or ransoms and plunder in time of war. It must be emphasised, however, that the surviving documentation involves only a small portion of the retaining arrangements made by the Black Prince. We know, for example, that in 1369 he spent a total of £1,537 on fees, annuities and wages from his revenues in Cheshire alone.[77] And a comparison of this total with the details of fees and annuities contained in the available retaining arrangements suggests that these involved only a small part of total expenditure in this area. Moreover, the large number of references to his 'bachelors' in his surviving registers implies that he must have maintained a much larger group of such retainers than other contemporary magnates. It is also important to bear in mind that the surviving indentures and letters patent relate to lifetime arrangements and that much of the prince's retaining must have been for limited periods or at his pleasure. In the last resort, however, it is essential to bear in mind that the Black Prince was the heir apparent to the throne. His practices, notably the substantial number of 'bachelors', must have been closer to those of the royal household than those of the magnates. Above all, his role of leadership in the kingdom's wars meant that men were so anxious to enter his service that the formalities of retaining were a secondary consideration in their dealings with him. And for this reason his retaining practices may embody relics of a time when such arrangments were looser and the indenture of retinue had not evolved into its conventional form.

Of the remaining indentures of the years 1330 to 1361 two belong to the house of Lancaster. Henry, earl of Lancaster (d. 1345), on 27 August 1333 granted to Philip of Castle Martin,[78] an annual rent of seventeen-and-a-half marks for life from his manor of Minsterworth in Gloucestershire in return for the good service that he had performed and would perform in future in peace and in war in all places where the earl himself might be. In time of war the earl would provide his mount; and in both peace and in war he was to receive shoes, provender and supplies for his horses and wages for his grooms like the rest of the earl's squires. He was given the right of distraint; but, at the same time, if he refused to serve on reasonable warning or failed to do so without reasonable excuse such as illness, then the earl had the right to retain the rent. The grant of the rent was made with warranty by the earl and his heirs for the squire's life. The indenture closed with the surrender of the rent (amount unspecified) which the retainer already had of the earl's grant for life elsewhere. This indenture displays features that have not so far been seen. The main one is the conjunction within the same document of a grant in return for past and future services with a retainer in peace and in war; it was the annuity that was the greater part of the retainer's reward for indentured service. And many of the detailed stipulations generally encountered in indentures, especially in time of war, are missing. It is especially interesting that the number of horses and grooms is not specified; and, although the retainer received his mount in time of war from the earl, there is no mention of his keep while he was serving. At the same time he was a squire and his other benefits resembled those that generally went hand in hand with *bouche de court*. The most likely suggestion is that earl and man took for granted the usages of the earl's household.

The indenture that this earl's son and heir, later duke of Lancaster, made with Sir Edmund Ufford on 1 March 1347 has a slightly more familiar form and character.[79] In time of war Ufford was to bring three men-at-arms, being himself mounted by the earl. He was to receive fodder and supplies for ten horses and wages for nine grooms, his chamberlain eating in hall. There was the usual provision for compensation in the event of any of his horses being lost on the earl's service. In time of peace he was to come with one squire, the number of horses and grooms being reduced to four and three respectively but the same conditions as in war applying to the latter and his chamberlain. The earl then granted to Ufford for the good service that he had done in the past and would perform in the future an annual rent of forty marks from his manor of Higham Ferrers in Northamptonshire, with the right of distraint and warranty by the earl and his heirs. Like that made by the earl's father in 1333, this indenture has several unusual features. Once again, the grant of an annuity in return for past and future services is found as the retainer's reward for service in peace and war. Here there is precision over the numbers of horses and grooms. But there is no mention of *bouche de court*. In the case of this indenture, however, there is reason to believe that this was intentional, since the fee of forty marks was quite high and there was no attempt to define benefits in terms of a comparison with other knights who served the earl. It is possible, though not certain, that Ufford was himself responsible for his own keep while on his lord's service.

One indenture survives for Thomas Beauchamp, earl of Warwick, made

with Sir Robert Herle on 20 April 1339.[80] It began with a precise statement
of the contingent in time of war – four men-at-arms. In time of peace Herle
served the earl as one of the 'bachelors' of his household (*de son hostel*).
He was to be paid his reasonable costs in journeying to and from the lord's
side and to receive *bouche de court* for himself and his squires, wages for
his grooms and fodder and supplies for his horses when there. In time of
war and for attendance at tournaments the earl would provide his mount,
there being the usual provision regarding the loss of his other horses on
the earl's service. Herle was to have the wardenship of Castle Barnard and
its appurtenances for term of his life, including forests as well as lands. He
and his officers were to have their keep (*buche*) within the castle and hay
for their horses. In this document we see some entirely novel features. A
retainer for life in peace and war was rewarded with the tenure of an office,
instead of an annual fee. It must be assumed that he would receive an
annual fee for the wardenship which, of course, made him an important
person in the administration of the earl's estates. Indeed, it is more than
likely that this office was granted in separate letters patent, the amount of
the fee being stated there. In its other provisions the indenture adheres to
the conventions more closely. It is worth noting that the earl and the knight
did not think it necessary to specify the privileges he would enjoy as a
'bachelor', the word itself sufficing as a definition, even embracing what
he would obtain for his own retinue and horses.

But, whatever the differences between the various indentures of these
years, all were substantial documents that attempted to cover at least the
important aspects of the relationships between lord and man. An indenture
made on 20 June 1340 between William Bohun, earl of Northampton, and
Sir William Taillemarche stands in complete contrast.[81] He granted Taillemarche the manor of Latchley in Essex for life, the tenant performing any
services due to the lords of the fee. In return he was retained for peace and
war, without further detail or qualification.

What emerges from an analysis of the life-indentures of the years 1330
to 1361, especially in contrast with those of the late thirteenth and early
fourteenth centuries, is a picture of complex variety.[82] It can be argued that
some of the conclusions about the Black Prince's retinue relate to a very
special case, since the heir apparent to the throne would not necessarily
behave like other magnates. But the indentures of the earls of Lancaster
also present a picture of complexity. Earl Henry in 1333 did not stick to
the pattern of the indenture he made in 1327; and those he and his son
and heir made in 1333 and 1347 respectively violated the legal distinction
between an annuity and a retainer's fee. These facts are all the more remark-

able because earl Henry's indenture of 1327 resembled more closely those made by his brother, Thomas. Moreover, the house of Lancaster had much greater administrative resources than other magnates and was in a good position to keep precedents.

Nevertheless, despite this picture of complexity, two features are to be found in common. One is the concern with the retainer's membership of a household when he came to serve his lord. Details might vary;[83] but in peace and in war he and his own entourage enjoyed benefits in the form of contributions to their maintenance, though these might vary from retainer to retainer. The second feature involves the existence of occasional apparent omissions or obscurities. Indentures rarely covered every detail of the relationship between lord and man with absolute precision. The explanation for this must lie in the fact that the relationship set out in the indenture was embedded in the structure of the lord's household. Literal precision on every point was superfluous, since there was always a body of usage which, in the event of uncertainty, could provide a fair basis for settlement. In the last resort no lord would engage in pettifogging with a retainer whose service and loyalty he wanted.

Viewed as a whole, the surviving life-indentures of the years 1330 to 1360 present a somewhat different picture from that so far depicted by the historians of 'bastard feudalism'. To be sure, virtually all involve the annual payment of a money fee; but equally important in the minds of those who drafted these documents, at least in terms of the space that was given to them, were the privileges and benefits that a retainer received as a member of his lord's household. It is especially interesting to note the way in which household relationships appear in these indentures. In one way or other the 'bachelor' constantly makes his appearance. A great retainer might bring his own 'bachelors'. Some were clearly 'bachelors' when they entered into indentures of retinue; and others acquired the status of 'bachelor' in peace or in war, or sometimes both, when their benefits as members of the lord's household were defined.

One particular impression emerges from a reading of the indentures of the late thirteenth and early fourteenth centuries, although it cannot be regarded as a firm conclusion supported by positive proof. Over fifty years ago A. E. Prince argued that the earliest contracts for military service between lords and men and between the king and his commanders were oral.[84] The later rejection of this view[85] has more recently been confirmed by the discovery of many more written contracts from the late thirteenth century. But a detailed study of many of the surviving life-indentures suggests that the possibility of an oral element in their composition should not lightly be dismissed. The evidence, it must be said, consists of written instruments. Even so, in reading some of these it is difficult not to feel that the actual texts emerged very directly out of oral discussions between the retainers and their lords, a clerk taking notes that were later expanded, or even writing out the indenture in a final stage of negotiation. This may well explain the loose, almost informal, character of, for example, the agreements between the earl marshal and John, lord Segrave, between Aymer de Valence and lord Berkeley and between Thomas, earl of Lancaster, and William, lord Latimer. It must be admitted that other indentures suggest the existence of basic forms and conventions in such agreements: the strong resemblances, even coincidences between those made by the earl of Lancaster with Sir Adam Swillington, Sir John Eure and Sir Hugh Menill are especially pronounced. The indentures that seem most strongly to have come fresh out of negotiation relate to especially important retainers. Even so, echoes of oral discussion can be detected in those of the earls of Lancaster between 1327 and 1347. Indeed, such a background may help to explain omissions and obscurities and the reliance on household usage they imply. This possible link between the written indenture and oral negotiation between lord and man is yet one more element in the picture of complexity revealed by a detailed investigation of the life-indentures that have survived before 1361.

Notes

1 For an earlier discussion see Lewis, 'Indentured Retinues'. Professor Lewis confined his attention to the fourteenth century which he tended to treat as a whole. Moreover, he did not have access to all the indentures now available.

2 The discussion in this and the following chapter is concerned with the indentures of retinue made by English lords (including those of the Welsh March). Except for purposes of occasional commparison, no attention is given to the extant Irish indentures, preserved among the Ormond deeds (*Ormond Deeds, passim*). In fact, though in the form of indentures, these for the most part are better regarded as treaties with Irish chieftains or gentry of the Pale.

3 This total does not include documents which other historians have placed in this category. The indenture printed and discussed by McFarlane, in 1965 (*Collected Essays*, pp. 45–55) is between two knights. Although it is 'an indenture of mutual retainer in peace and war' (*ibid.*, p. 47), it is between equals and neither is the lord of the other. *Pace* Saul, *Gloucestershire Gentry*, p. 91, the arrangements between Sir John Giffard of Weston and William Greenfield, archbishop of York did not

involve an indenture. The relevant document was a charter, being described as a *concessio* (*The Register of William Greenfield, Lord Archbishop of York, 1306–15*, Part I (Surtees Society Publications, vol. cxlv [London & Durham, 1931], ed. A. Hamilton Thompson), p. 168 [no. 385]). Though the use of *moretur* and the provisions of food and other maintenance for Giffard and his following are reminiscent of contemporary indentures, the grant is really one of hospitality for a knight who was the archbishop's nephew *quociens et quandocunque ad nos venire voluerit*. It was Gifford who decided whether to avail himself of his uncle's hospitality. Three documents cited as indentures in Jones, 'Mohaut–Bracebridge indenture', pp. 392–3 [nos. 10, 13–14] cannot be assumed to have been in this form, since they are known only from summaries and could have been charters or letters patent (*CCR, 1323–7*, p. 38; *Cal. Inq. Misc.*, ii [1307–49], nos. 970, 976).

4   Northumb. RO, Swinburne–Capheaton 1/36. For a receipt from Kellawe for his fee at Pentecost 1289, see *ibid.*, 1/44.

5   *Ibid.*, 1/37.

6   For details of Swinburne see *NCH*, iv, 254–8; xv, 206. There is some reason to believe that there was a crisis in his fortunes in 1278 (*ibid.*, iv, 256). Haughton was part of the lordship of Wark, then held by Alexander III, king of Scotland.

7   Denholm-Young, *Seignorial Administration*, pp. 23–4 (discussion) and 167–8 (text).

8   It was, however, abstracted in *Yorkshire Deeds*, ed. W. Brown (Yorkshire Archaeological Society, Record Series, xxxix, Leeds, 1909), p. 185 (no. 501). The original is now in Leeds City Council Archives, Gc/DZ 364.

9   BL, Add. Ch., 1531.

10   PRO, DL 25/92, calendared in *CDS*, ii, no. 1899.

11   PRO, E 101/68/1/1, printed in H. Gough, *Scotland in 1298* (London, 1888), pp. 260–61 and reproduced in *Speculum*, xxix (1954), facing p. 503.

12   Marshal–Segrave: *Ces sount les convenauntes;* Bluet–Martel: (after dating by regnal year) *Issi acquit parentre;* Grey–Tothill: *Hec est convencio facta;* Valence–Berkeley: (after dating by regnal year) *aconvenu est entre.*

13   Professor M. Altschul wrongly states that Martel was to serve as a knight (*A Baronial Family in Medieval England: The Clares, 1217–1314* [Baltimore, 1965], p. 279).

14   Apparently it was not the first indenture between the earl and Enfield. On 16 August 1294 the earl, described as going to Gascony on the king's service, was given a royal licence to grant to Enfield (not yet a knight) who was going with him for life an estate consisting of one and a quarter messuages and three carucates (*CPR, 1292–1301*, p. 84). Viewed in this light, the details of the indentures of 1307 suggest that the earl's need for his services had increased: the benefits provided cannot be attributed solely to Enfield's acquistion of knighthood in the intervening years.

15   Denholm-Young's term 'lances' (*Seignorial Administration*, p. 24) is misleading in the case of attendance in time of peace.

16   Whether one or two a year was not stated.

17   Reduced to thirty-two shillings if only two horses were brought.

18 *chaumbre de liverie en le houstel lavaundit Eymar.*

19 I have to thank Dr Robert C. Palmer for bringing this case and the one that follows to my attention.

20 PRO, CP 40/139/rot. 147.

21 *Ibid.*, CP 40/195a/rot. 301. Further details are lacking because non-performance of the retainer's duties was not (as it was in the other case) the issue. Guy Beauchamp, earl of Warwick, and his wife Alice, the sister and heir of Ralph de Tony successfully contested the case on the ground that de Tony was a minor at the time and thus they were not bound by the agreement.

22 It is worth noting that, apart from the commutation of his robe, there was no money fee in the case of Doylly.

23 This total does not include one between Prince Edward and Sir Simon de Hale, which Jones, 'Mohaut–Bracebridge indenture', (p. 393, no. 20) lists as an indenture made between them at some date before 23 August 1326. He does describe the actual document as a letter patent, apparently assuming from its words *nous avons retenuz* that there was also an indenture. But this language does not necessarily imply this (see above, pp. 60–2). Nor does the letter patent mention any grants for life that had been made to the retainer. Rather, in it the prince promised to grant lands worth 100 marks a year to his 'bachelor' *a avoir et tenir de nous fraunchement a li et a ses heirs perpetulement* (PRO, C 47/2/2/45). We cannot entirely exclude the possibility that there was a separate indenture of retinue. But it is more than possible that the prince was promising to reward a faithful 'bachelor' with an inheritance and that the word *retenuz* referred to an oral agreement or to his status as a 'bachelor'.

24 PRO, DL 36/2/p. 33. printed in Holmes, *Higher Nobility*, pp. 122–3.

25 The amount of the advance payment varied with the war's location – twelve weeks in the case of Scotland and Ireland, forty days in the case of Wales.

26 *quill serra renablement garni . . . et ove son plein des gentz darmes.*

27 *et touz les autres services contenuz en les endentures faites entre le dit conte et le dit monseiur William de sa retenance.*

28 Bodl. MS. Dodsworth 94, ff. 122v–23.

29 Bodl. MS. Dugdale 18, f. 39v. For a summary, see Dugdale, *Baronage*, i, p. 780.

30 Bodl. MS. Dugdale 18, f. 39v; Dugdale, *Baronage*, i, p. 580.

31 Twenty-six horses in the case of Swillington and twenty-eight in that of Eure.

32 The number was not specified; but the same benefit was also provided for *ses gentils gentz* – that is, his squires. The number of horses would, of course, impose limitations.

33 On such occasions *bouche de court* was provided, the provision of fodder and supplies and wages being scaled down to seven horses and as many grooms.

34 PRO, DL 25/1089; *ibid.*, DL 42/2/ff. 490–90v contains a copy.

35 Seven men-at-arms, twenty-four horses and the same number of grooms.

36 There is no mention of journeyings to and from the lord.

37 PRO, E40/11547, calendared in *CAD*, v, A. 11547.

38 PRO, E40/6404, calendared in *CAD*, iv, A. 6404.

39   PRO, E101/68/2/41. For summaries see Phillips, *Aymer de Valence*, p. 309.

40   *Ibid.*, E40/8019, calendared in *CAD*, iv, A. 8019.

41   The indenture belongs to the period of rivalry for power at court which led to the formation of the so-called 'middle party', for which see J. R. S. Phillips, 'The "middle party" and the negotiating of the treaty of Leake, August 1318: a reinterpretation', *BIHR*, xlvii 1973, (11–27).

42   Bodl. MS Dugdale 18, f. 39v; Dugdale, *Baronage*, i, p. 183.

43   Recompense was promised for horses lost in war in the service of the earl.

44   We cannot, of course, exclude the possibility that Dugdale was simply summarising at certain points.

45   Printed in Jones, 'Mohaut–Bracebridge indenture', p. 391, where there is also a discussion of Mohaut's career and background (pp. 385–8).

46   Printed in Dunham, *Hastings' Retainers*, p. 134 and summarised, *ibid.*, p. 56.

47   Lancs. RO, de Trafford deeds, DDTr/bundle 5/3 (Massy chs.). For comment on the connection with the influence of Sir Robert Holland. Lancaster's leading follower, see Morgan, *Medieval Cheshire*, p. 50.

48   See above, pp. 42–3.

49   Printed in Holmes, *Higher Nobility*, pp. 140–1.

50   *Ibid.*, pp. 136–40.

51   Phillips, *Aymer de Valence*, pp. 253–68 and 295–311.

52   Bl, Egerton R. 8724.

53   Baldwin, 'Household administration', pp. 198–9, further discussed, below, pp. 233–6.

54   A minor discrepancy between this statement and the texts can be found in the indenture between the earl of Lancaster and Sir Hugh Menill. But provender and wages were provided in peace for his horses and grooms respectively. Food and drink for the retainer himself may have been taken for granted. More likely, Dugdale's transcription is careless. Certainly the words *est demore ove le dit Conte* do not have the meaning of residence suggested by Maddicott (p. 43), since they were common terminology in indentures of retinue of this period.

55   Bodl. MS, Dugdale 18, ff. 39v–40.

56   *Perc. Chart*, pp. 273–4 (no. 738).

57   The manor was also granted by separate charter (*ibid.*, p. 273 [no. 737]) *pur sa demure od nous pur peas e pur gere, si come il est pleynementz contenuz en les endentures parentre nous.* Both the indenture and the charter laid down that Percy was entitled to resume the manor in the event of default of service on the part of Neville.

58   On these events see J. M. W. Bean, 'The Percies and their estates in Scotland', *Arch. Ael.*, 4th Ser., xxxv (1957), 948; R. Nicolson, *Edward III and the Scots: The Formative Years of a Military Career, 1327–1335* (Oxford, 1965), pp. 75 seq.

59   Bodl. MS Dugdale, 18, f. 40. On the Roddam family, see *NCH*, ii, 406–7; xiv, p. 283.

60   For details of the periods covered by these registers, see *BPR*, i–iv, Introductions. The material in one begins in 1346, in the three others in 1351. The prince's

preparations for his father's earlier expeditions to France are thus inadequately represented.

61   PRO, E 36/278/f. 48d; *BPR*, iv, 80.

62   PRO, E 36/280/f. 31; *BPR*, ii, 45. It is interesting to note that another copy entered in the same register as the cancelled indenture (presumably in error, since the register concerned did not contain entries relating to Devon) was preceded by an order to the prince's clerk and treasurer of the household to enter Sully in the rolls of array of the household (PRO, E 36/278/f. 50d; *BPR*, ii, 83–4).

63   His chamberlain was also to eat in hall or have wages of twopence a day.

64   PRO, E 36/278/f. 148d; *BPR*, iv, 80. For Freville's half see *HMC*, lxix (*Middleton*), 98.

65   See the details given above, p. 36, note 73.

66   See also above, p. 30.

67   PRO, E 36/278/f. 52; *BPR*, iv, 91.

68   PRO, E 36/144/f. 153; *BPR*, i, 163.

69   This is a paraphrase of *tiel regard faire a lui dont il se purra le mieltz soutenir al avenance de son estat.*

70   PRO, E 36/280/f. 24; *BPR*, ii, 34.

71   PRO, E 36/279/f. 251; *BPR*, iii, 475–6.

72   PRO, E 36/279/f. 251d; *BPR*, iii, 477.

73   *CPR, 1377–81*, p. 161; PRO, C66/300/m. 6.

74   PRO, Ches. 2/48/m 10; *DKR*, pp. 223–4.

75   Sir Richard Abberbury, Sir John Golofre, Sir Robert Roos and Sir William Thorpe. For the confirmation of Abberbury's letters patent by Richard II see *CPR, 1377–81*, p. 155.

76   Exactly the same arrangements were made with two knights – Sir Baldwin Berford (October 1367) and Sir Thomas Guysyng (October 1371) and one squire (William Wastneys, October 1371) (*CPR, 1377–81*, pp. 210, 249, 345; PRO, C66/301/m. 14 and -/30/m. 12).

77   Morgan, *Medieval Cheshire*, pp. 76, 163. For the number of 'bachelors' see above, p. 23.

78   PRO, DL 25/3937.

79   PRO, DL 27/155, printed in Fowler, *Henry of Grosmont*, p. 234.

80   BL, Add. MS. 28024 (the Beauchamp cartulary), f. 174.

81   PRO, DL 25/32.

82   This discussion has not included PRO, E. 101/68/3/68 (dated 12 July 1347) between William Montague, earl of Salisbury, and Geoffrey Walsh. It has many of the usual provisons of a life-indenture of this period – a fee of £10 a year, the retainer eating in hall with his chamberlain in time of war, fodder and supplies for horses, wages for grooms and similar provisions for time of peace. But it is not a life-indenture. Rather, no term is specified, though the annual fee was to be paid in quarterly instalments. The reason for ambiguity on this point probably lies in the fact the earl, though old enough to participate in a campaign, was still a minor, not receiving livery of his inheritance until 11 July 1349.

83 The sole exception to this generalisation may be Sir Edmund Ufford in time of peace. But the date of the indenture suggests that, although the conventional language regarding peace and war was used, he was really being recruited as a member of a war retinue, so that war conditions overshadowed the drafting.

84 A. E. Prince. 'The indenture system under Edward III', in *Historical Essays in Honour of James Tait*, ed. J. G. Edwards, V. H. Galbraith and E. F. Jacob (Manchester, 1933), p. 287.

85 See especially N. B. Lewis, 'An early indenture of military service, 27 July 1287.' *BIHR*, xiii (1935), 85–9.

III

The development of the indenture of retinue, 1361–1485

The years 1361 to 1485 are those to which the bulk of surviving life-indentures of retinue belong. Two magnates left a surprising quantity of such documents – one hundred and fifty-eight in the case of John of Gaunt, duke of Lancaster, and sixty-nine in the case of William lord Hastings. The major problem in studying the development of the life-indenture in this period is, therefore, to ensure that any conclusions are not biased by the dominance of the Gaunt and Hastings materials. Fortunately, however, enough has survived for other magnates to put the characteristics of the two large collections into some sort of perspective.[1] At the same time, if we chart the extent of survivals in chronological terms, a greater proportion of indentures of magnates other than Gaunt and Hastings has survived for 1361–99 than for 1399–1485. For that reason the analysis of life-indentures in the years 1361–1485 has been divided into three sections – the Lancastrian and the non-Lancastrian respectively in the years 1361–99, and those of the years 1399–1485.

(i) The Lancastrian indentures, 1361–99

With the exception of three stray retainers' halves, the surviving indentures of John of Gaunt are in the form of copies contained in three sources – the registers of his chancery that have survived for the years 1371–76 and 1379–83 respectively; the royal confirmations enrolled on the patent rolls of the Crown, nearly all of these following the seizure of the Lancastrian inheritance on the death of Gaunt in 1399; and a number of confirmations made by Henry IV in the year or so following his accession. The sheer bulk of this body of material makes it impossible to provide the close and detailed analysis of each document that was possible as well as necessary in earlier periods because of the paucity of survivals. Instead, the contents are summarized in tabular form in Appendix III. Except in a few cases (largely those of bannerets) this method gives an adequate summary of the information contained in the indentures.

Gaunt's years as duke of Lancaster embraced almost two generations. The evidence we have regarding his relationships with his retainers covers only portions of this period. And only in the case of the years covered by his registers – 1372–76 and 1379–83 – can we be reasonably certain that we have copies of *all* the life-indentures he made. Most of the copies recovered from confirmations on the royal patent rolls belong to the years 1387–99 – thirty six out of forty two. How important are these gaps in our evidence? The missing years include 1386 and 1387, those of the considerable effort to assert his claims to the throne of Castile by force; and, while some of the confirmations by Richard II and Henry IV involved life-indentures made during this expedition, we can be certain that they did not include all of them, our knowledge being especially defective regarding those made as part of the preparations for this expedition. At the same time it must be said that the periods 1371–74 and 1379–83 cover years in which the registers mirror Gaunt's involvement in the internal politics of the English kingdom as well as, in some measure at least, his Castilian ambitions, his marriage to Constanza of Castile having taken place in 1371. Above all, the total of his surviving life-indentures – fifty-six for knights and 102 for squires – is quite remarkable. It is useful to compare these figures with a list of Gaunt's retainers entered in the course of 1379–86 in his second surviving register.[2] This contains, apart from his son and heir, the earl of Derby, one other earl and three barons, a total of ninety six knights and 126 squires. It cannot be assumed that all of these were retained at the same time: some were marked in the margin as deceased or removed for other reasons and it is quite possible that some of those entered at the end of the respective lists of knights and squires were added to take the place of those no longer retained. Even so, on the law of averages, it seems unlikely that life-indentures were made which, if they had survived, would have altered the main conclusions that emerge from a study of those that have.

An especially prominent feature of all these documents is their tendency to leave certain issues undefined. In most cases the duke handled some of the retainers' benefits by promising to treat them on the same basis as their peers – other 'bachelors', knights or squires. It is especially interesting to note that the duke's and the retainer's respective shares of the 'profits of war' were treated this way in most cases, the indentures of only three

knights[3] and only eleven squires[4] containing specific statements regarding
the proportions of the division between lord and man.[5] In these respects
Gaunt's indentures are similar to those of the earls of Lancaster and other
magnates in the early fourteenth century.[6] It was accepted as a matter of
course that much could be left to usage and custom as well as the mutual
respect and loyalty that were part and parcel of the relationships between
lord and man. In the case of an administration like that of Gaunt, second
only to that of the Crown among secular powers in the kingdom, this
attitude could only have been strengthened by the quantity of precedents
available. We can be sure that the clerks who drafted Gaunt's indentures
were fully aware of the implications of the phraseology they employed;
and the knights and squires were well-informed about the treatment of
their peers. Because of the size of Gaunt's administrative staff it is probably
unwise to attach any importance to minor variations in language, since
clerks varied in competence as well as their taste for formulae. At least one
of the surviving indentures is badly drafted;[7] and in some other cases careful
study is necessary to extract the information required for tabulation Appendix III.[8]

By and large Gaunt's indentures conform with the pattern that emerged
among leading magnates in the early years of the fourteenth century: the
clearest similarity is with those of the earls of Lancaster. Beneath the minor
permutations in language and the occasional ambiguities or omissions it
is possible to detect a common pattern.[9] Nevertheless, Gaunt's indentures
differ from the earlier ones in one important respect: they reflect the effects
of two generations or so of war outside the boundaries of England, the
greatest expenditure of men and resources being within the kingdom of
France. Here there is more precision in defining the differences between
peace and war. In time of peace a retainer's fee was generally paid out of
landed revenues in England, the issues of a particular manor or local
receiver or those of the receiver-general. The details of war fees and war
wages given in Appendix III do not disclose the fact that generally any
additions in time of war to the peacetime fee came from another source –
the duke's war treasurer. It was also he who paid any wages in time of
war, whereas those paid for attendance on the duke's person in time of
peace came from the treasurer of the household.[10] The tendency to employ
general formulae and the apparent ambiguities embedded in these indentures mean that their language cannot give a complete picture of all the
usages involved in the payment of the duke's retainers in time of war. One
squire's indenture in particular gives us a glimpse, unique among these
documents, into the way a squire's wages could be handled in time of war.

John Massy was to receive 'such wages of war, food and drink *(bouche de court)* as other squires of his condition will take within the household *(dedeins court)* or otherwise such wages outside the household *(for de court)* as other squires will take on the campaign *(viage)*'.[11] He was clearly regarded as a household squire; but the conditions obtaining in time of war might be such that it could not be guaranteed that he would then receive the benefits normally available for such a squire. Language was therefore employed to cover an eventuality in which he would have to maintain himself outside the organisation of the duke's household. In view of the possibility of the dislocation of any household organisation or of any other administrative mechanisms and other disruptions that might intrude in time of war, it is certain that in practice many other squires must have received the same treatment as was promised Massy. The fact that this is the only surviving indenture to employ such terminology can safely be attributed to the punctilousness of a particular clerk or to the care with which an individual safeguarded his interests.

Because Gaunt was the most powerful magnate in England and one who was close to the throne, his retinue could be a source of attraction to other lords as well as their inferiors in social status and wealth. Membership of his retinue also promised to be a way to fame and fortune to knights who had already begun their careers in war or administrative service as well as to other knights and to squires who were on the threshold of their careers. Such ambitions explain features that are frequently encountered in Gaunt's indentures. In the case of knights attention was occasionally given to the possibility that the social importance or prowess of an individual would lead to his promotion to the status of banneret. The earliest of the surviving indentures relates to one of these, Sir Hugh Hastings.[12] His fee and contingent were more than doubled if he became a banneret, the former rising to 500 marks and the latter to twenty men-at-arms, six of them knights and twenty mounted archers.[13] In the case of John, lord Welles,[14] the fee in war was raised only very slightly from £30 to fifty marks; but, in addition to his own wages, the banneret took fees and wages for a contingent of up to twenty men-at-arms. In the third such case, Sir William Beauchamp,[15] who was a younger son of the late earl of Warwick, the war fee was increased from 100 marks to £100; but there was no limitation on the size of his contingent. The variations in the treatment of potential bannerets mirror similar variations in that of knights and squires. The greater the social importance of a would-be retainer and, we must assume, the stronger the duke's anxiety to recruit him because of his potential for leadership, the better the terms he was able to negotiate. Sir Hugh Hastings did better for himself than either a young lord (Welles) or the brother of a leading earl (Beauchamp) because he was an experienced warrior who had served in the French wars under the duke's father-in-law, Henry, duke of Lancaster. One of the surviving indentures relates to a rising lord – John, lord Neville of Raby[16] – whose son was to achieve an earldom. It is the most lengthy and complicated of all of Gaunt's indentures. Lord Neville's war fee was to be 500 marks, like that of Sir Hugh Hastings, with the same size contingent. Presumably this reflects, in some measure at least, one point of attraction he had for Gaunt as a retainer – the fact that he was the head of a northern family which had played a role in the Scottish wars of Edward III's reign second only to that of the Percies,[17] and had ambitions in an area – the extreme north – where Gaunt did not have the territorial influence he enjoyed elsewhere. In the event, indeed, of war with Scotland, the retainer's contingent was increased to fifty men-at-arms and the same number of archers at the duke's fees and wages. The indentures with Sir Hugh Hastings and John, lord Neville are two of the earliest we have of those of Gaunt's that have survived. Both, in fact, belong to the years before his marriage to the Castilian heiress. This may explain why they alone contain a provision that, if Gaunt were to go on Crusade *(sur les enemys Dieux)* and wanted his retainer's company, food and board were to be provided *(bouche de court)* – for the retainer and his two squires in the case of Hastings and for his 'bachelor' and two squires as well as himself in the case of lord Neville.[18]

The summaries provided in Appendix III present a basic pattern. But there are two points in particular that cannot be conveyed in such a tabular presentation. The first concerns the legal character of the retainer's annual payment (as distinct from any wages he might receive in peace or in war). In the case of nine of Gaunt's knightly retainers the legal distinction between a fee and an annuity appears to have been ignored, the retainer being given an annuity in return for his services in the past as well as those to be performed in the future.[19] In these cases the general statement with which indentures invariably began – that the retainer was retained with the duke for life in peace and in war – was followed by the grant of an annuity in the terms associated with such grants. In two cases – the earliest, Sir John d'Ipre the elder and the latest, Sir John Dabridgecourt – the terminology of this grant of an annuity is different from the others. D'Ipre was granted £20 a year from the issue of lands in Lancashire in return for his retainer and 'for the good and agreeable service that he has done to the said duke in the parts of Spain and elsewhere, and at the same time for him the better to maintain the order of knighthood which he took from him the day of the battle of Najera'.[20] In Dabridgecourt's case the language of the grant referred to past and future services in conventional terms;[21] but, after then giving details of an indenture that was now being surrendered, it went on to describe the grant of fifty marks a year as 'his fee'. Two of the indentures in this category also present differences in another area – those of Sir John d'Ipre the elder and Sir Walter Urswick. Neither contains any reference to obligations or benefits in time of war: the only language to indicate that the retainer was to serve for life in peace and in war was in the indenture's opening words. It is impossible to believe that the treatment given to these retainers was not deliberate. The distinction at law between the retainer's fee and an annuity was well enough known:[22] the duke, his retainers, and his chancellor and chancery clerks must all have understood that what was being granted was a financial interest more solid than a fee. There is, in fact, substantial information to indicate that these retainers were a specially favoured group. Sir John Marmion, Sir Richard Burley, Sir Walter Blount, Sir Thomas Banastre and (in an earlier indenture) Sir John Dabridgecourt were all 'bachelors' in time of peace, members of the inner circle of the duke's knightly retainers. Sir Walter Urswick and Banastre held posts of distinction in the duke's local administration.[23] In three cases – Sir Nicholas Longford, Sir John Marmion and Sir John Dabridgecourt[24] – there were earlier indentures which were surrendered at the time the new one was made: the transaction represented by the new indenture in each case suggests that the duke thought it expedient to bind them more closely to him. And in all these cases the retainer gained the right of distraint in the event of non-payment.

The second point of interest concerns only one indenture – that with a squire, William Barwell, made on 13 April 1383.[25] It contained no money fee at all and made no reference to war. Barwell was retained 'to serve the duke and do his business for his honour and profit in England for life, whenever reasonably required or summoned by the duke or his council'. When he attended the duke's household *(court)*, he was to receive food and drink and wages 'if commanded to appear by the duke'. It is unfortunate that, if similar indentures were made, none has survived.

The comparative bulk of the surviving indentures of John of Gaunt enables us to examine a question that cannot be addressed satisfactorily in the case of other magnates. Retainers (except in the case of William Barwell) were for peace and war. This terminology, especially in the light of the marked differences between the benefits available in peace and in war, suggests a clear dichotomy between these two situations. Which, then, was the more important in the motivation of those involved? Did Gaunt recruit

knights and squires primarily for peacetime service or for war? And for
those he recruited, which were more important – the benefits of the duke's
connections and patronage in time of peace, or the opportunities of fame
and fortune in time of war under his leadership? Any effort to answer these
questions from Gaunt's indentures is hampered by the fact that we are
dealing only with a group of surviving documents which lay down a body
of conditions but nowhere contain any description of the reasons why these
indentures were drawn up. It is, in fact, impossible to achieve any certain
insight into Gaunt's intentions. To be sure, for the greater part of his years
as duke he had ambitions on the Iberian peninsula, especially important
after his marriage to Constanza of Castile in 1371 and these remained a
powerful element in his policies, at least until after the failure of his campaign of 1386–87 when he surrendered his claims to the throne of Castile
in return for an annual subsidy.[26] But at that point Gascony became the
focus of his territorial ambitions outside England.[27] In dealing with Gaunt's
ambitions within England historians are faced with an ambivalence which
also perplexed contemporaries. But the most powerful magnate in the kingdom was also in line of succession to the throne. In a very real sense, indeed,
discussions whether Gaunt actually sought the throne or whether the earl
of March was the recognized heir presumptive to the throne of Richard
II are beside the point: a *coup* such as Gaunt's son achieved in 1399 had
never been inconceivable. It is against the background of these general considerations that we have to confront the gaps in our evidence. The register
of 1372–76 covers a period in which the possibilities of war in which Gaunt
asserted his wife's rights to the throne of Castile, affecting as this would
the English Crown's efforts in France, were inextricably bound up with
his participation in Engligh politics, as the eldest able-bodied member of
the royal family during his father's dotage and the physical decay of the
heir apparent, the Black Prince. In this context it is worth noting that indentures with eleven knights and twenty-two squires were made in the calender
year 1372, involving, apart from household benefits, a total expenditure
in peacetime of £485. This was the year in which Gaunt and his Castilian
wife made an offensive alliance with the king and queen of Portugal. And
in 1373 indentures with twelve knights and eight with squires preceded
Gaunt's departure from Calais at the end of July, the total peacetime expenditure of fees being £646 13s 4d. This evidence, circumstantial though it
is, suggests, especially in the light of the duke's readiness to make commitments from his revenues for the lives of those he recruited, that overseas
ambition, at this stage at any rate, was the driving-force behind Gaunt's
recruitment of additions to his permanent following. The position, even in

circumstantial terms, cannot be so clear during the rest of our period: the register of 1379-83 contains comparatively few indentures and it is unwise to gauge Gaunt's motives from confirmations enrolled on the royal patent rolls which represent only a portion of the indentures made outside the years of the two surviving registers.

Even so, some further comments are possible about the motives of retainers in joining the duke's service. In general terms it is quite clear that they expected larger financial payments in time of war, even though such service gave hope of profits from booty and ransoms. It must also be said that those who were recruited by Gaunt in the years 1372–73 must have been aware of the nature of the enterprise upon which he and they might be embarking In this area the confirmations made by Richard II and Henry IV do provide a little suggestive information. A total of seven indentures made with squires exists in this source for the years 1386–87: the dates indicate that all of them were made in the course of Gaunt's expedition and two, in fact, were dated in Castile and Portugal respectively.[28] The four indentures of 1388 – 89 were all dated in Gascony.[29] And all those we have for 1395 – one knight's and four squires' – were dated at Bordeaux.[30] From this information we gain a picture of gentry who had already followed the duke overseas, whether in the campaign of 1386–87 or its aftermath or later in the hope of benefitting from his regime in Gascony. It is more than likely that they had made contracts of service of limited duration with the duke or some of his captains. The existence of these indentures means that these individuals had earned the duke's attention and were judged worthy of a lifetime in his service.

There is, however, an element of anachronism in this discussion. By the late middle ages society in Western Europe had developed clear conceptions of the distinction between peace and war. But the moral values of its landed classes remained those of a warrior aristocracy. The indentures of John of Gaunt also deserve examination in this light. They have for many years been a major, probably the most important, source for those historians who have stressed the financial relationships that formed the basis of what they called 'bastard feudalism'. But even a cursory glance at the details tabulated in the following table[31] shows that a retainer's benefits ranged beyond a money fee, whether in peace or war. In fact, in the case of Gaunt's indentures it is difficult not to believe that a concern with the substitution of a money fee for one in the form of land has deflected the attention of historians from the need to study these documents as a whole. What emerges is a situation in which each retainer secured a mixture of benefits. One of these – the money fee – has a coherence that makes it stand out:

Table   Analysis of benefits in time of peace

Category	1371–74		1379–83		Confirmations by Richard II and Henry IV	
	Knights	Squires	Knights	Squires	Knights	Squires
Those with no fee						
with wages only	0	0	0	0	0	0
with keep only	0	4	0	0	0	0
with both wages and keep	3	3	3	14	1	3
Those with fees						
with wages only	11	14	0	0	0	1
with keep only	4	3	0	0	2	2
with both wages and keep	9	10	9	4	10	36
no keep or wages	3	6	0	0	0	0
Those with no benefits at all in time of peace	1	0	0	2	1	0

it was a fixed sum, the precise source from which it was to be paid being defined. The other benefits – food and drink *(bouche de court)* and wages – lacked the quality of coherence because almost invariably there was no valuation of them in money terms.

From this evidence it is quite clear that the benefits secured during service as a member of the duke's household formed at least a substantial portion of the financial opportunities available to a retainer in time of peace. More important, the payment of an annual fee in time of peace was not a *sine qua non* of the relationship between Gaunt and knight or squire he retained by indenture. In the register of 1372–76, 13 per cent. of the knights and 17.5 per cent. of the squires enjoyed no annual fee in time of peace: in that of 1379–83 the equivalent percentages are 25 and 70 per cent respectively. To be sure, this situation is much less marked in the case of the confirmations made by Richard II and Henry IV; but it must be remembered that these were made in time of peace and it was the very existence of a peacetime fee that made these confirmations necessary for most of the retainers concerned. Above all, side by side with these occasions when annual fees in time of peace are not present we must place the fact that the vast majority of Gaunt's retainers enjoyed *bouche de court* or daily wages, or both, whenever they attended the household in time of peace. It is apparent that in every one of Gaunt's indentures there was an effort on the part of both lord and man to maintain a balance between their respective needs – the lord's for service and the man's for reward. The bargain between lord and man appears more often than not to have involved an annual fee in time of peace; but this was not inevitable. And in every case the opportunity to be part of a great lord's household and receive benefits therein was a major consideration.

The position in time of war presents a more complicated problem. Two features of the indentures help to make this so. One is the tendency to employ rather broad language to describe benefits apart from the annual fee. The other is the fact that in time of war Gaunt might be receiving wages for his men from the king and some of the indentures reflect this fact in a quite precise way. Even so, there emerges a picture of the duke's retainers in time of war as a household at war. In the register of 1372–76, 16.7 per cent of the knights and 23.7 per cent of the squires received *bouche de court*: the percentage for those who received wages as well remained the same in the case of the knights and was 21 per cent in the case of the squires. It may be unwise to argue from similar figures in the case of the register of 1379–83, since it contains comparatively few indentures. But it may be useful to provide statistics for this source combined with those derived from the confirmations made by Richard II and Henry IV. In this case 66.7 per cent of the knights and 72 per cent of the squires enjoyed *bouche de court* in time of war or were promised wages and *bouche de court* in place of 'wages of war'. These proportions are remarkably impressive, since the conditions of warfare were bound to impose limitations on Gaunt's capacity to provide maintenance; yet in so many cases he felt obliged to make a commitment to do so.

This picture of a household enlarged by retainers in both peace and war is strongly supported by the appearance of the 'bachelors' when they entered into their indentures of retinue. In the register of 1372–76 the privileges of a 'bachelor' were attached to the *bouche de court* of one knight and to the wages of three others. In the case of the knightly retainers whose indentures survive in the register of 1379–83 and the confirmations made by Richard II and Henry IV, such precision is prevented by the employment so often of formulae that do not distinguish clearly between *bouche de court* and wages, especially one which promises both these benefits in the place of 'wages of war'. But, whatever the language used, twenty out of twenty-one knights became 'bachelors' in time of war.

Of course, the advantages gained by a knight or squire when he joined the service of so great a lord as John of Gaunt were in part a mixture of the political and psychological and lie outside the evidence available to the historian: they were brought out of the local societies in the neighbourhood of their estates into contact with a magnate who was at the centre of the kingdom's affairs in time of peace and in the forefront of its leadership in time of war. An indenture of retinue with John of Gaunt opened up vistas of gains from his patronage and influence which, if realised, might far exceed the financial gains guaranteed in the indenture. In some measure, of course, the hope of successful service and of contact with Gaunt himself was embedded in the retainer's membership of the household when he attended there. But each retainer when he negotiated the terms of his indenture must also have counted up the financial advantages of service within the household. For this reason it is tempting to attempt some sort of financial comparison between the benefits of an annual fee and those of wages and the retainer's keep.

In the case of a knight serving in the household of John of Gaunt the daily wage was one shilling.[32] The equivalent rate for a squire in one of his indentures of retinue, confirmed by the attendance rolls of his household,[33] was seven and a half pence,[34] a figure that can also be seen in *The Black Book* of Edward IV's household.[35] There is good reason to believe that *bouche de court* for a knight would have been regarded by Gaunt's

officials as falling between ninepence and a shilling a day. The former is
the daily value of a knight's *mensa* in the treasurer's accounts of the duke
of Glocester's expedition to Ireland in 1394,[36] while two shillings a day
was paid to a knight travelling on Gaunt's business to cover his wages and
keep.[37] Calculations in the case of a squire are slightly more difficult. An
inquisition ordered by the Crown in 1324 evaluated the maintenance of a
squire in the household of Edward II at three and a half pence a day.[38] And
in its model of a ducal household *The Black Book* of Edward IV assigned
£2,190 for a household of two hundred and forty domestics[39] – that is, an
average of three pence and a farthing each. The fact that these figures
remained at roughly the same level for a century and a half justifies their
use as a basis for calculation. But the majority of the domestics for which
The Black Book budgeted would have been at levels well below that of
the squire; and for this reason five pence a day might seem a more satisfactory estimate.

Clearly the ability of a knight or squire to profit from these benefits
depended on the length of time he actually spent within the household in
any year. 'Bachelors' must have spent a considerable time there, other
knights less, some, perhaps, attending the lord only during times of crisis
or emergency. But for the purpose of argument it is worth using the assumption of the *The Black Book* that the average period of service a year for a
squire of a duke was 213 days.[40] A knight who served for this period would
receive £10 13s in wages and receive keep to the value of somewhere
between the same figure and £8 – a total of between £21 6s and £18 13s
a year. The equivalent figures for a squire would be £6 13s 4d and £4 9s
– a total of £11 2s 4d. These totals are impressive in comparison with the
fees paid to many knights and squires. It is true that many knights would
not have the good fortune to earn these sums or anything approaching
them. But it is likely that many squires did spend substantial periods within
the household, since they were aspirants for knighthood and very often
heirs who had not yet come into their inheritances or were even younger
sons. Many of them, therefore, must have gained through daily wages and
their keep a financial package worth more than their annual fees.

The results of this discussion can be viewed from two different
standpoints. It is certainly possible to argue that what mattered was the
amount of time that knights and squires spent in the household. Furthermore, if Gaunt had sought to have all his indentured knights and squires
serving in the household for 213 days a year, the effects on his financial
position would have been crippling. This argument is certainly reinforced
by what we know of the costs in wages incurred by his heir, Henry of

Bolingbroke, when he called out a portion of retinue for three months in 1399.[41] On the other hand, Gaunt's retinue was exceptionally large; and there is every reason to believe that he could never have intended to summon the whole of it except in time of war or serious crisis. In fact, however, there is good reason to believe that service for as long as 213 days a year may have been a reality for any squires; and their wages and keep in themselves would not have been an excessive burden. For one of Gaunt's indentured squires the promise of wages and keep within the household for a substantial period of the year was in a real financial sense a large part of his living.

For the purpose, however, of an understanding of the complex of motives and attitudes that lay behind the making of Gaunt's indentures of retinue a discussion limited to the real extent of financial benefits within the household is misdirected. The truth is that these benefits were written into indentures; and the hope of acquiring them must have been in the retainer's mind just as the possibility of giving them have been in the lord's. A simple statistical analysis of the contents of Gaunt's indentures shows that historians' concern with the annual fee has diverted attention from the study of a retainer's benefits as a whole and thus warped our understanding of the relationship between lord and retainer. An examination of the value of household benefits in financial terms serves to strengthen this conclusion and to emphasise the hard financial reality that household benefits constituted in the relationship of lord and man.

(ii) Non-Lancastrian indentures, 1361–99

A total of twenty-six life-indentures has survived for the years 1361–99 apart from those of John of Gaunt. With a few exceptions, they do so in the form of copies enrolled in the form of confirmations on the royal patent rolls.[42] Four magnates provide the bulk of them – the Mortimer earls of March, five: Thomas Mowbray earl of Nottingham and (from 1397) duke of Norfolk, seven; Richard Beachamp, earl of Warwick, three; and Thomas, lord Despenser, three. If we add two in the case of the latter's father Edward, the Despenser family's total equalled that of the Mortimer earls of March. Two each survive in the case of other magnates – Edmund, duke of York and earl of Cambridge, and John Holland, earl of Huntingdon and duke of Exeter. In the case of each of the remaining magnates we have only single survivals. Just as the permanent attachment of the Lancastrian inheritance to the Crown brought about the survival of so many Lancastrian indentures, the circumstances of temporary acquisition of an inheritance by the Crown explain the survival of much of the non-Lancastrian material – two minorities in the case of the earl of March, exile in the case of the duke of Norfolk, and forfeiture in the case of the duke of Exeter.[43]

By and large most of this material presents a picture not remarkably different from that which can be seen in the surviving life-indentures of John of Gaunt or magnates in the earlier years of the fourteenth century. The same basic features are present – the payment of an annual fee, sometimes increased in time of war, household benefits (*bouche de court* and/or wages) in time of peace with detailed provisions regarding payments and other rights of lord and retainer in time of war. For this reason a detailed analysis of each indenture is not necessary; but two main issues require discussion – the differences between this group and other indentures of the fourteenth century, and the extent to which indentures have survived that do not conform with the general pattern.

In general, the majority of the indentures of this period gave full treatment to the benefits of the retainer enjoyed apart from his fee. Edmund, earl of March (d. 1381), made indentures with three knights and one squire. In the case of that made with Sir Hugh Cheyne,[44] the retainer was to receive food and board for himself, a chamberlain, two grooms and a page, with fodder and supplies for five horses,[45] his contingent being increased by only one groom in time of war. Sir John Bromwich was to bring with him in time of peace a company of one squire, one chamberlan and three grooms, with similar benefits:[46] the contingent was increased in time of war by three grooms and three horses. Both these cases show that an annual fee did not necessarily reflect the size of contingents in peace or war: despite the slight differences between them in this respect, Cheyne received an annual fee of forty marks while Bromwich's was more than double this (£66 13*s* 4*d*). The difference can only reflect the earl's estimation of their value to him. Bromwich, in fact, was an exceptionally important knight.[47] In contrast, in Cheyne the earl of March was securing the services of a younger man who then rose in the hierarchy of the Mortimer family's retainers. On 20 October 1397 earl Edmund's son and heir, Roger, entered into another life-indenture with Cheyne in which he was retained for life of the earl's council, the earlier indenture being confirmed at the same time.[48] Cheyne's contingent in time of peace was increased only slightly – to one squire, two yeomen, a groom and five horses, but he was now worth an increase of 50 per cent in his annual fee. In contrast, in the indenture he made with Sir Henry Conway on 1 August 1381 earl Edmund was adjusting the terms of an earlier indenture made with him when he was a squire.[49] He had now been knighted by the earl and undertook to perform service as a 'batchelor', the indenture providing for a company of one squire, a chamberlain and four grooms and six horses in time of peace, with an additional groom in time of war. His annual fee was increased from fifty marks to £40. The indenture made with a squire, Walter Bromwich,[50] followed the same lines, providing for a smaller company in view of his non-knightly status and a smaller annual fee (twenty marks).

The similarities between the main provisions of these indentures and those of other magnates are so marked as to make a summary of each of them superfluous. Thomas Beauchanmp, earl of Warwick, provided his knight Sir John Russell with £20 in time of peace and £40 in time of war,[51] food and board being provided in both peace and war.[52] One of the earl's squires, Walter Power, who was retained two days later,[53] came alone when summoned to the earl's side. He received a fee of £5 a year in peace, increased to £20 in time of war, with food and board when in attendance in time of peace, his benefits in time of war simply being defined in terms of those of other squires of his condition. Nine and a half years later Walter Power,[54] (presumably the same man) secured a fee of £10 a year in time of peace, the war fee remaining at £20, this time gaining the right to bring a yeoman to share in the benefits he had when attending in the earl's household.

When we turn to indentures made by Richard, earl of Arundel in 1379 and by Thomas, duke of Gloucester in 1395, the retainers being squires in both cases, there are some divergences from the general pattern. The earl of Arundel granted William Rees his manor of Ovesham in Essex for life, his contingent of a yeoman and two horses (increased by one groom in time of war) being at the earl's costs.[55] That made by the duke of Gloucester with William Cheyne differs little in substance but there are divergences in language.[56] The distinction between peace and war is not as clearly made as in other indentures, both being embraced within a general provision that Cheyne was to have 'for himself and a yeoman, his chamberlain food and board at all the times that he will be in the household *(courte)* of the said duke by the command and wish of the said duke', then proceeding to provide provender and supplies for three horses in time of war. The indenture then displays a peculiar feature in dealing with provision for horses in time of peace quite separately and using language that we do not find elsewhere: 'and in the time of peace when he will be in the country *(contre)* of the said duke', providing fodder and supplies or wages. We can only assume that such language reflects the special needs or concerns of this particular retainer. There is also a clause of a kind not usually found in the other indentures of the closing years of the fourteenth century. It laid down the retainer's obligations if the duke should decide to go on crusade, providing that he and his chamberlain would then have food and board 'without other fees or wages'.[57] In view of the indenture's date, it is reasonable to assume that the inclusion of this clause resulted from the effects on Gloucester's restless ambition of the invasion of Europe by the Ottoman Turks and Western chivalry's preparations for the Crusade that foundered at the battle of Nicopolis the following year.

The usual basic features can be seen in the two surviving indentures of Gloucester's brother, Edmund, earl of Cambridge and (from 1385) duke of York. The main difference between the indenture he made with Camoys Mavow on 1 January 1381,[58] and those of other magnates is that the retainer was thereby made one of the squires of his chamber *(destre un des esquiers de sa chaumbre)*, but, this apart, there are no remarkable features. A fee of twenty marks was promised in peace and war and, in addition, board and wages being provided in time of war. The indenture with Sir Thomas Gerberge (9 May 1388),[59] takes into account the fact that he was simultaneously being retained for life and was being appointed steward of the household during the duke's pleasure.[60] Both his duties as steward and his services as retainer were dealt with in the indenture. Gerberge was given a fee of forty marks a year for life. As steward he received the power to remove and appoint all household officers, taking wages of four shillings a day when conducting his duties together with food and board for himself, a squire, two yeoman and fodder and supplies for four horses. In time of war he was to accompany the duke, receiving for himself and his retinue such wages and rewards as the duke received from the king. But, despite the intrusion of a household appointment and its duties, the indenture followed the basic approach of others.

In general, then, a study of these life-indentures suggests that the earls of March and Warwick and other great lords treated their retainers in ways that did not greatly differ from those of the leading magnate of their time, the duke of Lancaster. To be sure, the relationship between lord and retainer in these indentures was defined in some areas which the Lancastrian indentures left vague; but, even so, the similarity to the treatment Gaunt gave to Sir Ralph Hastings or lord Neville of Raby is noteworthy. Where differences with Gaunt's indentures are to be seen, the practices of these contemporary magnates seem to hark back to the earlier years of the fourteenth century. In one respect, however, there is a marked adherence to one basic element in the relationship between lord and retainer – a concern with the retainer's benefits as a member of a household in peace and in war. In some of these indentures this appears more strongly than in others. Walter Power was retained to be 'menial' *(meynal)* with the earl of War- wick, a word, which, though it is rarely encountered in the surviving docu- ments of royal or baronial administration, echoes the close personal relationship between a lord and his following that was an accepted element in the courtly literature of medieval French society. Camoys Mavow became a squire of the duke of York's chamber, and the retainder of Sir Thomas Gerberge for life was amalgamated with an appointment as ste- ward of the duke's household.

Nevertheless, at the same time as we interpret these indentures along these lines we can also detect a change of emphasis in the relations of lord and man away from what we see in the indentures of John of Gaunt. To be sure, such an assessment must be argued with caution, because the number of these indentures is small. Even so, the concern we see for the explicit definition of matters left vague in the Lancastrian indentures requires explanation. It may well be, in some cases at any rate, that this was a response to the retainer's efforts to extract a good bargain. In the case of the four knights, and even the squire, whose indentures with him have survived, the earl of March felt impelled to give his retainer the right of distraint, as did the earl of Warwick in the case of Sir John Russell and Walter Power and the duke of York in the case of Camoys Mavow. But it was also laid down by the earl of March in his contracts with Sir Hugh Cheyne and Sir John Bromwich that he had the right to resume the annual fee if service was refused without reasonable cause. The earl of Warwick had to agree that neither Sir John Russell nor Walter Power would have to serve in time of war except in the company and presence of the earl. But the most impressive evidence of concern with the definition of rights relates to the profits of war, an area in which Gaunt and his clerks were almost always content with vague principles, obviously relying on custom and usage. In his indenture of 1381 with Sir John Bromwich the earl of March explicitly reserved to himself the third part of any ransoms or other profits and required that no ransom be arranged without his agreement. A third share was similarly reserved in his indenture of 1373 with Walter Bromwich, the earl reserving to himself the ransom of any 'chieftain', prom- ising a reasonable reward to the squire. The earl of Warwick's indenture with Sir John Russell provided that, if he took a prisoner, the earl would treat him as he would any of his 'bachelors' who were retained for life. The earl's first indenture with Walter Power used similar language for a squire; but that made eleven years later explicitly reserved for the earl a third of all the winnings of the retainer and his men, also laying down that no ransom was to be arranged unless licensed by the earl. Richard, earl of Arundel, reserved his third share in the case of William Rees and even imposed this when he allowed his squire to go on a campaign from which he himself was absent. The duke of Gloucester also required his third in the case of William Cheyne; and he explicitly reserved for himself the ransom of any 'royal person, chieftain or lieutenant of war', promising in such cases reasonable treatment for the retainer and his men. And, despite the importance of Sir Thomas Gerberge in his affairs, the duke of York felt it necessary to require for himself a third of Sir Thomas's winnings and a third of the thirds Sir Thomas received from his men's winnings, reserving for himself 'any chieftain or peer of the realm, town, castle or fortress of our enemies', promising a fair reward in such circumstances. It is noteworthy that in all these cases the language employed to deal with the profits of war varied; and in only one case – that of Sir Thomas Gerberge – is there any reference to profits of war from sources other than ransoms of individuals. Why is there comparative precision in this area in the case of these magnates, but vague principle only in nearly all of Gaunt's indentures? The answer can only lie in the greater power and influence of John of Gaunt. On the one hand, a retainer's desire to enter the following of the greatest lord in the realm would discourage him from driving too hard a bargain. On the other hand, the duke could rely on the customs and usages of the largest household and estate administration in the realm, apart from that of the Crown, and would feel confident that, in the event of any disputes with his men over their profits of war, Lancastrian tradition and power would together provide satisfactory protection for his interests.

When we turn to the remaining indentures of this period, any image of conformity disappears. To begin with, the surviving indentures of other magnates and lesser lords are shorter, sometimes quite abrupt, documents. Thomas Mowbray, earl of Nottingham and duke of Norfolk provides one of the two comparatively large groups. Within it alone there are marked variations. In the earliest indenture (6 February 1389),[61] Sir Thomas Clinton received an annual rent of £20 from one of the earl's manors, with right of distraint. In return, he was to travel and go on campaign (*chivachera*) where the earl went 'within the realm of England' and to stay with the earl 'within our household' with two yeomen 'to do us honor and service'. Peacetime benefits in addition to the annual rent simply involved *bouche de court*. In wartime he and his men were to receive such wages and rewards as were paid by the king, together with food and drink 'for campaign or tournament (*pur le viage ou tourne*)'. On 7 May 1389 and 26 May 1391 the earl entered into indentures with Sir Robert Legh[62] and

Sir Richard Basset[63] in quite similar terms. Service was limited to journeying and campaigning within England; but the annual fees were lower – twenty marks,[64] and ten marks respectively. Legh was already one of the earl's 'bachelors'. In peace he received food and board for himself, a squire and a yeoman;[65] in time of war he was to serve with wages and rewards such as the earl received from the king. The basic difference between his indenture and that of Sir Richard Basset is that the latter now became a 'bachelor', receiving the appropriate benefits in time of peace.

In comparison, the indenture made with Sir John Inglethorpe on 26 April 1396 was more brief.[66] After providing an annual rent of £20 the indenture turned to the time of war when Inglethorpe and his men were promised wages as paid by the king. In time of peace he was to receive such wages as were paid to other 'bachelors' of his estate, the word 'bachelor' clearly supplying all further definition required. A contract with a squire, Richard FitzNichol,[67] (27 April 1397) was briefer still, providing only an annuity of ten marks in time of peace and, in addition, in time of war, wages as paid by the king to one of his degree. In another indenture (23 February 1390),[68] Mowbray followed a practice similar to that of the duke of York in the case of Sir Thomas Gerberge. He appointed Richard Burgh his chamberlain for life. At the same time he granted him an annual rent of £20 for his good service in the past and in the future, stating that he was retained by this grant for life in peace and war. He was to travel and campaign with the earl when required within the realm of England, staying within the household with one yeoman and taking food and board for both of them and wages for his horses: the same conditions were to apply in time of war when he and his servants were also to have such wages as were paid by the king. This indenture, like some of those of John of Gaunt, ignores the legal distinction between an annuity for past and future services and a retaining fee, using the former in place of the latter. A last variation in Mowbray's retaining practices can be seen in the grant of an annuity (10 October 1393) to a squire,[69] John Husthwaite, 'for the good service that he will do us in time to come if God pleases . . . for term of his life in time of peace', terms which are reminiscent of Gaunt's indenture with William Barwell.

In the case of the Despenser indentures we are dealing with a father and son, the latter's minority lying between them. Two have survived for Edward, lord Despenser, lord of Glamorgan and Morgannwg,[70] both of them extremely curious in comparison with those of any other magnate for this or any earlier period. On 16 November 1372 he granted to Sir Thomas Arthur[71] by letters patent indented an annual 'pension' of £20 'for the good and laudable service he has performed and will in future per-form',[72] with power of distraint. In return Arthur

> freely promises to stay in his fealty of the said lord Edward through the whole of the said time in time as well of peace as of war whenever he has been properly (*debite*) summoned by him or by anyone else on his part in return for the said pension of £20 and this at all the lawful and usual expenses in the household (*curia*) of the said lord Edward and also at his lawful expenses in coming and returning on every occasion he is sent for by him for his business.

An identical indenture, except for a pension of twenty marks, was made with a squire, Nicholas Bernak,[73] just over a week later (25 November).

This pair of indentures does more than provide examples of the use of an annuity for services past and future where a retaining fee would have been more advantageous to the lord. For the first time we encounter the concept of lawfulness used to define the retainer's services and the lord's demands. And this language is thought sufficient definition in itself. To be sure, the retainer was guaranteed his expenses in the lord's household and in journeying to and from there. But the phrase 'licit and usual' is enough to describe these; there is no mention of food and drink, let alone what was available for the retainer's following. Nor is there an precision at all in the treatment of war as distinct from peace. Indeed, while it would be wrong to assert a firm conclusion on this point, the impression is left that these indentures were more concerned with peace than war. It is tempting to suggest that this simply reflects the needs of a Marcher lord who would feel it superfluous to engage in precise definitions of foreign service. This explanation gains some support from the fact that Sir Thomas Arthur's 'pension' was to be paid from the lord's exchequer in Cardiff castle; but against this must be set the payment of Nicholas Bernak's from a manor in Buckinghamshire.

In his three surviving indentures[74] lord Edward's son and heir Thomas (created earl of Gloucester in 1397) did not follow these precedents. His were more conventional in general format and in the way they defined mutual obligations. On 29 September 1395 an indenture with John Willi-cotes required him to serve his lord in time of war in campaigns outside England, taking, beyond his annual fee of £10, such fees and wages as his lord paid men of the condition and degree of the retainer and his follow-ing.[75] If commanded to come to his lord within any part of England and Wales with a requested number of men on reasonable warning, he and they would have appropriate wages while serving. In any event (presumably if the lord's written or oral command did not specify an exact number) he was to bring with him anywhere in England and Wales one yeoman, one groom and three horses, receiving customary benefits for himself and these. On 1 October 1396 the indenture made with William Daventry displayed a broad similarity with its predecessor;[76] but there were distinct differences. It began where its predecessor concluded by laying down the obligation to come when summoned anywhere in England and Wales on reasonable warning with three horses and two servants, taking wages coming and departing and food and board for him and his servants and horses while serving. He was to bring additional men if required, who were to be at his lord's wages. If his lord took part in a campaign outside the kingdom of England at the king's wages, he was bound to go with him at appropriate wages; and he could not accompany anyone else without his lord's leave. He was bound to go with his lord on Crusade if so required, when he and his men would have food and board 'without other wages'. The third indenture was three years later (27 October 1399). William Hamme agreed in return for the same fee as Willicotes to follow his lord in any war outside the kingdom of England on the king's service if required, he and his men taking fees and wages appropriate to their estate.[77] But in that event he would not receive anything of his annuity during the period of the campaign. If his lord wished to journey to the isle of Rhodes or any other parts outside the realm of England or outside Wales, he was required to accompany him at his lord's expense. He was also to attend his lord anywhere in England or Wales when commanded with a yeoman, a groom and three horses, taking wages for him and his men and appropriate benefits for his horses. He was also bound to come bringing such smaller or a larger company as was specified in his lord's commands. All three retainers of lord Thomas were given powers of distraint.

These three indentures reveal concerns on the part of lord Thomas and his clerks which were missing in those of his father. There are clear distinctions between simple attendance with a small contingent in the lord's household and, on the one hand, service in England and Wales that required a larger contingent and, on the other hand, service in the king's wars overseas. But the treatment of service in England and Wales does have echoes of lord Thomas's father's indentures, in that this is not attributed to peace or to war. Though there is a basic similarity in the concerns of lord Thomas's indentures, they did not adhere to a common form, there being variations in particular in the order in which matters were handled. All three indentures mention the possibility that the lord might go on Crusade. We gain a glimpse, as in the case of the duke of Gloucester, into the impact of the advance of the Ottoman Turks on the conscience of the chivalry of Europe. The indentures with William Daventry and William Hamme contain differences in language that may reveal the changing fortunes of the struggle against the Turk: the former was drawn up in the aftermath of the defeat at Nicopolis and employs language that simply envisages a renewal of the struggle, whereas the latter has a precise location in mind – the isle of Rhodes.

The last magnate of this period for whom we possess more than a single indenture is a very special case. John Holland, earl of Huntingdon and (from 1397) duke of Exeter was a half-brother and close courtier of Richard II. Both his indentures (22 and 24 September 1399 respectively) were made within the week in which decisions were made among the magnates about the way in which Richard II was to be deprived of his throne.[78] Just over three months later the duke was to lose hs life as a result of rebellion against the usurper Henry IV. All the circumstances suggest that these indentures formed part of an effort to recruit a following, either in order to strengthen the duke's standing in the new regime or, more likely, to recruit support as part of a plan to use force to overturn Henry of Bolingbroke's *coup*. Certainly the terms give support to the latter suggestion. The two squires, Thomas Trenarake,[79] and Thomas Proudfoot, promised 'to remain with the said duke to be with him before all living men save our liege lord for peace as well as for war'. At the time these indentures were made 'liege lord' could refer only to Richard II; and it is worth noting that this language, rather than 'our lord the king', was used. Moreover, in their closing words both indentures stated that the squires had taken an oath on the Gospels to perform their undertakings. In time of war the squires were promised appropriate wages and rewards for their condition and in the event of being sent for on other occasions. While in the duke's household they would receive wages.

The single surviving indentures of these years equally fail to conform with any conventions. On 29 March 1361 William Montague, earl of Salisbury, retained Edward Sommers with singular terseness.[80] He granted him a manor for life in return for his good and 'agreeable' service in the past and in the future. The squire promised on his side to stay with the earl in peace and in war, taking during the latter 'payment and allowances for his men and horses'. On May 1370 Humphrey Bohun, earl of Hereford, Essex and Northampton, granted his squire William Stapleton a rent of £20 a year for life out of his lands in Huntingdonshire 'for his good and agreeable service which he has done us and will do as well in peace as in war wherever we may be'.[81]

An indenture made between James, lord Audeley of Red Castle and

Heyleigh, and Sir John Massy on 23 September 1377,[82] clearly arose out
of negotiations, perhaps a dispute, concerning their interests in the manor
of Tatton. This was held in fee by Massy, but Audeley apparently received
an annual rent of 60s, also in fee. In the indenture Audeley surrendered
and quitclaimed this to Massy, his heirs and assigns. Massy granted and
confirmed to Audeley in exchange two messuages and thirty-six acres of
land in the township of Wrenbury. In addition, he was 'retained with the
said Sir James, saving his retainer and service to his liege lord'. Whenever
he 'journeyed' by Audeley's command, he was to have reasonable wages
of him. On 22 June 1385 Walter, lord FitzWalter, made an indenture with
Sir Alexander Waldon,[83] in which he granted him an annual rent of £10
for life (with power of distraint). On his part Walden promised to go with
his lord anywhere in the king's wars 'before all others', taking wages and
rewards such as were paid to other knight's of the lord's retinue and also
food and drink for himself, his chamberlain and a page.

These four indentures present in microcosm the picture of complexity
we see within the larger collections. Montague and Bohun used annuities
granted for past and future services as retaining fees; and Bohun's indenture
did nothing at all to identify the conditions of service apart from the conventional language of a grant of annuity, giving no indication that, when
the retainer appeared in response to his lord's summons, he could expect
additional benefits. While Audeley did promise wages during active service,
its language was otherwise vague. Of the four, FitzWalter's is the most
conventional; but it contains no references to the conditions of peacetime
service.

In two other cases we encounter indentures in which lords sought retainers outside the ranks of the gentry. On 13 January 1387 Roger, lord Clifford
granted a messuage and lands in Whinfell in Cumberland and the office
of forest bailiff there to Roger son of William at an annual rent of thirty-
seven shillings for life.[84] 'And the said Roger will serve us as well in war
as in peace taking from us as much as other men of his condition will take
for war.' There are no details of peacetime service. On the basis of these
terms it is reasonable to assume that lord Clifford was recruiting from the
upper level of his manorial peasantry with the needs of defense against the
Scots in mind.

In an indenture of 27 January 1392 Sir Ivo FitzWarin granted lands
and rents (including some in reversion) in several places in Dorset to Ralph
son of Ralph Brit for life.[85] Brit was to pay an annual rent of one rose to
Sir Ivo and also one mark a year to Sherborne Abbey (presumably the
overlord for some, or all, of these holdings). He was retained for life in

peace and war as a squire, taking such clothing (*vesture*) as other gentlemen (*gentiles*) took from the lord. In peace he was to attend FitzWarin when summoned, receiving food and drink for himself and his yeoman (*valet*) and hay and provender for two horses. If he followed his lord to the king's wars, he was to receive the king's wages and rewards for himself and his archer, with appropriate shipping. This indenture has several novel features. There is the grant of a tenancy for life instead of an annual fee; and, while other examples of such a practice exist, it is unusual to encounter a complex group of holdings, including a reversion. The details indicate that these were manorial freeholdings, or rents from them; and it is impossible to assess the value of the life-grant that Brit received in these terms. There are, indeed, some resemblances to the Clifford indenture. To be sure, Brit was a squire; but, in view of the sort of holdings granted to him, it is difficult not to feel that he belonged to that indeterminate group between the upper levels of the peasantry and the lowest ranks of the gentry. The indenture also contained an additional clause that was unusual. If Brit became too ill or too infirm or old to perform his service, he was to retain the holdings for life. At the same time a concluding clause emphasised his duty to perform his obligations if fit. In other respects the indenture echoes the terms of those of a conventional character. FitzWarin, a leading member of the gentry who was also a London mercer, was anxious to ape his social superiors and to cut a figure when he journeyed between his various manors in the south and west of England. Although the contingency of war service was mentioned, it seems certain that FitzWarin's primary concern was peacetime attendance by his squire. It was Brit's refusal to perform this obligation that led to his being dispossessed and to the litigation that has preserved a copy of the indenture.

Conclusions covering the whole range of non-Lancastrian indentures in the years 1361 to 1399 are hardly possible in the way they were for those of John of Gaunt. The only firm impression is one of complex diversity; and the only firm conclusion can be that it is unwise to rely upon the Lancastrian indentures as much as historians have. It is, indeed, foolish to give the Lancastrian survivals any sort of primacy in view of the fact that special circumstances led to their survival in comparatively large numbers. In the case of the non-Lancastrian indentures it is true that their survival is due in most cases to the special circumstances created by minorities or forfeitures. But against this it is important to bear in mind that some fees held for life may have been paid out of the revenues of receivers and, because they did not issue from specific manors or lands, were much less likely to be the subject of a successful attempt to secure royal confirmation.

In consequence, the details of divergence from the Lancastrian pattern we have seen may be part of an even larger picture the rest of which has disappeared from view.

It is certainly possible to suggest that outside the house of Lancaster the payment of an annual fee in both peace and war was at least a frequent practice and that the retainer was often given the right of distraint. This apart, each lord made his bargain in his own way and this might even vary from retainer to retainer. It is equally possible to say that most of the indentures of this period gave substantial attention to the retainer's service in the lord's household and to the benefits he and his following enjoyed while there. But this element in the handling of peacetime service was not universal. It is, for example, missing in each of the cases where only a single indenture has survived for a magnate. On the basis of the general obligation of peacetime service embeddded in two indentures belonging to the early years of this period – those of the earls of Salisbury and of Hereford and Essex – it might be argued that household obligations cannot be ruled out and may even have been taken for granted; but in the case of lords Fitz-Walter and Clifford the content of the indentures indicates that they could not have been expected. Nor is it possible to reach solid conclusions about the role of war as distinct from peacetime service in these non-Lancastrian indentures. To be sure, war bulks large in those that gave special attention to the division of the profits of war. But these were especially thorough in their treatment of all the mutual obligations of lord and man. The Despenser indentures, those of lord Thomas, the son, as much as those of lord Edmund, the father, suggest that the needs of these particular lords could not be handled by means of the conventional distinction between peacetime and wartime obligations. There were also those lords who recruited retainers without any peacetime service in mind – the duke of Exeter who planned for the possibility of rebellion, the lord FitzWalter and (though less definitely) the earls of Salisbury and of Hereford and Essex who were making preparations for the king's wars.

(iii)   1399–1485

The surviving life-indentures of the years 1399 to 1461 may be conveniently divided into two sections – those that generally conform with the main patterns of the fourteenth century, exemplified best in the indentures of John of Gaunt, and those that are markedly different from these. The latter group is dominated by the sixty-nine indentures of William, lord Hastings, which comprise over 70 per cent of its total.

Copies exist of the three life-indentures made by the future Henry V when Prince of Wales – two with squires (15 November 1408) and the other with Richard Beauchammp, earl of Warwick (2 October 1410)[86] In all three the language used to define the basic relationship between lord and retainer in peace and war is reminiscent of that in the indentures of John of Gaunt. Unlike most of the latter, however, these define the lord's right to a third share of his retainers' profits of war and in this connection explicitly except captives of royal blood and leading commanders from ransoming by the retainer. Wages were promised in all three in the event of service in the king's wars. Only in the case of the earl of Warwick is the retainer given household benefits, the earl, four of his squires and six of his yeomen securing *bouche de court* when attending the household at the prince's summons. While the two squires' fees were at a normal level (ten marks), the earl obtained the enormous sum of 250 marks a year.

A similar conformity with the main patterns of the previous century can be found in the case of Humphrey Stafford, earl of Buckingham (and duke from 1444). The texts of three of his indentures survive in the form of copies made by a Welsh antiquarian of the seventeenth century.[87] In four other cases we have brief summaries of the details of which suggest that they also were in the same form.[88] The full transcript we have of the indenture with Sir Edward Grey (20 April 1440) tailors its fee to the retainer's status: as long as he remained 'at the degree of bachelor' he was to receive £40 a year, but this was to be increased to 100 marks if he became a baron. As 'bachelor' he was to be ready to come at the earl's request 'and with him to ride in all parts on this side of the sea' with one squire, four yeomen, one groom, one page and seven horses or any larger contingent requested by the earl, food and drink being provided for him and his men and provender and supplies for his horses, all being paid their reasonable costs in journeying to and from the earl's side. In the event of war 'be it on this side of the sea or beyond' he was to bring the number of men-at-arms and archers commanded by the earl, receiving appropriate wages. The earl's indenture with seven other retainers seem to have been similar. The fullest text survives in the case of Sir John Mainwaring (5 September 1441) and this was virtually identical in general terms. It is, however, quite clear that the financial treatment of Sir Edward Grey was exceptional. Even his knight's fee of £40 was markedly higher than those of the other knights: all were £10 except for that of Sir Richard Vernon which was £20, and even William Fiennes, lord Say and Sele, received £10. In some sense Grey's higher fee reflected the importance of a knight who might in the foreseeable future become a baron; but it may also take his status as 'bachelor' into account.[89]

In one other case only do we have an indenture that conforms with this type. On 15 October 1415 John, duke of Bedford, retained Sir Robert Plumpton for life for an annual fee of twenty marks.[90] Somewhat more than in most indentures of its kind, most of its terms were concerned with war service. Plumpton and his men were then to receive appropriate wages, his own fee being abated for any period of such service that amounted to a quarter of a year or more. In time of peace he was to serve with a squire and two yeomen, in the duke's household or in attendance in his company, when he and his men were to take food and board.[91] There can be little doubt, especially in view of the importance of the duke of Bedford in his brother Henry V's campaigns in France, that Plumpton was recruited primarily for war service. In particular, the indenture mentions the duke's right to a third of Plumpton's winnings and of a third of his men's. Similar clauses can also be found in two of the earl of Buckingham's indentures – those with Sir Edward Grey and Sir John Mainwaring.

When we turn to the other fifteenth century indentures, the impression of diversity that emerged from those of the fourteenth century is both extended and deepened. In the case of Henry Percy, earl of Northumberland (d.1408) we see a retaining relationship emerging out of a dispute over land. An indenture,[92] made with Sir William Curwen on 8 May 1401, provided for the entailment of the manors of Workington, Seaton and Thornthwaite in Derwentfells on Sir William, with remainder in default of his issue on the earl in tail, with further remainder in default of his issue to Sir William's father for life, with final remainder to his right heirs. In return the earl and his son and heir granted an annuity of twenty marks for life to Sir William, 'through which annuity the said Sir William is retained for the whole of his life in chief by the said earl and his son in time of peace'. After the provision of an annuity for Sir William's son, a clerk, until he was provided with a benefice by the earl, a further annuity was granted to Sir William's son Christopher for life 'for which annuity the said Christopher shall be with the said earl and his said son for the term of his life in time of peace'. If Christopher became a knight, 'he shall then be in chief with the said earl and with the said son of the said earl', his annuity being increased from £5 to ten marks. The dispute between the Percies and the Curwens seems to have emerged out of the former's absorption – as a result of a settlement by the earl's second wife that took effect on her death in 1398,[93] – of the Lucy estates in Cumberland, consisting mainly of the honour of Cockermouth of which the Curwens were feudal tenants. In any *rapprochement* between the earl and a leading feudal tenant it clearly made sense in terms of contemporary practice to confirm the bond of lordship by means of a retaining relationship. It is quite likely that other leading families sometimes engaged in such practices. But two other aspects of this episode are especially interesting. One is that the Curwens were retained for peace, there being no mention at all of war. This is especially remarkable in view of the proximity of the Scottish border and the Percies' interest in the Wardenship of the West March. The other is the appearance of the phrase 'in chief' (*en chief*). This is a unique survival. The obvious explanation is that it imposed on the retainer the obligation of loyalty to his lord before all others save the king. It is interesting that this obligation was not imposed on Christopher Curwen until he became a knight.

The other early fifteenth-century indentures of the other great northern family – the Nevilles – reveal a range of approaches. A total of six survive for Ralph Neville, earl of Westmorland (d. 1425), all from the years 1400– 8. Three,[94] all belonging to February 1400, apparently emerged from re- arrangements that were required as a result of Henry IV's grant of estates from the duchy of Lancaster and the earldom of Richmond to the Neville earl. The terms suggest that the three squires involved had either previously been retained by the king or had been receiving annuities for life from the landed revenues concerned. In particular, the annual fees were remarkably high for squires – £100, 110 marks and £50. Because of the previous con- nection with the king, each indenture specifically laid down that the earl's right to the squire's services was contingent on his not being required by the king, his service with the earl being by royal licence. These details apart, the terms are quite terse in each case. Wages appropriate to the squire's condition were to be paid in time of war. Each squire was to be ready to serve fully armed, mounted and arrayed. The earl was to receive the third of the profits of war gained by the squire and by his men who were at the wages and costs of the earl. None of the squires was permitted, royal service apart, to serve anyone else without the earl's license. In two other inden- tures with squires made some years later (24 April 1406 and 21 June 1408)[95], the basic description of the obligations of the retainer to be ready to serve at all times was the same. But there were differences. The fees in these cases (forty shillings and five marks, respectively) were somewhat low. In the case of the profits of war, while the basic rule regarding the earl's third share was stated in the same terms, there was an explicit reser- vation to the earl of any captain or man of rank (*home destat*) for whom he would pay a reasonable reward to the captor. There was no clause reserving the squire's service to the earl alone.

In strong contrast there stands the agreement with Sir Thomas Grey, lord of Heton, on 6 August 1404.[96] It is reminiscent of the Percy indenture with the Curwens. In this case, however, the Neville earl did not grant a fee or annuity. Instead, the indenture stated that he had purchased the office of constable of Bamburgh castle from the king and this was now granted to Grey for life by royal letters patent.[97] In return, Grey released all actions against the earl. In time of war he was to serve at the wages appropriate to his degree, these not affecting his fee as constable. The clause dealing with the profits of war simply stated that Grey would be treated like others of his estate and degree. The fact that the agreement brought a period of dispute to an end is emphasised by the last clause in which Grey pledged his faith to perform its terms. These details show that this indenture represents a special case; and the features displayed in common over a period of eight years by the five squires' indentures suggest that the Neville earl operated a basic formula for the making of indentures of retinue. At the same time there were variations. And the Grey indenture reinforces the view that an indenture of retinue did not necessarily emerge from a simple negotiation in which a lord recruited a follower. There is, however, one feature which all six of the earl of Westmorland's indentures have in common – the total absence of any reference to household benefits in either war or peace.

Two indentures survive in the case of Henry, lord Beaumont (d. 1413), the one quite different from the other. On 5 April 1412 he granted two messuages with two bovates of land to a trumpeter at a yearly rent of forty shillings,[98] 'for the good and agreeable service . . . which he has done to me and will do to me and my heirs . . . provided that at all times (he) shall be bound to serve in his office me and my heirs for term of his life aforesaid'. This contract deserves attention for several reasons. Neither the usual words stating a retaining relationship nor any reference to peace or war can be seen in it. It can, of course, be argued that the very duties of a trumpeter would involve duties in both peace and war. The grant of lands at a rent (reminiscent of lord Clifford in 1387),[99] involved future service to lord Beaumont's heirs as well as himself. The other indenture (14 December 1412) does mention retaining but in very sparse language.[100] A minstrel was retained for life in peace and war in return for forty shillings a year, with power of distraint, there being no mention of other terms of service. The duties of a trumpeter and a minstrel clearly put them in the lord's household; and it is inconceivable that such low fees as these two were paid would provide adequately for their maintenance when in the household in time of peace or when on campaign. But it was thought unnecessary to make further provision in writing for such needs.

The grant by letters patent by William, lord Zouche (24 September 1414), to John Clifford of an annual rent of eight marks for life was less brief.[101] It was made for 'good and agreeable' service in the past and in the future, providing also food and board for the retainer, one groom and the equivalent for two horses. The power of distraint was given for these benefits as well as the annual rent. But beyond these details we learn nothing. It is not clear whether Clifford was a permanent member of the household staff. If he was, the absence of any mention of peace or war is explained. With two other indentures we return to terser language. On 18 June 1424 Edmund, earl of March and Ulster, retained his kinsman John, lord Talbot and Furnival,[102] in return for an annual rent of £100, with power of distraint. The transaction took the form of letters patent in which in return for lord Talbot's 'laudable service' he was retained for life without further definition or description of his obligations or of the lord's. It is not impossible that the letters patent (as also in the case of lord Zouch) were accompanied by a separate indenture but there is no mention of this. And there is no reference to peace or war. In an indenture with Sir John Cressy (12 November 1429),[103] Thomas, lord Roos, granted him twenty marks a year together with the demesne of a manor, both for life. In return Cressy was retained 'to do him service for term of his life in England'. In addition, he was to receive food and board for himself, a squire, a yeoman, a groom and four horses for all the time that he was in his lord's 'presence and service of the said lord in England'. This contract is conventional in that it explicitly involves household benefits; but these are defined in unusual language. There was, however, no mention of peace or war; and the retainer's service is limited to England.

It is unwise to generalise on the basis of a group of indentures consisting of the odd couple and single survivals for individual lords. But the chronological approach to the surviving indentures of the fifteenth century now brings us to survivals, the quantity of which permits some sort of interpretation, at least within the practice of the magnates concerned. And this is especially helpful because, in addition to the large collection for William, lord Hastings, groups of indentures have survived for the three most powerful magnates in the politics of mid-fifteenth-century England — Richard, duke of York, and the Neville earls of Salisbury and Warwick.

Most of the survivals in the case of Richard, duke of York, belong to the autumn of 1460 – that is, the eve of his open claim to the throne before the Lords in Parliament in October 1460. But two earlier ones have survived. On 28 July 1450 the earl of Ormond,[104] was 'witholden and belaft' with the duke for life, to do him service in peace and war, in Ireland or whenever he might be in England, 'to be with him against all creatures of whatsoever estate, preeminence or condition' next to the king. The fee was one hundred marks a year , to be paid according to the terms of letters patent under the duke's seal. There was an explicit provision that it would cease if the earl did not perform the promised service. In another indenture (30 January 1453),[105] a squire, George Darell, was 'belaft and witholden . . . to do true and faithful service unto my said lord the duke and with him for to be against all earthly creatures of what estate preeminence or condition so ever they be next the king our soverign and his issue kings of England'. He was to have £10 a year from the issues of a manor in Wiltshire until provided with an office or 'other reasonable reward' of twenty marks a year. A total of four indentures,[106] all dated 2 October 1460, were in the same terms as this, with virtually indentical language,[107] except in two respects. First, the reference to the king and his issue was missing,[108] Second, service was also owed to the duke's son and heir, Edmund, earl of March.

There are also minor differences between the squires' indentures and that with Ormond. Unlike theirs, his does not contain any reference to 'the faith of his body', possibly because such language was beneath the dignity of an earl who had territorial interests in England as well as Ireland. The squires' indentures do not contain any clause declaring the grant of their annual fees null and void in the event of a failure to perform the promised service; but in their case the duke's need to increase his following in the years to which they belong would have made such a provision counter-productive. More important, a comparison of all these indentures reveals the influence of political developments at the time they were made. That with the earl of Ormond was made when the duke of York was in virtual exile as the royal lieutenant in Ireland; a contract of service with the heir of the most powerful of the magnates of Ireland strengthened both his position there and his influence in English politics if his fortunes there improved. The absence of any reservation of the squires' loyalty to Henry VI or his heirs in 1460 was the direct result of York's decision to claim the throne. But, these matters apart, all these indentures follow the same pattern; and this deserves two comments. The first is that none of these indentures was the only document involved in the transaction concerned. In each of them reference is made to letters patent granting the fee or annuity and setting forth the terms of the grant. In the case of one of the squires recruited in October 1460 – Simon Milburne – we are fortunate in having the letters patent he received,[109] under the same date as the

indenture. In these the annuity was granted 'for good and laudable service
... performed to us before these times and for his life according to the
force, form and effect of certain indentures between us'.[110] It can be argued
that the concurrent use of an indenture and letters patent simply reflected
administrative practice.[111] The duke's receivers and manorial officials were
used to executing grants of fees and annuities according to the terms of
letters patent; and no doubt enrolments of the latter were kept quite separate
from the collection of the duke's halves of his indentures. Letters patent
thus had a financial function in the duke's administration, whereas indentures
had only to be consulted for a political purpose, the raising of the
duke's supporters when the need arose. But this argument does not provide
an adequate explanation. It is quite true that it was administratively
convenient to make grants of all fees and annuities in the form of letters
patent, whether or not an indenture of retinue was involved. But the effect
of a letter patent was to give greater protection to the retainer's financial
interest, since the appropriate receiver or manorial official could hardly
doubt his obligation to pay when the time came. The text, however, of the
letters patent that have survived in the sole case of one of the squires
retained in 1460 shows that the issue was more complicated. Past service
was specifically stated to be a ground for the grant of the annuity concerned;
and, despite the statement that the terms of an indenture of service
were the other basis of the grant, the language used put the retainer's
annuity within the confines of the legal doctrine that distinguished between
annuities for past and future services and simple retaining fees.[112] In short,
even if the retainer failed to perform the promised service, in law he could
not be dispossessed. It is difficult not to feel that, when the duke of York
followed the practice we see in the case of Simon Milburne, he was granting
letters patent as well as making an indenture as part of the price he was
paying for political support.

The second comment on York's indentures is that their descriptions of
the services owed by those retained are remarkably general, especially in
comparison with the indentures of fourteenth-century magnates. The only
concern for precision is displayed in the stress on the retainer's duty to
serve the duke against all others. Admittedly, the indenture with the earl
of Ormond specified that the service was in peace and war in both Ireland
and England. But this can be explained in terms of his special Anglo-Irish
role. In the case of the squires there is no mention at all of peace or war.
But this, of course, can be explained in terms of the constant threat of civil
war, which was present even when the indenture was made with George
Darell in 1453, a circumstance which must have made the conventional

references to peace and war in indentures seem superfluous. Most important of all, however, is the total absence of any reference to household
benefits or any other additional obligations of the duke towards his retainers when they responded to his summons.

A total of seven indentures has survived for the Neville earls of Salisbury[113] and Warwick. Four relate to the father, Richard, earl of Salisbury
(d. 1460). All use the same basic language to describe the man's obligations
as we encounter in those of the earl's father, Ralph, earl of Westmorland,
except that English is used instead of French. The retainer was to be 'well
and conveniently ('covenably') horsed, armed and arrayed, and always
ready to ride, come and go with, to and for the said earl at all times'. But,
this apart, there were marked differences. The indenture with Sir Thomas
Dacre (22 April 1435),[114] gave him a fee of twenty marks a year during
the lifetime of the earl's mother, Joan, countess of Westmorland, the amount
being increased to £20 on her death or on that of lord Dacre, his father. The
earl was clearly anxious to keep down the burden on his revenues but was
nevertheless prepared to pay an additional price to have a peer as one of
his retainers. In the case of Ralph, lord Greystoke (10 July 1447),[115] the
amount of the fees was not mentioned, it being merely stated that it should
be the same as he had held from the late Richard Beauchamp, earl of Warwick from his lordship of Barnard castle. Sir James Strangeways[116] was not
give a money fee but the issues and profits of the manor of Hundburton
in Yorkshire which were granted him in a separate deed of gift. Only in
the case of Sir Thomas Strickland (1 September 1448)[117] was there a simple
money fee – ten marks. Greystoke, Strangeways and Strickland were to be
paid wages in time of war. But even on this point there were differences.
'Costs' as well were mentioned in the case of Strangeways; while Strickland
was to have his annual fee 'abated' during the period of war wages. In the
case of Dacre there was no mention at all of payments over and above his
annual fee.

There were also variations in the retainers' obligation to serve the earl.
Strickland was to be ready to go 'unto all places on this side and beyond
the sea', but in the case of Greystoke and Strangeways France was explicitly
excepted. Dacre's indenture contained nothing at all about the areas of
service. While all four indentures imposed an obligation to serve the earl
above all others, 'saving his allegiance' to the king, that of Greystoke also
added the exceptions of Katherine, duchess of Norfolk, Robert, bishop of
Durham and Greystoke's own 'kin and allies at and within the third degree
of marriage'. There were also minor variations in the treatment of the division of the profits of war,[118] the language on this point in all four indentures

implying that the retainer's men would be at the 'wages and costs' of the earl. In the case of Greystoke alone a final clause stated that the indenture would be of no value if his fee was unpaid.

These details illuminate the range of bargainig that could occur in the negotiations over an indenture, even if the lord was as powerful as the Neville earl of Salisbury. There was a basic formula which linked these indentures with those of an earlier Neville generation. But the earl was ready to make substantial concessions in the case of a knight whose services he was especially anxious to acquire. This is especially marked in the case of Ralph, lord Greystoke. All four of these retainers were northerners; and, while it is impossible to generalise on the basis of only four indentures, the details do illustrate the earl's efforts to expand his following in the north in the years following the successful exclusion of the elder Neville line from the bulk of the family's inheritance. Certainly the contents of these indentures suggest that it was this motive, rather than the needs of war, that explain the indentures with Greystoke and Strangeways, since service in France is excluded. There is nothing in the indentures with Dacre and Strickland to suggest that peacetime lordship was more important than the need to recruit in time of war; and the location of the family holdings of both men does indicate that they had a role to play in the defence of the West March.

The three indentures of the son, Richard, earl of Warwick (d. 1471) were made within two days of one another – two on 27 April 1462,[119] and one on 28 April.[120] The only noticeable difference from his father's is the size of the fee – five marks – presumably because these retainers were not knights and did not belong to substantial families, the fathers in two cases being still alive.[121] In 1462 Richard, earl of Warwick, was the new Yorkist king's leading commander in the extreme north of England, engaged in driving out the Lancastrians in a campaign that would not end for another two years. In April 1462 he may well have been trying to exploit his greatly increased power in national politics and his role of military leadership to increase his following among the Cumbrian gentry. At any rate, we know that he made at least one other indenture with a Cumbrian squire in the same two days as the three that have survived.[122]

The main differences between these Neville indentures and those of Richard, duke of York, lie in two areas – the use of phraseology concerning peace and war and the way the Nevilles spelled out their retainers' obligation to provide an armed force at the lord's command. But otherwise they share with York's an assumption that the words 'belaft and witholden' and a statement that this bound the retainer to serve his lord against all men save the king were sufficient description of the retainer's duties. As in York's, there is no concern with household benefits, though the retainer is assigned wages during war services. The emphasis is not on any relationship involving the household but on the retainer's obligation to follow and be loyal to no one else. A single surviving indenture of Henry Percy, earl of Nothumberland (d. 1489),[123] suggests that he also followed the same approach. Its terms coincide with York's rather than the Nevilles', because it does not refer to the retainer's obligation to bring a body of armed men when summoned by his lord; but the services explicitly involved both peace and war.

Ever since Professor W. H. Dunham brought to light the indentures of the Yorkist peer, William, lord Hastings (d. 1483), it has been recognised that they present a complete contrast with any others we know. Their hallmark is the absence of a retaining fee whether in peace or in war: 'only two of Lord Hastings' sixty nine extant indentures . . . record money fees. Instead this peer contracted to be 'good and favorable lord' to his men who were neither tenants nor, literally, "feed" retainers.' On these grounds Professor Dunham has detected a pronounced change in the relationships of lord and man in the late fifteenth century, 'good lordship' taking the place of the money fee. 'The final substitution of what medieval men called good lordship – aid, favor, support, and preferment – for the fee created a more refined, certainly a more subtle relationship, one that could be advantageous and effectual only in a more sophisticated society.'[124]

The historian of the relationships of lord and man in late medieval England must constantly beware of the temptation to generalise on the basis of evidence that exists simply because it has survived. The comparatively enormous number of lord Hastings's indenture, therefore, should not deflect us from the realisation that they relate to only one magnate. In fact, only Richard, earl of Warwick, Richard, duke of Gloucester, and Henry Percy, earl of Northumberland, among the other peers of the Yorkist period have left us any indentures of retinue; and the combined total for all of them is a mere eight. But this general warning apart, there are good reasons for rejecting the sweeping interpretation that Professor Dunham has advanced from the Hastings evidence. In effect, it is impossible to avoid the conclusion that lord Hastings's indentures constitute a special case.

In discussing these documents as part of a wider examination of the Wars of the Roses, K. B. McFarlane pointed out that they were not distributed over the whole reign of Edward IV.[125] All but six of the sixty-seven indentures without money fees belonged to the years 1474–83, the very period when Hastings stood closer to the king than any other peer outside the royal family. And the trust which Edward IV placed in Hastings made him a politician whose 'good lordship' was especially attractive. A local gentleman who wanted to find a protector could not have found a better candidate to approach. Indeed, it would often have been worth sacrificing the advantages of an annual fee to gain the favour of so great a lord. At the same time there is good reason to believe that lord Hastings would have preferred to offer his influence rather than his money. Edward IV's gratitude to a loyal supporter immediately after his accession and then Hastings's rise in his favour, cemented by his loyalty during the vicissitudes of Warwick's rebellion and the Lancastrian restoration, had brought elevation to the baronage and great territorial wealth. But it is likely that Hastings was cautious in the use he made of his new-found wealth and loath to encumber his landed revenues with a body of fees and annuities for life.

Nor is it wise to assume from the absence of fees from the indentures of retainers that none were paid to them all. We have seen in the case of Richard, duke of York, that his indentures were accompanied by letters patent. And there are grounds for believing, at least in the case of some of his Yorkshire retainers in the late 1460s, that Richard, earl of Warwick, followed a similar practice: a receiver's account of his Yorkshire estates in 1464–65 describes payments of retainer's fees in several cases but proceeds under each to recite a copy of a grant of annuity for past and future services.[126] It is not inconceivable that lord Hastings went one step further, entering into indentures of retinue that did not mention a fee at all but granting annuities by separate letters patent.

All these are *a priori* arguments against building an interpretation of the Yorkist period on the basis of the extant Hastings indentures. But there are also grounds founded on what we actually know of the practices of contemporary lords. Richard, earl of Warwick continued the practice of retaining by annual fee that he was operating in 1462: the contemporary chronicler, John Warkworth,[127] tells how, when tensions developed between him and the king, he 'took to him in fee as many knights, squires and gentlemen, as he might, to be strong'. At his death in 1489 Henry Percy, earl of Northumberland, was spending roughly a quarter of his gross income on fees and annuities, much as his father had done.[128] It is reasonable to assume that, if the indentures of retinue of these magnates had survived on a scale comparable with those of lord Hastings, the majority, perhaps all, would be found to involve money fees.

In fact, the texts of the indentures provided by Professor Dunham can themselves provide a better perspective. A study of their terms leads to two main conclusions. First, as Professor Dunham himself notes, two of Hastings' indentures do contain money fees. Moreover, in sixty-four out of the sixty-nine indentures, involving sixty-two out of sixty-seven retainers,[129] Hastings promised the costs and expenses incurred by them and by those they brought with them when responding to his summons.[130] To be sure, as in the case of the Nevilles' indentures, there is no mention of any of the particular benefits we encounter elsewhere, especially in the fourteenth century. Nor on the basis of the language of Hastings's indentures can it be assumed that his men and their followers received their keep while in his service. The second main conclusion is that the language used to express the basic relationship between lord and man is strongly reminiscent of that of both Richard, duke of York, and the Neville earls. Professor Dunham has divided the Hastings indentures into twenty-six basic categories, each embodying a formula of which he has printed the text.[131] In the case of his Forms F, K, and V the language is almost identical. Form F is the best example: the retainer 'is belaft and retained for the term of his life with the said lord and him aid and his part take against all other persons . . . his ligeance only except. And at all times shall come to the said lord upon reasonable warning accompanied with as many persons defensibly arrayed as he may goodly make or assemble at costs and expenses of the said lord . . .'[131] These three Forms comprise a total of twenty-three indentures. In fact, if we look at the remaining indentures, we encounter only four Forms, comprising a total of a mere four indentures, that do not impose an obligation of personal service which in real terms replicates the requirements of Form F. In short, in sixty-five of the sixty-nine Hastings indentures the obligations of the retainer are, the absence of money apart, reminiscent of those of the Yorks' and the Nevilles'.

In one other respect Hastings's indentures have more in common with those of York than the Nevilles'. In the case of two indentures[132] the retainer's obligation is strengthened by means of language similar to York's – 'by the faith of his body' and 'upon his faith and honour of knighthood'.[133] Fifty-seven indentures fail to mention peace or war.[134] And the retainer's duty to ride to his lord's assistance is specifically confined to England in forty cases.

There are, in fact, solid grounds for believing that it was not the French wars but the possibility of civil war and the need for local influence that mattered in the thinking of Hastings and his men. It is especially interesting to note that twelve of the indentures that mention peace and war also limit the retainer's service to England. A total of thirty-two of the sixty-nine surviving indentures of lord Hastings belong to the years preceding Edward IV's expedition to France in July 1475, in which Hastings was one of the leading commanders. But of these twenty-eight confine the retainer's service to England. The dates of three of York's surviving indentures indicate that they formed part of a recruiting programme, intended to back his claim to the throne. But in Hastings's case the motives must have been more complicated. In the first place, there was the need to have men to assist Hastings's own lord, the king, if his throne (or his issue's succession to it) were threatened. Sixty-three of Hastings's sixty-nine indentures were made during the years after 1471, in the aftermath of a crisis in the fortunes of Hastings and his king: although Hastings's lord, the king, had ultimately been victorious, similar events were still more than conceivable. In the second place, Hastings wanted to bolster his own power in time of peace: he needed in the shires where he had his estates a following that was commensurate with his territorial power there and with his position at Westminster. A great courtier needed the opportunity to display his power of patronage as much as lesser men hungered for its benefits.

Viewed in this way, lord Hastings's indentures display a connection with those that were contemporary as well as with those of preceding generations. Are they so remarkably different from those of John of Gaunt that provide no fee in time of peace?[136] And it can be argued that, except in terms of the absence of any provisions relating to benefits in the lord's household, there is a basic similarity between them and the indenture between Gaunt and his squire William Barwell.[137] Those of Hastings's indentures that confine the retainer's service to England adopt the same approach as some of those of the lords Despenser and Thomas Mowbray, earl of Nottingham and duke of Norfolk.[138] In fact, the importance of lord Hastings's indentures in the history of the relationships between lord and man does not lie in a strong contrast with what had gone before. Rather, we should think of a spectrum of relationships, with some of those of the fourteenth century at one end and his at the other. And it would be wrong to define this spectrum along chronological lines: at no point in the fourteenth or the fifteenth centuries is a silence resulting from a failure to survive compelling historical evidence.

This conclusion is supported by what we know of the retaining practices of Richard, duke of Gloucester, the future Richard III. Receiver's accounts of the Neville lordship of Middleham in Yorkshire which he held by virtue of his marriage show that in 1471 he retained a knight and a squire, and in 1473 another knight, all for money fees.[139] One indenture of Gloucester's that has survived in the original, made with William Burgh (4 October 1471),[140] virtually repeats the language employed by Gloucester's father-in-law, Richard Neville, earl of Warwick, providing an annual money fee and wages during service. One other case shows Gloucester emulating the practice followed by his father, Richard, duke of York, in October 1460.[141] In letters patent (22 December 1474),[142] he confirmed a previous grant by Richard Neville, earl of Warwick, to Thomas Hutton of £5 a year from the lordship of Penrith, this being made for past and future services, Gloucester's grant and confirmation being made 'in consideration of the good and acceptable service . . . rendered to us aforetime and according to the force, form and effect in certain indentures between us'. A petition made to Gloucester by another squire, Gerard Salvin,[143] shows that the duke had a reputation for granting money fees: '. . . I offer my service to your lordship, and if you will please to take me, you shall find me true and at your pleasure, considering my true intent and service that intend to do towards your good Grace, it shall please you to grant me a fee yearly . . . '

It is equally clear, however, that Gloucester's retaining practices were not confined to the methods revealed by these documents. It may be unwise to lay a great deal of emphasis on the terms of an indenture made with another squire, Robert Ratcliffe, associated with the ex-Clifford lordship of Skipton which was also in Gloucester's hands (15 January 1480),[144] since it survives in a copy which may have been abbreviated. But, if we accept its evidence, we encounter a form much closer to the practices of lord Hastings. There was no annual fee, the squire simply being 'bound to serve . . . in the wars for the term of his life at the costs of the said duke'.

Even more reminiscent of the methods employed by lord Hastings are two other indentures. The terms of that made with Henry Percy, earl of Northumberland,[145] clearly emerged from a dispute between the two magnates over their respective spheres of influence and followings, since the duke promised that

> he shall not ask, challenge nor claim any office or offices or fee that the said earl hath of the King's grant, or of any person or persons, at the making of these presents, nor interrupt the said earl or any of his servants in time to come. And also the said duke shall not accept nor retain into his service any servant or servants that was or at any time since hath been with the said earl retained of fee, clothing or promise.

The indenture's reference to the 'appointment' made between the duke and the earl by the king and the lords of his council in the preceding May shows that the settlement was made under royal pressure; but the form of a retaining relationship between lord and man was employed for this purpose. The earl promised the duke that he would be 'his faithful servant, the said duke being his good and faithful lord, and the said earl to do service unto the said duke at all times lawful and convenient when he thereunto by the said duke shall be lawfully required'. Although there is no reference to service at the duke's costs, in other respects these are distinct echoes of the language of lord Hastings' indentures.

More remarkable is an indenture made by Gloucester with Elizabeth, the widow of Thomas, lord Scrope of Masham (14 January 1476).[146] By this she agreed that her son, the new lord Scrope of Masham,

> shall from henceforth be belaft, witholden and retained with the said duke and wholly be at his rule and guiding. And also that all her servants, tenants and inhabitants in and upon any of the lands late her husband's shall hereafter at all times belonging to the said duke and to give their faithful attendance for the which the said duke agreeth and by these presents granteth to be good and loving lord to the said Elizabeth, Thomas her son and all her said servants, tenants and inhabitants.

This indenture is a unique servival among those known indentures from late medieval England; and it is quite impossible to assess how far Gloucester and other lords at other times who enjoyed his scale of power employed similar methods. The agreement was clearly intended to secure some sort of control over the following of the Scrope lord of Masham; and his mother cooperated with Gloucester in the hope of securing his protection of her son's inheritance and his future patronage for the heir. The 'good lordship' which so dominates the indentures made by lord Hastings was clearly a flexible concept which could cover both other magnates who had been rivalling Gloucester in power and influence and also be used to define a relationship with another peer who was an inferior in both territorial power and age. Even though a mere four of Gloucester's indentures have survived, these and other scraps of evidence demonstrate that he employed several methods of retaining, ranging from the traditional money fee to the promise of 'good lordship'. His practices provide a microcosm of those employed in late fifteenth century England.

Throughout this discussion of the development of the indenture of retinue attention has been confined to the retainers of the titled nobility, mainly the most powerful of the kingdom's magnates. But in the Yorkist period which has given us the indentures of lord Hastings there also survive two documents which demonstrate that retaining by means of indentures had percolated deep down within the lowest levels of the gentry class. On 27 January 1468 a Westmorland squire, Thomas Sandforth of Ascom, made an indenture with William Bradley of Snipe, described as a 'yeoman'.[147] Bradley was 'witholden, belevyt and become ye said Thomas man' for term of his life 'and ye said William, his friends and all that he

may cause and strive *(strevyn)* shall take true and faithful service with the
said Thomas as oft as he shall make the said William sufficient warning
against all manner of men except the sovereign lord the king'. In return
Thomas promised to be his 'good and tender master' and to pay him 13s4d
a year. Sandforth made another indenture fifteen months later (27 April
1469) with John Clibburn of Bampton,[148] 'gentleman', in similar terms.
Clibburn promised his help 'as oft as when he shall be sufficiently required
against all other men', except the king, Rowland Clibburn his father, his
brother and his father-in-law, Sir Thomas Curwen, and all the latter's children 'and by this indenture him to fulfil in all his power as well with all
his men and tenants. . . and assist ye said Thomas as by his own person'.[149]
In this case the annual fee – forty shillings – reflects the local importance
of Clibburn as a member of a leading local gentry family. Clibburn was
also promised a gown every year of Sandforth's clothing. Sandforth also
undertook on his side 'to assist and maintain ye said John Clibburn as his
man'. From the dates of these two documents it is reasonable to infer that
the deterioration in the relationship of Edward IV and the earl of Warwick
and the growing possibility of civil war was leading to contingency planning by gentry in one of the earl's areas of territorial influence. Sandforth
himself had been retained by Warwick for life in April 1462;[150] and in
1468–69 it was in his own interest to strengthen his following among
fellow gentry and leading peasant farmers.

How frequent arrangements of this kind were it is impossible to say,
though the evidence of the Paston correspondence suggests that similar
episodes may have occurred in East Anglia at this time. To be sure, landed
gentry did not have the financial resources for retaining that the magnates
enjoyed; and this must certainly have imposed limitations on the use of
fees to recruit supporters. At the same time one letter in the Paston correspondence describes how the anxiety to cut a figure in local politics could
outweigh financial realities.[151] In Sandforth's case we see a local gentleman
who was definitely aping in a quite literal sense his superiors in wealth and
social status, because he was retaining for life in return for an annual fee.
And what is especially interesting about these two indentures is the way
he did this. There are resemblances beween his language and that of his
own lord the earl of Warwick. Moreover, the annual fee apart, there is an
even stronger resemblance between his indentures and those of lord Hastings in his promise to be 'good and tender master' to Bradley and to 'assist
and maintain' Clibburn. Nor could he have regarded these as empty for-
mulas: the differences between them reflect the social differences between
the two retainers.

The historian of the indenture of retinue in late medieval England is the victim as well as the beneficiary of the collections of those documents that have survived. Time and again a strong note of caution has to be sounded, drawing attention to the dangers of basing arguments on the quantity of survivals and assuming that the indentures that have disappeared had the same characteristics as those that have survived. It is, for example, quite clear that even in the fourteenth century the money fee was not always granted in time of peace and that its absence in the indentures of William, lord Hastings, was not a sudden or radical innovation. Even so, despite the difficulties inherent in our evidence, a few general conclusions about the development of the indenture of retinue are possible.

To begin with, there is every reason to distrust the generalisations that have been current for many years. The complexities of the body of phenomena which made up what historians have labelled 'bastard feudalism' are such as to throw doubt upon the usefulness of this term. It is equally clear that we must also discard the view that retaining in England in the late middle ages involved a relationship in which a cash nexus had replaced one of landholding. By fastening attention on the obvious financial elements in indentures of retinue – the fees and the wages – the balance that should be drawn between these and other elements is distorted. If, indeed, there is any common element in the surviving indentures of retinue from the late thirteenth to the fifteenth century, there is a much stronger case for finding it in some form of membership of the lord's household. The most detailed picture of the retinue as part of the household comes from the indentures of John of Gaunt; but, especially if other indentures of the late thirteenth and fourteenth centuries are studied in the light of the solid conclusions possible from Gaunt's, a common pattern can be observed, with comparatively slight divergences from it. The core of the relationship between lord and man in time of peace lay in his availability for summons to his lord's side at any time; and his presence there would give him membership of the household. The annual fee was one reward he could receive but daily wages or food and drink – in the case of many retainers both together – were others. War conditions could sometimes make it difficult to make the firm undertakings about such benefits that were possible in time of peace. Even so, there is enough information in most cases, especially of the leading magnates, to show that in war the retainer was a member of a household at war. Within the household retinue of great lords there was, at least in the fourteenth century, a group of 'bachelors', the word denoting a close relationship between a lord and a knight. Many were already 'bachelors' when they entered into indentures of retinue: many who did not already enjoy this status acquired its privileges when at their lord's side in time of peace or in time of war. The appearance of the 'bachelor' in one way or another in so many indentures of retinue of the late thirteenth and fourteenth centuries can only strengthen an interpretation that emphasises the importance of the household in the body of benefits conferred in indentures of retinue.

When we move into the fifteenth century, we encounter evidence that does not appear to justify the same confidence in the importance of the household relationship. In the middle years of the century the duke of York, the Neville earls of Salisbury and Warwick, William, lord Hastings, and Richard, duke of Gloucester, did not offer *bouche de court* or use the vernacular term for this or any other household benefits. And, though the Neville earls at least did pay wages during the retainer's perod of active service, they did not do so in terms of household arrangements. By the middle of the century the term 'bachelor' appears to have disappeared from indentures of retinue.

These arguments can, of course, be criticised on the ground that they are based on an examination of formal documents and thus neglect realities. In practice, it may be suggested, when a retainer joined his lord and, in company with his following, he and they became members of an enlarged household. This may well be true. But, even so, it remains a fact that these great lords of the middle of the fifteenth century did not bother in their indentures of retinue to employ language that set out any role for the household or to make commitments about benefits resulting from temporary membership of it. If the household still had a role, it was quite an informal one. Indeed, the change can be seen in the terminology that was intended to encapsulate the basic notions of the relationship between lord and man. Throughout the fourteenth century the word 'retained' is generally accompanied by (to give the literal meaning) 'remains' [*demore*), the latter word emerging from the notion of a stay within the household. Its use implies that, even if the retainer were not at any time physically a member of the household, he remained subject to the obligations of loyalty and obedience that would apply if he were. By the middle of the fifteenth century the word 'retained' is accompanied by 'withholden', or the formula is 'belaft and withholden'. This language has no echoes of the household in it: rather, its meaning is remarkably similar to that which we encounter in the words 'retaining fee' or 'retainer' in descriptions of relationships in today's society.

It would be wrong to think that this change was a sudden one: in a sense its roots can be seen in the earliest surviving indentures. The very existence of an indenture of retinue and its delineation of mutual obligations meant that a relationship existed in some measure outside the household. But by the middle of the fifteenth century the change had been recognised. Historians have been correct in emphasising the role of 'good lordship' in the relationships of lord and man in fifteenth-century England. But its role can only be understood if it is realised that it replaced a firmer body of mutual obligation primarily located within the lord's household. The history of the relationship of lord and man in late medieval England is one of a decline in the importance of the household.

Notes

1 Others may, of course, exist, but they have not so far been traced.

2 *JGRB*, i, 6–13. For a fuller discussion of this list, see App. II. App. III contains two knight's indentures ([a], nos. 3, 50) and eleven squires' ([b], no. 43, 78, 79, 80, 83, 84, 85, 86, 92, 93, 94, 95) which were discovered in the first of Henry IV's registers as duke of Lancaster (PRO, DL42/15), in the course of research for the present study.

3 *JGRA*, i, 293 (no. 782); *ibid*, i, 298–9 (no. 788); *ibid*, i, 330–2 (no. 832).

4 *Ibid*, i, 299–300 (no. 789); *JGRB*, i, 21–2 (no. 45); Lewis, 'Gaunt indentures', pp. 88, 96–7 (nos. 2, 10–4).

5 For further discussion of this matter see App. I.

6 Without such understanding the war benefits of Sir Thomas Dale could not be construed (App. III (a), no. 28).

7 *JGRA*, i, 315–16 (no. 809). *Cf. ibid.*, 344 (no. 850).

8 A frequent omission is a provision relating to the payment of wages for the journeys to and from war; but, even when this omission occurs, a study of the text as a whole suggests that this benefit was provided.

9 However, it is difficult to be quite as confident as Professor Lewis when he writes of 'a general tendency towards standardisation and simplification in the substance of the contracts' (Lewis, 'Gaunt indentures', p. 80). Another view is suggested in the paragraphs that follow.

10 E.g., *ibid.*, p. 102 (no. 22).

11 App. III (6), no. 64.

12 App. III (a), no. 1.

13 A few details of him and his family may be found in A. Goodman, 'The military subcontracts of Sir Hugh Hastings, 1380', *EHR*, xcv (1980), 114–15. The Sir Hugh discussed there was the son.

14 App. III (a), no. 7.

15 *Ibid.*, no. 18.

16 App. III (a), no. 4.

17 For the Nevilles see *Comp. Peer.*

18 In the case of Hastings the text (though slightly defective) indicates that he

need only go if fit to travel.

19 Full references will be found in App. III (a). They were: Sir John d'Ipre the elder (no. 2); Sir Nicholas Longford (no. 10); Sir John Marmion (no. 15); Sir Walter Urswick (no. 16); Sir Richard Burley (no. 19); Sir Thomas Fog (no. 22); Sir Walter Blount (no. 27); Sir Thomas Banastre (no. 30); and Sir John Dabridgecourt (no. 39).

20 Almost fourteen years separate the two indentures.

21 In the case of Banastre, however, there is the interesting addition of the phrase *pur son corps* after the formula for past and future service.

22 The case law was rather more substantial than Lewis, 'Gaunt indentures' p. 81, n. 6 indicates. See above, pp. 14–6.

23 See *JGRA*, *sub* Index, and Somerville, *Duchy*, *sub* Index.

24 In his case copies of the original as well as of the replacement survive (App. III (a), nos. 40, 52).

25 App. III (b), no. 60.

26 See P. E. L. R. Russell, *The English Intervention in Spain and Portugal in the Time of Edward II and Richard II* (Oxford, 1955).

27 For the latest discussion see (with references to earlier literature) M. G. A. Vale, *English Gascony, 1399–1433*, (Oxford, 1970), pp. 27–8.

28 Lewis, 'Gaunt indentures', pp. 94–7 (nos. 8, 9, and 14).

29 *Ibid.*, pp. 97–98 (nos. 15–18).

30 *Ibid.*, pp. 105–107 (nos. 15–18).

31 Based on App. III. Similar statistics are not possible in the case of the indentures surviving after 1383 because of the sort of language employed in them to describe war benefits. But the term 'bachelor' is frequently found in conjunction with the duke's commitment to pay war wages. Indentures from 1371 are included from *JGRA*.

32 East Sussex RO, Glynde 3469/5, 11; *JGRA*, ii, 89 (no. 1082).

33 *JGRA*, i, 299–300 (no. 789).

34 East Sussex RO, Glynde 3469/5, 11. See also *JGRA*, ii, 118 (no. 1146).

35 *Black Book*, p. 95.

36 BL, Add. MS. 40859A. The difference between the annual fee for knights with *mensa* and that for those without was £13 6s 8d.

37 *JGRA*, i, 89 (no. 1082).

38 *Berkeley Charters*, pp. 155–6.

39 *Black Book*, p. 95.

40 *Ibid.*: *cum venerint computamus cum vacacionibus eorum extra per finem ad plenam recepcionem monete; potest estimari quod quilibet contentetur cum x marciz.* This results in 213.33 if divided by 7½d.

41 See below, p. 173.

42 The summaries in the *Calendar of Patent Rolls* vary considerably in quality. In addition, litigation has preserved the terms of an indenture made by Sir Ivo Fitz-Warin. See above, pp. 94–5.

43 Forfeiture explains the single survivals in the case of Thomas, duke of Glouces-ter, and Richard, earl of Arundel. But it accounts for only one out of the three in the case of Richard, earl of Warwick.

44 *CPR, 1401–5*, p. 229; PRO, C 66/369/m. 24 (2 November 1376).

45 'or reasonable wages', presumably money for the horses' keep.

46 *CPR, 1381–85*, p. 99; PRO, C 66/312/m. 28. Strictly speaking, these were

letters patent of indenture.
47 See the details in Saul, *Gloucestershire Gentry*, p. 93.
48 *CPR, 1401–5*, p. 229; PRO, C 66/369/m. 24.
49 *CPR, 1381–85*, p. 119; PRO, C 66/312/m. 12.
50 *CPR, 1381–85*, p. 116; PRO, C 66/312/m. 15 (4 April 1373).
51 *CPR, 1381–85*, p. 238; PRO, C 66/314/m. 6 (29 March 1383).
52 *et avera bouche a court ove liveree pur luy mesmes un chamberleyn et trois garzons ou gages al afferant et feyn provendre et ferure pur cynk chivalx en maniere come autres de son estate ove le dit counte prendront.* As sometimes happens in Gaunt's indentures as well, this language does not preclude the payment of wages in addition to food and drink. No doubt it was assumed that these came from the king.
53 *CPR, 1381–85*, p. 277–78; PRO, C 66/315/m. 6.
54 *CPR, 1391–96*, p. 465–66; PRO, C 66/340/m. 29. There is, however, no reference to an earlier indenture.
55 *CPR, 1396–99*, p. 255; PRO, C 66/348/m. 29. The treatment of the retainer himself in time of war is not absolutely clear if the language is interpreted literally. In peace he enjoyed food and drink with his yeoman, but in time of war the description of benefits does not mention the latter. It can only be assumed that the payment of wages was taken for granted.
56 *CPR, 1399–1401*, p. 117.
57 Since this exception had to be made explicitly, the payment of wages on other occasions, at least in war, is implied. The language of this indenture on this point gives further support to the view that indentures were not always explicit in this area.
58 *CPR, 1405–8*, p. 16; C 66/373/m. 23.
59 *CPR, 1405–8*, p. 12; C 66/373/m. 25.
60 The language does not preclude separate letters patent of appointment; but, since this contract was in the form of letters patent indented, it is likely that this was the only form it took.
61 *CPR, 1399–1401*, p. 28; PRO, 66/354/m. 15.
62 *CPR, 1405–8*, p. 29; PRO, C 66/373/m. 15.
63 *CPR, 1399–1401*, p. 196; PRO, C 66/358/m. 10.
64 When the earl's inheritance was increased by descent, this fee was to be raised to ten marks.
65 This provision was preceded by the statement that he would be allowed 'his costs *(coustages)* for the time that he remained with us in the same way as other bachelors will be allowed'. The fact that this was deemed necessary, as well as details of food and drink, indicated that the latter did not comprise all the benefits involved. The term *coustages* must therefore indicate wages.
66 *CPR, 1399–1401*, p. 193; PRO, C 66/358/m. 13.
67 *CPR, 1399–1401*, p. 224; PRO, C 66/359/m. 36.
68 *CPR, 1399–1401*, p. 234; PRO, C 66/359/m. 28.
69 *CPR, 1399–1401*, p. 7; PRO, C 66/354/m. 33.
70 Both are in Latin, not French.
71 *CPR, 1399–1401*, p. 244; PRO, C 66/359/m. 18.
72 *pro bono et laudibili servicio suo impenso et ad totam vitam suam imposterum impendendo.*
73 *CPR, 1381–85*, p. 181; PRO, C 66/313/m. 12.

74 The *Calendar of Patent Rolls* summary of these indentures is much more sparse than in the case of their predecessors.

75 *CPR, 1399–1401,* p. 189; PRO, C 66/358/m. 17.

76 *CPR, 1399–1401,* p. 182–3; PRO, C 66/358/m. 4.

77 *CPR, 1399–1401,* p. 263; PRO, C 66/359/m. 4.

78 *CPR, 1399–1401,* p. 244 and 255; PRO, C 66/359/mm. 9 and 18.

79 *CPR, 1399–1401,* p. 255 is incorrect.

80 PRO, E326/4915.

81 *CPR, 1370–74,* p. 261; PRO, C 66/288/m. 23.

82 Chesh. RO, DET/303/14. The summary in Morgan, *Medieval Cheshire,* p. 76 is inaccurate.

83 *CPR, 1385–89,* p. 307; PRO, C 66/323/m. 6.

84 *CPR, 1385–89,* p. 311; PRO, C 66/323/m. 3. The indenture is in Latin.

85 The indenture is recited in a case of novel disseisin (for which see above, pp. 23–4), its date being given at a previous point in the record (BL, Add. R., 74138).

86 Dunham, *Hastings' Retainers,* pp. 138–9.

87 In National Library of Wales, Peniarth MS, 280D, compiled by Robert Vaughan.

88 The texts are all printed in A. Compton Reeves, 'Some of Humphrey Stafford's military indentures', *Nottingham Medieval Studies,* xvi (1972), 88–91. I have not included the last entry in this article, since it is the indenture of retainer of a physician.

89 One cannot be certain of this. The word may have been used to define knightly status in contrast with that of a baron. Vaughan's transcript may not be complete or entirely accurate.

90 *Plumpton Corr.,* p. xlii, n.g.

91 There is no mention of horses.

92 For the text (with translation) see F. W. Ragg, 'De Culwen', *Trans. Cumb. West. A.A.S,* New Ser., xiv (1914), 398–400.

93 See Bean, *Percy Estates,* pp. 8–9.

94 *CCR, 1399–1402,* p. 104–5, 115–6; PRO, C 54/245/m. 16d, 17d. 23d. They were John Pirian, Nicholas Ardwich and Anthony Ritz.

95 Richard Otway (*HMC, Tenth Report,* Part IV, p. 226; John Thorp (T. Madox, *Formulare Anglicanum* [London, 1702], p. 97 [no. 176]).

96 *PRO, E326/3515 (CAD,* ii, 412).

97 *CPR, 1401–5,* p. 412.

98 *CPR, 1413–16,* p. 137; PRO, C 66/392/m. 15.

99 See above, p. 94.

100 *CPR, 1413–16,* p. 132; PRO, C 66/392/m. 22.

101 *CPR, 1413–16,* p. 387; PRO, C 66/398/m. 16.

102 *CPR, 1422–29,* p. 332; PRO, C 66/419/m. 21.

103 *CPR, 1429–36,* p. 330; PRO, C 66/435/m. 18.

104 *Ormond Deeds,* iii, 167–68 (no. 177).

105 PRO, C 146/6400, calendared in *CAD,* vi, (C. 6400).

106 Longleat MSS. 10491 (Thomas Holcote), 10492 (Henry Hakluyt), 10493 (name destroyed) and 10494 (Simon Milburne). In each case the annuity was ten marks.

107 The word 'diligent' is also added to describe the service.

108 For comments on the way the indentures illuminate York's intentions, see McFarlane, *Collected Essays*, pp. 236–7.
109 Longleat MS. 1095.
110 The letters patent are in Latin, the indenture in English.
111 Copies of other letters patent issued by the duke which refer to separate indentures will be found summarised in *CPR, 1461–67*, pp. 94, 121 and 129 (PRO, C 66/494/m. 4 and -/495/mm. 3 and 10).
112 See above, pp. 14–15.
113 An indenture between Salisbury and Sir Henry Threlkeld (*Trans. Cumb. Westm. Arch. Soc.*, New Ser., ix, 283–4) is for six months only.
114 Northants. RO, FitzWilliam (Milton) MSS, no. 2049.
115 *Ibid.*, no. 2052.
116 *Ibid.*, no. 2051. for an account of Strangeways's career see Roskell, *Parliaments and Politics*, ii, pp. 279–306.
117 Copies of this indenture (which is in the muniments at Sizergh Castle) are in Denton, *England in the Fifteenth Century*, p. 290 and Scott, *Stricklands*, pp. 67–8.
118 See below, App. I.
119 C. L. Scofield, 'An engagement of service to Warwick the Kingmaker, 1462', *EHR*, xxix (1914), 720 (Christopher Lancaster son and heir of Hugh Lancaster, esquire); PRO, E 327/185 (Robert Warcop the younger, son and heir of Robert Warcop the elder). For a copy of Warcop's half see Madox, *Formulare Anglicanum*, pp. 104–5 (no. 185).
120 PRO, E 326/6415 (Thomas Blenkinson, esquire).
121 On his father's death Lancaster's fee was to be increased to £5.
122 A warrant to the earl's receiver in Westmorland survives, dated 28 April 1462, directing payment of five marks a year to Thomas Sandforth for life (Cumberland and Westmorland RO, Carlisle, AS 59). This is an example of a 'letter dormant' (*litera dormiens*). See below, Ch. V, p. 195 no. 85.
123 Ragg, *art, cit., Trans. Cumb. Westm. A. Soc.*, New Ser., xiv (1914), 402. The indenture has two curious features. It is not stated that the grant of the fee is for life and, indeed, it does not specify any term at all. The explanation must be that the earl had not yet been restored to his inheritance. Indeed, he had not yet the right to call himself earl of Northumberland until 25 March 1470. But the events that followed showed that his expectations were justified (Bean, *Percy Estates*, pp. 109–10) and Edward IV's intentions may well have been known to him: the king was clearly proceeding slowly in order not to drive John Neville (who had been given the earldom in 1464) into active support of his brother the earl of Warwick. In addition, the indenture is not dated by the regnal year. Whatever his expectations of restoration from Edward IV, Henry Percy may not have forgotten his family's Lancastrian background, preferring to avoid explicit support of Edward IV.
124 Dunham, *Hastings' Retainers*, pp. 9–10.
125 K. B. McFarlane, *Collected Essays*, p. 249.
126 PRO, SC 6/1085/ 20. The above arguments assume that this is virtually the same practice as the duke of York's. There is, however, the possibility that each of these payments was an annuity in strict terms, granted simply for past and future services. The accountant may be using the term *retentus* in a loose sense, meaning a follower bound to the earl by ties of loyalty. But, if this is the case, it does not affect the argments above concerning the Hastings indentures.

127 Warkworth, *Chronicle*, pp. 3–4.

128 Bean, *Percy Estates*, pp. 129–30.

129 In the case of two retainers there are two indentures each, made at different times (Dunham, *Hastings' Retainers*, p. 121).

130 All except Forms A, H, O, Y, Z, each involving only one retainer. (*Ibid.*, pp. 123–33).

131 Forms A, B, D, E, G, H, I, J, M, N, P, S, T, V, W and X.

132 *Ibid.*, pp. 123–4.

133 See above, p. 102.

134 Dunham, *Hastings' Retainers*, (Forms, H, Q, S, T, U and V).

135 Forms B, C, F, G, H, J, K, N, Q, S, W.

136 See above, p. 80; App. III, *passim*.

137 See above, p. 77.

138 See above, pp. 89–91.

139 PRO, SC6/1085/20. See also A. J. Pollard, 'Richard Clervaux of Croft: a North Riding squire in the fifteenth century', *Yorkshire Archaeological Journal*, 1 (1978), 163.

140 C. S. Perceval, 'Notes on Documents belonging to Sir John Lawson, Bart, of Brough Hall', *Archaeologia*, xlvii (1882), 195.

141 See above, pp. 102–3.

142 C. H. Hunter Blair, 'Two letters patent from John Hutton near Penrith, Cumberland', *Arch. Ael.*, 4th Ser., lix (1961), 569. The phrase *per vim et effectum* in the photograph of the manuscript is not accurately transcribed.

143 R. Surtees, *The History and Antiquities of the County Palatine of Durham* (4 vols., London, 1816–40), iv, 114–15.

144 T. D. Whitaker, *The History and Antiquities of the Deanery of Craven in the County of York* (3rd edn., London, 1878), p. 211.

145 Printed in Dunham, *Hasting's Retainers*, p. 140.

146 Printed and discussed in L. C. Attreed, 'An indenture between Richard Duke of Gloucester and the Scrope family of Masham and Upsall', *Speculum*, lviii (1983), 1018–25. The comments in *ibid.*, p. 1018, n. 2 fail, however, to distinguish between the indenture in the proper meaning and other kinds of legal document.

147 Cumb. Westm. RO, AS63.

148 *Ibid.*, BM. 119.

149 Portions are illegible.

150 See above, n. 122.

151 *Paston Papers*, i, 80 (no. 48); *Paston Letters*, ii, 313.

IV

The forms of relationship between lord and man: the problem of origins

The internal workings of lordship present one of the most elusive phenomena a historian can encounter. The sources, both administrative records and chronicles, are replete with references to great lords – their exploits in war, their role in royal government and their benefactions to the church. Through all this information runs the assumption that the existence of a following was both a source and a demonstration of the power of the great lords of the realm. But precision about the relationships between them and their followers is lacking before the appearance of the indenture of retinue in the late thirteenth century. To be sure, there survive many records of grants of land before this – *laens*, then 'books' of land in the Anglo-Saxon period, and charters of enfeoffment from late in the reign of William the Conqueror onwards; but this body of evidence in no way throws light on the heart of the problem. In a sense, when a lord granted land to a follower, they were on either side approaching the end of a major, if not the most important, phase in their relatioship, since the follower was being rewarded for services he had already performed. Life-grants, it is true, lacked permanence. Until the late twelfth century, although many knights' fees had descended in the same family for generations the lord had enjoyed some freedom of manoeuvre in combating his feudal tenants' claim that continued occupation by heirs amounted to hereditary tenure. Nevertheless, once royal justice had intervened and produced procedures that protected the tenants' rights, a lord whose ancestors had rewarded their followers with grants of land in fee simple had to content himself with services and the incidents of feudal tenure – relief, aids, wardship and marriage. A lord, of course, could still protect his interests and those of his heirs by making a grant that was specifically for life. But this put the

follower at a disadvantage in comparison with those who enjoyed hereditary tenure. In any event, none of these considerations is relevant to the
fundamental problem in the understanding of lordship – the relationships
that compelled lords to reward their followers in a tangible way, so con-
crete, at least after the Norman Conquest, as to create throughout the kingdom a system of land tenure on which rested the authority of the Crown,
and after that create a system of money payments.

In the study of any historical problem it is inevitable that hard data will
receive more attention than issues that are ill- documented. And most of
the solid information in English history after the Norman Conquest comes
from the records of royal government. For the king the great lords of his
kingdom were either instruments or opponents of his will and policies. In
his dealings with them awareness of the sources of their power in terms
of men was an important element in the formulation of policy; but the
records of the Crown necessarily recorded decisions and actions, rather
than the motives that led to them. For this reason from the end of the
twelfth century onwards, when regular series of chancery enrolments begin,
they provide little to assist the historian of lordship. He can only work
backwards from an understanding of all the elements involved in the
relationships between lord and man in the period when great lords themselves left records – that is, from the late thirteenth century onwards.

The problem of the origins of the financial elements in lordship we see
in late medieval England has received some attention in the past forty years
or so, especially in the writings of K. B. McFarlane and Bryce D. Lyon.
Their arguments depend on accepted notions of the system of feudal tenure
under which the Crown obtained military resources from its subjects. It
was against this background that these and other historians shared in varying degrees the view that the thirteenth century was a period in which the
Crown to all intents and purposes abandoned the feudal host as an effective
means of raising even a portion of the troops needed in time of war. Instead,
in this interpretation, it turned to the contract system of military service
by means of which contracts were made with leading commanders who in
their turn recruited their contingents by making subcontracts. It was a system of paid service, in a sense making mercenaries out of the king's own
subjects. Recent research has served to emphasise the extent to which this
system was a mainstay of the Crown's military resources by the beginning
of the fourteenth century.[1]

Both the content and the chronology of the contract system of military
service appeared to provide enough to explain the development of the
indenture of retinue from the late thirteenth century onwards. It had fully

arrived a little time before the appearance of the earliest surviving indentures of retinue for life; and, like the indenture of retinue, it involved a
written contract in the form of an indenture. In the classic discussion of
'bastard feudalism' in 1945 McFarlane traced the practice of retaining by
indenture back to the recruitment by contract involved in Edward I's Welsh
campaign of 1277.[2] To be fair, his approach was essentially descriptive of
the forms of relationship and he did not set out to provide a complete
explanation of origins. Bryce Lyon was more firm in his view of the origins
of the indenture of retinue. He found his solution in a study of the money
fief *(fief-rente)*, the practice of granting a money fee instead of land in
return for feudal service, this interest in legal terms being indistinguishable
from a feudal holding of land except in its consisting of revenues. Like the
other rulers of Western Europe from the eleventh century onwards the
kings of England employed this device for purposes of military recruitment
as well as diplomacy: and its use continued well into the period in which
the contract system took hold. For Lyon the *fief-rente* was 'transitional
military institution which helped to bridge the gap between non-paid feudal
service and contractual non-feudal service'.[3] He claimed that, 'The *fief-
rente*, the antecedent of contractual service, epitomized the transition from
the time when feudalism provided the armies of western Europe to when
it was but a sentimental memory of such as Froissart.'[4] In contrast with
the views of McFarlane and Lyon are those of H. G. Richardson and G.
O. Sayles who see the contract system as no more than a variant of the
Crown's practice of employing mercenaries which went back at least to
the years immediately after the Norman Conquest.[5] They denounce the
view that contracts for military service first appeared under Edward I: 'We
can see no ground for any other conclusion than that such contacts have
had a continuous history at least from the eleventh century onwards,
though the forms with which such contracts were clothed underwent
change.'[6]

None of these interpretations is adequate as an explanation for the forms
of relationship between lord and man in late medieval England. A fundamental objection to all of them is that they are directed against only one
of those forms – the indenture of retinue – and fail to deal with either
livery or the granting of annuities. Equally important is the basic difference
between royal contracts of military service and the subcontracts then made,
on the one hand, and, on the other hand, the indenture of retinue for life.
Such contracts and subcontracts were made for limited periods, generally
the duration of a campaign and in most cases for no more than a year. It
is these arrangements that have given rise to the concept of a 'contract'

system of military service. But knights and squires sought, and were often
granted, the benefits of an indenture for life. To be sure, it can be argued
that contracts and subcontracts for limited periods led naturally and inevitably to indentures of retinue for life, because it would be in the interest of
lords to maintain a nucleus of knights and squires who, when their lords
made contracts with the king for a campaign, would be available to recruit
the men-at-arms and archers that had been promised the king.[7] But there
is much that is unsatisfactory in this explanation. First, it ignores the extent
to which indentures of retinue for life were concerned with service in time
of peace. Second, it is based on the assumption that the lords who entered
into indentures of retinue for life with their knights and squires lived in a
period when the possibility of a call from the king to service was always
likely, if not imminent. This may, indeed, have been the situation in the
case of the Scottish wars of the early fourteenth century or in the middle
of the century, when Edward III's ambitions in France appeared to have
become the dominating element in his relations with his subjects. But it is
much more difficult to argue the existence of a similar situation before
Edward I's effort to conquer Scotland began or between the English defeat
at Bannockburn and the assertion of Edward III's claim to the throne of
France. Third, when a lord made an indenture of retinue for life, he generally parted with a portion of his landed revenues for a period of time that
was beyond limitation by him if his retainer performed the promised services. It is not easy to believe that lords would be ready to do this simply
for the convenience of easy and speedy recruitment if and when the king
requested that they bring a contingent on a campaign he was planning.

Perhaps the most telling of all the possible objections to existing explanations of the origins of 'bastard feudalism' is that, with the sole exception
of that of Richardson and Sayles, they assume a dichotomy between the
developments of the late middle ages and those of the centuries traditionally
viewed as the 'high middle ages'. McFarlane was critical of the concept of
'bastard feudalism' advanced by Plummer; but he retained the phrase while
substituting an interpretation of his own. Indeed, he did not free himself
of the shackles imposed by Plummer's views and in some measure wrote
within their limits. The very phrase 'bastard feudalism' to which he gave
renewed currency assumes a contrast between it and 'feudalism'. In present-
ing a contrast between feudal institutions and what came after Lyon stands
out by his reliance on the role of a money economy, viewing the medieval
period as a whole as one in which a natural economy gave way to one based
on the use of currency. When he published in 1957 there was already an
air of *déja vu* about any explanation in any field that sought refuge in the

deus ex machina of the 'rise of a money economy'.[8]

It is in this context that attention should be given to interpretations that are best regarded as 'riders' to that of 'bastard feudalism' as a body of military arrangements based on money instead of land. On the basis of a suggestion made by Professor T. F. T. Plucknett in 1949,[9] it has been argued that the abolition of subinfeudation by the statute of *Quia Emptores* (1290) made 'bastard feudalism' 'inescapable'.[10] It is a notion that fulfils no useful purpose in the search for the origins of the relationships between lord and man in late medieval England.[11] First, it is based on a misunderstanding of the statute. Grants for life involving subinfeudation remained possible under its terms. Indeed, such grants are occasionally encountered in indentures of retinue during the fourteenth century. Second, the earliest indentures of retinue for life belong to 1278. They are not, it must be said, in the form to which the majority of those made belong; but the earliest of these comes from 1297, a date so close to that of the statute as to make suspect the attribution of any role to it in the development of the indenture of retinue. Third, there is abundant evidence, both in the treatise known as *Bracton*,[12] and in the existence of an action of annnuity by the middle of the thirteenth century,[13] to indicate that lords did not have to wait for the statute of *Quia Emptores* before they could grant annual payments from their revenues, Last, any effort to ascribe a role to *Quia Emptores* in this area misconstrues the nature of the 'bastard feudalism' it seeks to explain, since it is concerned with annuities and indentures of retinue and ignores the existence of grants of livery.

The most recent interpretation is that offered by Professor Scott Waugh. It has the merit of taking the practice of granting annuities into account. Indeed, it is that which lies at the heart of Waugh's explanation of the origins of the indenture of retinue. He sees this in practices developed by lords in the late twelfth and early thirteenth centuries[14] – changes in the administration of their estates, triggered by the effects of inflation, on the one hand, and, on the other hand, encouraged by the development of written contracts involving regular money payments, this in turn facilitated by the growth of royal justice and the creation of a jurisdiction over the obligations created in this way:

> lords tried to rationalise their feudal relations. They used written documents to define precisely the content of those relations, and they used cash payments to conserve their resources. Through these devices, lords hoped to restore the discretion over rewards and clients that they were losing over fee land and tenants.[15]

He provides a wealth of illustrative material to demonstrate the existence of formal legal arrangements in which lords undertook to make annual payments of money in return for specified services, such arrangements being tantamount to what were later described as contracts. Against this background Waugh regards the indenture of retinue itself as 'contractual retaining'.

There are, however, serious defects in this interpretation. First, it has a somewhat *post hoc, propter hoc* character. To be sure, there is substantial evidence that the payment of annuities and other forms of financial reward for services were in vogue in the decades preceding the first appearance of the indenture of retinue. But the latter required a particular kind of service: the connexion between this and service of other kinds is not established. In fact, the details adduced of 'contractual' arrangements involve a miscellaneous collection of methods, including grants of wardships and annuities that were to be paid to clerks until they were provided with benefices. It is hardly surprising that lords were paying money for services by the end of the twelfth century, in view of what we know about the role of England in European trade and industry or the financial concerns of the government of Henry II and his sons. Nor is it helpful to draw attention to grants of wardships in return for services. Wardships were also sold outright or given away without conditions of any service being attached. In fact, among all the surviving indentures of retinue of late medieval England there is only one case of a wardship being used in place of the retainer's fee; and this appears to have been a special case, since the retainer was the uncle of the ward.[16]

Another criticism of Waugh's theory lies in the contents of the surviving indentures of the late thirteenth and fourteenth centuries. The range and content of their clauses cannot be reconciled with his conclusion:

> by the end of the thirteenth century, when Edward I's ambitions in Wales, Scotland and Gascony placed new military demands on English lords they did not have to invent a new system of military service. They simply adjusted the system of contractual retaining which they had developed for administrative service to military needs. All that was involved was a change of the wording of the phrase concerning service.[17]

In particular, this statement ignores the detailed attention given to household benefits in the surviving indentures.

There is, however, a much more fundamental body of objections to Waugh's interpretation. He claims that there are 'well over a hundred cases involving a clear indication of a contractual relationship between a lord and client before 1300, at least twenty-five of which pertain to the reign of Henry III'.[18] But this statement itself implies that three-quarters of these known examples belong to the years 1272–1300. The crucial issue is whether there is anything to indicate that 'contractual' arrangements were being made over military service in the reign of Henry III, since our earliest two indentures of retinue belong to 1270 and the two earliest for life (not involving military service) to 1278.[19] Within his total of 'contractual' arrangements Waugh describes two documents as 'military deeds'. But an examination of the contents of these show that they can hardly count as indentures of retinue or as precursors of such agreements. In 1272 (a date that is anyway late for the argument) Roger Darcy promised to make Ingram of Oldcotes a knight, also undertaking to provide clothing and maintenance for him for life, the same benefits being promised for his squire and two grooms.[2] It is quite true that the provisions concerning maintenance are reminiscent of some of the features of indentures of retinue of the late thirteenth and fourteenth centuries; but there is nothing to indicate duties of a military character. A knight did not necessarily go to war. The other example is more useful to Waugh's argument, since it belongs to the reign of John and refers to war. According to a case in records of the *Curia Regis* in 1220 the plaintiff was given arms by the defendant, who took his homage and promised him four marks a year from his chamber 'at the time when the lord king John came from Poitou'.[21] But it is important to bear in mind that we know these details from the case stated by the plaintiff some years later in litigation and that the defendant lord, while admitting giving arms, taking homage and promising promotion denied granting any charter or promising any money. Even if a military relationship was involved, the details provided reveal nothing resembling the features of the later indenture of retinue. A final criticism of Waugh's theory is that it does nothing to explain the practice of granting liveries.

At this point it is worth asking whether another approach to the problem would be more worthwhile. *A priori* there is much to be said for working backwards from the documents surviving from the late thirteenth and fourteenth centuries in order to produce an explanation based on the firm foundations of those relationships between lord and man that can be delineated in reliable detail. In the indentures of retinue concerned benefits received in the lord's household bulked as large as the payment of money fees. Does this not suggest that we search in the lord's household for the origins of the forms of lordship we encounter in late medieval England? This suggestion is certainly supported by evidence that the household was often the source of the payments made in the arrangements in the first half of the thirteenth century discussed by Waugh. The plaintiff who brought an action in 1220 claimed that his lord, as well as giving him arms, and taking his homage, had promised him four marks a year from his chamber. A number of the other 'contractual' arrangements cited by Waugh in the period before 1272 involved annual payments from the chambers of the lords concerned.[22] And, when in 1272 Roger Darcy promised to make Ingram of Oldcotes a knight, he undertook to provide maintenance and clothing for life, for him, his squire and two yeomen, details which suggest he was to become a household knight.

A decision to investigate along these lines gains further support if we move into the area of current knowledge of lords' followings in time of war. We have long been aware that as a force in politics and society the great lord's household was present from the very beginnings of English history in the Anglo-Saxon conquests.[23] And recent work on the role of the household of the greatest lord of all, the king, in war suggests that it was the core of the kingdom's military resources from the time of the earliest kings of England. A recent study of the military household of the Anglo-Norman kings demonstrates that the Crown's employment of mercenaries was intended to enlarge and strengthen resources that were already in existence in the royal household.[24] There is every reason to believe that a similar organisation existed under the Angevin kings. The most recent study of the kingdom's war effort in the reign of Edward I in Wales and Scotland and against France has demonstrated the importance of the king's household knights.[25] An examination of the wardrobe book of the royal household in 1338–40 shows that a similar situation existed in Edward III's campaigning in Flanders in these years.[26]

Nor is the suggestion that the origins of late medieval retaining be sought in the lord's household surprising. Despite the paucity of information, there is enough to justify the view that, whether in royal government or in the administration of great lords' estates, there occurred from late Anglo-Saxon times onwards a body of changes in which a household, originally a warband and then in more settled times a centre of government, shedded responsibilities that in due course became the functions of separate institutions. The less peripatetic the king's household or that of one of great subjects became, the more coherent these developments appeared. For instance, in the case of the Crown the handling of the kingdom's revenues moved out of the household and into what became the Exchequer, staying in a fixed place; or, in the case of justice, this aspect of royal authority ceased to be exercised from a peripatetic court but settled down at Westminster. In the case of the king's leading subjects receivers took over the functions of administering landed revenues that had hitherto been handled by the steward and other household officers. Thus, instead of seeing the origins of retaining in 'contractual' arrangements involving annual payments in return for service, it may be more sensible to treat both these phenomena as developing from a long-term change in the structure and role of the lord's household. In other words, the structure of retaining that was in place by the beginning of the fourteenth century had descended from relationships that over a century before had been located within the household. These considerations certainly justify an effort to search for household origins in the evidence relating to the three main forms of the relationships between lord and man in late medieval England.

(i) The annuity

Our detailed examination of the origins of the main forms of the relationship between lord and man in late medieval England must begin with the annuity because it is the one for which the earliest solid evidence has survived. For the most part we have to rely on information culled from the early records of the courts of common law. It is quite clear that royal justice had to develop in the course of the first half of the thirteenth century a jurisdiction over disputes arising out of the non-payment of annuities. A writ of debt already existed; but this was not a satisfactory recourse for claims over annuities. In the case of an action of debt a plaintiff sought the payment of cash that was owed to him. But in litigation over the non-payment of annuities what was required was not merely the payment of arrears but also an assurance that payment would continue in future years under the terms of the original grant.[27]. By the middle of the thirteenth century the necessary procedures were in place. A plaintiff could choose between two writs of annuity. One was known as *ex camera*, dealing with an annuity paid out of the grantor's chamber. The other was *ex tenemento*, applying to annuities due from lands or rents.[28]

The functions of the writ *ex tenemento* are clear enough. But that *ex camera* presents a more complicated picture, since legal historians have attributed a fictional character to it, arguing that the source of payment of an annuity was so conceived because annuities were regarded as incorporal things which had to belong in some fixed place.[29] It is, however, more likely that the phrase *ex camera* originally denoted, at least in the beginnings of common law jurisdiction, the actual source of payment. The assumption was that the lord's chamber was the centre of his financial administration. To be sure, at the lowest levels of landowning a lord might not possess a clearly articulated household administration composed of several distinct offices. But the grants of annuities preserved in the plea rolls of the first half of the thirteenth century,[30] often describe the source as the grantor's chamber in terms that do not suggest that it was a totally fictitious location. The essential point, however, is that, even if a chamber did not exist, it was considered necessary to assume its existence in order to denote revenues under the grantor's control: his role was naturally construed in terms of the organisation of his household.

In the light of these comments it is tempting to suggest that the writ *ex camera* must have appeared earlier than that *ex tenemento*. It must be said, however, that there is no certain support for this suggestion. Indeed, the practice of paying annuities out of landed revenues must have gone back towards the beginning of the thirteenth century, since the compilation we know as *Bracton*, belonging to the third decade, stated, 'There is likewise a certain kind of rent, which is paid by someone, to be derived from a certain thing, with distraint or not, which is not called a service, but is as it were a free tenement upon enfeoffment.'[31]

A ruling by royal justices in 1293 was bound to lead to a decline in the use of the writ *ex camera* and at the same time to a strengthening of any tendency to pay annuities out of landed revenues. It was laid down that a writ of annuity *ex camera* had to be brought in the shire where the lord was physically present.[32] From now on, if a lord wanted to give an annuity both as a reward for past service and as an inducement for the future, he would be well-advised to arrange for its payment from landed revenues, since this would free the grantee from serious inconvenience if non-payment occurred and litigation was threatened. Indeed, a grant from landed revenues in the state of the law after 1293 would count as a special testimony to the lord's commitment to his man's interest. From 1293 onwards the lord's household as a source of annuity payments was bound to decline.

By the beginning of the fourteenth century lords generally granted annuities in terms that simultaneously embraced services performed in the past as well as those to be performed in the future. In the details that have survived in legal proceedings and original deeds relating to grants before 1272, such terms are unknown and any references to services at all in general terms is rare. But it is more than likely that grants were being made for both past and future services by 1272, since the two indentures of retinue made by William de Swinburne in 1278 granted rents 'for services performed to me and to be performed'.[33] And the practice had certainly created a legal problem by 1307, since in that year royal judges had to draw a distinction between the obligations of lords under grants of annuities for past and future services and those incurred under indentures of retinue.[34]

Annuities paid in these terms from landed revenues remained an endemic feature of lordship throughout the fifteenth century and beyond. But the fact that most of those we know of were paid in this way should not obscure the real nature of the distant origins of the practice. The form of payment and, indeed, the practice of formalising the arrangement in a legal instrument were results of a change in the structure of the administration of the lord's finances that seems to have occurred in the late twelfth and early thirteenth centuries and led to the household's loss of all-embracing financial functions. Within this context annuities in the form we encounter them in the years after 1300 were the product of interraction between two forces – the appearance of new doctrines and procedures in the courts of common law and the mutual self-interest of lords and men.

(ii) The indenture of retinue

The problem of the origins of the indenture of retinue is more complicated than that of the annuity's beginnings, since we are not able to rely on the evidence of rulings in the courts of law and records of the royal courts of justice. Instead, we are dependent on a limited number of surviving indentures the availability of which is due largely to the rare and haphazard survival of the administrative records of the king's subjects. Moreover, the study of the origins of retaining by indenture involves more than one issue. There is, of course, the need to explain why lords chose this particular means of recruitment rather than any other. At the same time, however, while the historian of lordship has to give primary attention to the indenture for life because it is this practice which throws the best light on the nature of the relationships between lord and man, it is also necessary to bear in mind that a substantial proportion of the surviving indentures are short-term engagements, generally for a period covering the duration of a campaign.[35] There was, in addition, some retaining at the lord's will or pleasure.[36] The paucity of evidence for the period of origins compels us to use both life – and short-term indentures, but the basic difference between them must always be borne in mind. It is tempting to suggest that the appearance of the short-term indenture preceded that of the form for life, lords responding to the pressure engendered by competition with other lords for followers. But there is no evidence to support this suggestion: and a very short time – a mere eight years – separated the first surviving examples of either kind of engagement.

The best way to approach the origins of the indenture of retinue is to work backwards from 1297, since it is from that year that there survive three life-indentures which display the same sort of features as we encounter in most such documents during the next two centuries. It is, however, quite clear that the practice of making life-contracts in indenture form had been known for at least a generation. Two indentures imposing on followers a general obligation to serve and assist their lord for life, made by a Northumbrian landowner, survive from 1278.[37] It is true that, while these grant annual fees in return for service, the precise nature of that service is nowhere specified and there are none of the details of military service or household benefits that we find in later indentures. But the fact that a member of the knightly class on the border with Scotland made such agreements in indenture form indicates that the practice of making contracts of this kind and form was then quite well known throughout the whole kingdom.

It is also quite clear that the practice of making written contracts for limited terms of military service was accepted by 1270. Two contracts have survived, both belonging to July of that year, in which the future Edward I recruited a total of fifteen knights for his crusade to the Holy Land, one being with one subcontracting follower, the other with two.[38] The terms are identical, a lump sum of 600 marks being paid to each of the three individuals for a year's service. Dr Lloyd has shown from the evidence of the Pipe Roll of I Edward I that these two contracts were part of a larger body of similar arrangements, there being a total of eighteen such followers, each with his contingent, in the retinue that left England with the lord Edward.[39] He also employed similar methods of recruitment on his journey to the Holy Land.[40] There is also evidence that by this time the practice already existed of paying for military service out of landed revenues. On 1 February 1271 by means of letters patent the lord Edward's brother, Edmund, earl of Lancaster, granted to his knight Sir Robert Turberville, the manor of Minsterworth for a term of three years.[41] It is not clear whether the letters patent were the only form the contract took; but, if so, earl Edmund's practice was not remarkably different from what can sometimes be ecountered a century or so later.

Unfortunately, when we move backwards from 1270–71, we lack such solid documentation. Enough, however, exists to indicate that retaining in a technical sense (though not necessarily in the form of an indenture) had already existed for over a century or so. The accounts of Marcher estates held by the lord Edward,[42] record wages paid to serjeants who had been 'retained' to guard the castle of Abergavenny from 28 October 1256 to 30 November 1257. There is also an indication of peacetime retaining in *The Rules of Robert Grosseteste*, drawn up as a body of advice for the countess of Lincoln between 1240 and 1242. The language used is especially important, since the advice is based upon the bishop's understanding of general practice.

> Order that no one be accepted or retained *(retenu)* to be of your household
> *(maysnee)* within it or outside it, without good reason for believing them to be
> faithful, knowledgeable, diligent in the work for which they have been engaged,
> and above all, honest and of good character.[43]

And there survives one indenture which, though undated, can confidently
be assigned to 1252, in which William de Wydendon demised all his
lands in the parish of Wycombe to Sir Philip Basset for seven years
from Michaelmas 1252, the lessee paying the chief lords of the fee eight
shillings a year. In return 'the aforesaid Philip will retain the said William
in his service to the end of the said term if he wishes or will place him in
the service of some good man for that time'.[44] During his term of service
he was to receive food and clothing as one of Basset's squires and another
horse in the event of his own dying. In the case of this cotract, there was
no payment of fee by lord or man. On the contrary, the man leased land
in order to enter his lord's service. But in other respects there are elements
that point the way to the indenture of retinue. The indenture form was
used; there was the promise to maintain the man as a squire; and there
was to be recompense for a dead horse. It is impossible to believe that
Philip Basset and his squire, together with those who witessed their indenture, would have found this form of agreement between lord and man at
all strange. Both this document and the advice given to the countess of
Lincoln are important because they reveal peacetime retaining as distinct
from arrangements for war campaigning.

In fact, we can secure solid information three-quarters of a century earlier
than the date of *The Rules of Robert Grosseteste*. One of the most important sources for the history of chivalry in England and France – the verse-life
of William Marshal – reveals some form of retaining in the latter half of
the reign of Henry II. The author used the word *retenir* on seven occasions,
the editor translating it as 'to hire a knight' *(prendre [un chevalier] a sa
solde)*.[45] The poem describes how the young king Henry retained the best
of the young men and how his example encouraged other great lords to
seek to do the same.[46] Another passage throws light on the structure of
such retaining. In his description of the young king's following at one tournament the author tells us that his knights numbered eighty, each of them
receiving twenty-five *sous* a day for each of those he brought with him.
Since the young king had fifteen bannerets, there were, we are told, more
than two hundred knights maintained by the young king.[47] This passage
can only be understood in terms of a following brought by leading knights

that differed very little, if at all, from those we see depicted in the earliest surviving indentures. Daily wages paid by a lord were channelled through his retainers to their own followings. Admittedly, we are here discussing an aspect of a highly mobile knightly society in which young knights and those aspiring to knighthood travelled far and wide to enter the service of leaders whose prowess and connexions would bring them winnings in tournaments and other rewards. Their anxiety for such career-openings may have meant that the engagements they made with their lords were oral, not written. Even so, the basic features of retaining by means of contracts and sub-contracts were present.

There are, however, two considerations which suggest that such contracts were generally made in writing in the late twelfth century. First, it is reasonable to follow in the footsteps of Richardson and Sayles and infer from the Crown's use of mercenaries that written contracts of service must have been made with mercenary captains.[48] Second, what we know about the organisation of military service from the Crown's subjects in the closing years of the twelfth century and the early years of the thirteenth suggests that English lords may well have made written agreements with English knights for limited periods of service in the king's wars. It was in the reigns of Richard I and John that the practice began of requiring much smaller contingents than the total of knights owed by tenants-in-chief. The precise arrangements by which a tenant-in-chief raised the small quota of knights he was requested to produce may well have varied.[49] In the case of some of the most powerful of them it is not at all unlikely that the members of the quota were elected in a court of feudal tenants;[50] but such an arrangement depended on the functioning of a feudal jurisdiction that had not been so eroded by the consequences of subinfeudation as to make such efforts still feasible. It is equally, if not more, conceivable in the case of many lords, even including some of the most powerful, that the quotas were furnished by hiring knights. If so, the likelihood of written agreements is strong.

Some details compiled by Bryce Lyon from royal records in the reign of John give support to these hypotheses.[51] In the case of fifteen knights whose fees from the king can be found in the Chancery and Exchequer enrolments it is possible from the same sources to compile in each case a list of payments made to the knight for wages in addition to annual fees, *dona* covering miscellaneous expenses and sums in recompense for horses lost and armour damaged in the king's service. These items concern matters that were the subject of specific clauses in the indentures of the late thirteenth and early fourteenth centuries. It is thus difficult to believe that written contracts of some kind, approximating to some of the earliest indentures of retinue, did not exist by this date. Indeed, thorough methods of accounting had been employed for generations in the royal Exchequer. It is inconceivable that royal officials would have made payments of this kind without the warrant of written agreements.

But did such written agreements take the form of indentures? This form of document had a long history. When Henry I in 1101 made a life-contract with Robert, count of Flanders, it took the form of a chirograph, the older form of, and term for, an indenture.[52] And the popularity of this form of agreement must have increased with the expansion of royal justice in the late twelfth century and its adaptation of the chirograph in the regular series of 'feet of fines' that began in 1195. Indeed, the closing years of the twelfth century and the early thirteenth were a period of 'take-off' in the expansion of lay literacy in England.[53] Within the knightly class, largely because of the expansion of royal justice, knowledge of legal instruments became more sophisticated; and by the end of the thirteenth century royal courts of law followed procedures that took this situation for granted. In particular, by the middle of the century they would only recognise a contractual agreement if it had been made under seal.[54] In these circumstances an indenture was bound to be the form of agreement two parties would tend to favour, since it guaranteed for both of them an authentic instrument that would be accepted as evidence in the kingdom's courts of law.

Nevertheless, these arguments do not exhaust all the issues involved in the origins of the indenture of retinue. In view of the absence of solid documentation for most of the thirteenth century it is difficult to form any judgement about the extent to which lords engaged in retaining in this form. Some suggestions can certainly be advanced on the basis of the forms of contract that have survived. In 1270 the lord Edward made contracts with three followers in the form of charters in which the payment for service took the form of lump sums.[55] But the following year his brother the earl of Lancaster granted a manor to a knight, who was about to cross the sea, by letters patent.[56] In 1278 William de Swinburne chose the indenture form for the agreements he made with two followers.[57] Stronger evidence that practices varied comes from the year 1297. Of the three life-indentures from that year each takes the form of an indenture, being both indented and sealed interchangeably; but there is still marked variation in language.[58]

Considerable variations can also be observed in those contracts of this period that were not for life. That between Theobald Walter and John Neville (2 April 1296) in which the latter undertook to serve in Scotland was indented and sealed interchangeably,[59] while the 'quasi-life' agreement

between Aymer de Valence and Thomas, lord Berkeley (7 July 1297) was
not described as an indenture, though in that form.[60] In contrast, however,
when Sir Edmund of Stafford engaged Philip of Hartshill to serve with him
in the war between Edward I and the king of France (3 October 1297) he
did so in the form of letters patent.[61] In these non-life contracts there is
also a lack of precision over the terms of service. In the case of that between
Theobald Walter and Neville service was to be 'during the war between
the noble lord Edward king of England and the king of Scotland', similar
language being used the following year by Sir Edmund Stafford. That
between Aymer de Valence and lord Berkeley was for peace and war but
did not say how long the service was to last. All this suggests that there
was as yet no consensus about the form a contract of service should take.
Caution is certainly desirable in pressing this conclusion, because of the
diversity that can be seen within the development of the indenture of retinue
throughout the fourteenth and fifteenth centuries. At the same time, however, the indenture form did become general during the first two decades or
so of the fourteenth century; and the examples that have survived from
those years display rather more precision than can be seen in 1296–97.

Is it, then, possible to argue that the indenture as a form of contract for
military service took root in those years (1294–97) because of the demands
made by Edward I on the military resources of his kingdom in order to
wage campaigns in Scotland, Gascony and Flanders? It is worth noting
that, of the total of sixteen indentures known before 1307,[62] including those
that were not for life as well as those summarised in legal proceedings,
two were made by Henry III's son and heir, the lord Edward, two by leading
magnates – the earl marshal and Aymer de Valence – and the rest by members of the lesser baronage and the knightly class. These details fit the
suggestion that the lesser baronage and those below them in the landowning hierarchy were now employing practices already in use among leading
magnates; and the variations we observe would have been a natural consequence of this situation. But for several reasons this argument must be
treated with reserve. It ignores the possibility that the surviving contracts
may not be a fair sample of those that were made. Nor can the indenture
form have been new to the knightly class: in 1252 Sir Philip Basset used
it for a contract of service. Even so, the fact remains that, the two belonging
to 1278 apart, the surviving life-indentures before 1307 all belong to 1297
and, of the four that were not for life,[63] two belong to the years 1296–7
and one to a Marcher lord's expedition of 1287. Furthermore, all these
documents emerge from Edward I's wars of ambition outside the boundaries of his English kingdom. If, then, we argue on the basis of all this

documentation, it is difficult to resist the conclusion that the scale of Edward I's demands for men from 1294 onwards did force some sort of extension of methods of recruitment by indenture that were already known. In this context it is reasonable to assume that the contracts of service made in these years would have given full attention to the needs of service in war and the different circumstances of service in Scotland, Gascony and Flanders. Certainly the three surviving life-indentures can be shown to distinguish between peace and war and to mention the possible area of campaigning to which the retainer might have to follow his lord. And one of these life-indentures – that between the earl marshal and Segrave – mirrors the crisis in the relations of Edward I with his subjects at the time it was made.[64] Similar features can be detected in the other contracts of these years. Those made by Theobald Walter,[65] and Sir Edmund Stafford referred specifically to the Scottish and French wars respectively; and the latter issued the letters patent concerned at Ghent.[66]

There are also good reasons for believing that this group of survivals is a remnant of a much larger group belonging to the years 1294–7. We know of two other life-indentures from legal proceedings[67] – those made by William Cressy (19 September 1294) and Robert de Tony (16 July 1297). Moreover, an examination of royal licences to alienated enrolled on the Patent Rolls shows that five licences were granted in 1294, four of them in August, to tenants-in-chief who were going on the king's service to Gascony.[68] Each of these involved grants of land or rents for life, on a scale approximating to what can be seen in the earliest surviving indentures of retinue. In 1297 two such licences were granted, both to tenants-in-chief going overseas on royal service.[69] The difficulties in securing royal licences to alienate at this time,[70] suggest that tenants-in-chief would have preferred to reward followers from lands held of mesne lords, with the consequence that many other such arrangements are hidden from our view.

None of this is surprising. The scale of the king's demands at this time far exceeded those for his earlier campaigns which had been confined to Wales; and by the summer of 1297 his problems of recruitment were aggravated by the need to carry the war against France into Flanders as well as Gascony. To be sure, there is every reason to believe that indentures of retinue had a history that began well back before 1294. At the same time it is necessary to remember that the realm had not been involved in overseas war on a scale commensurate with that of 1294–97 since the Bouvines campaign of 1214. It was not until 1294, therefore, that lords would have had the opportunity to employ indentures of retinue on any scale as a means of responding to the duty of serving the king overseas as well as in territories on the frontiers of England. The dimensions of Edward I's war effort in the years 1294–97 – in particular, the possibility of service in Wales, Scotland, Gascony or Flanders – imposed on lord and man requirements of precise definition that made the indenture of retinue an especially advantageous form of agreement for both sides.

But why did some lords go beyond agreements for limited periods and choose, instead, to make indentures for the life of the retainer? It is tempting simply to seek an answer in the interaction of two influences. On the one hand, every indenture emerged from a process of bargaining. On the other hand, the extent to which a lord would yield in offering terms would depend on the importance of the prospective retainer; and in the circumstances of 1294–97 one element in this must have been the latter's capacity to lead on campaign and, before that began, to assist in the recruitment of the lord's contingent. In such a situation it was inevitable that some specially favoured or important retainers would secure terms for life. But there is more to this problem than is supplied by an answer along these lines because another question is involved. Why did the commitments made for the retainer's life involve grants of land or landed revenues, instead of annual payments from the lord's household? The failure to use the latter is especially noteworthy in view of the commitments that were simultaneously made in indentures for the provision of *bouche de court* for the retainer and also for his following, benefits that lay within the household. There is no information that bears directly on this question. Nevertheless, it is possible to point to a body of circumstances that together provide an explanation. Great lords like the earl marshal or Aymer de Valence must always have had large followings by contemporary standards, though not on a scale commensurate with that of Thomas of Lancaster. But even for magnates at their level the sudden transformation of a peacetime household into one organised for war must have raised serious problems of organisation; and these would have been proportionately greater at the lower levels of the landowning hierarchy, since their castles and manor houses would have been smaller than those of magnates.

The response of the lords in these circumstances varied. Two of the surviving life-indentures of 1297 confer benefits on the retainer as a member of his lord's household, even in the case of a small Marcher lord. And similar features on a substantial scale can be seen in Aymer de Valence's agreement with lord Berkeley and in the plea roll records summarising the indentures made by William Cressy and Robert de Tony. In contrast, however, the life-indenture made by Sir John Grey of Rotherfield and the contracts for limited service made by Walter Butler and Sir Edmund Stafford do not mention household benefits at all. These, it must be said, emerged from efforts at recruitment on the part of lesser men, all of whom had particular military needs in mind – service in the king's wars overseas in the case of Grey, and campaigns in Scotland and Flanders in those of Butler and Stafford respectively. And, while Grey made an agreement for his man's life in peace and war, he prepared for the contingency that his choice of man would prove unacceptable for the royal army. Even so, when we move to the surviving life- indentures of the years after 1297 through to the end of the fourteenth century, the role of household benefits almost invariably bulks large. What emerges is a picture of a retainer who, when on his lord's service, whether in peace or war, was part of an enlarged household.

The truth is that lords and their followers belonged to a society in which service was inevitably conceived in these terms; and the values that were part and parcel of such thinking transcended the difference between peace and war. The lord's household, apart from staff who in modern terms would be described as 'domestics', consisted of knights and squires, some of whom supervised provision for the immediate needs of the lord and his family, while others, not necessarily present at his side throughout the year, gave counsel and assisted in the administration of his estates. Even at the end of the thirteenth century the values that nurtured the relationships between the lord and his household had been forged centuries before in the warrior-band. The concepts of 'peace' and 'war,' were accretions imposed by the authority of kings and the teachings of the church. When the lord followed his king to war, he and his followers inevitably thought of the group under his command as an enlarged household. Moreover, the practical problems of command and campaigning were bound to strengthen such attitudes, since in real terms it would be difficult to distinguish between knights and squires of a peacetime household and those of their status who joined the lord for war. What mattered was the fact of membership of the lord's following.

It is not easy to secure confirmation of these arguments, apart from the attention given to household benefits in indentures of retinue. But there is some useful information. The details of the lord Edward's preparations for his crusade to the Holy Land in 1270 show that his contingent was essentially his household enlarged by short-term contractual arrangements.[71] In the case of Thomas of Lancaster we possess a book of his daily household expenses from Michaelmas 1318 to Michaelmas 1319, a period that includes his participation in Edward II's siege of Berwick-on-Tweed. In it we can see the expenses of household maintenance fluctuating day by day and week by week, reaching their highest levels as the royal army approached its destination and during the siege itself.[72] In a very real sense it was a household at war. In the, same financial year the war fees of two retainers – William, lord Latimer and Sir Nicholas Segrave – for the quarter that included the siege were paid out of the wardrobe.[73]

These arguments and details explain why household benefits for the retainer were so marked a feature of the surviving indentures of retinue of the late thirteenth and fourteenth centuries. But it remains necessary to explain why part of these benefits so often consisted of fees paid direct out of landed revenues instead of household sources. The explanation for this involves several factors, long-term as well as short-term. To begin with, there must always have been a tendency for lordship to extend outside the immediate household. No doubt in the years in wich feudal tenures were emerging after the Norman Conquest this tendency was masked, because lords were granting fees of land on terms that created a real bond between them and their tenants. But, when the inheritance of feudal holdings became an absolutely established principle and disputes in this area moved into the royal courts, the personal bonds between lord and man were bound to be eroded as long as they were based on the tenure of land: homage did still exist, but it was now a matter of form and ritual, rather than an expression of a real personal relationship. Such tendencies were strengthened by the growth of subinfeudation which led both to the disintegration of holdings and to an increase in the number of lords from whom a man might hold his lands. In particular, those ties of lordship that depended on the lord's rights of wardship and marriage were weakened. When a man held from several lords, the identity of the lord who would exercise the wardship of the heir's body and the right of marriage would be decided by the complicated issue of priority of enfeoffment,[74] the inheritance being broken up during the heir's minority by the rights of wardship claimed by other lords. And, if a man held only a minute portion of land from the Crown in chief, its right of 'prerogative wardship' was then exercised over all the feudal holdings of the deceased, together with the wardship of the body and the marriage of the heir. What real ties survived between lord and man because of feudal tenure must have been weakened still further in the thirteenth century by the tensions caused by the tenant's freedom of alienation.[75]

Yet, while these changes were occurring, the lord's need for a following remained. And even for the leading earls who had both the revenues and the accommodation to maintain large followings permanently within their households such resources must sometimes have failed to provide enough in the way of demonstrations of power and sources of armed support in times of crisis in their relations with other magnates or with the king. Furthermore, leading magnates held inheritances spread over many counties. The household would move from castle to castle or manor-house to manor-house through the course of the year: at any point it might be several days' journey from an area where the immediate impact of the lord's authority was required. In view of these circumstances it is reasonable to suppose that leading lords, at any rate once the power and influence they enjoyed through feudal tenures began to be eroded, sought to maintain followings outside the household. In some measure, of course, such a lord's need for resources of local influence might be met by giving offices in the administration of his estates to members of local gentry families, and our knowledge of seignorial administration by the end of the thirteenth century suggests that this was an important resource. Office in the lord's administration must often have been a way of cementing the ties of loyalty between a lord and a local gentry family, whether or not it held of him by feudal tenure. Even so, even in time of peace it is unlikely that this method of recruiting a following would in itself have satisfied the needs of magnates in thirteenth-century England.

It is no surprise, therefore, to find in *The Rules of Robert Grosseteste* as early as 1240–42 that a distinction was drawn between those retained within the household and those retained outside it.[76] By the end of the thirteenth century the royal courts of law were reinforcing any tendencies to create relationships with a following outside the household. It was still possible to pay fees to such followers directly out of the cash revenues of the household, whether through the chamber or the wardrobe. In 1292, however, it became clear that a fee or annuity paid in this way might be a source of trouble for a retainer who had received such a grant for life. The common law judges laid down that in the event of non-payment he would have to bring his writ of annuity against the lord wherever he might be physically present, taking the view that 'his chamber is where he himself is'; and in the event that the instrument of grant made no specific reference to the source of payment, the writ would have to be brought in the county where the contract was made.[77] In the case of great lords who moved from one part of their estates to another or spent time at the royal court or even out of the kingdom, this doctrine could subject retainers to considerable inconvenience or even damage a lord's capacity to gather a following. Indeed, the inconveniences for lords and men in the case of indentures of retinue more than annuities must have been especially apparent from 1294 onwards when the king's wars took them outside the kingdom for long periods.

In the absence of documentation we can only engage in educated guesswork about the impact of these influences. But in the case of the most powerful magnate of the early fourteenth century there are convincing indications that retainers' fees were still partly financed out of the household. The wardrobe account of Thomas of Lancaster for 1313–14,[78] includes a total of £623 15s 5d 'in divers fees paid to divers earls, barons, knights, squires this year'. This total must have been for peacetime service, since it refers to 'fees', not wages, and the earl had not taken part in the Bannockburn campaign of that summer. An account of 1318–19 shows that £561 13s 4d was spent during this year on fully paid retainers' fees.[79] If we take partial payments into account, the figure rises to £663 6s 8d.

The explanation of the origins of the indenture of retine that best fits the known facts is thus one which accepts the existence of written contracts of military service at least as early as the late twelfth century. It is probable that these existed among the mercenaries hired by the Crown, at least involving mercenary captains and the leaders of the bands they hired. We cannot exclude the possibility that English magnates employed written contracts to recruit the king's own subjects when the conditions of their own military duties to the Crown required the raising of contingents outside a feudal framework; and any tendency towards this must have been strengthened by the development of the 'quota' system of military service in the first half of the thirteenth century. At the same time, however, the small size of the contingents for which leading tenants-in-chief were now responsible was bound to mean that any use of written contracts from this standpoint was on a rather limited scale.

Against this background two influences interacted to produce the arrival of the indenture of retine in the form we encounter it at the end of the thirteenth century. On the one hand, there was the pressure of the ambitions of Edward I on the military resources of his kingdom, on a scale unparalleled since 1214. On the other hand, in this situation great lords were forced to reorganise their own resources for raising men. Because the household had always been the core of the great lord's following, the indenture of retine that were now made emerged out of an effort to maintain a balance between the lord's need to have a following at his side at all times and the demands of the king's wars that might at any time necessitate an expansion of the retine.

It was also the demand for military service in wars of aggression that led to the existence of indentures for limited periods as well as those for life. It is, of course, more than likely that lords exercised caution in making indentures for life since these would constitute a long-term drain on their peacetime revenues. It is, therefore, reasonable to suppose that during the period when the king's needs for his wars were being felt by the great lords of his kingdom, most of the indentures made were for limited periods of service. But, even when a lord decided to offer benefits for life because the retainer concerned was especially powerful or influential, he was careful to take into account the need for service in the king's wars. And, whatever the precise details of his negotiations with the individual, the indenture he then made brought him within an enlarged household following.

The development of the indenture of retinue thus moved outwards from within the lord's household. And the language employed to define the basic relationship between the retainer and his lord until the middle of the fifteenth century bears the marks of household origins. Through this whole period the word 'retained' was generally accompaied by *demore* (literally, 'stay with'), a word that had its roots in the notion of physical presence at the lord's side.[80] So basic were such ideas in contemporary conceptions of the relationship between lord and retainer that the same language was used in indentures that recruited for single campaigns or other limited periods,[81] even though the lord offered no household benefits in such contracts and the relationship was not intended to go into peacetime. In this sense the indenture of retinue of late medieval England was a remodelled survival of bonds that went back to the warbands of centuries before when a lord's *familia* and his warrior following were synonomous.[82]

(iii) Livery

The beginnings of livery lie shrouded in mystery. By its very nature it is the least likely of all the forms of relationship between lord and man to appear in the available records. There can, however, be no doubt that the practice of clothing members of the lord's household in robes provided by him went back before the beginning of the thirteenth century and that the silence of our sources means simply that an accepted and usual practice was not worthy of attention.

It is tempting to have recourse to *a priori* argument and to suggest that the desire of lords to clothe their followers in distinctive uniforms must have existed even earlier. It would have been an especially visible way of 'upholding the lord's honour' *(honur garder)* in the language of *The Rules of Robert Grossesteste*. And any tendency to such display must have been encouraged by the tournaments that had becme part of the life of royal court and landed society by the middle of the twelfth century. The feats

of arms narrated in the verse-life of William Marshal took place against
the background of more settled government in France and England under
the rule of Louis VII and Henry II; but tournaments occurred at least
through the first half of the twelfth century and the propensity of leaders
to distinguish their men from those of others must also have existed then.
In the case of English lords, it should be added, there were opportunities
for buying high quality cloth at the kingdom's fairs and an industry that
could provide cloths of varying colours was already flourishing.

There is, in fact, one piece of evidence that suggests that livery must
have been a well known practice by the middle of the twelfth century. A
royal confirmation of 1154–62 set out the terms of an agreement between
Robert de Valoignes and William de Bacton. One of these reveals a form
of livery outside as well as within the household: Robert

> will find necessities in sufficiency for the same William and one man of his and
> two of their horses in his household for the whole life of William and garments
> *(vestes)* of cat or rabbit for the same William. If the household of Robert dis-
> pleases William and he prefers to remain outside it, Robert will give him annually
> while remaining outside twenty shillings and one mantle of cat.[83]

An incident at the deathbed of William Marshal in 1219, described in
the verse biography written shortly afterwards, is narrated in terms that
treat livery as a customary practice at this time. The suggestion was made
to Marshal that the robes and furs stored in his household should be sold
to raise money for the redemption of his sins. He replied that it would
soon be the feast of Pentecost when his knights had a right to these robes;
and they were thus distributed in due course.[84] The story leaves no doubt
that the practice of giving knights robes at Christmas and Pentecost was
a fundamental part of Marshal's relationship with his household. As in the
case of Thomas of Lancaster a century later, the knights' robes were lined
with fur. Admittedly, there was no mention of any robes provided for the
lower ranks of the household; but this omission may simply reflect the
lower monetary value which made them a less obvious source of money
for the redemption of Marshal's sins. Although it made no reference to
distributions twice a year, the advice given to the countess of Lincoln in
1240–42 in *The Rules of Robert Grosseteste* provides confirmation of the
practice for both knights and squires: 'Order your knights and your gentlemen *(gentis homes)* who wear your livery *(vos robes)* that they ought to
put on that same livery every day, and especially at your table and in your
presence to uphold your honour, and not old surcoats, and soiled cloaks
and cut-off cloaks'.[85] *Gentis hommes* may, indeed, include yeomen as well

as squires. In this context it is also worth noting part of the terms of a final concord in which William Beauchamp in 1259 acquired a messuage and two carucates: as well as making a life-grant of the holding to the grantor he promised him for life two robes a year 'as for his other squires' (*sicut aliis armigeris suis*).

This evidence, however, does not stand alone in our sources for early thirteenth century England. In 1218 a leader of a gang of robbers in Yorkshire bought cloth worth a hundred marks to clothe his following of fifteen men, in the words of the record of the Yorkshire eyre, 'as if he had been a baron on an earl'.[87] Although we have no information about cloth prices in the area at the time, an average of almost £4 9s a man suggests that his intentions were on the scale of the disbursement of both winter and summer liveries, a fact that may explain the record's comment. This apart, the episode suggests that livery had now been extended outside the households of the magnates and that it was being used in a way little distinguishable from what we encounter in the late fourteenth and fifteenth centuries – for example, when a local squire employed it to recruit a following.[88] There is also good reason to believe that livery was a frequent method of recruitment on the part of rebels in the period of baronial reform and rebellion (1258–65), being used, for example, by the young Simon de Montfort in the months preceding the battle of Evesham.[89]

The very existence of livery within the great household created temptations for both the magnates of the realm and for the lesser landowners from whom they recruited their followers. The fact that retaining by indenture was an outgrowth of the household meant that retainers received livery on terms which were, as far as we can tell, indistinguishable from those applied to others of their estate and degree within the household. But there was inevitably embedded in this practice a tendency to give livery to men who were not retained or members of the household but were anxious to be brought into the shadow of a great lord's authority. For the lord to do this cost him no more than the cloth and its making up into robes and in return he could hope for loyalty and assistance in his affairs. For the beneficiary there was the hope of his lord's protection and the opportunity to impress his neighbours with his powerful connexions. Similarly, lesser landowners who could not afford to grant out fees or annuities on any scale, if at all, might be tempted to ape their political and social superiors and create connexions and alliances for themselves at the mere cost of robes. The extent to which such tendencies proliferated depended on political conditions both kingdom-wide and locally – above all, the power and personal authority of the ruler. Once, however, livery began to be used in these ways outside the household, it became apparent that there were less expensive means of attaining these ends than robes, even when these were given once, not twice, a year. Hence by the end of the fourteenth century caps and emblems were also part of the practice of livery.

There is no simple explanation, or even body of explanations, for the emergence of the relationships between lord and man which historians have labelled 'bastard feudalism'. Indentures of retinue and livery shared an origin in the household. But, beyond this simple fact, the processes of origin were different. While both moved outside the household, they did so in different ways and for different reasons. Indentures of retinue had appeared by the end of the thirteenth century as a result of complex forces, mainly the interaction of legal changes and the military needs of the Crown, the wars of Edward I beyond the frontiers of his kingdom acting as the catalyst that led to the appearance of indentures of retinue in the form that is generally encountered for the next century and a half. In the first stage of its move-ment outside the household livery maintained its original features, partly because it was one of the benefits bestowed on indentured retainers. But in due course robes were joined by emblems and caps, livery taking on the dimensions of power on the cheap.

At first sight the granting of annuities differed from the other two main forms of relationship because it was not anchored in the household. But a study of its origins demonstrates that the practice had once existed there. This, however, was not due to its role in household arrangements *per se* but to the need for a mechanism for making annual payments. Even so, some of those rewarded for their services in this way had served in the household; and, more important, annuities moved out of the household at roughly the same time as retaining.

What mattered in all these forms of relationship was the fundamental nature of the relationship between lord and man, its core consisting of values nurtured for centuries in the household, embodying the duty of loy-alty on the part of the man and that of reward on the lord's. In this analysis there is a real continuity between the *gesithcundman* of the beginnings of Anglo-Saxon history, the later thegn, and then the knight, granted land by the lord, and the late medieval retainer who held an annual fee for life. It is true that in the case of some Anglo-Saxon thegns and all post-Conquest feudal tenants eventually lands held as life-grants became hereditary, whereas the late medieval retainer held his money fee for life. But the development of inheritance occurred because kings and lords transferred life-grants to the heirs of the deceased. And in late medieval England an indentured retainer might be following in the footsteps of his father.[90] Nor is it wise to stress the difference between a holding of land and a money fee, since in late medieval England there were certainly retainers whose indentures conferred grants of land for life.[91] There are, indeed, important differences between the several phases in the develoment of lord's followings through the middle ages; but these can be explained in terms of the consequences of the development of royal government, the legal position of great landed inheritance and the nature of their administration.

Arguments along these lines are strongly supported by the presence of the 'bachelor' in late medieval England. There is, as we have seen, more than sufficient documentation to establish a link between this household knight and the indentured retainer. And there is a basic similarity between the 'bachelor' of the thirteenth century and, if we move backwards in time, the household knight of the Norman period and the Anglo-Saxon thegn who served in his lord's household. The registers of the Black Prince and John of Gaunt, for example, contain many orders sending 'bachelors' and other retainers on errands; and the description of the duties of an Anglo-Saxon thegn that have come down to us assume that he was often used in the same way.[92] The picture we gain from Bede's letter to bishop Egbert of a Northumbrian kingdom in which young warriors were denied the opportunity to settle down and marry because they had no hope of acquiring land has echoes in it of one element in the meaning of 'bachelor' – the unmarried knight.[93] There is thus every reason to believe that in one way or another the several forms of lordship we encounter in late medieval England mask relationships that go back into the darkest ages of English history.

These relationships were always subject to pressures that came neither from lords nor their men. By the end of the twelfth century these took the form of conditions created by the growth of royal government and, by the end of the following century of the organisation of the resources of the kingdom of England for the purpose of war outside its frontiers. There is every reason to believe that both the practice of granting annuities as a reward for and in expectation of service as well as the indenture of retinue appeared before the impact of foreign war occurred in the reign of Edward I. In the social and institutional framework of thirteenth century England there were good reasons why the relationships between lords and men should be defined in these ways. The evidence that exists for the period between the defeat of Bouvines in 1214 and the beginning of the wars of aggression waged by Edward I does not permit us to view the connexion between the contract system of military service and the indenture of retinue as one of cause and effect. Indeed, there are grounds for believing that the contract system revealed in the records of royal government in the late thirteenth century was an adaptation of the methods used in the employment of mercenaries by the Anglo-Norman and early Angevin rulers. There were also similarities between it and the recruitment of knights for tournaments in the late twelfth century.

Once, however, the Crown began to make contracts for raising men with its leading subjects and subcontracting was disseminated through the kingdom, this method of recruitment was bound to have some effect on the form of the written agreements that were already made between great lords and their followers. It is fair to suggest that it encouraged the use of the existing indenture form; and, since from the late thirteenth century onwards, the need to raise men for the king's wars was a contingency that had always to be borne in mind, it was inevitable that it be reflected in the drafting of indentures, leading to clauses that took into account both the advantages and the hazards of wartime service. But what occurred was essentially a process of adjustment, not the creation of a new relationship. If we are to summarise in simple terms the connexion between the contract system of military service, the practice of rewarding followers with annuities and the indenture of retinue, they are all best viewed as different species of a genus which was a lordship anchored in the household.

Notes

1 See especially Prestwich, *War;, Politics ad Finances,* pp. 41–66.
2 McFarlane, *Collected Essays,* pp. 24–6. There is a note of caution embedded in McFarlane's language. His discussion in his Ford Lectures twenty years later (*Nobility,* pp. 102 seq.) does not deal with the issue of origins.
3 Lyon, *Fief to Indenture,* p. 262.
4 *Ibid.,* p. 265. For an earlier statement of Lyon's views see his article, 'Some feudal antecedents of the indenture system', *Speculum,* xxix (1954), 503–11. A strong note of criticism was sounded by J. O. Prestwich in his review of the book in *History,* xliv (1959), 48–50.
5 I substitute 'contract' for 'indenture' in Lyon's 'indenture system', since the indentures of retinue discussed in the previous two chapters were distinctly different from contracts made for a campaign or similar short period.
6 Richardson and Sayles, *Governance,* p. 463.
7 For the most recent elaboration of this argument, see Saul, *Gloucestershire Gentry,* p. 83.
8 See especially the article by M. Postan, 'The rise of the money economy', *Econ. H. R.,* xiv (1944), reprinted in his *Essays on Medieval Agriculture and General*

Problems of the Medieval Economy (Cambridge, U.K., 1973).

9   Plucknett, *Legislation*, pp. 107–8.

10   Holmes, *Higher Nobility*, p. 83. See also Lewis, 'Decayed and non-feudalism', p. 160.

11   For an earlier version of these arguments see Bean, *Decline of Feudalism*, pp. 306–9.

12   See below, p. 130. See also Bean, *Decline of Feudalism*, pp. 308.

13   Waugh, 'Tenure to contract', pp. 828–32.

14   *Ibid., passim.*

15   *Ibid.*, p. 819.

16   See above, p. 58.

17   Waugh, 'Tenure to contract', p. 820

18   *Ibid.*, p. 820, nn. 1–2.

19   The long list of references assembled by Waugh in *ibid.*, p. 820, n. 1, in support of the statement in the text of the article is misleading, since it contains a number of contractual arrangements that did not involve any sort of service. Aside from those that involve wardships or temporary annual payments until a clerk was presented to a benefice, several concern grants of annual money payments in return for the conveyance of lands and tenements in fee (*Historia et Cartularium Monasterii Sancti Petri Gloucestriae*, ed. W.H. Hart [Rolls Series], i, pp. 187–8, 213–4 [nos. 73, 120]; *Beauchamp Cart.*, pp. 61–2, 126 [nos. 101, 217]). *Perc. Chart.*, p. 375 (no. 878) consists of a grant of an annual rent to be held of the grantor and does not mention any non-feudal service or any other consideration. PRO, E210/1034 (*CAD*, iii, 527) is an obligation that does not involve any annuity or service.

20   Brand, 'Oldcotes v. d'Arcy', pp. 64–104.

21   *Curia Regis Rolls*, viii, 393

22   PRO KB26/165/m. 3;   /E159/60/m. 1d;   /Just. 1/278/m. 26d. In 1278 William de Swinburne also made annual payments from his chamber (see above. p. 42). See also the plaintiff's claim in *Curia Regis Rolls*, viii, 67, discussed above, p. 127.

23   This subject is illuminated by R. Abels, *Lordship and Military Obligation in Medieval England* (Berkeley, Los Angeles, 1988).

24   J. O. Prestwich, 'The military household of the Norman kings', *EHR*, xcvi (1981), 1–35.

25   Prestwich, *War, Politics and Finance*, pp. 41–66.

26   *The Wardrobe Book of William de Norwell, 12 July 1338 to 27 May 1340*, ed. M. Lyon, B. Lyon and Henry S. Lucas, with the collaboration of J. de Sturler (Brussels, 1983).

27   For a useful summary see Waugh, 'Tenure to contract', pp. 828–32.

28   *Brevia Placitata*, ed. G. J. Turner (Selden Soc., vol. lxvi, London, 1931), pp. 31, 95, 106–7, 109–12.

29   *Ibid.*, pp. cxxxi–ii.

30   PRO, KB26/165m. 3; *ibid.*, E159/60/m/ 1d; *ibid.*, Just.1/278/m. 26d; *Curia Regis Rolls*, viii, 67.

31   *Bracton De Legibus et Consuetudinibus Angliae*, ed. G. E. Woodbine and translated with revisions and notes by S. E. Thorne (Cambridge, Mass., 4 vols., 1969–77), iii, p. 59.

32   *YBRS, 20, 21 Ed. 1*, p. 320

33   See above, p. 42. The Latin phrase is *pro servicio suo mihi impenso et impen-*

dendo.
34 See above, p. 14.
35 A substantial collection is to found in PRO, E101/68/3–9.
36 *Cf.* above, pp. 29–30.
37 See above, pp. 42–3.
38 Richardson and Sayles, *Governance*, pp. 464–5; S. Lloyd, 'The Lord Edward's crusade, 1270–2: its setting and significance', in *War and Government*, p. 126.
39 *Ibid.*
40 *Ibid.*
41 *CPR, 1266–72*, p. 515; PRO, C66/85/m. 14d.
42 *in vadiis trium serventium coopertorum retentorum* . . . (PRO, SC 6/1094/11/m. 5, printed in 'Ministers' Accounts for the Lordships of Abergavenny, Grosmont, Skenfrith and Whitecastle 1256–7' *South Wales and Monmouth Record Society*, vols. ii–iv (Cardiff, 1950–7). Sergeants, a janitor and a guard were also retained for the war (*retentorum pro guerra*)
43 *Walter of Henley*, pp. 401–2. I have altered the editor's translation. The meaning of the words *dedens ne dehors* is hardly adequately conveyed by 'in or out of doors'. The language of the original is, in fact, reminiscent of Gaunt's indentures with several squires (App. III(b), nos. 64–8).
44 PRO, E 40/391, calendared in *CAD*, i, (A. 391).
45 *Guillaume Le Maréchal*, ii, 380.
46 *Ibid.* i, 97 (ll. 2663–6). Cf. ii, 38:

Par l'envie le giemble rei
Pristrent li halt home conrei
Des bons chevaliers retenir
E essaucier e maintenir.

47 *Ibid.*, i, 172 (ll. 4750–76). Cf. iii. 62. The important passage is ll. 4759–73:

Quatre vinz, c'est ore del mains
Quer a prover vos prenc en mains
Qu'il en remaint sey tanz ariere,
Quer qui unques portout baniere
E ert ove le giemble rei,
A toz cles qu'il menout o se,
Avieent vinten sout lo jor,
Fust a esrer, fust a sejor,
Des que il moveient de lor terre.

Merveille ert ou l'om puet ce querre,
Ne mais que Dex li devisont
Les biens qu'il li abandonout.
Quinze i out banieres portant.
Por ce vos plevis en por tant
Que bien erent deux cenz & plus.

48 Richardson and Sayles, *Governance*, p. 463.
49 For the most recent study, see I. J. Sanders, *Feudal Military Service in England* (Oxford, 1956), pp. 50–90.

50   This happened in the case of the knights of St Albans Abbey in 1257 (Matthew Paris, *Chronica Majora*, vi, 375–6).

51   Lyon, *Fief to Indenture*, pp. 234–35. 'Fee' translates the *feodum* of these records. There is no warrant for Lyon's translation *fief-rente* which, in the light of his general thesis, has misleading connotations. Cf. the comments in the review by J. O. Prestwich in *History*, xliv (1959), 49.

52   *Diplomatic Documents preserved in the Public Record Office*, ed. P. Chaplais (Oxford, 1964), p. 4.

53   For a recent summary see M. T. Clanchy, *From Memory to Written Record: England, 1066–1307* (London, U.K., and Cambridge, Mass., 1979), esp. pp. 65–67.

54   See Plucknett, *Common Law*, p. 634.

55   Ricardson and Sayles, *Governance*, pp. 464–5; BL, Addit. Ch., 19829.

56   CPR, *1266–72*, p. 515; PRO, C66/85/m. 14d.

57   See above, p. 42.

58   See above, pp. 43. seq.

59   *The Red Book of Ormond*, ed. N. B. White (Dublin, 1932), p. 103.

60   See above, p. 43.

61   Printed in G. Barraclough, 'The earldom and County Palatine of Chester', *Transactions of the Historic Society of Lancashire and Cheshire,* ciii (1951), 54.

62   See the list in Jones, 'Mohaut–Bracebridge indenture', pp. 391–2, 393–4. This must be corrected, however, to transfer the Bluet–Martel indenture to the life category and by the additions of the Grey–Tothill indenture brought to light and discussed above, pp. 43. seq.

63   Jones, 'Mohaut–Bracebridge indenture', pp. 393–4, excluding the Valence–Berkeley indenture (no. 4) which as been treated above as quasi-life.

64   See above, pp. 44, 48.

65   *Red Book of Ormond*, p. 103.

66   Barraclough, *art.cit.*, p. 54.

67   See above, pp. 47–8.

68   CPR, *1292–1301*, pp. 84–6, 169. In one case in August 1294 a tenant-in-chief demised lands worth ten marks each to a father and son who were going in his place to Gascony. In another case in August 1294 a grant was made in fee simple to a follower who was going on the king's service to Gascony with the tenant-in-chief (*ibid.*, p. 84).

69   In May 1297 another licence, involving land worth £20 a year, permitted a grant for the life of the follower and for the six years following his death, the licence being given on condition that the tenant-in-chief and the man go with the king overseas or elsewhere and stay there at the king's command (*ibid.*, p. 249).

70   See Bean, *Decline of Feudalism*, pp. 70–9.

71   Lloyd, 'Lord Edward's crusade', in *War and Government*, p. 128.

72   PRO, DL 28/1/14. A transcript made before the original deteriorated is in Manchester Reference Library, MS. LI/48/2/3.

73   Maddicott, *Thomas of Lancaster*, pp. 46–7.

74   On this see Plucknett, *Legislation*, pp. 112–5.

75   Bean, *Decline of Feudalism*, pp. 86–89; D. W. Sutherland, *The Assize of Novel Disseisin* (Oxford, 1973), pp. 91–5

76   *Walter of Henley*, pp. 401–2.

77   YBRS, 20, 21 Ed. I, p. 320

78   Baldwin, 'Household administration', p. 199.

79   Maddicott, *Thomas of Lancaster*, pp. 46–7.

80   This is clearest in the Irish indentures. John Neville *moram traxit familiarem* with Theobald Walter (*Red Book of Ormond*, p. 103). See also the use of *mora* in *Ormond Deeds*, ii, (no. 33), 23 (no. 36), 23–24 (no. 37), 26 (no. 39), 143–44 (no. 205) and 150 (no. 219).

81   *E.g.*, *morabitur* in the contract for the campaign of 1287 between Peter Maulay and Edmund Mortimer (N.B. Lewis, 'An early indenture of military service, 27 July 1287', *BIHR*, xiii (1935 – 36), 89).

82   Even in the late twelfth century the word *familia* could be used in a military context. See, for example, the ways in which it was employed by Gerald of Wales in his narrative of the conquest of Ireland. It was used on a number of occasions to mean a military force (Gerald of Wales, *Opera*, ed. J. S. Brewer, J. F. Dimmock and G. F. Warner (Rolls Ser., 8 vols.; London, 1861-91), v. 286, 308, 329, 334, 348). It could also denote a garrison (*ibid.*, v. 329, 333, 339, 340).

83   B. Dodwell, 'Some charters relating to the Honour of Bacton', *A Medieval Miscellany for Doris Mary Stenton* (Publications of the Pipe Roll Society, lxxvi [New Series, xxxvi], London, 1962), p. 160.

84   *Guillaume le Maréchal*, ii, 311–12 (ll. 18675–730). Cf. *ibid.*, iii, 262–3.

85   *Walter of Henley*, p. 403.

86   *Beauchamp Charters*, p. 62 (no. 101). It is interesting to compare this language with that of two charters contained in *Hatton's Book of Seals*, pp. 363–6. They are assigned by the editors to 1153–84 and c. 1200 respectively; but both are spurious. The latter contains no reference to robes; but the former contains language remarkably similar to the Beauchamp arrangement, William, earl of Warwick granting the office of master cook in his household together with land 'with all appurtenances that pertain to the master cook, that is, in robes and in horses as my squires have in my household, in the same way as Richard his father had in the household of my father and in mine'. The charter of c. 1200 grants the same office to the son of the earlier grantee; but it contains no reference to robes. In view of this latter omission and the spurious character of both charters, it would be unwise to suggest that the term 'robe' was employed in the mid-twelfth century to describe the garment that a lord gave his knight or squire. But the origins of robes as a standard form of livery are worth further investigation. The Latin word was a borrowing from the vernacular. According to *The Oxford English Dictionary* the stem was that of the verb 'rob', the original meaning being 'spoils, booty'. It is tempting to suggest that the granting of robes was a survival of the ancient practice under which the warrior-leader distributed a share of plunder to his followers.

87   *Rolls of the Justices in Eyre for Yorkshire in 3 Henry III (1218–19)*, ed. D. M. Stenton (Selden Soc., vol. lvi, London, 1937), p. 424.

88   See especially below, pp. 177–8, 209.

89   *Cal. Inq. Misc.*, i, 216, 261 (nos. 705, 853). The large number of references in the same period to rebels who were members of lords' households suggests that livery must have been an endemic feature of the rebellion (*ibid.*, i, 191–2, 195, 198, 215, 228, 240, 259–60, 266, 281, 283, 311 (nos. 627, 632, 644, 650, 695, 746, 789, 850–1, 871, 932, 936, 1024).

90   For examples of fathers and sons who were simultaneously retained by John

of Gaunt see *JGRB*, i, 7–8 (Hungerford, d'Ipre and Roucliffe) and below, App. III(a), nos. 2, 45.

91 See, e.g., above, pp. 47, 57, 64, 86, 94–5.

92 This is best illustrated by a compilation on status belonging to 1002–3:

> And the thegn who prospered, that he served the king and rode in his household band on his missions, if he himself had a thegn who served him, possessing five hides on which he discharged the king's dues, and who attended his lord in the king's hall, and had thrice gone on his errand to the king.

(translation in *English Historical Documents, c. 500–1042*, ed. D. Whitelock (London, 1955), 432.

93 Bede, *Opera*, ed. C. Plummer (2 vols.; Oxford, 1896), i, 415.

V

The role of retaining

By the close of the thirteenth century the tentacles of lordly influence extended well beyond the limits of the household through the employment of formal relationships that also lay outside the structure of feudal tenure. In one sense the thirteenth century witnessed the institutionalisation of such relationships: whatever tendencies towards the formalisation of indentures of retinue and of annuities for past and future services can be discerned before the end of the twelfth century, by 1300 contemporaries must have been well aware of these forms of relationship between lord and man. But the existence of these in itself did not mean that they were extensively employed. Moreover, the real differences between the several forms of relationship available to lord and man imposed choices on them. For these reasons it is necessary to investigate the actual extent to which retaining in these ways was employed in late medieval England. Any such investigation must employ a wide interpretation of the word 'retaining'. Annuities for life were the most advantageous of the financial benefits of lordship from the standpoint of the follower; and, quite as much as the retainer's fee, an annuity imposed the obligation of loyalty on the recipient. For these reasons any discussion of the scale of retaining must include annuitants as well as indentured retainers.

(i) Indentures of retinue and aunnuities: the problem of scale

For an assessment of the extent to which indentures of retinue and grants of annuities were employed we have to rely on the surviving records of the landed classes. These necessarily reflect the actions of the lord, and not those of the recipient, since very few records of the gentry who composed the bulk of the recipients have survived and, even when they do, they consist largely of manorial accounts which were in no way concerned with any revenues from fees and annuities.[1] In the case of lords most of the material relates to leading magnates and in general consists of the accounts of local receivers or of receivers-general together with some valors – that is summaries of the revenues of a group of estates and of direct expenditure from these by manorial officials and receivers in a stated financial year. In using these records it is essential to bear in mind their deficiences as sources of information. Those that happen to survive are only a small portion of those that existed. Even the valors are not free of the risk of a deficiency imposed by the nature of the accounting system of which they formed a part.[2] An accounting official whether a manorial bailiff or reeve or a receiver,[3] rendered an account of monies that he had actually received or spent. In consequence, the details of expenditure do not necessarily include payments that were due but not actually made. This is certainly unlikely in the case of a valor drawn up by especially thorough auditors; but not all were of the same standard. More important, however, is the possibility that an account of a particular receiver or receiver-general does not provide full details of all the payments for which he was responsible. There is thus always the possibility that the financial records on which for the most part we have to rely do not provide all the requisite information about the fees and annuities they mention. Indeed, they sometimes fail to distinguish between the fees paid to indentured retainers and the annuities granted for past and future services.[4]

Once again, it is the history of the house of Lancaster that provides the most sensible approach to the chronological division of problems of the scale of retaining, since the seizure of the throne by the greatest lord of the fourteenth century, the duke of Lancaster, in 1399 makes it possible to divide our discussion into the fourteenth and fifteenth centuries respectively.

The fourteenth century

Our knowledge of the dimensions of retaining in the fourteenth century is dominated by the records of the house of Lancaster, since it is two heads of that house – Thomas, earl of Lancaster (d. 1322) and John of Gaunt (d. 1399) – that provide the bulk of our evidence for the century.

The retinue of earl Thomas has received considerable attention. In 1927 Professor J. F. Baldwin used his wardrobe account of 1313–14 to argue that he had a retinue of some 210 knights and 112 squires.[5] He based this calculation on the quantity of cloth bought for the liveries of these two groups, assuming that eight yards would be required for a knight's livery and six for a squire's. In 1970 Dr J. R. Maddicott criticised this calculation on two main grounds – first, that the assumptions about the quantity of cloth required were purely arbitrary and, second, that no account was taken of the need for both summer and winter liveries. In the light of these criticisms and of information surviving in other sources, Maddicott argued that Lancaster's retinue consisted of no more than fifty to fifty-five knights.[6] There are, however, serious flaws in these criticisms of Baldwin. First, there is information to suggest that Baldwin's assumptions about the amount of cloth required for the liveries of a knight and a squire were not excessive.[7] Second, a reading of the wardrobe account of 1313–14 shows that it does contain quite separate totals for cloth purchased for the summer liveries of the various ranks of the retinue, in addition to those totals used by Baldwin.[8]

In fact, the size of Lancaster's retinue is a much more complicated problem than either Baldwin or Maddicott suggested.[9] Recent comments on the household of Lancaster's father-in-law, Henry Lacy, earl of Lincoln, in 1304–5 provide another approach through their use of information about the value of the cloth which the king purchased for a single knight's livery at this time[10] – four marks (£2 13s 4d). The assumption that the munificence of a leading earl would not fall greatly short of that of one who was of royal blood and was more wealthy than he, must be a reasonable one. On this basis the winter figure of £460 1s 3d for Lancaster himself, the bishop of Agen, his knights, clerks, squires, officers, grooms, archers, minstrels and carpenters,[11] was for a total of 172 persons. A similar calculation for the total expenditure on summer liveries for barons, knights, clerks, squires and officers produces a total of 129 persons. The margin between the figures of 172 and 129 can be explained in terms partly of the lighter weight and (possibly) smaller quantity of the cloth for the warm season, partly in terms of a smaller list of ranks for which purchases were made. More important, there is reason to believe that the retinue may have expanded between Christmas 1313, the season of the granting of winter liveries, and Pentecost 1314, the beginning of the summer season: whereas the number of cloths purchased for squires for winter liveries was twenty-eight, for the summer it has risen to thirty-six. For this reason the Christmas and Pentecost totals should be considered separately. The winter calculation of 172 must be adjusted substantially upwards, since only the single liveries of the earl himself and the bishop of Agen could have exceeded those of single knights in the amount and quality of cloth used and lower ranks must have received less in terms of both quantity and quality.[12] It is reasonable to assume that the knights and clerks received roughly similar treatment and that of the squires was equal to that of the officials but superior to that of the other ranks. In the light of thee considerations it is difficult not to feel that, while Baldwin's figures were excessive, the total number of knights must have been higher than Maddicott's fifty to fifty-five. If we assume that each knight's winter livery cost four marks, the amount spent on fifty-five would have been £146 13s 4d, just below thirty-two per cent of the total spent on all liveries. To suggest a figure for knights alone would be sheer guesswork, but it is difficult to avoid the conclusion that in Christmas 1313 the number of knights and squires combined in Lancaster's retinue would have been in excess of 120. And, because of a definite increase in the number of squires, the total must have been larger by the summer of 1314, perhaps exceeding 150.

These arguments must be placed in the full perspective of our knowledge of a great lord's retinue at this time. It is unwise to assume that the earl's wardrobe bought only that amount of cloth required for the liveries of those in the retinue at the time of purchase. Quite apart from the possibility of some waste, there was the likelihood that others would be recruited in the months immediately following the purchases. Furthermore, not all the liveries issued by the earl were intended for retainers directly recruited by himself. In the case of another earl or baron or even a knight of exceptional importance, he might have agreed to provide liveries for some of the retainer's own retinue: for example, in the case of the knights of William, lord Latimer, the earl undertook to provide his own liveries for them in time of parliament.[13] At any rate, the conclusion that earl Thomas's retinue of knights and squires must have exceeded a total of one hundred and fifty by the summer of 1314 provides an estimate that is easier to reconcile with two other sources than any lower one. First, there was contemporary comment on the size of Lancaster's retinue which viewed it as alarmingly large.[14] Second, there is the evidence of the daily accounts of the earl's household for 1318–19 in which by the summer and autumn of 1319, the period of the York parliament and then of the expedition to lay siege to Berwick-on-Tweed, the number of horses in the earl's household was often over one thousand and sometimes exceeded twelve hundred.[15]

Thomas of Lancaster's disbursements on his following were not confined to retaining fees or the provision of liveries. Firm indications exist that he made lavish grants of annuities and lands for life. Our information comes from two lists of his muniments made by royal clerks after his defeat and execution in 1322.[16] Both include fees and grants of land made in indentures of retinue for peace and war. If these are excluded, and allowances made for the slight duplication between the two lists, it is clear that he had made grants of annuities and lands for life to a total of £241 10s 8d.[17] In addition, grants of land had been made to a total of £450 or so. It is impossible to be certain that all of these grants were by way of reward for services, past or future. But, when rents paid by the grantees are mentioned, their low level indicates a deliberately beneficial element. And in a number of cases the grantees were the earl's household servants.

It is tempting to attempt some sort of calculation of the proportion of his revenues that Thomas of Lancaster devoted to the maintenance of a following.[18] But the sparsity of evidence relating to the size of his retinue, especially between 1314 and 1322, precludes such an effort. We cannot be sure that the lists of his grants of lands and annuities we do possess provide a full picture; nor do we enjoy complete certainty about the size of his retinue, let alone a full list of all his retainers. Moreover, the political situation between the summer of 1314 and his defeat in 1322 makes it all too likely that his retinue expanded during these years. Even so, a very rough impression of scale is feasible. The two lists of his grants we do possess, one earlier than the other, contain the names of twenty-nine retainers who received peacetime fees totalling £849.[19] In addition, four others held life-grants of land. This total of thirty-three must be reviewed in the light of the knowledge we have of the size of the total retinue of knights and squires in 1313–14 and the liklihood of its expansion in later years.[20] It is thus difficult to avoid the conclusion that Lancaster's expenditure of the indenturing of his retinue of knights and squires in time of peace and on annuities by 1322 must have been well in excess of £2,000 a year and, in the light of what we know about his landed revenues, may well have consumed more than a fifth of his gross income.[21]

The active political career of John of Gaunt spanned almost twice the time of that of earl Thomas, a predecessor in the Lancastrian inheritance. For this reason alone the size of his retinue presents a more complicated problem. But, that apart, the only list of his retainers that has survived from roughly the middle of his tenure of the inheritance requires detailed examination in the light of the extant financial records of his administration, which are much more substantial and complete than those of earl Thomas's. Because of the complexity of this problem its discussion is handled in Appendix II. The results of this investigation indicate that, at least by the time of his death in February 1399, John of Gaunt possessed a retinue of indentured knights and squires which may have been half as large again as that of Thomas of Lancaster at its maximum. Moreover, it appears to have consumed at least one-quarter of his net disposable revenues after all the local administrative expenses had been met.[22] Circumstantial though the evidence may be, it suggests that this retinue had been growing during Gaunt's years as duke, the point of 'take-off' occurring during the preparations for the expeditions of 1372 and 1373 to France. In Gaunt's case a much higher proportion of his revenues was spent on annuities for past and future services in comparison with that of Thomas of Lancaster. Precise totals are impossible. But from 1372 to 1375 he made eighty such grants totalling £363 1s 3d, virtually all of which were for life.[23] Like earl Thomas, Gaunt made many of such grants to members of his household; and most of them were small sums. It is, however, quite clear that he was in the habit of granting annuities for past and future services of considerable value to important individuals. Of the total granted in the years 1372–74, seven, totalling £160, were each above twenty marks a year.[24] Nor was the practice of granting such large annuities a recent one. The Register of 1372–76 contains references to five annuities granted in earlier years which totalled £220.[25] In the years 1372–5 the total of sixty-one new annuities granted amounted to £361 1s 3d, an average of just below £6; but in the years 1380–2 the twelve new ones amounted to £344 16s 8d, an average of almost £28 15s. The valors of the 1390s certainly give the impression, in comparison with those of the late 1380s, that the amount spent on fees and annuities continued to increase. By the end of the financial year 1393-94 these items consumed over £3,000 a year out of gross revenues of £12,000–13,000. It is unfortunate that we cannot chart grants of annuities in the years that followed; but what information we have about the making of new indentures of retinue suggests that the total involved in this item of expenditure continued to increase. By Gaunt's death in February 1399 his need to retain a following by means of indentures of retinue and grants of annuities had imposed financial obligations that must have consumed over a quarter, and, perhaps, almost a third of his disposable revenues from his lands in England and Wales.

A priori Thomas of Lancaster and John of Gaunt would seem to be exceptional among the magnates of fourteenth-century England in both the size of their retinues and the scale of their expenditure on them, since no one else could rival them in terms of wealth,[26] and, because of their royal blood, both were more deeply involved than others in the disturbed politics of their times. However, evidence does exist to permit some sort of assessment of the size of the retinues maintained by other magnates in this period. In one case only – Edward Courtenay, earl of Devon – do we have anything similar to the retinue-list surviving for Gaunt. There exists

a roll that lists those who received robes of livery from the earl in 1384–
85.[27] It thus provides the names of all the members of the earl's household
in the respective categories of rank. If we remove the earl himself, there is
a total of eight knights and forty-three squires. While this total contains
the earl's indentured retainers, it is far from certain that all the knights
and squires concerned fell into this category. Included, for example, are
three members of the Courtenay family – Sir Peter and, among the squires,
Richard and Hugh. It is more than likely that the list contains some who
were simply household officers. If these considerations are taken into
account, the retinue of the earl of Devon would appear to be very much
smaller than Gaunt's, especially in its number of knights. This impression
is confirmed by the six receivers' accounts that have survived for the period
of earl Thomas's tenure of his earldom.[28] None of these contains any references to indentures of retinue. The few annuities (called 'pensions') that
are mentioned are not handled separately from other disbursements, a fact
which certainly suggests that they were not an important burden on the
revenues handled by the receivers. Nor is it possible when 'pensions' were
paid to be certain that they were not the salaries of administrative officials.[29]
Only in the case of two accounts can the totals of payment that were probably annuities in the strict sense be compiled with any confidence. In 1381–
82 two 'pensions' totalled £4, the same amount including three in 1405–6.[30]

A Courtenay earl of Devon does not provide the best contemporary standard by which to judge the size of non-Lancastrian retinues or the scale
of expenditure on them, since he was one of the least wealthy of the earls.
Some information can be gleaned about the practices of more important
magnates. In the case of Thomas of Lancaster's contemporaries this is
hardly possible. Recent studies have discussed the retinues of Lancaster's
father-in-law, Henry Lacy, earl of Lincoln (d. 1311), and of Aymer de Valence, earl of Pembroke. In Lincoln's case it has been shown that the cloth
he ordered for his liveries in 1305 was probably intended for two bannerets,
twenty-five knights and forty-five to sixty men-at-arms, or squires.[31] In
Pembroke's case, the evidence indicates forty to fifty knights and men-at-
arms between 1297 and 1299, rising to sixty by 1307, and reaching a peak
figure of 124 in 1315.[32] But a simple comparison of these figures with those
for Thomas of Lancaster is not possible. There is nothing to indicate that
all these knights and squires were retained for life, or even retained directly
by Lincoln or Pembroke. In the manorial and receivers' accounts of the
earl of Lincoln that survive for 1295–96 and 1304–5 there are only two
possible references to indentures of retinue for life and these are not certain.[33] In the case of the earl of Pembroke the information that forms the

basis of the estimates of the size of his retinue comes from campaigns and only four of his indentures (two with the same person) exist.[34] In the case of Bartholomew, lord Badlesmere (d. 1322) we have a list of his muniments which names four persons with whom he had made indentures of retinue;[35] and it may certainly be argued that, if more had existed, at least some of them would have found their way into what appears to be a comprehensive catalogue of this lord's muniments. Care must be used, however, in arguing in these terms about the retinue of the earls of Lincoln and Pembroke or lord Badlesmere, since their period was one in which much retaining remained within the household. Even so, in the case of earl Thomas of Lancaster a substantial proportion of the cost of the retinue in time of peace had been transferred to the revenues of manorial officials and receivers;[36] and, in the case of the earl of Lincoln for whom such evidence has survived, the virtual absence of any mention of retaining is a powerful argument. Certainly the king as well as other contemporaries regarded Thomas of Lancaster as the lord of a retinue of quite exceptional proportions.

In the case of leading magnates who were contemporary with John of Gaunt we are on slightly firmer ground. Some evidence survives for those who were the leading 'appellants' in the crisis of 1387–88 – Thomas, duke of Gloucester, Richard FitzAlan, earl of Arundel and Thomas Beauchamp, earl of Warwick. In the case of all three information exists in the records of the Crown – confirmations of their grants issued after the seizure of their lands in 1397 and the surveys then made. Care must be exercised in using such sources, since it may be argued that only retainers with special influence at the royal court could secure confirmations of their fees or annuities after their lords' forfeitures. But it can also be argued that it was in the king's interests to detach from the families of these earls the loyalties of any of their retainers. Furthermore, the surveys of the forfeited estates were intended to provide a complete record of outgoings from their revenues. It is, therefore, interesting to note that in the case of these magnates remarkably few indentures or annuities for life came to light in 1397. In the case of the duke of Gloucester,[37] and the earl of Arundel,[38] single indentures surfaced, each with a squire; and in the case of the earl of Warwick no such document was confirmed by the king after his forfeitures.[39]

It is possible to check the information gleaned from these sources against other evidence. In the case of Thomas, duke of Gloucester, we have the accounts of his war-treasurer for the expedition he took as the king's lieutenant to Ireland in April–September 1392.[40] His retinue consisted of fourteen knights and thirty-nine squires with their respective contingents of archers and men-at-arms. The details of pay and benefits are extremely full; and it is clear from these that, of the whole contingent of knights and squires, only one – Sir Walter Clopton – was retained by the duke for life. It is reasonable to assume that for an expedition which demonstrated his importance in the realm the duke would have made a special effort to bring those he had retained for life. In the case of the earl of Arundel some receivers' accounts have survived for his Welsh estates.[41] None of these contains any mention of indentured retainers or their fees. And in only one case is there payment of annuities – the Clun receivership in 1386–7 where £15 was paid to Sir Hamo Peshale and £5 to a friar. The total is remarkably small in comparison with that of £760 for which the receiver accounted. And the absence of retaining fees or annuities from the account of the receiver of the lordship of Holt in 1387–8 is especially remarkable in view of his payments for the garrisoning of its castle during the period when Aubrey de Vere, duke of Ireland, was present in the Marches on the eve of his defeat by the 'appellants' at Radcot Bridge. No receivers' accounts have survived for the earl of Warwick who forfeited in 1397; but there is one of a receiver-general of his son in 1402–3.[42] It is especially useful since earl Richard's livery of his inheritance on coming of age fell within the year of the account; and for this reason, and in view of the favour extended to the family by Henry IV which might have led to the continuation of life-payments during the minority, it might be expected to contain references to any life-indentures made by the late earl. But no retaining fees were paid to knights: there were three fees, totalling £15, paid to squires, only one of which can definitely be described as being in return for his retainder.

In the England of Richard II the nearest rival to John of Gaunt in wealth and, because of his descent from an elder son of Edward III and his presumptive claim to the throne, in political influence, was the Mortimer earl of March. An assessment of his retinue's size is especially difficult because during most of the reign of Richard II the earl was a minor. Earl Edmund died at the age of twenty-nine in 1381 and had enjoyed a limited time to build up his retinue since coming of age in 1373. He did engage in some retaining for life. The royal patent rolls after his death contain a total of three confirmations of his indentures of retinue.[43] It would be wrong to assume that this total includes all such contracts, since some years after his son's death Henry IV confirmed an indenture he had made with Sir Hugh Cheyne in 1376.[44] But, if the earl's retaining had reached substantial proportions, it is reasonable to assume that it would have been reflected in the scale of royal confirmations. His son earl Roger had even less opportunity to build up a retinue, since he died in 1398 only four and a half years after receiving livery of his inheritance. In his case, however, a survey of his revenues in England and Wales,[45] made by the Crown after his death, enables us to form a reasonably firm estimate of the extent of his expenditure on a permanent following.[46] If we exclude payments which were obviously made as a result of family settlements,[47] and add the total of £40 paid to Sir Hugh Cheyne which is omitted, we have a total of £226 for fees and annuities. Even though this list is not complete, it is still remarkable that it comprises only six per cent of the total net revenues concerned.[48]

Information on other magnates of Richard II's reign is even more sparse. The most substantial body of material relates to Thomas Mowbray, earl marshal and of Nottingham, from 1397 duke of Norfolk, for whom we have a total of seven indentures, ranging over the years 1389–97.[49] This is fairly impressive in comparison with what we know about other magnates apart from John of Gaunt. The peacetime fees for five knights totalled £80 a year, and those of two squires £26 13s 4d.[50] In addition, after his death twenty-nine life-annuities, totalling £283, were confirmed by Henry IV.[51] It is difficult to assess the proportion that these totals formed of all the retaining payments made by Mowbray. It is unwise to place much emphasis on Henry IV's anxiety to recruit support after his accession, since Mowbray was never forgiven for the quarrel of 1398. Even so, there was a substantial number of confirmations after Mowbray's death and there was even one after the rebellion of the young earl marshal in 1405. It is certain that, if we judge by the evidence of the confirmations surviving in the royal patent rolls, Mowbray retained by indenture and granted annuities on a greater scale than his erstwhile allies, the duke of Gloucester and the earls of Arundel and Warwick; but the scale of his peacetime expenditure revealed by royal confirmations is by no means remarkable, especially in comparison with that of John of Gaunt. Firm conclusions are difficult to reach in the case of another contemporary – Thomas, lord Despenser (created earl of Gloucester by Richard II in 1397). Confirmations by Henry IV after his execution and forfeiture for treason in 1400 reveal a total of four indentures, including one made by his father.[52] The knight retained by the father (as far back as 1372) had an annual fee in peacetime of £20; in the case of the three squires recruited by the son the total of the peacetime fees was £30. The circumstances of Despenser's treason and forfeiture may suggest that only those with access to special favour at the royal court received confirmations of their retainers' fees from the Crown. For this reason the actual total of Despenser's indentures may have been much larger than is disclosed by the patent rolls of Henry IV and there may also have been annuities that were not confirmed. Similar considerations apply in the case of the two indentures of Despenser's fellow-traitor, John, earl of Huntingdon, which Henry IV confirmed.[53] These had been made in the very week in which Richard II had lost his throne and were clearly part of contingency planning for a rebellion that actually took place a few months later.

The fifteenth century

Because of the nature of the available evidence, an effort to estimate the scale of retaining in England after 1399 presents problems different from those encountered in the preceding century. Especially in the last three decades of the fourteenth century there survives a comparatively enormous group of indentures; and, even if we exclude the extraordinarily large collection left by John of Gaunt, slightly more survive for the twenty-two years of the reign of Richard II than for the sixty years or so between 1399 and 1461. However, in the fourteenth century, with the exception of those of John of Gaunt, it is not easy to find receivers' accounts or similar financial documents to compare with the indentures. But in the fifteenth century rather more material exists in the form of accounts and valors. At the same time the royal patent rolls no longer yield confirmations on a scale anywhere approaching that of the previous century. For this reason we cannot in the case of any fifteenth-century magnate make any attempt to assess the extent of retaining on the basis of confirmations made by the Crown after death or forfeiture.

This point is remarkably well illustrated in the case of the Percy earls of Northumberland. For the earl who died at the first battle of St Albans in 1455 we possess some receivers' accounts – a single one for the Northumberland estates in 1442–43, two for those in Cumberland in 1441–42 and 1453–54, four for the estates in Sussex in the years between 1426–27 and 1452–53, together with a valor for the estates in Yorkshire in 1442–43. What we have is enough to show that by the time the third earl died in 1455 fees and annuities that were not connected with the administration of the estates were consuming at least a third of gross revenues. The evidence of the receivers' accounts for Sussex, the two for Cumberland and scraps of information relating to the Northumberland estates after the year of the sole surviving receiver's account for that county, all indicate that this situation was the result of growth over a period of two and a half decades. The total amount of fees and annuities charged on the Cumberland receivers' revenues doubled between 1441–42 and 1453–54.[55] In Northumberland in 1442–43 these charges consumed fifteen per cent of the revenues for which the receiver was accounting.[56] In the Yorkshire valor of 1442–43 the equivalent figure was roughly one-quarter.[57] And on the Sussex estates there was a threefold increase between 1426–27 and 1452–53.[58]

These details need to be put in their proper perspective. It is necessary to take into account the fact that the earl of Northumberland was Warden of the East March in the years 1417–35, his son and heir (earl from 1455) holding the same position from 1440 until his death in 1461.[59] In both these periods it is more than likely that the revenues of the Wardenship received from the Crown bore the burden of other retaining fees, although it is quite possible these were not for life. This may well explain why the amount expended in Northumberland in 1442–3 was both lower, and took a smaller portion of local revenues, than those in Yorkshire. On the other hand, the Percy earls' profits from the Wardenship would have compensated for the expenditure on fees and annuities from landed revenues.[60] It is impossible to decide what proportion of fees and annuities was devoted to indentured retainers. The Northumberland account does make two specific references to indentures of retinue; but it is all too likely that other 'fees' and 'annuities' that had no further description also comprised such payments.[61]

Some information exists on the extent to which the Percy earl who died in 1489 directed his landed revenues to the maintenance of a retinue. He had been restored in stages to the inheritance forfeited by his father in the years 1469–71.[62] It is quite clear that he sought rapidly to recruit a following. By his death in 1489 fees and annuities for life consumed one-quarter of his gross revenues from land.[63] It can, of course, be argued that this situation, like that exhibited by the financial records of his grandfather, can be explained in terms of the special position occupied by the Percy earl in the north of England, where territorial wealth in Cumberland and Northumberland made him the most powerful magnate in the Border region. But, as it stands, this explanation involves oversimplification. Fees and annuities consumed a very high proportion of the earls' revenues in Sussex.[64] The truth is that the Percies' ambitions in the north of England made them important figures in national politics: even in Sussex, where their estates *per se* put them in the upper gentry group of wealth, they had to act as leading earls.

Much more information exists for Humphrey Stafford, earl (and from 1444 duke) of Buckingham (d. 1461). In his case we have two valors of all his lands in England and Wales for 1441–42 and 1447–48, together with a number of receivers' accounts. In addition, there are some details in other sources (mainly in the form of copies or summaries of indentures) about one peer, eleven knights and squires who were retainers of this magnate. All this material has recently been the subject of investigation.[65] It is quite clear that the duke never retained or granted annuities on the scale of the Percy earls of Northumberland. The valor of 1441–42 listed fees and annuities totalling £465 14s that were actually paid:[66] if those not paid are added, the total rises to £505 13s 4d.[67] Of the recipients nine were named as knights and twenty-six as squires. For the valor of 1447–48 the total charged is roughly the same – £485 9s 1d. Neither of these lists can be complete, since, for example, eleven additional fees granted between 1442 and 1447 are known from elsewhere.[69] From other sources we know that Buckingham had retained a further total of at least six knights and eighteen squires by 1447:[70] the totals of their fees amounted to £100 and £133 6s 8d respectively.[71] It is thus reasonable to infer that the total of annuities paid out in 1441–42 and 1447–48 was rather more than that of fees to indentured retainers.[72] What is especially interesting about the case of the duke of Buckingham is the contrast it presents with that of the Percies in the extent of retaining in the 1440s and 1450s. In Buckingham's case the total spent on fees and annuities stayed fairly stable between 1441–42 and 1447–48. After the latter date the situation is less clear. But from sources other than receivers' accounts we know that a total of twenty-six fees and annuities were granted by the duke between 1448 and 1460, totalling £139 a year. At least some of these must have taken the place of fees and annuities vacated by death or other causes. In fact, the surviving receivers' accounts do not show any growth in these items after 1447–48. Indeed, in the case of the receivers' accounts for the duke's manors in Warwickshire and Staffordshire there occurred a pronounced reduction in the total paid out by the late 1450s.[73] At any rate, there can be no doubt that, when the Percy earls of Northumberland substantially increased their expenditure in fees and annuities, the duke of Buckingham made no appreciable efforts in this direction.

In mid-fifteenth-century England two magnates possessed territorial wealth and political importance on a scale that surpassed those of the Percy earls of Northumberland and the duke of Buckingham. One was Richard, duke of York (d. 1460) who laid claim to the throne two months before his death and whose son assumed it as Edward IV. The other was Richard Neville, earl of Warwick. His acquisition of the inheritance of the Beauchamp earls of Warwick through marriage to their heiress put him in the ranks of the leading magnates while his father Richard, earl of Salisbury (d. 1460) was still alive. His father's death brought him his Neville inheritance; and this was followed by grants of forfeited Lancastrian estates, including substantial portions of the Percies' so that by the end of 1464 he was the most powerful magnate in the Yorkist kingdom with territorial wealth, which, though well below that enjoyed by John of Gaunt, equalled, if not exceeded, that of Richard, duke of York. It is unfortunate that the financial records surviving for these magnates are sparse and limited. In the case of Richard, duke of York, we have a valor for his Welsh and Marcher estates from 1442–43.[74] Out of gross revenues (including all casualites) of £4195 12s, fees and annuities unconnected with the administration of the estates amounted to a mere £373 18s 10d.[75] Moreover, one fee alone – that of the earl of Shrewsbury – amounted to £200. To be sure, in 1442–43 the duke was involved in the administration and defence of Henry VI's holdings in his kingdom in France and had not yet entered on a struggle for power in England that might be expected to lead to some expansion of expenditure on a following. We possess some information of the extent of such expenditure by the duke from his holdings in England. In 1441–42 his receiver-general paid out a total of £201 13s 4d for eight annuities, three persons taking most of this amount.[76] His receiver in Somerset and Dorset in 1449–50 paid out a total of £73 13s 4d for three annuities,[77] one alone amounting to nearly all of this sum.[78] Accounts for the same receivership in 1451–52 and 1452–53 indicate no change.[79] All these details suggest that, prior to an active political campaign in England to maintain his interests against the faction that controlled the court, Richard, duke of York was paying out fees and annuities on a scale that was, in proportion to his income from land, roughly commensurate with that of the duke of Buckingham. It is unfortunate that none of his financial records survive after 1452–53. We know from several extant indentures that he recruited followers by these means;[80] and a total of six life-annuities granted by him, amounting in all to £60 were confirmed by his son Edward IV after 1461.[81] But it is quite impossible to assess the scale of his expenditure on fees and annuities during the decade preceding his death in December 1460.

The Neville earls are best discussed together, although the father did not enjoy the territorial wealth amassed by the son. The available information is slight. A receiver's account for the lands of Richard, earl of Salisbury, in the south of England for 1445–46 reveals one annual fee of £5,[82] apart from the fees of lawyers retained by the earl, a total that is infinitesimal in comparison with the £861 odd for which the receiver was accounting. Luck has preserved the portion dealing with some of the fees and annuities from the account of the earl's receiver for the Yorkshire lordship of Middleham in one of the financial years 1456–59, possibly 1456–57.[83] The list of payments is not complete, but as it stands it contains twenty

knights and squires retained by indenture for service in peace and war.[84]
An assessment of the proportion that fees and annuities formed of the earls
revenues from this lordship is difficult since this section of the account is
incomplete and the rest of it is missing. But some assistance can be obtained
from a complete account of the same lordship in 1464–65 in the time of
Richard, earl of Warwick. In this fees and annuities totalled £181 6s 8d.[86]
Two were annuities, amounting to a total of £8: the remaining twenty-two
payments were fees paid to knights and squires retained for peace and
war.[87] In view of the fact that seventeen of Warwick's annuitants and
retainers were not mentioned in the surviving portion of the account of
his father's receiver,[88] and these included members of families with strong
associations with the Nevilles, it is quite possible that the earl of Salisbury
was retaining from his Yorkshire revenues on a scale greater than that of
his more wealthy son six to eight years later. Unlike his father, however,
Warwick had made most of his grants for life – one of the two annuities
and sixteen of the twenty-two retaining fees. On this evidence, it is quite
clear that the burden of fees and annuities on Warwick's Yorkshire estates
in 1464–65 fell well below that on all the revenues of the Percy earls of
Northumberland in the previous decade: the total of the payments involved
consumed 14.6 per cent of the revenues of £1,220 for which the receiver
accounted. It is difficult to be certain that this proportion remained so low
in the late 1450s, since, quite apart from the indications that the earl of
Salisbury had retained on a more considerable scale, Warwick's Yorkshire
estates now included the lordships of Craven and Topcliffe which had
belonged to the attainted earl of Northumberland.[89] We cannot, therefore,
exclude the possibility that the expenditure of the Nevilles from their Yorkshire lands of fees and annuities approached the proportions displayed by
the Percies' financial records. In the case of Richard, earl of Warwick the
dimensions of his expenditure revealed in 1464–65 must have grown as
the rift developed between him and Edward IV and he moved into rebellion: it was in his account of these years that the contemporary chronicler
Warkworth described the lavish distribution of fees by the earl in order to
gain support.[90]

What information we have about other magnates of fifteenth-century
England is sporadic and diffuse and less useful than that for the Percy and
Neville earls or the dukes of Buckingham or York, since it cannot so easily
be located within a political context. The fullest information relates to
Richard Beauchamp, earl of Warwick (d. 1439).[91] In 1409–10 he had
engaged in some retaining and granting of annuities. Three manors had
been granted away for life, two knights were retained at £20 each and five

squires for varying fees, the total, excluding one fee paid out of household revenues, being £41 13s 4d.[92] It is possible that this retaining reflects the young earl's involvement in the campaigning against Owen Glendower in Wales under the leadership of the prince of Wales. Over the next two decades he continued his military career, being a leading commander in France; and for that reason any discussion of the available evidence has to take into account the possibility that some retainers were paid in France and did not show up in the English accounts. This, indeed, may explain the contrast between the accounts of his receiver-general in 1417–18 and in 1420–21. In the former year the receipts amounted to £5,366 19s 9d, including £166 13s 4d for part of his soldiers' wages in Calais. This contingent included one knight and eight squires. In the account of 1420–21, out of total receipts of £2,918 2s 1d, including war wages of £306, a total of £123 6s 8d was paid for annual fees to one knight, thirteen squires and six yeomen ('valets').[93] An incomplete valor of the earl's estates which belongs to the years shortly after his death in 1439 suggests either that fees paid in France had meanwhile been transferred to his revenues in England or that he had increased the scale of his expenditure on fees and annuities since 1420–21. Such charges amounted to £492 (21.6 per cent) out of net manorial revenues of £2,273 or so, involving the greater part of the Beauchamp and Despenser inheritances, if we exclude the latter's lordship of Glamorgan.[94] The scale of expenditure approaches that of Gaunt and the Percies; and the explanation may lie in the dispute over the Berkeley inheritance in which the earl's wife was a claimant. But the incomplete state of the valor makes it impossible to be certain of this.

The account of the receiver-general of John Mowbray, earl marshal and duke of Norfolk, in 1429–30 presents similar problems,[95] since the possibility exists that some fees were paid in France.[96] The total of fees and annuities charged on the account was £298 8s 4d. Almost all these payments were of annuities for past and future services, granted for life: only two persons were retained in peace and war – a knight for £13 6s 8d a year, and a caretaker for £4 5s 6d.[97] The total revenues from the estates for which the receiver-general accounted amounted to roughly £2,430; but this must represent a sum substantially below the real net value of the estates, since the totals for some manors or lordships were unduly low or even non-existent. The description of one of the annuities listed in the account is especially curious. A Master Forester held his office 'while he conducted himself towards the lord well and faithfully in the said office'. However, the annuity which appeared to be his compensation for the office had been granted for his good service in the past and in the future 'as well as in time of peace as in war'.

What little we know about some other magnates indicates that the scale of their expenditure on fees and annuities was even lower. Despite his growing importance as a politician and a courtier, William de la Pole, earl of Suffolk, in stating deductions from his income for the tax of 1436 claimed only four annuities, totalling £150 from an income of £1,817 before deductions.[98] It was, of course, in Suffolk's interest to claim as large an amount of annuities as possible on such an occasion; but the possibility does exist that, at this date at any rate, some were charged on his lands in France. However, this possibility did not exist in 1453–54, the year from which an account of the receiver-general of his widow, Alice, duchess of Suffolk, survives.[99] In view of the continued importance of the family in East Anglian affairs and the duchess's own involvement in them in the interests of her son and heir, we would expect this account to reveal a substantial proportion of fees and annuities granted by her husband before his death in 1450. But the total of six annuities, all for life, amounted to only £34 out of a total just below £1,100 of that year's revenues entered into the account. One piece of evidence survives in the case of James, earl of Ormond, who was also earl of Wiltshire and played a leading role on the side of the court faction in the events of the late 1450s. The receiver of his estates in Suffolk paid a total of £22 for four annuities out of just over £180 of that year's receipts.[100] The valor of the English estates of Edmund Grey, lord of Ruthin and (from 1464) earl of Kent, exists for 1467–68. Both the recent career of this magnate and the date of this document lead to the expectation that it would reflect the scale of ambitions that had recently been achieved through a comital title and the territorial gains granted in return for support of the Yorkist king and, also, perhaps, the beginnings of the rift between Edward IV and the Nevilles. But fees and annuities totalled only £100 or so, only 9–10 per cent of the net revenues of the earl's lands in England, out of gross revenues of £900–1,000.[101]

The results of this analysis of the surviving financial records of English magnates in the fourteen and fifteenth centuries must remain impressionistic. In one case only – John of Gaunt – can we be entirely confident in charting the scale and growth of fees and annuities over the greater part of a lord's tenure of his inheritance. In the case of his predecessor in the same inheritance – Thomas of Lancaster – there are solid grounds for believing that at his death in 1322 his expenditure on a following approached that of John of Gaunt at the end of his life. There is only one other case of a family – that of the Percy earls of Northumberland – in whose case we can be confident that the total expenditure on fees and annuities approximated to that of John of Gaunt, though this conclusion has to be based on a smaller body of documentation. In one case – Richard Neville, earl of Salisbury – it is possible to state that his expenditure on these items from his revenues in Yorkshire by the end of the 1450s equalled that of the Percies; but there is no evidence that this was true of the rest of his estates and, indeed, there is a single account which indicates that such expenditure was minimal on those in the south. Moreover, his son and heir, Richard, earl of Warwick, devoted a smaller proportion of his revenues in Yorkshire to fees and annuities than his father had, even though his holdings there had been augmented. Enough information has survived for other magnates, including the most wealthy in the fifteenth century – Stafford, duke of Buckingham and Richard, duke of York – to suggest that fees and annuities consumed comparatively small portions of their revenues, apparently less than ten per cent.

It must be said that totals obtained from receivers' accounts do not necesarily provide a complete picture. It is possible that a receiver did not make a payment that was due and for that reason omitted all mention of his obligation from his account. Moreover, the possibility must also be taken into account that some payments were made out of household revenues. At least one receiver's account mentioned such an occurrence.[102] But it is unlikely that this consideration should alter conclusions from the available financial records. There were compelling reasons, in existence since the late thirteenth century, why fees and annuities should be paid direct from landed revenues.[103] Moreover, it is quite possible that some magnates followed the opposite policy and paid the fees of some of their houshold officials out of receivers' revenues.[104] Against these possible reservations, however, must be placed evidence from a quite different source. There survive statements of the fees and annuities granted for life out of their revenues by fourteen of the parliamentary nobility at the time of their assessment for the income tax of 1436.[105] Only three were making such payments in excess of ten per cent of their incomes after the deduction of ordinary expenses. In one case – Reginald, lord de la Warr – the proportion was high, over 30 per cent; but in the other two cases – John, earl of Huntingdon, and John, lord Scrope of Masham – it was much lower, 13.77 and 12.56 per cent respectively. Since these fourteen peers represent one-third of the temporal peers so taxed in 1436, these figures confirm the impression that it was rare for expenditure on a retinue in the form of payments for life to exceed 10 per cent of a lord's revenues.

It is unfortunate that the details encountered in the financial records of the nobility rarely permit us to distinguish between the fees paid to inden-

tured retainers and the annuities granted for past and future services. Such
information is available in the case of John of Gaunt and in that of the
Yorkshire estates of Richard Neville, earl of Salisbury in the late 1450s;
but firm conclusions on this point are not possible in the case of the family
whose expenditure in fees and annuities as a whole equalled that of Gaunt
– the Percy earls of Northumberland. It is, however, clear that only in the
case of Gaunt and the Neville earl can we be certain that more was spent
on indentured retainers than annuitants. In terms, however, of a lord's
capacity to rely on his following this is not an important conclusion, since
it was an annuity that was the most desirable of the benefits available from
a lord. Even so, it serves to emphasise that indentures of retinue were not
necessarily the most important element in the relations of lord and man in
late medieval England.

The conclusion that heavy expenditure on fees and annuities appears to
have been the exception, rather than the rule, hardly fits the stereotype of
the 'overmighty subject' which has been dear to so many historians, or
even their employment of notions of 'bastard feudalism' to explain the
power of certain magnates in the politics and society of late medieval England. But this is hardly surprising if attention is given to the financial
realities faced by any lord. A magnate who granted out fees and annuitiees
on a substantial scale thereby reduced the revenues available for his family
and household and the luxurious display that was also part of the panoply
of lordship. It can be argued that those cases of exceptionally heavy expenditure that occurred were made possible by additional sources of revenue
or were made necessary by ambition. Thomas of Lancaster's retinue was
a product of the conditions of civil war and, indeed, by his death may have
been a major cause of his financial difficulties.[106] The extent of the ambitions of John of Gaunt within the kingdom of England is difficult to determine, though it is likely that he was always concerned about the possibility
that a contest might arise, as six months after his death it did, over the
throne. But there can be no doubt of his ambition to acquire the throne
of Castile and, when this aborted, to secure a principality in Gascony. In
the case of the Percy earls of Northumberland there are convincing indications of their desire to dominate the Border; and the revenues they obtained
from the Wardenship of the East March must have made their expenditure
on fees and annuities more feasible.

In the case of the most powerful of all these magnates we can investigate
further, since evidence exists to throw light on the scale of expenditure
involved on one important occasion when the Lancastrian retinue was summoned for service. Peacetime expenditure of fees and annuities had two

functions: it extended a lord's authority outside the immediate area of his estates and it provided a body of men on which the lord could call in time of crisis. But, once he summoned his men for service, a lord incurred financial obligations that were in addition to the payment of fees and annuities. The records of the administration of the Duchy of Lancaster in the years 1399–1401 show that Henry of Bolingbroke, after securing the throne as Henry IV, paid out a total of at least, and perhaps over £3,000 to the retinue that accompanied him during the three months between his landing in Yorkshire in July 1399 and his acceptance as king at the end of September 1399, this total including £256 spent on the garrisoning of the duchy's main castles.[107] This sum was not far short of a quarter of the gross revenues of the duchy of Lancaster at the time of his father's death.[108] The scale of this expenditure is placed in a more impressive perspective by the fact that it involved only a portion of the retinue of Gaunt at his death. A total of £1,650 15s 1d was paid to fifteen knights (two of whom were 'bachelors'), twelve squires, one yeoman and eleven others of lesser rank. Each of these brought a body of followers with him; and, even if the total of knights, squires and others is raised upwards to take into account the additional £1,100 or so spent on the remainder of the retinue, it is clear that the greater part of Gaunt's following did not come out in support of their lord's heir.[109] It is impossible to say whether this was because of deliberate decision on the part of some retainers or because of Bolingbroke's failure to request their help.[110] Nevertheless, the scale of the expenditure that did occur demonstrates that the calling out of a retinue for any length of time could impose a serious strain on any magnate's revenues. For the so-called 'overmighty subject' civil war was an exorbitantly expensive business.

These conclusions must be placed in a wider perspective. The survival of at least some quantity of the financial records of the leading magnates, and the paucity of equivalent documentation for the knights and squires, leads inevitably to a tendency to underestimate the importance of the gentry in the functioning of late medieval society, reinforced as this has been by the assumption that a large porportion of them owed some of their incomes to the financial benefits of lordship. In one case – the records of the income tax of 1436 – we are able to make a rough comparison between the wealth of the nobility and that of the gentry. The total net income of the parliamentary peerage – including widows holding dower-interests and minors – assessed for this tax amounted to some £45,000.[111] To be sure, this total is incomplete as an estimate of the net wealth of the whole parliamentary nobility in two respects: it omits the incomes of a number of widows and, more important, applies only to holdings in England, as distinct from Wales and the March.[112] But it is still useful to compare it with that of £151,000 for knights, squires and other non-titled landowners. It is unlikely that the impression this comparison provides would be remarkably altered by the addition of the missing noble widows and, indeed, it is likely that non-noble widows as well are missing from the surviving returns, while the absence of totals for Wales and the March applies to nobles and non-nobles alike. It is quite true that the incomes at which some of the knights and squires were assessed included such fees and annuities as they held through grants from magnates. But, whatever the limitations of the statistics available from the income tax returns of 1436, it is impossible to avoid the conclusion that the parliamentary peerage held a comparatively small portion of the landed wealth of England. In particular, the landed incomes of the leading magnates were dwarfed by the total wealth of the knights and squires, Individuals may well have benefited handsomely from the financial benefits of lordships;[113] but they must have formed a minority within the gentry as a whole. Retainers' fees and annuities could have been only one element in the power and influence of the magnates of the realm.

(ii) The sources of power

The conclusion that in the case of most magnates the burden of fees and annuities was limited, and even in some cases slight, leads to an adjustment of views of the sources of power enjoyed by the 'overmighty subject' of late medieval England. To be sure, the extent to which a magnate employed force to gain his ends or fomented lawlessness or even engaged in civil war, was governed by the Crown's capacity to maintain order. But in certain periods in the history of late medieval England the Crown's authority was weakened or even collapsed; and the sources in these years contain striking illustrations of the desire of leading magnates to increase their followings. The figures we find in the chronicles for the size of armies during periods of civil war must be treated with severe caution. But, when we turn to the period of the 'Wars of Roses', for example, we have some sources that deserve respect. According to one of John Paston's correspondents the earl of Devon arrived at the May parliament of 1450 with 300 men and the earl of Warwick with more than 400.[114] In February 1456 John Bocking, writing to Sir John Fastolf, announced the arrival of the duke of York and the earl of Warwick for parliament accompanied by 300 men, all in coats of mail.[115] In February 1458, at a point when the political situation had developed into a serious crisis, another of Fastolf's correspondents described the arrival of the duke of York 'with his own household only to the number of 140 horse' but told how the earl of Salisbury had come with 400 horse in his company, including eighty knights and squires, the duke of Somerset having already arrived with two hundred horse.[116] These totals do not seem unreasonable in the light of those provided for the duke of York's household, since this does not seem unduly large in comparison with that revealed by the accounts of the duke of Buckingham.[117]

The information provided by the magnates' financial records leaves little doubt that knights and squires retained for life in peace and war, together with such men as were brought with them to the lord's service, could have forced only a minority of the large companies known to have accompanied leading dukes and earls to some of the parliaments in the years of crisis preceding the Yorkist *coup* of 1461. It is worthwhile to note the margin between the eighty knights and squires who followed the earl of Salisbury in 1458 and the total force of 400 horse of which they formed a part. Moreover, on the evidence of our knowledge of Salisbury's disbursements on retainers in the case of his Yorkshire estates at this time it is difficult to believe that all eighty knights and squires were retained by indenture for peace and war.

In some measure a great lord's following on occasions such as are depicted in the Paston correspondence or in times of actual civil war must have come partly from his household. In February 1458 the duke of York had household men to the number of 140 with him; and by this time the duke of Buckingham may well have been able to produce a contingent of household men on roughly the same scale. In 1439 he had a riding household of fifty-six; and by 1456–57 additional recruitment had brought the total of eighty-five. If we can make some allowance for knights and squires whose indentures imposed on them the duty of household service when required and assume that these brought attendants with them, the total body may well have been on the scale of York's. But there remains a gap between such figures and the totals we encounter in our sources. In fact, even if he brought out all his household men and all the knights and squires retained by indenture, a leading duke or earl would still have to raise additional men, at least for the needs of civil war.

This conclusion is strongly supported by some information we have about leading magnates' retinues in the late thirteenth and early fourteenth centuries. According to a list that probably belongs to the autumn of 1297,[118] Roger Bigod, earl of Norfolk and earl Marshal, had a household, excluding clerks, of five bannerets, nine knights, six squires and fifteen others of lower rank. Since the list of bannerets includes John, lord Segrave, with whom an indenture had been made a few months earlier,[119] there can be little doubt that the list includes all those knights and squires with whom the earl had made indentures of retinue. At the same time a comparison between the number of bannerets and knights in the light of the Segrave indenture indicates that the list does not include the companies of squires and other ranks brought with them by indentured retainers. It belongs to a period when rebellion was narrowly averted. Its details suggest that, if the earl had been forced to raise arms against the king, neither his standing household nor his group of indentured retainers would have provided him with a sufficient following. Another piece of evidence relates to Thomas of Lancaster in 1318–19, a year when he participated in the king's siege of Berwick-on-Tweed. the daily accounts of his household reveal the number of men and horses that had to be fed from its resources. At the time when he was moving northwards to join the king, the numbers of men fluctuated well above the 1,000 level, some times exceeding 1,200.[120] These totals are 8–10 times the size of the number of knights and squires in receipt of robes from his wardrobe in 1313–14;[121] and, although it is reasonable to assume that political conditions had led by 1318–19 to a further increase, there must remain a large gap between the number of indentured retainers and the size of the forces in attendance on the earl. In some measure this can be explained by the presence of knights, squires and other ranks which the terms of their indentures required the earl's knights and squires to bring with them; but what information we have about Lancaster's indentures suggests that this can only be a partial explanation.

To what sources of manpower, then, did lords turn in times of crisis or civil war? The most obvious is the enlisting of men on a temporary basis in return for grants of livery and daily wages. The employment of wages is, for example, attested by the act of parliament which attainted the Yorkist leaders in 1459, describing how they had rebelled 'with other knights and people, such as they had blinded and assembled by wages, promises and other exquisite means'.[122] The employment of livery for similar purposes is certainly implied by the efforts of the Crown and the commons in parliament from the late fourteenth century onwards to prevent the spread of livery outside the household.[123] Grants of livery for short-term purposes can be illustrated from the Paston correspondence even in time of peace. In 1467 Sir John Howard gave out 'jackettes' to sixty-nine men for the great tournament held between lord Scales and the Bastard of Burgundy.[124] In June 1469 Sir John Paston wrote to his brother describing his efforts to recruit a following in his livery for the king's visit to Norfolk.[125] It was natural enough in time of local or national crisis or civil war to transform methods that provided for ostentatious display into a means of recruitment for less lawful purposes. One of the most remarkable illustrations of this phenomenon can be found in a dispute between the officials of the cardinal archbishop of York and the tenants of the duchy of Lancaster's forest of Knaresborough over the payment of tolls at the local fair. If we can believe the archbishop's opponents, he had 'kept his town of Ripon at fair times at night, like a town of war, with soldiers hired for their wages' for the past three years. At the time of that year's fair in May 1441 his officials continued this state of local war 'with soldiers waged thither out of Tyndale and Hexhamshire and of other parts nigh unto Scotland, into the number of 200 men of arms, riding and coming from the said parts unto Ripon like men of war . . . taking some 6d a day and 12d a day', with food and drink ('bouch de court').[126] Although there was no specific reference to the archbishop's livery, it is implied in the description of these soldiers' accoutrements. Some of the best examples of such practices are to be found in a newsletter describing the great lords' reactions to the crisis caused early in 1454 by the madness of Henry VI. It tells how the duke of Buckingham had ordered 2,000 'bendes and knottes, to what extent men may construe', a reference to livery in the form of neckgear. In Somerset the earl of Wiltshire and lord Bonville were offering sixpence a day to any man who would serve them.[127] Most of these illustrations of the employment of livery or wages for short-term recruiting are to be found in the Paston correspondence. Other periods of crisis or rebellion in late medieval England do not unfortunately yield evidence of this kind; but there is no reason why great lords' conduct in these years should have differed from that of the middle years of the fifteenth century. The use of livery or wages in this way was, of course, a repetition of the means great lords employed to raise men who under contract to supply a contingent for the king's wars. There is also good reason to believe that, when the bonds of royal authority collapsed, such methods were not confined to the magnates. An account of the misdeeds of a Norfolk gentleman,[128] apparently intended to form the basis of an indictment, complained that

> notwithstanding that all the livelihood that the said Ledham hath passed not £20, besides the repairs and outcharges, and that he hath no cunning nor true means of getting of any good in this country as far as any man may conceive, and yet keepeth in his house daily 20 men, besides women and great multitude of such misgoverned people as be resorting to him, as is abovesaid, to the which he giveth clothing, and yet besides that he giveth to other men that be not

dwelling in his household. And of the said 20 men there passeth not 8 that use occupation of husbandry; and all they that use husbandry, as well as other, be jacked and 'salettid' ready for to war.

Some of the references in mid-fifteenth century sources are especially valuable for the light they throw on the form taken by grants of livery at this time. Robes were still in use. A letter written by John Paston in June 1469 shows that the duke of Norfolk adhered to this practice.[129] But there are strong indications that the signs or badges that had already begun to be substituted for robes by the end of the fourteenth century had proliferated. In February 1454 the duke of Buckingham intended the use of neckgear ('bendes and nottes').[130] In 1483, after the seizure of power by Richard III with the aid of the duke of Buckingham, the contemporary Warwickshire antiquary, John Rous, commented that so many men had not worn the same badge since the time of Richard Neville, earl of Warwick,[131] thus implying the latter's use of badges also during his rebellion against Edward IV and his restoration of Henry VI. It was thus no coincidence that the statute of 1468 was the first piece of legislation to list signs and badges as forms of livery and retaining.[132] Nor is it surprising that a growth in the use of such livery had occurred. It must have been much cheaper than the provision of robes, a consideration of substantial appeal during a period of intermittent armed conflict when magnates had to put substantial numbers of men into a state of warlike preparation at short notice.

The use of signs and badges occurred in peace as well as in war. But another practice – the taking of oaths as a means of creating a bond of lordship – was primarily a peacetime affair. It is quite likely that such oaths had been in use for centuries, if only as a stage on the route that led to office or an indenture of retinue or an annuity. At any rate, the fact that the practice was mentioned for the first time in Edward IV's 'articles' of 1461,[133] may suggest that it had been growing in recent years . One reference to it can be found in the Paston Correspdence. In June 1469 John Paston described how three men, two of whom had received gowns from the duke of Norfolk that season 'are sworn my lord of Gloucester's men'.[134]

But a delineation of a great lord's sources of power in late medieval England that simply stresses the role of livery and daily wages as a means of enlarging the resources available through the household, indentured retainers and annuitants is incomplete. It is also necessary to take into account the role of holdings of land as sources of men. The greater the lord, the greater the range of patronage available to him in the form of offices, and the greater the number of peasant tenants who could be called upon to provide the rank-and-file of a private army.

Historians have long been aware of the complexity and professionalism of the bureaucracy with which the magnates managed their estates and revenues,[135] but, since the personnel of local administration was generally chosen from the ranks of local gentry, a magnate's bureaucracy could serve to anchor his authority in local society by creating a body of dependents within its leadership. In every case there was a range of offices moving upwards from the local manorial bailiff to the receivers and stewards of groups of estates, together with the constableships of castles. While offices at the local manorial level were not substantial income-producers, the fees paid by the leading dukes and earls to their receivers, stewards, master foresters and constables were often at the level of those paid to knights and squires retained by indentures of retinue. For most leading magnates of late medieval England some information exists, sometimes quite substantial, to show how such offices provided sources of patronage for local gentry. Quite frequently grants of such offices were virtual annuities for past and future services, since they were given for life and their duties could be handled by deputies: indeed, in the case of stewardships the need for legal knowledge may even have made this desirable. But this feature also meant that pluralism occurred, a magnate rewarding a favourite knight or squire with a succession of offices, just as he might grant more than one annuity. In some cases – the surviving registers of John of Gaunt provide many examples – such offices were specifically granted, like annuities, in return for services performed in the past and to be performed in the future.[136] The array of such patronage in the case of a leading duke or earl could be immense, being equal to the landed incomes of other members of the parliamentary peerage. In the case of John of Gaunt in the 1390s it amounted to approximately £2,000 a year.[137] In that of the estates of Richard, duke of York, in Wales and the March in 1442–43 the total was £575.[138] At the time of the death of the fourth earl of Northumberland in 1489 fees paid in connection with the administration of his estates amounted to £612 a year.[139] Both John of Gaunt and the Percy earls of Northumberland in the mid-fifteenth century spent sums in retaining fees and annuities that were well in excess of those fees connected with the administration of their estates. But for all the other magnates for whom information has survived the opposite was true, retaining fees and annuities often being dwarfed by the annual outlay on administrative offices.

Nor were retainers and annuitants, on the one hand, and administrative officials, on the other, totally separate categories of personnel. In the case of John of Gaunt, for example, some knights were already important administrative officials when they entered into indentures of retinue with him,[140] and others who were retained were given administrative offices at later stages in their careers.[141] Occasionally, indeed, in the case of the receivers' accounts of some magnates it is difficult to distinguish a man's functions as retainer from those of his administrative offices.[142] Those, of course, who held important offices in a magnate's estate administration came from the same social background as the knights and squires who were retained by indenture. But this fact should not lead to the conclusion that the bonds of loyalty between lord and man were confined to those who held high administrative office. A lord might also use manorial officials as sources of local leadership in his interests. For example, in the private war between the Percies and the Nevilles which erupted in the north in 1453–54 the bailiff of the Percy manor of Pocklington played a leading part in the so-called 'battle' of Stamford Bridge.[143]

The value of a magnate's bureaucracy as a source of power was not confined to the dissemination of his patronage through the local societies in the neighbourhood of his estates. In addition his local officers could in collaboration with his indentured retainers and annuitants, serve as recruiting officers when he wanted to raise men by means of grants of livery and daily wages. An obvious area of such manpower was his manorial tenantry. A glimpse into such recruitment is provided by the newsletter of January 1454 which survives in the Paston correspondence:

> my lord [presumably the duke of Norfolk], at his coming hither, shall come with a good and cleanly fellowship, such as is likely and according to his estate to have about him . . . And over that, that my lord have another good fellowship to await on him, or else soon after him, in like wise as other lords of his blood will . . . for the more readiness of such fellowship to be had ready, that my lord send sad and wise messengers to his servants and tenants in Sussex and elsewhere, that they be ready at London against his coming, to await on my lord.[144]

Indeed, the private armies that fought when civil war did occur in late medieval England could only have been feasible if tenants had served, presumably wearing their lord's liveries and receiving wages. But the precise nature of the lord's capacity to raise his tenants presents a complicated problem.[145]

It is quite clear that in some areas of the kingdom much more was involved than a peasant's traditional loyalty to his lord. In the areas of Cumberland and Northumberland that bordered on Scotland there is firm evidence that manorial tenants had imposed on them by custom the obligation to maintain arms and horse and serve in the defence of the kingdom, a situation best attested in the survey which royal commissioners made of the Percy estates in the north on their acquisition by the Crown in 1537.[146] A similar situation obtained in some of the great lordships of the Welsh March.[147] In those of Chirk, Bromfield and Yale, military service was due from unfree as well as free tenants and was not confined to Wales but extended at the lord's will to England and Scotland, the lord paying for such service outside the lordship.[148] References to similar customs in the north and west are not difficult to explain. In the case of the Scottish border it is quite likely that the custom became entrenched in the two centuries following the English defeat at Bannockburn and, indeed, its development may have been intensified by the rise of the authority of the Wardens of the Marches in the area. It is, however, clear that the custom was a general one, forming part of local custom as a whole, and did not involve the insertion of conditions to this effect in leases or in conveyances of customary land in the manorial court. In the case of the Welsh March the lords of the late middle ages were the heirs to the authority exercised by Welsh princes before the Norman conquest of the area. It is reasonable to assume that the emergence of the Marcher lordships as fully defined judicial entities in the generation following the Edwardian conquest led to an adaptation of basic custom for current military purposes. At any rate, in the case of Chirk,[149] a reference to the wages paid in the Scottish wars of Edward I suggests that the military obligations of the tenantry were defined in the last decade of the thirteen century and certainly before 1307. There is, however, some ground for believing that in some areas of the Welsh March a lord was able to call on his tenants without the assistance of customs stated in these terms. In May 1318 Hugh Despenser the younger leased to Rees ap Griffith for seven years the castle of Dynevor and the land of Cantred Mawr in return for an annual rent of 500 marks and the promise of men when required for war in Scotland or elsewhere.[150] Two features of this agreement are especially interesting. While the reference to service in Scotland implies the king's wars there, there is no specific reference to this; and Despenser's ability to require service elsewhere implies that he had his own needs, as distinct from the king's, in mind. Equally remarkable is the lack of any definition of the size of the tenant's contingent. This suggests that Despenser was relying on the lord's ability to raise his tenants, Despenser's own in the case of the lands he had leased and those of Rees ap Griffith himself. This arrangement may be exceptional in that it belongs to a period when the process of definition of the rights of Marcher lords which began with the Edwardian conquest was not yet complete. Even so, it provides a glimpse into conditions that had existed for centuries and into conditions of lordship which could not be encapsulated in a simple definition of custom.

We are on much less firm ground when we seek to analyse the military obligations of tenants to their lords elsewhere in the kingdom. By the middle years of the sixteenth century landlords in various parts of England were inserting in their tenants' leases clauses that imposed duties of military service in the king's wars.[151] This phenomenon was apparently a quite different one from the customs which can be traced in the Border country a generation earlier, since it involved a deliberate leasing policy as distinct from a custom that affected a whole area, embracing the manors of different lords.[152] The information available suggests that the practice was not a universal one.[153] But did such practices exist in earlier centuries? Of all the surviving indentures of retinue only one – that made by lord Clifford in 1385 – involved a peasant tenant and his holding.[154] And, if such practices were frequent, it is odd that no other examples have survived, especially since minorities and forfeitures would have led to royal confirmation of at least some such arrangements. It is true that in many manors freeholder tenants would often have held small portions of land by military tenure; but in strict legality this would always have involved the payment of scutage, not personal service. Nor would agrarian conditions from the time of the Black Death onwards have made it easy to impose military service as one of a tenant's obligations. Landlords needed to secure as high a financial return from their land as possible in conditions in which peasant demand for land was declining, or at best stagnant, while tenants would not have been anxious to take up holdings on terms which involved military service. In short, the conditions we find on the borders with Scotland and in the Welsh March lordships do not appear to have parallels elsewhere in the kingdom. Nevertheless, it is reasonable to assume that traditional ties between lord and peasant, afforced by continuity of administration, must have assisted lords who turned to their tenantry as sources of recruitment. To be sure, even on the Scottish border and in the Welsh March military obligations existed only for defence and the king's wars respectively. A tenant who followed his lord into violence in local politics or into civil war risked the vengeance of the royal law. But in practice it must often have been difficult to resist pressure from the lord's bailiff or steward or the constable of his castle. Indeed, we know of one case – the lordship of Ellesmere on the eve of the Shrewsbury campaign of 1403 – where tenants felt compelled to follow their lord's steward into rebellion even though their lord was under age.[155]

A lord's capacity to exploit these resources needs to be put in the context of the geographical distribution of his lands. The roles of certain families in English politics in the middle ages suggest that it is not enough to make an equation between the size of a magnate's territorial holdings and the human resources in the form of his local bureaucracy or tenants who might join his forces. In all the episodes of political tension or rebellion as far back as late Anglo-Saxon times decisive roles were played by magnates whose bases of territorial power lay in the north of England or in Wales and the March. Sometimes a great lord would hold most of his estates in one of these regions. John of Gaunt, for example, was the dominant land-owner in Yorkshire, Lancashire and the north Midlands, while the holdings of the Percy earls of Northumberland were by the beginning of the fifteenth century concentrated in Northumberland, Cumberland and Yorkshire. Although the Stafford dukes of Buckingham held manors in most shires of England the greater part of their revenues came from lordships in the March of Wales. Similarly, Richard, duke of York, was the owner of large holdings in Yorkshire, East Anglia and the West Country; but two-thirds of his landed revenues came from the Welsh March. In the few years that followed the seizure of the throne by Edward IV, Richard, earl of Warwick, succeeded in expanding his family's original bases of power in Yorkshire and Cumberland, while his marriage had brought him a decade or so earlier the great lordship of Glamorgan. Each of these magnates played a role in politics that involved the recruitment of rank-and-file followers in addition to the resources provided by indentured retainers and annuitants. The terri-torial strength of each of them was concentrated in a way that could only strengthen their hold on the loyalty of their tenants. Nevertheless, an explanation of their capacity to raise men in these terms alone would be inadequate, since there were other elements in the situation.

One of these was continuity in the structure of lordship over a period of centuries. To be sure, holdings changed hands. Richard, duke of York, was the heir of a Mortimer uncle, while Richard, earl of Warwick, held the lordship of Glamorgan through his marriage to the heiress of the Beauchamp and Despenser families. The Percies had held most of their Yorkshire holdings since the late eleventh century and most of those in Northumberland since the early fourteenth; but it was only in 1398 that the honour of Cockermouth in Cumberland became theirs absolutely. The territorial power of the Stafford dukes of Buckingham had a twofold origin – an heiress's third-share of the inheritance of the Clare earls of Gloucester who died at Bannockburn and the land settled on his youngest surviving son by Edward III. The history of other great families in late medieval England shows other great lordships changing hands in similar ways through the vicissitudes of birth, death and marriage. Even so, as territorial holdings all these great lordships had stayed intact through centuries, the authority into which new lords stepped when the inheritance became theirs had been maintained over local tenants, feudal as well as manorial, over the same period. It was this, and the personal capacity of a new lord to exploit such authority, that mattered, rather than the nature of his relationship with a family that had died out in the main line.

In delineating these features of the structure of lordship and political power in late medieval England we are moving in an area of knowledge for which no solid documentation exists. Even so, it is reasonable to suggest that conditions in the north and on the Welsh March provided the great lords of these areas with sources of manpower that extended beyond the confines of their own estates. The tendencies to lawlessness in these areas were encouraged by the presence of a number of franchisal jurisdictions that lacked any overriding authority, a situation well known to historians who have studied the achievements of the early Tudor monarchs in government. It is not unreasonable to assume that such conditions provided sources of recruitment in time of civil war. For instance, the opponents of the archbishop of York in 1441 claimed that his hired soldiers came from Tyndale and Hexhamshire, two of the northernmost franchises.[156] In the case of the great lords of the Welsh March the unruly gentry of the shires of the Principality and their tenants must always have been a source of men. The March itself even in the late fifteenth century retained its reputation as a 'land of war'.[157]

Thus there can be no simple definition of the sources of power enjoyed by the magnates of late medieval England. The lord's following had three nuclei – his household, his indentured retainers, both these merging when his retainers were summoned to his service, and his annuitants. Moreover, both indentured retainers and annuitants served as recruiting agents; but the same function was also performed by those administrative officials who were not also to be found in these two categories. In this complex of manpower the role of indentured retainers and annuitants should not be exaggerated, since only a handful of magnates in the fourteenth and fifteenth centuries spent a substantial proportion of their revenues on these categories of follower. And even they, when faced with an urgent need to make a impressive display of their power or to prepare for civil war, found it necessary to turn to recruitment by means of livery and daily wages. In their efforts at such undertakings they relied in substantial measure on the administrative officials of their estates and on the links of traditional loyalty between them and their tenants.

(iii)   **The limits of lordship**

A great lord's sources of power in late medieval England were by no means absolutely firm. From the earliest time for which we have information – the disturbances of Edward II's reign – down through the so-called 'Wars of Roses' we can trace examples of retainers who deserted their lords for others. On the eve of the final confrontation with the king that led to his defeat and execution Thomas of Lancaster, despite his pre-eminent territorial wealth and power, lost the support of some of his retainers.[158] In the same period Aymer de Valence, earl of Pembroke, failed to retain the loyalty of the Berkeleys, father and son, who had become his retainers in 1297. Indeed, in 1318 they took part in an attack on some of his islands and by the spring of the following year were in the service of Roger Mortimer, lord of Wigmore.[159] Outside periods of civil war knights and squires can be found who were retained by indenture but held annuities or offices of other lords. An often-quoted example is that of Sir Thomas Hungerford, the Speaker in the parliament of 1377, who was at the time chief steward of the estates of John of Gaunt in the south and, definitely by 1379, retained by him;[160] but he had also been the steward of the estates of the earl of Salisbury since 1365, the grant of this office emphasising the closeness of his relationship with the earl by stipulating that his fee was to continue even if he were unable to act as steward, provided he remained the earl's retainer and councillor.[161] Especially remarkable cases are supplied by successive heads of the family of Stafford of Grafton in the middle years of the fifteenth century. In 1448–49 Sir Humphrey held an annual fee of forty marks a year from the duke of Buckingham,[162] but he also enjoyed large fees, each of twenty marks, from James Ormond, earl of Wiltshire, and Cecily, duchess of Warwick, and other fees, ranging between ten marks and forty shillings from Sir Andrew Ogard and four local churchmen – the bishop of Worcester, the abbots of Evesham and Pershore and the prior of Worcester.[163] Within twelve months or so of succeeding his father his heir (also Humphrey) enjoyed a somewhat different list of fees, the grantors in the case of one earl – Wiltshire – and three churchmen being the same as had rewarded his father, though in the case of the earl of Wiltshire's fee there had been a reduction by one-half. Unlike his father, he seems to have secured a fee from the leading magnate of the area of his estates – Richard Neville, earl of Warwick.[164] But the most interesting feature of Humphrey Stafford's dealings with lords is the reward he paid to the servant who brought him the livery of Ralph, lord Sudeley.[165] It is important to note that there is no evidence that either Stafford was retained by indenture with any of the lords concerned: it is possible that the term 'fee' employed to describe these payments in their surviving financial records might quite properly have been replaced by 'annuity'.

There were also incidents which show that loyalty to a lord's heir or to his family was not always maintained in the aftermath of his death. The events that followed the death of John of Gaunt in February 1399 are especially remarkable. In the months following his seizure of the Lancastrian inheritance Richard II confirmed over fifty of the grants made by the deceased duke, in most cases on condition that the grantee would be retained with the king only.[166] Of those who received such confirmations nine were knights, and thirty squires, who had been retained by Gaunt by indenture.[167] Both they and others who had received annuities, lands and offices for life from Gaunt accepted the king's patronage despite his breach of the undertakings he had made to the heir in seizing the inheritance and the real possibility that the heir would seek to recover his rights. Within a few months of this episode we encounter the case of two squires who had been retained for life by John, earl of Huntingdon, and whose fees were confirmed by Henry IV shortly after their lord's abortive rebellion. The circumstances of these confirmations suggest that they had deserted their lord and stayed loyal to the new king.[168] The most well-known of such illustrations is the situation that occurred after the arrest and execution of William, lord Hastings, by Richard, duke of Gloucester, in 1483. Immediately after their lord's death, 'All the lord chamberlain's men became my lord of Buckingham's men'.[169]

In the light of such information historians have regarded the lordship of late medieval England as prone to dissolve into shifting loyalties, seeing in this a reason for the disorder that erupted when the monarchy was weak. But some of the illustrations of shifting loyalties that are available need to be put in their proper perspective. The duties of Sir Thomas Hungerford as steward of the earl of Salisbury did not necessarily conflict with those he had as one of the two chief stewards of John of Gaunt, since the duties of a steward could be, and often were, carried out by deputies. It is true that Hungerford was a member of the council of the earl of Salisbury and retained by him; but there is nothing to indicate that the language employed in his appointnment as steward in which his relationship to the earl was described in these terms meant anything more than obligation to be loyal in his capacity as councillor.[170] Provided Hungerford obeyed Gaunt's summons to attend him, his obligations as an indentured retainer would be fulfilled. The cases of the pluralism of Sir Humphrey Stafford of Grafton and of his son contain nothing to suggest that they were retained by any of the lords from whom they received fees or annuities. Indeed, these two cases point to the dangers of an approach to such evidence which assumes that every grant of an annuity or even a retainer's fee involved exactly the same sort of relationship. It is reasonable to assume that the duke of Buckingham, the earl of Warwick and lord Sudeley were seeking the support of the Staffords of Grafton in local or national politics. But the motives of the great churchmen who gave them fees must have been rather different. They realised that disputes might arise which might affect their interests and wished to assure themselves in advance of help from this family. Such arguments serve to emphasise the fact that a multiplicity of fees and annuities did not necessarily imply a conflict of interest.

Other examples of shifting loyalties need to be placed in their political contexts. It is unwise to study the loyalties of lordship simply from the standpoint of the obligations of the follower. Loyalty and service were given in return for benefits that extended beyond the payment of a fee or annuity or the granting of livery. There was nothing necessarily improper or unnatural in the conduct of a man who left his lord because the latter could not assist or protect him, provided he did not seek to keep his fee or annuity. In 1318 the Berkeleys, father and son, turned against the earl of Pembroke because he had done nothing to help through influence at court the father's claims to a share of the Clare inheritance.[171] In the last resort, for example, Humphrey Stafford of Grafton had to choose between the duke of Buckingham and the earl of Warwick who were the two powerful lords in Warwickshire and chose the latter because he was territorially the more powerful in that shire.[172] It is especially noticeable that the most impressive of the examples of apparent disloyalty to a lord or his family involved a struggle against the resources of the monarchy. The retainers who deserted Thomas of Lancaster in 1321–22 weighed the consequences of their continued loyalty to him in a situation in which there were doubts about his judgment and capacity for leadership and strong reasons to fear that the king and his supporters would be victorious. Similarly, those Lancastrian retainers who agreed in the spring and early summer of 1399 to serve no one except the king had to weigh the consequences of loyalty to an exiled heir against the wrath of a king who might not stop at the cessation of their financial benefits. In 1483 the retainers of the dead lord Hastings had every reason to believe that, even if Richard, duke of Gloucester respected the interests of the heir, their interests and security were at risk. In this situation adherence to the most powerful of Richard's allies was a policy of self-preservation.

There are, indeed, good reasons for avoiding the temptation to stress the impermanence of the ties of lordship in late medieval England. It is impossible to assess the extent to which those illustrations that can be adduced of such tendencies were exceptional. More important, even during the confused period of the 'Wars of the Roses' when loyalties to lords were especially under stress the values of aristocratic society continued to be dominated by a man's moral obligation to remain loyal to his lord. Even in the highly competitive society in East Anglia revealed in the Paston correspondence we find that, when John Paston recommended (2 March 1476) someone to William, lord Hastings, for an appointment in his household, he took care to point out that the duchess of Norfolk had no objection to his entering Hastings's service, 'But that notwithstanding, as I informed your lordship, he is not so retained neither by fee nor promise but that he may let himself loose to do your lordship service when ye will receive him and so will he do.'[173] Thirteen years later the poet Skelton condemned the cowardice of those followers who had done nothing to save their lord, the earl of Northumberland, from his death at the hands of a mob:

> Alas! his gold, his fee, his annual rent,
> Upon that sort was ill-bestowed and spent.[174]

Such standards of conduct were of ancient origin and had not changed in the intervening centuries. They are to be found in the speech in which Wiglaf upbraided his fellows for not going with him to the help of Beowulf: 'I remember that time at which we drank the mead, how in the beer-hall we pledged ourselves to our lord, who gave us the rings, that we should repay him for the war-equipments, the helmets and hard swords if any need like this befell him.'[175] And between the poet of *Beowulf* and Skelton lay the Latin poet of the battle of Bannockburn who wrote, singling out one particular retainer, of the treachery of those who failed to come to the rescue of the earl of Gloucester.[176]

Nevertheless, even in the world of *Beowulf* the loyalties of lordship were in competition with the pressures of self-interest. Like the Anglo-Saxon warrior, a knight or squire in late medieval England joined a retinue to advance himself; but he did so in a society in which the pressures of both loyalty and self-interest were greatly different from those of early Anglo-Saxon England. On the one hand, in many cases the choice of a lord was dictated by a family tradition built up over generations. In such a situation loyalty had been nurtured by the satisfaction felt by generations of a family with their lords' exercise of lordship. On the other hand, the society of late medieval England was one in which loyalty to a lord, even if nurtured by generations of family tradition, was subject to erosion. Unlike the warrior of early Anglo-Saxon England who served in the hope of a grant of land, the late medieval knight was either the owner of an inheritance or, like many squires also, the heir to one. In the last resort he would choose the security of his interests as landowner over his duties to a lord. Moreover, the lordship of late medieval England operated in the context of the authority and institutions of a monarchy. This provided sources of patronage in the form of gifts of lands and revenues from the Crown and also offices at Westminster and in the shires. In time of war lordship operated within an environment which had originally given rise to its values and practices; but in time of peace it became a vehicle of search for royal patronage. The potential for dissatisfaction with a lord's leadership on the part of a follower was no longer confined to war. There was also the larger context of the king's political power. If a king had the character and personality to control and to manipulate the resources of his Crown, no retainer would readily follow his lord in rebellion, especially since the law of treason might deprive him and his family of their inheritance. If the king was weak, the resources of royal patronage might become the prey of baronial factions; and in this situation both an individual's self-interest and the need to protect the inheritance might easily lead to changes of loyalty. It is no coincidence that some of the most impressive changes of allegiance among retainers are found either in the face of royal power or in times of its total collapse.[177]

In late medieval England the oldest source of power available to a lord – the men of his household – was still in use. By the end of the thirteenth century it is clear that the households of great lords were undergoing a structural change. At any one time the group in attendance on the lord would consist partly of officials and servants who were permanently in residence, partly of those who attended for limited periods in response to the lord's summons. Some of these were 'bachelors', others knights and squires retained by indenture of retinue, each such knight and some squires bringing their own followings with them. But the financial costs of maintaining such an enlarged household as well as problems of accommodation must always have imposed limits on a lord's capacity to use these means of expanding his following. In addition, the most effective means of ensuring that a knight or squire would always obey his lord's summons to attend his person was to make an indenture with him for his life, an arrangement which imposed a lasting burden on a lord's landed revenues. It is not surprising, therefore, that in the fourteenth century only Thomas of Lancaster and John of Gaunt appear to have used indentures of retinue on a substantial scale and that in the following century their examples were emulated only by the Percy earls of Northumberland

and (possibly) the Neville earls of Salisbury and Warwick, in additions to William, lord Hastings.

Occasions arose when lords wanted to raise contingents on a scale that greatly exceeded that of the household, even when enlarged by indentured retainers. One might be the need to raise a large contingent for the king's wars. Others might arise from the pressures of national or local politics – the need to impress other lords and their followers in time of parliament or to overawe opposition within the area of a lord's territorial influence. In the last resort a lord might want to raise the standard of rebellion. What information we have about the size of the contingents magnates took to the king's wars or raised for the purpose of their ambitions in national or local politics demonstrates that only a comparatively small proportion of their followings was provided by household members, indentured retainers and the latter's own followers. The raising of substantial forces must always have involved short-term recruitment. In this, to be sure, a lord would rely on permanent followers as recruiting agents, these also including the officials of his estate administration. Through these means men were hired in return for daily wages and grants of livery. In a formal sense such arrangements were an extension of household usages, because it was the wearing of livery that demonstrated attachment to the lord's following. But in practice such grants of livery were a manipulation of one of the ancient practices of the household. and it is equally true that without such methods magnates would not have been able to serve the king effectively in time of war or to assert their political ambitions within the kingdom in time of peace or civil war. Lordship in late medieval England was thus an amalgam of several elements. The lord's permanent household and his indentured retainers were two of these. There can be no doubt that indentures of retinue and annuities were fundamental mechanisms in the extension and maintenance of territorial influence and political connections; but it is equally clear that in the last resort they could not provide the resources of men on which a lord's success might ultimately have to depend.

Notes

1 For an exception see the receiver's account of Sir Humphrey Stafford of Grafton in BL, Add.R., 74171.

2 Their form and content vary considerably. See C. D. Ross and T. B. Pugh, 'Materials for the study of baronial incomes in fifteenth-century England', *Econ. H. R.*, 2nd Ser., vi (1953), 185-94 and R. R. Davies, 'Baronial accounts, incomes and arrears in the later middle ages', *ibid.*, xxi (1968), 211-29.

3 There is, however, an important difference between the manorial official and

the receiver. The former's receipts were checked by the lord's auditors against a rental which set out the rents for which he was responsible. The receipts of the receiver were similarly checked against the acquittances he gave manorial officials. But the auditing of his obligations, as distinct from his actual expenditure, was a more complex problem. The need, therefore, to have a clear statement of the receiver's permanent annual obligations must have been a major reason for the compilation of valors. The nature of the system, however, meant that the primary concern of the auditors was with what was due to the lord. Those who had money due to them from the revenues handled by the receiver occupied a second place in the auditor's concerns.

4 This is, for example, true of the valors of John of Gaunt. See App. II.

5 Baldwin, *Household administration'*, p. 192.

6 Maddicott, *Thomas of Lancaster*, pp. 44–5. The question of the number of squires is, however, ignored.

7 Baldwin, 'Household administration', p. 192 allowed 8 yards of cloth for a knight's robe and 6 yards or less for a squire's. The livery roll of the earl of Devon seventy years later provided 5¾ yards for the earl and each of nine knights while three of the squires were each allocated 4½ yards (BL, Add., R. 64320). It is probably wise to treat these figures with caution, since the totals for the whole listings of knights and squires are crossed out and cannot be reconciled with the individual figures. Even so, it is fair to assume that the amounts allocated to individuals are reliable. To be sure, these figures are less than those assumed by Baldwin. But the margins of difference are not great, especially if we bear in mind that the wealth of the earl of Devon was markedly inferior to that of Lancaster.

8 *Et. CCC.xlv.li.xiij.s.viij.d in. lxv. pannis de colore croceo pro baronibus et miltiibus in estate* . . . (Baldwin, 'Household administration', p. 199).

9 It is unwise to place emphasis on the fact that the household account book of 1318-19 mentions thirty-nine retainers who received two allowances for themselves and their followers (as in Maddicott, *Thomas of Lancaster*, p. 45). This must have happened because their indentures entitled them to benefits on this scale: there must have been others who received less. In any case, an argument based on the presence of these thirty-nine knights and their benefits in account book is weakened by their absence from the lists of those who received letters from the earl in the course of 1318–19.

10 Prestwich, *War, Politics and Finance*, p. 63.

11 The respective figures are: knights, 70; clerks, 15; squires, 28; officials, 15; grooms, 19; archers, 5; minstrels and carpenters, 4.

12 This is supported by the evidence of the wardrobe account which mentions 120 pieces of silk for the lining of the knight's robes and seventy-five lambs' furs for that of the squires' robes. While the robe of a knight may have taken more than one piece of silk, that of a squire is unlikely to have taken more than one lamb's fur.

13 Holmes, *Higher Nobility*, p. 123.

14 See the references in Maddicott, *Thomas of Lancaster*, pp. 43–4.

15 DL 28/1/14; Manchester Reference Library, LI 48/2/3 (a copy made before the condition of the original deteriorated).

16 See Holmes, *Higher Nobility*, pp. 134–42. That printed *ibid.*, pp. 139–40, appears to be based on a collection of documents earlier than the one that formed the basis of the other list (*ibid.*, pp. 134–40). It does not include the retainer of

William, lord Latimer; and in the case of Sir Peter Leybourne it mentions a fee whereas the other list adds a grant of property. There are thus grounds for thinking that earlier the collection of documents was made well before 15 May 1319 (the date of the earl's indenture with lord Latimer).

17 This figure does not include the total of lands and rents worth 1,000 marks a year granted to the earl of Warenne [(*ibid*, p. 134), because this was part of the settlement of the dispute between the two magnates (see Maddicott, *Thomas of Lancaster*, pp. 234–7).

18 *Cf., ibid.*, pp. 46–7.

19 It is assumed that the phrase *pur son service etc*, where it occurs in the surviving texts refers to peace and war, since it is found in the case of William, lord Latimer and two others – Sir Henry Glastonbury and Sir Peter Leybourne – who are mentioned in such terms in the other list.

20 *Cf.*, Maddicott, *Thomas of Lancaster*, p. 47.

21 On the basis of figures suggested *ibid.*, pp. 22–3.

22 For the annual totals, see below, App. II.

23 Only five, amounting to a total of £10 6s 8d, appear to have been at the duke's pleasure.

24 The total includes an increase of twenty marks on a previous grant to Katherine Swynford.

25 Katherine Swynford, £13 6s 8d; Sir Richard Scrope, £40; Sir Walter Blount, £66 13s 4d; and Sir Walter Beauchamp and Sir Richard Burley £66 13s 4d each. There were also nine smaller annuities, totalling £26 16s 8d.

26 The only possible rival in the case of earl Thomas – the Clare earl of Gloucester – died at the battle of Bannockburn in 1314, his estates eventually being divided between three co-heirs.

27 BL, Addit. R., 64320.

28 1379–80 (BL, Addit. R., 64317); 1381–82 (Devon RO. CR 543); 1388–89 (*ibid.*, CR 500); 1396–97 (BL, Addit. R., 64321); 1398–99 (*ibid.*, 64322); and 1405–6 (Devon RO, CR 536). All these related to the estates in Devon and Cornwall. In addition there is an incomplete account for Cornwall for 1391–92 (*ibid.*, CR 534).

29 E.g., £24 to the earl's steward in Devon 'in full payment of his pension' in 1405–6. In the same year the receiver's fee was described as his 'pension'.

30 For 1396–97 it is possible to construct a total of £38 6s 8d for five annual payments; but one of these – £26 13s 4d to John Prestcot – was given no description, only half being paid.

31 Prestwich, *War, Politics and Finance*, p. 63.

32 Phillips, *Aymer de Valence*, p. 254.

33 Nicholas Leybourne and his brother Robert (Prestwich, *War, Politics and Finance*, p. 63). But the accounts refer to these payments as *pro annua firma ei debita ad terminum vite per scriptum comitis* in 1304–5. Such language, especially in view of the word *firma*, by no means necessarily implies a contract of service (*Two 'Compoti' of the Lancashire and Cheshire Manors of Henry de Lacy, earl of Lincoln, XXIV and XXIII Edward I*, ed. P. A. Lyons (Chetham Soc., cii, Manchester, 1884, p. 67).

34 Phillips, *Aymer de Valence*, pp. 295–311.

35 BL, Egerton R. 8724, m. 6.

36 See the references in Maddicott, *Thomas of Lancaster*, pp. 43–4.

37　*CPR, 1399–1401*, p. 117. See above, pp. 86–7. .

38　*CPR, 1396–99*, p. 255. See above, p. 86. For several manors granted for life by the earl see *Cal Inq.Misc.*, vi, 119, 122, 136, 214.

39　See above, p. 86 for indentures that appear from confirmations made before the earl's forfeiture.

40　BL, Add. MS. 40859A.

41　Clun, 1386–87 (Shropshire RO, 5521A/8); Holt, 1387–88 (PRO, SC6/1234/5); Oswestry, 1394–95 (Shrewsbury Public Library, Craven Collection 8391); Clun, 1394–95 (*ibid*, 8392).

42　BL, Egerton R., 8770.

43　*CPR, 1381–85*, pp. 99 (Sir John Bromwich), 116 (Walter Bromwich) and 119 (Sir Henry Conway), the last being made only four months before the earl's death. For discussion of the indentures, see above pp. 85–6.

44　*CPR, 1401–5*, p. 229.

45　PRO, SC11/23. For some details see Holmes, *Higher Nobility*, pp. 62–3.

46　The surviving records do not deal with the earl's Irish estates. But since he died in an effort to restore order as the king's lieutenant, it is highly unlikely that he enjoyed much in the way of revenues there or that these estates were charged with fees and annuities.

47　Those made in tail to the earl's brother Edmund and 100 marks to Sir Henry Percy (Hotspur) who was married to the earl's sister.

48　The accounts of a receiver-general and of the receiver of the honour of Clare for 1398–99 (PRO, SC6/1112/6 and 8) contain nothing to contradict this calculation.

49　*CPR, 1399–1401*, pp. 7, 28, 193, 224–5, 234; *Ibid.*, *1405–8*, p. 29. In one case – Sir Thomas Clinton – there was the further grant of an annuity of twenty marks for the lives of him and his wife after the death of the earl's grandmother (who held part of his inheritance) (*ibid.*, 1399–1401, p. 28). In the case of Sir Robert Legh who was a 'bachelor', there was to be an additional ten marks once the earl's inheritance was increased (*ibid.*, 1405–8, p. 29).

50　*Ibid.*, *1399–1401*, pp. 7, 39, 50, 91, 105, 109, 121, 126, 133, 145, 170, 191, 200, 220, 223–5, 234, 241, 259, 263, 273, 294, 325, 330, 335. Two manors were also granted for life (*ibid.*, pp. 160, 273). It is worth noting that, of the total of £280, £192 consisted of annuities granted in the period February 1396–October 1398. Annuities totalling just over £80 were granted in September–October 1398, presumably being intended to build up loyalty to his interests and those of his heir during the life-exile to which he had been sentenced by Richard II. The above total does not include annuities totalling £45 that had been granted to his grandmother, Margaret, countess Marshal (*ibid.*, 1399–1401, pp. 132, 145, 152, 156, 160, 182, 278).

51　There is a receiver-general's account for 1399–1400 (BL, MS. Harley 892). But this relates to the period of the earl's exile and the picture it gives of income must be far from complete.

52　For the father's see *CPR, 1399–1401*, p. 244 and for the rest *ibid.*, pp. 182–3, 189, 263. Another of his father's was confirmed by Richard II (*ibid.*, 1381–85, p. 181).

53　*Ibid.*, *1399–1401*, pp. 244, 255.

54　For a full discussion see Bean, *Percy Estates*, pp. 85–98.

55 *Ibid.*, p. 91.
56 *Ibid.*, p. 89.
57 *Ibid.*, p. 91.
58 *Ibid.*, p. 88.
59 R. L. Storey, 'The wardens of the marches of England towards Scotland, 1377–1489', *EHR*, lxxii, 613–4.
60 For the extent of such profits, see Bean, *Percy Estates*, pp. 105–7.
61 The material for the Stafford earl (later duke) of Buckingham confirms this. In particular, an examination of two payments in the valors for 1441–42 and 1447–48 (Staffordshire RO, D. 641/1/2/17; Longleat MS. 6410) and the available references to his indentured retainers (Rawcliffes, *Staffords*, pp. 232–8) indicate that by no means all the fees paid to indentured retainers were described in the financial records in precise terms that make this clear.
62 Bean, *Percy Estates*, pp. 109–10.
63 *Ibid.*, pp. 130–31.
64 *Ibid.*, pp. 128–30.
65 Rawcliffe, *Staffords*, pp. 232–5, 238–40.
66 Staffordshire RO, D. 641/1/2/17 (dorse).
67 One hundred pounds to the duchess of Buckingham has been deducted. The duke's half-brother, John Bourchier, is included.
68 Longleat MS. 6410. There is, however, no list of names with their offices.
69 Rawcliffe, *Staffords*, p. 75.
70 *Ibid.*, pp. 73–4, 238–40.
71 This total excludes Buckingham's eldest son.
72 Precise totals of those retained by indentures are not possible, since the terms of some grants are unknown. But those definitely retained by indentures for service in peace and war consisted of one peer, three knights and one squire, their fees totalling £63 6s 8d (if we exclude a physician).
73 *Ibid.*, p. 76.
74 PRO, SC11/818.
75 There was also a total of rents and farms released to tenants, amounting to £10 13s 3d.
76 BL, Egerton R., 8782.
77 PRO, SC 6/1113/10. This does not include £100 to his sister, the countess of Eu. Payments under letters of warrant involved another £25 10s 0d paid to Sir William Oldhall in recompense for lands granted him in Gloucestershire. Arrears were also paid of annuities from the preceeding year.
78 £66 13s 4d to Sir John Popham.
79 PRO, SC6/1113/11; BL, Egerton R., 8784.
80 See above, p. 102.
81 J. M. W. Bean, 'The financial position of Richard, Duke of York', *War and Government*, p. 197, n. 79.
82 PRO, SC6/1122/3. There was an annual fee (without further description) of £5; in the case of another of 40s only half was paid because the man was dead. The fees of lawyers retained as counsel amounted to £23.
83 Pollard, 'Salisbury retainers', p. 55.
84 For a full discussion see *ibid.*, pp. 57–66. the text is printed on pp. 66–8. The Yorkshire receiver's account of the earl of Warwick is PRO, SC6/1085/20.

85 An annuity of £20 paid to the earl's brother William, lord Faucomberg, is not included. The statement that the annuity and retaining fees were 'granted *per litteras dormientes* (the same as letters close)' is inaccurate in several respects. Annuities were generally granted by charter or letters patent, and retainers' fees by indentures. *Littere dormientes* were warrants for payments which, once issued and until countermanded, imposed on the receiver the obligation to make payments at specified times. In other words, they were 'standing orders'. The term is employed in the receivers' accounts of other magnates in this period – for example, those of the duke of Buckingham.

86 In addition to his retaining fee, of £13 6s 8d (which included his fee as steward of Richmondshire) Sir John Conyers had been granted a farm in the manor of Crakell worth £6 1S 4d a year.

87 Richard Pigot, sergeant at law, was retained *de consilio* at £2 a year and for service in peace and war for £4.

88 *Cf.,* Pollard, 'Salisbury retainers, p. 64, where the absence of the names of Warwick's retainers from the list of his father's is not taken into account.

89 This is not noted *ibid.,* pp. 65–5.

90 Warworth, *Chronicle,* p. 4.

91 See C. D. Ross, *The Estates and Finances of Richard Beauchamp, Earl of Warwick* (Dugdale Soc., Occasional Papers, no. 12, Oxford, 1956), which, however, does not use the receivers' accounts in BL, Egerton R. 8772–3.

92 There was also the fee of one squire. It is not possible to assume that this figure equalled the total of the annual fees owèd to these retainers, since in some cases the account does not mention the amount of the annual fee.

93 Ross (*op. cit.,* pp. 15–16), which, however, includes yeomen.

94 Grants for manors for life too are included.

95 Arundel Castle Muniments, A. 1642.

96 Although written in a good hand on a roll of several membranes, this document may well have been a draft, since no totals are provided under the respective headings.

97 The amount actually paid was £17 6s 8d less, one fee of £6 13s 4d being halved as result of the retainer's death midyear.

98 PRO, E. 163/7/3/2/2, cited in *Fifteenth-century England,* p. 102.

99 BL, Egerton R. 8779.

100 PRO, SC/1003/22.

101 *The Grey of Ruthin Valor,* ed. R. I. Jack (Sydney, 1965), pp. 53–4 and 56.

102 This was the account of the receiver-general of the earl of Warwick in 1409–10 where the fee of one squire was paid *in quaterno hospicii forinseci* (BL, Egerton R., 8772).

103 See above, p. 130.

104 See Rawcliffe, *Staffords,* pp. 195–8, a list which relies on estate valors to a substantial extent. A list of members of the household, ranked under the headings of their offices with their annual fees, is written on the dorse of the valor of the estates of the duke of Buckingham in 1441–42 (Staffs. RO, D. 641/1/2/17).

105 For what follows see *Fifteenth-century England,* pp. 101–2.

106 Maddicott, *Thomas of Lancaster,* p. 38.

107 These details are taken from four valors (PRO, DL 29/728/11987–90). Only one of these, however, includes totals for one year in both north and south parts.

The evidence of these documents can be supplemented from the register of the Lancastrian chancery which began with the accession of duke Henry to the throne. This contains a list of warrants directed to several receivers, each providing the name of the knight or squire concerned and the amount of the payment for the services of himself and his retinue (*ibid.*, DL42/15/ff.70–1). Most of these warrants and the greater part of the total involved related to the northern states. But it is unlikely that duke Henry called on or received the services of southern retainers to the same extent as those in the north. His journey from Yorkshire to Westminster lay largely through the north and the Midlands, touching only on the fringes of the West Country. He did move along the Marches of Wales and, therefore, may have called on retainers residing in this region and paid from Lancastrian lordships in Wales. But this group of retainers had always been small in comparison with those from other areas of Lancastrian power. For these reasons it is unlikely that, if our information on this matter from all sources was totally complete, the estimate of £3,000 would have to be revised upwards very much.

108 See the table in Somerville, *Duchy*, p. 94.

110 *Cf.* below, p. 171.

111 We have scarcely any information about the extent to which fees and annuities were paid from the landed revenues of the gentry. The information we have about the Vernons of Derbyshire indicates that such payments were hardly a serious drain on their resources and the individual payments were below the level of those paid by magnates (S. M. Wright, *The Derbyshire Gentry in the Fifteenth Century* (Publications of the Derbyshire Record Society, viii, Chesterfield, 1983), pp. 249–50).

112 H. L. Grey, 'Incomes from land in England in 1436', *EHR*, xlix (1934), 630. For criticisms see T. B. Pugh and C. D. Ross, 'The English baronage and the income tax of 1436', *BIHR*, xxvi (1953), esp. 13–4. There is, in fact, good reason to believe that the 1436 assessments underrate both the number of gentry and the total of their landed incomes. But, while those of the income tax of 1412 when they survive for individual counties give a more reliable picture, it is not possible to provide kingdom-wide comparisons. See my article, 'The income taxes of fifteenth century England', forthcoming. For useful comments on the role of fees and annuities in the incomes of some Warwickshire gentry, see Carpenter, 'Beauchamp affinity', p. 519.

113 *Cf.* Saul, *Gloucestershire Gentry*, p. 98, where it is stated that 'it may be fair to guess that nearer two-thirds than one half of the gentry were retained' in fourteenth-century Gloucestershire. The information on which this estimate is based, however, does not distinguish between retaining for life and that for limited periods. Elsewhere (*ibid.*, p. 102), however, Saul concludes that 'there were numerous unattached gentry'.

114 *Paston Papers*, ii, 37 (no. 451); *Paston Letters*, ii, 148.

115 *Paston Letters*, iii, 75.

116 *Paston Papers*, ii, 532 (no. 883); *Paston Letters*, iii, 125.

117 Rawcliffe, *Staffords*, pp. 68–9. Seventeen squires and gentlemen, twelve senior and thirty-nine lesser yeomen, thirty-eight pages and one herald, apart from waiting women, chaplains and clerical staff (*ibid.*).

118 *Documents illustrating the Crisis of 1297–98 in England*, ed. M. Prestwich (Camden 4th Ser., xxiv, London, 1980), pp. 157–8 (no. 154).

119 Denholm-Young, *Seignorial Administration*, pp. 167–8, discussed above, pp. 65 seq.

120 PRO, DL28/1/14; Manchester Reference Library, MS. LI/48/2/3 (transcript).

121 See above, pp. 156–7.

122 *Rot. Parl.*, v, 348.

123 See below, pp. Ch. VI, *passim.*

124 *Paston Letters*, iv, 279.

125 *Paston Papers*, i, 400 (no. 240); *Paston Letters*, v, 29.

126 *Plumpton Corr.*, Introd., liv–v.

127 *Paston Letters*, ii, 297.

128 *Paston Papers*, i, 80 (no. 48); *Paston Letters*, ii, 313.

129 *Paston Papers*, i, 545 (no. 351); *Paston Letters*, v, 32.

130 *Paston Letters*, ii, 297.

131 J. Rous, *Historia Regum Angliae*, ed. T. Hearne (Oxford, 1745), p. 216.

132 The 'articles' of 1461 did, however, refer to 'livery of sign, mark token of company' (see below, p. 211).

133 *Ibid.*

134 *Paston Papers*, i, 545 (no. 333); *Paston Letters*, v, 32–3.

135 The duchy of Lancaster during the time of John of Gaunt provides the fullest available body of information, for which see Somerville, *Duchy*, pp. 90–110 and 363–84. For the dukes of Buckingham, see Rawcliffe, *Staffords*, pp. 45–65 and 195–217, and for the Beauchamp earls of Warwick Carpenter, 'Beauchamp affinity', *parsim.*

136 E.g., *JGRA*, i, 98, 119, 150, 160, 175–6, 182, 184, 187, 201–2, 208–10, 213, 217–8, 220–1, 225–7, 229, 231–4, 238, 240, 243–4, 246, 255, 257, 258–62 (nos, 225, 279, 347, 381, 427, 443, 452, 460, 500, 503, 521–2, 527–29, 543, 560, 565, 570, 573, 586–7, 591, 596, 603, 606–7, 609, 613, 626, 636, 650, 652, 656, 662, 696, 702, 708, 712, 717, 721, 724–5); *JGRB*, 11, 301, 303–5, 308, 310, 312, (nos. 958, 965, 967, 970, 975, 987, 998, 1004, 1007–8). The offices concerned varied considerably in importance, but *JGRA*, i, nos. 225, 279, 347 involved the constableships of castles.

137 This calculation is based on the valors and other materials discussed in App. II. See also Somerville, *Duchy*, pp. 91–2.

138 PRO, SC11/818.

139 Bean, *Percy Estates*, p. 129.

140 Sir John d'Ipre the elder (App. II, no. 2; Somerville, *Duchy*, p. 372); Sir Walter Urswick (App. III, no. 16; *JGRA*, i, no. 426); (almost certainly) Sir Richard Burley (App. III, no. 19; *JGBR*, i, no. 565). It is quite possible that this was also the case for Sir William Hawley (App. III, no. 35; *JGRB*, i, no. 80) and Sir Walter Hungerford (for whom see below, note 160).

141 Sir Thomas Ilderton (App. III, no. 12; *JGRB*, i, no. 264); Sir Thomas Travers (App. III, no. 17; Somerville, *Duchy*, p. 380). The case of Sir Walter Blount is uncertain (App. III, no. 27; *JGRA*, i, no. 382). It is quite likely that the lists provided in this and the preceding footnote could be considerably extended if more registers had survived.

142 E.g., the case of Sir John Conyers where the Yorkshire receiver's account of Richard, earl of Warwick, in 1464–65 does not distinguish between his fee as steward of Richmondshire held for life and that for his retainer in peace and war (PRO, SC6/1085/20). See also the interesting example of the master forester of the earl marshal cited above, note 97.

143 Bean, *Percy Estates*, p. 96.

144 *Paston Letters*, ii, 298.

145 See *CPR, 1401–5*, p. 253 for the case of a steward of the lordship of Ellesmere who compelled the tenants to follow him against the king in the Shrewsbury campaign of 1403. It is worth noting that the lord (Strange of Knockyn) was a minor at the time.

146 Bean, *Percy Estates*, pp. 56–7 and references cited.

147 See T. P. Ellis, *Welsh Tribal Law and Custom in the Middle Ages* (2 vols., Oxford, 1926), i, pp. 339–411. *Cf.*, however, *The Survey of the Honour of Denbigh, 1334*, ed. P. Vinogradoff and F. Morgan (London, 1914), p. lxxiii, where the absence of date relating to military service is stressed. But this argument is not convincing since in the case of one entry (*ibid.*, p. 295) it is explicitly stated that tenants 'will go with the lord in the army of the lord if the lord wished (*si dominus voluerit*)'. This aspect of the law and custom of the March is not discussed by R. R. Davies, *Lordship and Society in the March of Wales, 1282–1400* (Oxford, 1978).

148 *The Extent of Chirkland*, ed. G. P. Jones (London, 1933), pp. xxvii–viii, 66–7; *The First Extent of Bromfield and Yale, A.D. 1315*, ed. T. P. Ellis (Cymmrodorion Record Ser., xi, London, 1924), pp. 29–30, 58, 60, *et al*; BL, Addit. MS. 10013, ff. 21v, 57, 69v, 131, 97, 114v, 123, 131, 151v, 160, 168.

149 *Extent of Chirkland*, pp. 66–7.

150 PRO, E 40/4878; *CAD*, iii, 116 (A4878). If war broke out in Wales, Rees was discharged from paying his rent for as long as he was prevented from receiving the issues of the lands leased to him.

151 For some discussion of military service from tenants in the Tudor period see L. Boynton, *The Elizabethan Militia, 1558–1638* (London, 1967), pp. 31–3; Cooper, *Land, Men and Beliefs*, pp. 91–3.

152 It is tempting to speculate whether a desire to create a reservoir of military service from his tenants lay behind the policy under which the fifth Percy earl of Northumberland introduced the customs of his Cumberland estates into those in Northumberland and Yorkshire (Bean, *Percy Estates*, pp. 56–64). To be sure, this effort can be quite satisfactorily explained in terms of a heightened interest in revenues from entry fines. But what we know of the earl's relations with the Crown suggest that he may have been anxious to ensure that he was able to supply the king's military demands in time of need and may even have seen potential political advantages in a military relationship with the peasants on his estates. *Cf.* M. E. James, *A Tudor Magnate and the Tudor State. Henry, Fifth Earl of Northumberland* (York, 1966).

153 The details given by Boynton (*op. cit.*, p. 32), especially the views of Bacon cited there, suggest that the practice was by no means a national one. But Cooper, *Land, Men and Beliefs*, p. 92, suggests that 'such practices were common in the first half of the century'. The details he provides suggest, however, that while the lords involved were not 'ancient feudal magnates (*ibid.*, p. 93), they were all anxious to rise in royal favour through service in war.

154 See above, p. 94.

155 *CPR, 1401–5*, p. 253.

156 *Plumpton Corr.*, Introd., pp. liv–v.

157 Davies, *op. cit.*, p. 68.

158 Maddicott, *Thomas of Lancaster*, pp. 295–7.

159 Phillip, *Aymer de Valence*, pp. 261–7.

160 He is entered ninth among the knights in the list of 1379–86 (*JGRB*, i, 7), but his indenture was not entered in the register covering the years 1372–76. He was, therefore, retained either before 1372 or between 1376 and 1379. His son was also in the same list (*ibid.*, i, 7). The father had been appointed chief steward and surveyor of all Gaunt's lands in Wales and twelve shires in the south of England in August 1372 (*ibid.*, i, 269). There is circumstantial evidence to argue that his connection with Gaunt must have preceded this appointment (Roskell, *Parliament and Politics*, ii, pp. 27–8). He was described as a 'bachelor' in February 1380 (*JGRB*, i, 61 [no. 180]).

161 Roskell, *Parliament and Politics*, ii, 26, citing *CPR, 1364–67*, p. 169.

162 Rawcliffe, *Staffords*, p. 240.

163 McFarlane, *Nobility*, pp. 108–9, citing BL, Add. MS., 74168.

164 *Ibid.*, 74171.

165 *Ibid.*, Add. R., 74174.

166 *CPR, 1396–99*, pp. 534–71. For further details see below, p. 228, note 45.

167 Lewis, 'Gaunt indentures, pp. 90–112.

168 See above, p. 93. Both squires had taken oaths on the Gospels to keep the promises they had made.

169 *Stonor Letters*, ii, 161. This statement has been described as 'highly ambiguous', it being suggested that it applied to Hasting's indentured retainers rather than his household men (C. D. Ross, *Richard III* [London, Berkeley, Los Angeles, 1981], p. 111, note 17). But it is difficult to believe that contemporaries in such circumstances were so legalistic as to employ a distinction between indentured retainers and the household.

170 The terms of the indenture with Salisbury clearly indicate this. In the event of Hungerford's inability to perform the duties of his stewardship on reasonable grounds, he was to continue to receive his annual fee and *'soit devers nous et de nostre consail et avisant es busoignes que nous touchent,'* (PRO, C66/272/m. 22). The summary in *CPR, 1364–67*, p. 169 is less explicit.

171 Phillip, *Aymer de Valence*, pp. 263–4.

172 Carpenter, 'Beauchamp affinity', p. 518; McFarlane, *Collected Essays*, p. 251.

173 *Paston Papers*, i, 600–1.

174 John Skelton, *The Complete Poems*, ed. P. Henderson (2nd edn., London, Toronto, 1948), p. 7.

175 *Beowulf*, trans., J. R. Clark Hall, new edn., revised by C. L. Wren (London, Toronto, 1948), p. 7.

176 *The Political Songs of England, from the Reign of John to that of Edward II*, ed. T. Wright (Camden Soc., Ser. I, vi, London, 1839), pp. 263–5.

176 For details of such consequences during a period of collapse in royal authority – the so-called 'Wars of the Roses' – see McFarlane, *Collected Essays*, pp. 244 seq.

VI

The policy of the Crown,
1390–1504

For the kings of late medieval England the retinues of their great subjects were sources of both power and danger. It was the magnates' retinues that provided leadership in the form of lords, knights and squires for the king's wars and at the same time the system through which archers and other infantry were raised. Retinues could, however, perform similar functions in time of rebellion; and even in time of peace the good lordship that a retainer expected from his lord could lead to his support of lawlessness and abuses in the administration of justice, since a lord might use his retinue to manipulate the procedures of the common law in the regions of his territorial influence and even to overawe his opponents with the threat of force. 'Maintenance' – the effort to influence the outcome of litigation in a court of law – and 'embracery' – the intimidation of a jury – were rooted in the procedures of the common law in late medieval England. The final resolution of both civil and criminal cases depended on the verdicts of juries, whether convened by the sheriff in response to a writ from Westminster or empanelled by justices of *nisi prius* or oyer and terminer and gaol delivery. Moreover, by the middle of the fourteenth century the system of local justice had developed in a direction that especially favoured the spread of 'maintenance' – the evolution of the justices of the peace. These local gentry either had ties to the local magnates in the form of retaining fees, offices or traditions of family connection or, if no such ties existed, might find themselves under pressure to exercise their duties in the interests of a powerful lord. In this situation effective government in the shires required constant vigilance. In the hands of a effective king legislation promulgated in parliament could provide a means of defining and publicising methods of control. But in late medieval England a king's authority depended on a balance of mutual respect between him and his leading subjects. In this the vigour of his personality and the determination to enforce his will were powerful elements; but his government had also to involve an awareness of the resources of his leading subjects. Several aspects of royal authority played their part in the achievement of this balance of power. One was the policy of the Crown towards the maintenance of retinues by the magnates. Efforts to prevent the abuse of local power to which these resources lent themselves had to go hand in hand with a recognition that by these means the great men of the realm could provide men for the king's wars.[1]

(i) 1390–1461

From the late thirteenth century the Crown in parliament had legislated against 'maintenance'. The series of statutes began in 1275,[2] and further efforts followed in the course of Edward I's reign. There can be no doubt that the conflict between Edward II and the 'Ordainers', the confrontations with Thomas of Lancaster and then the struggle over the ambitions of the Despensers explain the absence of parliamentary legislation in the years between the death of Edward I and the accession of Edward III. But the parliamentary campaign was renewed with another statute in 1327.[3] It is reasonable to infer both from this, and a parliamentary petition against retaining *de pace* in 1330,[4] that royal authority in the shires had weakened in the course of the previous reign and 'maintenance' had become a more serious problem. A statute of 1330 moved from prohibition of the practice to a structure of control, giving full powers to the justices of *nisi prius* and oyer and terminer and gaol delivery, acting on their own initiative as well as in response to complaints.[5] As yet, however, although indentures of retinue, annuities and liveries had existed for more than a century, none of the parliamentary legislation had made any specific references to these practices. From the beginning interference by the magnates in the administration of justice had been singled out but there was no mention of their methods or the sources of their power. It was only in the reign of Richard II that such precision developed.

One reason for the appearance of a parliamentary campaign against the evils of retaining in the last two decades of the fourteenth century lies in the existence of the office of justice of the peace.[6] Though its beginnings can be traced back earlier, it was the reign of Edward III that witnessed the clear emergence of the commissions of the peace that were the basis of the authority of the local justice. In the course of its evolution a struggle for control of this system between the magnates and the gentry ended in

the victory of the knightly class. By the time this had happened the gentry
who sat in the Commons in time of parliament were ready to add grievances
over the administration of justice in the shires to those fuelled by taxation
and incompetence in the prosecution of the war in France. Their readiness
to speak out against the abuse of power by the magnates can be more
readily understood in the light of our knowledge of the nature of the
retinues of the time. The available evidence indicates that no magnate had
retained for life on anything approaching the scale of John of Gaunt and
that only a minority of knights and squires could have been retained for
life, or received annuities, over the whole kingdom. Present knowledge of
the realities of politics and the structure of the upper levels of landed society
in late medieval England presents a picture of a substantial 'independent
gentry'.[7] One can suspect, but not prove, however, its role in earlier legislation against 'maintenance', especially in the statutes of 1327 and 1330,
since these followed two decades in which civil war, when not in existence,
was constantly threatened. There can certainly be no doubt that the existence of this 'independent gentry' is a major part of the explanation for
the magnates' failure to take control of the commissions of the peace. In
the reign of Richard II its readiness to identify the causes of 'maintenance'
led to a campaign in the Commons against 'livery'.

This campaign began with a statute of 1377 which for the first time
identified the evils of 'livery' by forbidding the granting of caps or other
uniforms for the maintenance of quarrels or confederacies but it did not
identify the lords of the realm as perpetrators of such practices.[8] Rather,
the statute was aimed at their men. In 1384, however, the Commons complained only about the activities of the liveried retainers of the great lords.[9]
This had no effect. A more strongly worded complaint was made in the
Cambridge parliament of 1388 about the interference of the followers of
great lords in the workings of justice.[10] At this point, in fact, the political
situation was more favourable to such efforts on the part of the Commons.
The king had survived the attempt of the Lords Appellant to wrest authority completely from him, if not dethrone him altogether, and was actively
seeking means of embarrassing the great lords.[11] The regime of the Appellants was discredited by the defeat by the Scots at Otterburn. And any
complaints about 'livery' by the Commons were palpably not mere rhetoric,
since the brief warfare of 1387 and the ensuing struggle for power at
Westminster had encouraged lawlessness throughout the realm. One of the
most notorious incidents occurred when this parliament was sitting and
involved as its leader a squire of the earl of Derby.[12] Despite an offer by
the lords to punish offenders and not give liveries to known malefactors,

the Commons demanded the outright abolition of all liveries. The demands of the Commons, in fact, had given the king part of the programme for the improvement of justice which was one element in his justification for the resumption of his authority in May 1389. He himself had responded to the Commons' demands by offering to cancel his own grants of livery; and, while he did not intervene openly against the lords, this initiative resulted in a commitment by them to produce some sort of reform by means of discussions between the king and his council.[13]

The confrontation between lords and Commons was renewed in the parliament of January 1390. In his account of this parliament the St Albans chronicler Thomas Walsingham began with a summary of a debate in which the Commons complained of the absence of the promised reform.[14] The lords eventually withdrew from a position of total refusal to accept any change in the law and agreed that livery should be limited to those retained for life by indenture and, in the case of yeomen and archers, to those who permanently resided in their lords' households. But even this concession did not satisfy the Commons who in another petition demanded that liveries should be confined to household servants, kinsmen and officials.[15] Their agitation in this area was, in fact, only part of a larger body of grievances over the administration of justice, including the ease with which murderers were pardoned.[16]

From these events reform did emerge, presumably because it was clear that, if nothing was done, the Commons would renew their campaign and also because it was in the king's interest to curtail the power of the lords. On 12 May 1390 a proclamation was issued concerning grants of liveries by lords. Professor Storey has demonstrated that, although this was a reform which emerged from the parliament of 1390, it was not a statute in the sense of an enactment made in parliament 'at the request' or 'with the assent of' the Commons.[17] Nor is there any evidence that it emerged from a meeting of the great council. To all intents and purposes, the ordinance adopted the concession made by the lords in the parliament preceding.[18] First, it aimed at some measure of control by clearly defining the status of those who alone could have the right to give liveries. No prelate or simple knight[19] or squire was allowed to do so. Second, dukes, earls, barons and 'bannerets' were forbidden to grant 'livery of company' unless it was given to a knight or squire retained for life in peace and war by indenture or serving as a member of his household. Third, such lords were forbidden to give livery to anyone of the rank of squire unless the recipient was 'a familiar abiding in the household'. Both the preamble and the enacting clause of the ordinance show clearly that it was conceived in response to complaints about the prevalence of 'maintenance'. This practice was expressly forbidden: in company with the rest of the king's subjects lords were enjoined to desist from it and were also commanded to eject 'maintainers' from their retinues. Precise penalties for breach of the ordinance were not laid down; but offenders were threatened with 'imprisonment, fine and ransom or being punished in other manner as we and our council may be advised'.

The dethronement of this piece of lawmaking from its previous status as a statute helps to explain why it left no records of prosecutions in its wake.[20] In 1393 the Commons complained that it was disregarded. They petitioned that the justices of assize and of the peace should have authority to inquire into the wearing of liveries and to punish those who had worn them against the law.[21] In effect, they regarded the ordinance as having the force of law and made requests intended to repair an obvious defect in it – the absence of definite procedures for enforcement at the local level. The king agreed to the Commons' petition. Although no statute has survived, one would appear to have been promulgated, since in 1397 another petition of grievances referred to the failure to enforce it.[22] If, indeed, efforts at enforcement had been made,[23] they might well have run into a problem of legal interpretation, since the terms of the ordinance of 1390 (re-enacted, presumably in the status of 1393) employed a dichotomy between those retained for life by indenture of retinue, on the one hand, and members of the household, on the other, that was difficult to maintain in the case of squires. A squire so retained was forbidden to wear livery. But what was the position when he joined the household on his lord's summons and during the time he remained there? The terms of statutes promulgated in 1393 and 1397 indicate this, since they forbade the wearing of livery by anyone below the rank of squire unless he was *continually* resident in his lord's household, implying that squires might wear it during periods of temporary residence.[24] There is, however, no evidence that this issue was ventilated.

In fact, the ordinance of 1390 and (presumably) the statute of 1393, were political ploys on the part of a king who had turned the deepfelt discontent of the Commons over the contribution of livery to the decay of justice in the realm into a instrument for the restoration and maintenance of his own authority. The king himself was not bound by the statute; and from October 1390 a form of livery – the badge of the white hart – was one of the means by which he was building up his own following, particularly in Cheshire.[25] The two ancillary statutes of 1393 and 1397 which forbade the granting of livery to anyone below the rank of squire who was

not continually resident in a lord's household had the indirect effect of
bolstering royal power, since they belong to years when the king was building up his private army of Cheshire archers. At the same time there was
one magnate in the realm who would suffer markedly less than any other
if efforts were made to enforce recent legislation – John of Gaunt. His
financial resources enabled him to maintain a retinue of knights retained
by indenture for peace and for war that dwarfed all other retinues save,
possibly, the king's.[26] That apart, he had a larger group of household officials and servants than other magnates. Indeed, on the basis of the available
evidence it is fair to state that Gaunt's total following may well have been
larger than that of all other dukes and earls combined. To be sure, these
are considerations that have to be examined at two levels – that of legal
interpretation and that of political realities. In the case of the former, it
must be stressed that a large portion of Gaunt's retinue consisted of squires
who were forbidden to wear livery under the legislation of 1390 and 1393.
But, as we have seen, there are grounds for believing that they were permitted to do so while serving for periods of duty in his household. In terms
of the realities of the political situation in the kingdom it is reasonable to
assume that Gaunt would have followed this interpretation. It is more than
difficult to conceive of the king's uncle and the most powerful magnate in
the realm being prosecuted for breaches of the law against liveries.
Moreover, it is likely that Gaunt would have benefited from the legislation
of 1390–93 because of its effects on other magnates and the possibility
that they would be discouraged from granting liveries and engaging in
unauthorised retaining, a circumstance that could only enhance the comparative dimensions of his retinue. To be sure, Gaunt had intervened to
put down the Commons in 1384 with the assertion that the punishment
of offenders who wore liveries should be left to their lords.[27] But the situation had got out of hand during his absence from the kingdom between
1385 and 1389. In any event, there can be no doubt that he suffered less
than any other magnate from any discouragements against retaining and
liveries created by the legislation of 1390–93.

The first parliament of Gaunt's son and heir, Henry IV, saw a wide-rang-
ing attempt at legislation which remained the basis of the law for the rest
of the Lancastrian period.[28] A statute was promulgated at the end of the
parliament of October 1399 which had two main bodies of provisions.
One was concerned with the prohibition of liveries throughout the kingdom. In its first clause the statute forbade any lord to give his livery to
any knight, squire or yeoman. But this was qualified, after a series of clauses
dealing with the king, by one under which lords of any condition, tem-

poral or spiritual, were forbidden to give livery of cloth except to 'their household men *(menielx)* and officers and those who are of their council' of either the civil or the common law. In its second body of provisions the statute specifically defined the king's authority to give livery. He was authorised to grant it to any of the temporal lords he chose and to those knights and squires who were members of his household or were retained by him and drew an annual fee for their lives. In this language the statute echoes that of the ordinance of 1390 and (presumably) that of the statute of 1393. In a sense, therefore, the king put himself under the terms of earlier legislation by accepting a definition of his own right to give liveries. Two further clauses reinforce this interpretation. Those who held livery of the king were forbidden to wear their liveries in the areas or shires where they resided or elsewhere in the realm without the king's presence, a proviso that simultaneously strengthened the king's ability to control his retainers and sought to avoid abuses of local authority by means of the wearing of the king's livery. And the *valettus* called 'yoman' was singled out in a clause which explicitly forbade him to wear livery granted by anyone, including the king, on pain of imprisonment and ransom at the king's will. Lords who gave liveries in breach of the statute were to be fined at the king's will, while knights or squires who received them were to forfeit them together with any fees. For the first time procedures against unlawful liveries were placed clearly within the jurisdiction of the Court of King's Bench. For the first time also there was some recognition that the granting of liveries could not be entirely separated from the needs of war and defence. Those holding the offices of constable and marshal of England were given authority for their retinues to wear ther liveries in time of war on the frontiers and marches of the realm and those lords who went overseas on war campaigns were given the same permission.

It is unfortunate in the case of this statute that we are not able to rely, as in the case of the ordinance of 1390, on background information supplied by the chroniclers. It is thus impossible to claim with entire confidence that in promulgating the statute of 1399 the government of Henry IV was responding to complaints from the Commons. But in any event the gentry's concerns about 'maintenance' were well enough known; and it was in the interests of a usurper king to appear sympathetic on such issues. It was equally in his interest to prevent lawlessness that might well give opportunities to magnates bent on rebellion. There is solid evidence of the king's awareness of this. On 23 April 1400 the mayor and sheriffs of London were ordered to proclaim the statute and to arrest all yeomen whom they found in breach of it and commit them to prison.[29] Efforts at enforcement were also made in the north of England in the summer of 1404, probably to help quell the lawlessness fomented by the rebellion of the Percies. On 5 July the mayor of York was ordered to proclaim that, by the advice of the council, no one except the king was to give livery of fellowship.[30] It is interesting to note that this proclamation was not simply a repetition of the statute of 1399. Rather, it ordered the proclamation of its main provisions, on the ground that 'in divers statutes and ordinances made in divers parliaments of the king and of former kings it is contained that no knight etc. shall wear such livery save under certain conditions therein mentioned'.

There was, however, more behind this statute than the concern about lawlessness on the part of a usurper king. In effect, it gave the king a monopoly of grants of livery in time of peace, apart from those given to members of his subjects' households. In this the statute operated a distinction between livery 'of fellowship' which the king alone could grant and livery 'of cloth' for his subjects' household men, presumably the robes given at Christmas and Pentecost. Since the former is mentioned in the beginning clause of the statute and the latter in the last, the exception for livery 'of cloth' in the case of household men has the appearance of an afterthought. It is tempting to speculate whether the Crown had originally intended to secure an outright prohibition of all liveries save the king's and that the exception in favour of livery 'of cloth' was added as a result of pressure from the Lords. At any rate, there are other indications in the text of the statute that it may have been adapted to take into account concerns expressed during the meeting of parliament or to avoid opposition. Henry IV enjoyed through his duchy of Lancaster resources of men and money that, those of the Crown apart, dwarfed those of any magnate. And the last years of his predecessor had exhibited the consequences for the king's subjects of a royal power that was deliberately based upon the creation of a retinue. It is against this background that we should interpret that clause in the statute which confined the king's right to give livery to those retained by him for life by indenture in return for an annual fee and to members of his household. The clause which forbade the wearing of livery by the king's retainers in the areas or shires where they resided unless in the king's presence obviously ministered to a concern that their connection with the court might be used to overawe their neighbours. Whether or not in response to pressure from Lords and Commons, the king had to agree to careful definition of his monopoly of liveries.

The last decade of the fourteenth centry thus saw the creation of a body of statutory law that the Crown could employ against the abuse inherent in the granting of liveries. Other statutes in the decade or so after 1399 made minor changes. A statute of 1401 both glossed the terms of that of 1399 and improved the procedures for enforcement.[31] Dukes, earls, barons and bannerets were permitted to wear the royal livery throughout the kingdom while knights and squires could do so while going to and from the royal household. The authority permitted the king in the granting of livery was now extended to the Prince of Wales. The power to inquire into breaches of the law held by the judges of the King's Bench was now extended to those of the Court of Common Pleas and justices of assize, oyer and terminer and of the peace. In 1406 a further statute put the existing law on firmer foundations by simultaneously confirming both the statute of 1377 and that of 1399, explicitly stating that no spiritual or temporal person was to give livery 'of cloth' except to members of his household.[32] And for the first time penalties were firmly defined. Anyone granting livery in breach of the law was to forfeit 100s for each such grant and the recipient was to pay 40s. No information has survived to explain why the threat of fine and imprisonment at the king's pleasure was now removed.

The existence of continued activity over liveries in parliament suggests that they remained a matter of concern. But both the succession of efforts at legislation and the absence of evidence of sustained endeavours at enforcement indicate that none of the legislation against liveries was strictly observed. Even so, to say that the law in this matter was 'more honoured in the breach than in the observance' would be excessively dismissive of the legislation. If a strong king wished to issue a warning to potential law-breakers within the ranks of upper landed society, or if conditions in a particular area got out of hand, the legislation gave him a weapon; and in contemporary terms the financial penalties imposed in 1406 were by no means low. The successful prosecution of a number of grants of livery could make serious inroads into the incomes of those outside the ranks of the magnates, especially those of the knightly class, while the 40s penalty on recipients amounted to the net value of a freehold franchise for shire elections for parliament when this was defined in 1430. The statutes were available if required. In effect, the legislation against liveries played a role in the maintenance of royal authority in England analogous to that of the statutes of *praemunire* in its relations with the Papacy.

There are solid indications that Henry V was well aware of this; and in his reign at least the statutes against liveries were real presences in the background of his relations with his subjects. On 5 November 1413, within just over six months of his accession the king ordered the sheriffs throughout his realm to proclaim that article in his father's statutes that forbade lords to grant liveries.[33] Complaints against lawlessness in the Leicester

parliament of April–May 1414 were followed by a royal progress in Staffordshire and Shropshire in company with the Chief Justice of the King's
Bench which singled out for prosecution the unlawful granting of liveries.
Although no records of prosecutions have survived, seven Shropshire gentlemen were indicated for granting a total of fourteen liveries at various
dates and places in 1412–13.[34] In the case of one important Shropshire
squire, Thomas Corbet of Leigh, there was a prosecution for the granting
of liveries to two yeomen.[35] He admitted one offence; in the case of the
other his claim that the recipient was his receiver and continually residing
in his household may not have been genuine, since he secured a royal pardon. The royal concern over such activities in Shropshire probably arose
over lawlessness fomented by the aftermath of the rebellion of Owen Glendower in Wales which had affected the county. In the case of Staffordshire
the major target of the progress was a leading landowner whose wealth
put him well into the upper reaches of the kingdom's gentry – Edmund
Ferrers of Chartley,[36] who had been engaged in a private war with another
local family, the Erdeswikes of Sandon. To recruit support he had granted
liveries to six local squires, and twenty-one yeomen and others. He denied
doing so in the case of six and in the case of the others sought to claim
that the law did not apply to him, since, like his ancestors before him since
the Conquest, he held by barony. If not a genuine misunderstanding of the
statute of 1406 and the legislation it confirmed under which he was being
prosecuted, this was an attempt to hide behind the provisions of the ordinance of 1390. In this prosecution as well as Corbet's the Crown seems to
have been anxious for a firm demonstration of its authority rather than
punishment, since Ferrers received a pardon. But the details of the case
also drive home the nature of the potential that liveries had for the forment-
ing of lawlessness. Ferrers reached beyond the ranks of the squires and
yeomen of local rural society: of the total of twenty-seven to whom he
gave his liveries, nine were townsmen of Lichfield.[37]

There are other indications of Henry V's firmness in such matters. For
example, his services to the king did not save a royal squire who was constable of Rhuddlan castle from being indicted for granting liveries to eight
persons.[38] In the next parliament after the progress and prosecutions of
1414, that of November 1414, the king pardoned all offences against the
statutes against liveries that were committed before 8 December of that
year; and another such pardon was granted in the parliament that met in
March 1416.[39] No doubt the king's readiness to overlook transgressions
of this kind on the part of his nobility and gentry owed much to his desire
for their cooperation in his designs on France. But these acts of royal grace

in parliament, following as they did a number of prosecutions, were a reminder of the need to obey the law.

In the reign of Henry VI, despite a long minority and then the presence on the throne of an ineffective personality the existence of legislation against liveries was not forgotten. When the Crown granted general pardons, offences against the 'statute of liveries', clearly a reference to that of 1406, were frequently included;[40] and some pardons were given for offences against this statute alone.[41] The short-lived attempt at firm government during the first Protectorate of Richard, duke of York, led to indictments of the sons of the Percy earl of Northumberland and their adherents following their granting of liveries during their feud with the Nevilles in the north in 1453–54.[42] And on 12 April 1457, under the threat of insurrection, the government of Henry VI ordered sheriffs throughout the realm to proclaim *inter alia* that no one of any estate whatsoever should give out badges or liveries contrary to the statute.[43]

Under Henry V an impressive new departure in policy occurred which was not in the form of ordinance or statute and lay totally outside the tradition of legislation and efforts at its enforcement. An examination of the confirmations made on his accession by the king of the offices and annuities granted by his father reveals that these were invariably made on condition that the recipient was retained by no one save the king. Furthermore, this policy was maintained in the king's own grants for the rest of his reign.[44] This was a shrewd exploitation of the patronage at the disposal of an effective king. It did much more than simply reinforce the legislation against liveries. For the first time the Crown launched a policy that was intended to control retaining *per se*. The threat of forfeiture of any office or annuity held of the king was a powerful inducement not to join the indentured retinue of one of his subjects. And, since the patronage at the disposal of the king was so much greater than that of the greatest lord in his realm, it effectively reduced the opportunities for retaining available to his leading subjects.

It is impossible to say how this policy arose. There may be indications that Richard II was moving in such a direction in the last months of his reign. On most of the occasions when he confirmed indentures of retinue made by John of Gaunt he did so on condition that the retainer would not be retained by anyone save the king, following the same practice in the case of offices and annuities.[45] But this practice was not invariably followed. It is difficult to form a firm judgment about this king's motives, since the events that led to his loss of the throne soon intervened and the majority of Gaunt's retainers, annuitants and office-holders received no such confirmations. Certainly the practice was followed in the majority of the known confirmations; and the explanation may lie in an anxiety to break any possible connections between the individual concerned and the exiled Henry of Bolingbroke. In contrast, when Richard II organized his own retinue on the basis of the earldom of Chester, no such policy was followed.[46] What information we have, therefore, suggests that the use of royal powers of patronage to exercise a means of control over retaining was the invention of Henry V. It vanished at the beginning of the reign of his son and successor Henry VI; but it did make a very short-lived reappearance in July 1454 when the council gave Richard, duke of York, as Protector of the realm, 'power and authority to give the king's livery of colors to eighty gentlemen after his discretion, they and every of them to be sworn to be afeed without [with] no man but with the king without his special licence'.[47] It was no doubt the memory of Henry V's policy that inspired Sir John Fortescue in *The Governance of England* to recommend that 'no man have any office of the king's gift, but he be first sworn that he is servant to none other man, or take his clothing, or fee while he serveth the king'.[48]

(ii) 1461–1504

In the first parliament of his reign in 1461 the new Yorkist king Edward IV took action along lines that went back to the ordinance of 1390 and the agitation that produced it. He did not follow the normal route of statute-making but, instead, introduced a group of 'articles' that announced his intention to enforce the law relating to 'maintenance' and other abuses; and the lords then swore before him in the Parliament Chamber that they would endeavour to enforce them.[49] No doubt this approach of cooperation with the lords in the maintenance of the kindom's laws was regarded as tactful by a young king who had just seized the throne by force and had still to fight to keep it. Even so, the 'articles' did have novel features. They distinguished between 'livery of sign' and 'livery of clothing'. No lord spiritual or temporal, or anyone of lower degree, was henceforth to 'give livery of sign, mark or token of company'. In the case of 'livery of clothing' it was laid down that it should not be given by any lord or person of lower degree 'save to his household and menial men, officers and councillors learned, spiritual and temporal'. Exceptions were permitted under certain circumstances. There could be the 'special commandment by the King to raise people for the assisting of his resisting of his enemies, or repressing of riots within his land'. And the Wardens of the Marches towards Scotland could give livery north of the Trent, whenever it was necessary for the defence of the Marches.

Edward IV's intervention at the beginning of his reign is best regarded as an attempt to remind his subjects of existing legislation. The statutes of Richard II and Henry IV were in no way repealed. And in one important respect royal authority was reasserted, since there was an explicit recognition of the king's right to licence the granting of liveries. The 'articles' of 1461 are best regarded as an important part of an effort to maintain order on the part of a king who was uneasy about the security of his throne and well aware that lawlessness might encourage rebellion. The 'articles' were intended to deal with an immediate situation, not to produce lasting reform.

The major contribution of Edward IV to the legislative campaign against the dangers inherent in retaining occurred in the parliament of 1468. Indeed, the novel features of the statute of that year were to dominate the law in this area well into the Tudor period.[50] After a preamble which put the statute squarely in the tradition of legislation against liveries, it was laid down that

> no person, of whatsoever degree or condition he be, by himself or any other for him, from the feast of the Nativity of St John the Baptist, that shall be in the year of our Lord 1468, give any such livery or sign, or retain any person other than his menial servant, officer or man learned in the one law or the other by any writing, oath or promise.

All retainings by indenture before that date were declared null and void 'other than to be the household servant or officer or of his [the lord's] council for lawful service done or to be done'. Any one who made grants of liveries or indentures of retinue after that date was to pay a penalty of 100*s* for each such grant or act of retaining; and a further penalty of 100*s* a month was imposed on both lord and man while the grant or retainer remained in force. In contemporary terms these were very stringent penalties that might well nullify any financial benefits a man gained by his service and substantially increased the costs of his retaining for the lord: 100*s* was between a half and the whole of the annual fee most frequently granted to squires and between twenty-five and forty per cent of the figures most frequently encountered in the case of knights. The judges of all the courts of common law, including justices of the peace, judges of the palatinates and other privileged franchises and even urban authorities, were given authority to hear complaints of breaches of the statute and to try the accused. Information that led to successful prosecutions was to be rewarded with half the penalties imposed. Both the thorough range of jurisdictions empowered under the statute and the financial incentives it promised informers created, at least in principle, the capacity to destroy retaining outside households throughout the kingdom.

The novel features of this statute clearly lie in its prohibition of retaining as well as livery, this being made especially explicit by the specific mention of indentures of retinue among those devices of lordship now put outside the law. The exception in favour of household servants and officials, which appeared in the ordinance of 1390, which was in the statute of 1399 and reappeared in the 'articles' of 1461, was now repeated and extended to retaining by indenture as well as livery. The approach of the statute was remarkably radical, especially in comparison with previous legislation. In 1485–86 Chief Justice Hussey gave an account of the conduct of the lords in Edward IV's reign (presumably in the light of his experience as attorney-general) which leaves no doubt that in his mind all retaining and giving of liveries outside the household were illegal.[51] A further piece of legislation by Edward IV was certainly based on such a view.[52] In the parliament of 1472–75 the king dealt with the fact that any retaining or granting of liveries by his son and heir, Edward, Price of Wales, would fall within the terms of the statute. Accordingly it was ordained that

> the said Prince should be at his liberty to retain and give his honourable livery and sign at his pleasure, and that the persons so retained, or to whom such liveries or signs is (*sic*) or shall be given, may be retained and receive, wear and use the same livery or sign, without any let, impeachment, pain, contempt or forfeiture of any penalty comprised in any of the statutes

which prohibited such practices.

The sweeping nature of the statute's provisions, however, required that some attention be paid to a feature of the relationship between lord and man that had not so far appeared in similar legislation – the granting of annuities, as distinct from indentures of retinue or liveries. These were specifically excepted from the terms of the statute:

> Provided always that this act extend not nor be prejudicial to any gift, grant or confirmation, made or to be made, of any fee, annuity, pension, rent, lands or tenements, made by the King, or any other person or persons, for their counsel given, and their lawful service done or to be done, and for no other unlawful cause, nor to none other unlawful intent, albeit the person or persons to whom such gift, grant or confirmation is or shall be made be not learned in the one law nor in the other.

This exception, of course, could only weaken the statute. The obligation of loyalty to a lord applied in the case of annuitants as well as those retained by indenture of retinue or receiving livery; and there is every reason to believe that annuities granted for past and future services were a powerful force in cementing the bonds of lordship and might well in certain circumstances foment lawlessness and abuses of justice. Moreover, the strict legal distinction between an annuity and a retainer's fee was not always observed in the drafting of indentures of retinue.

The origins and purpose of this statute have received substantial attention in recent years. The discussion was opened up by Professor W. H. Dunham who made its terms the basis of an examination of the lawfulness of retaining in the Yorkist and Tudor periods, stressing the contrast between the statute's apparent prohibition of retaining and the contemporary reality of such activity on a substantial scale on the part of the king's leading supporter and courtier, William, lord Hastings. In Dunham's view the contrast provides a key to the understanding of the statute. He accepts that this legislation must have been drafted by the king's councillors and judges,[53] and that there is no evidence of opposition to it among the lords in parliament. Hence he asks the question: 'Why should the lords temporal, mighty as they were in 1468, have approved the enactment of a law which would have been, had it applied to them, a self-denying ordinance?' To this he answers: 'Either hypocritically they passed a law that they had no intention to abide by; or else they understood that the "lawful service" clauses would permit them to have non-resident retainers.'[54] The 'lawful service' clauses are two – one which used the phrase 'for lawful service done or to be done' in stating an exception from the abolition of existing liveries or retainings and the provison that excepted annuities from the terms of the statue. He explains the substantial retaining that occurred on the part of the lord Hastings by drawing attention to an effort on the part of those who drafted his indentures to bring the services involved within a concept of 'lawful service'. But he also suggests, in view of the total absence from the surviving records of any licences to retain or give livery by Edward IV both before and after 1468, that the statute was not intended to apply to peers of the realm.[55] In so far as he explains its appearance in the year 1468, Dunham looks to a desire to maintain law and order. In this and in his stress on the importance of the idea of 'lawful service' he, in fact, places the statute within the tradition that produced the ordinance of 1390 and later legislation against liveries.

None of these arguments is convincing. They assume in the first place, that lord Hastings's indentures were typical of those of the Yorkist period. But any such inference is based on the failure of those of other magnates to survive in quantity. And the few that do exist do not contain phrases at all reminiscent of the concept of 'lawful', as distinct from 'unlawful' service.[56] In the second place, Dunham's interpretation strains the text of the statute. The main clause, declaring outside the law any liveries and retaining to all except officials and members of a household, contained no mention of 'lawful' or 'unlawful' service. Such language in the case of the proviso excepting annuities for past and future services from the operation of hte statute can only be construed in a sense that removes this concession when the services involved were 'unlawful'. To be sure, language about 'lawful service' is employed in that clause of the statute that declared null and void all retainings made before 24 June 1468. But Dunham's interpretation of this overlooks the nature of the legal problems facing those who drafted the statute. Before it became law, retaining, as distinct from livery, was legal. Both in terms of the propriety of the motives of those who had hitherto engaged in retaining and because of the need to avoid hostility to the retroactive terms of the statute, it was necessary to employ language implying that at least some of such retaining had been for 'lawful' purposes. In the event that cases of retaining before 24 June 1468 were brought to trial, the onus would be on the accused to prove the 'lawful' intent of his activities. In the third place, Dunham does not take into account the character of annuities and the existence of lawyers' distinction between them and the retainer fee. Those who drafted the statute had to take a realistic view of the relationships of lords and men. The very nature of grants made for services performed in the past and to be performed in the future made it extraordinary difficult to make an outright prohibition of them. An annuity might be granted to a lord's old nurse or the widow of a retainer; but even such grants were not entirely immune from the obligations and benefits of lordship. In this society there could be no absolute distinction between a lord's charity and the exercise of his lordship. For this reason the statute made it clear that the exempted gifts and annuities must be for services that were 'lawful' and 'for no other unlawful cause, nor to no other unlawful intent'. Such language gave the king's justices the authority to hear complaints about such grants and annuities and apply the statute's penalties if the intentions behind them were found to be 'unlawful'. An interpretation of the statute's language in these terms makes in unnecessary to invent a hypothesis that it was not intended to apply to peers.

Another explanation for the statute has been argued by Professor J. G. Bellamy,[57] out of a discussion of a feud in Derbyshire that involved leading lords and gentry – the earl of Shrewsbury, lord Grey of Codnor, lord Mountjoy and Sir John Gresley – and led to prosecutions for the granting of liveries in 1468. There can be little doubt that Edward IV exploited these events in order to bolster his authority. The indictment of both lord Mountjoy and Sir John Gresley for grants of livery made as long ago as 1461 can certainly only be explained in terms of the king's desire 'to demonstrate to the nation the illegality of the giving of livery on a casual basis'.[58] The cases were removed into the King's Bench, a move which enabled the king to achieve a balance between publicity for the prosecutions in the very centre of the realm's affairs and his personal control over cases that involved lords whose loyalty was essential at a time when the earl of Warwick was building up his power and might explode into rebellion. In the public forum of the King's Bench Edward IV was able to secure pledges of good behaviour from the lords concerned without alienating them. In the light of these facts Bellamy suggests, 'It must have been the feud in Derbyshire which prompted the official bill on livery in the parliamentary session of 1468.' The difficulty, however, with this interpretation is that it does not take full account of the terms of the statute of 1468. The prosecutions were directed against livery, whereas the statute was aimed at retaining as well and made the radical departure of prohibiting outside lords' households this form of relationshp between lord and man.

In fact, the prosecutions of 1468 and the statute of that year shared the same background of political unrest: both must have been responses on the part of Edward IV to the political ambitions of Richard, earl of Warwick. It can be no coincidence that the month of June 1468 saw the pledges of good behaviour given in the King's Bench by lords indicted for the granting of liveries, the promulgaton of the statute outlawing retaining and the departure of the king's sister for her marriage to the duke of Burgundy, the last an event that increased the chances of open rebellion on the part of the earl of Warwick. The contemporary chronicler John Warkworth wrote how,[59] when the rift between Warwick and the king first developed, the earl 'took to him in fee as many knights, squires and gentlemen as he might, to be strong'. And it is against this background that we should place an ordinance of the mayor and common council of the city of London, dated 23 September 1467, laying down that no freeman or officer of the city was to take or use the livery of any lord or other magnate under penalty of losing his freedom and office for ever.[60] It is more than likely that this was prompted by the ostentatious display of his power and wealth by the earl within the city, described by *The Great Chronicle of London* under the year 1468–69.[61] It is quite reasonable to assume that, faced with the display of Warwick's capacity to retain by indenture as well as by the danger that liveries would also proliferate, Edward IV determined to produce a firm legislative prohibition of both practices. The stringent financial penalties enjoined by the statute and the encouragement given to potential informers would, it was hoped, cut at the root of Warwick's power: if the earl himself was not deterred, at least lesser lords and gentry might be discouraged from breaking the law. Edward IV's readiness to take some form of action against liveries at the very beginning of his reign and the character of his regime, especially after 1471, may, indeed, suggest that, even if the quarrel with Warwick had not occurred, efforts to strengthen existing legislation would have been made; but it was the danger that Warwick was preparing for rebellion that explained both the form and the timing of the legislation of 1468.

Once the statute of 1468 had been promulgated, it remained the basis of the law relating to livery and retaining down to 1504. It is anachronistic to approach its effects, as Dunham does, by contrasting its terms with the reality of the continued employment of retaining. Nor is it reasonable to accuse lords who continued to retain of 'hypocrisy'. This charge is also anachronistic, since it assumes a view of this legislation that belongs in more modern times. In contemporary terms in fifteenth-century England a statute in this area could not be viewed as a piece of absolute law that must always be enforced with total rigour. Those who agreed to it would assume that they were helping to create a weapon of royal authority, the actual employment of which would depend upon the king's will at any given time. In this situation a lord who stood close to the inner counsels of the king would see no problem in continuing to retain.

These considerations help to explain why there was no simple pattern of enforcement during the rest of Edward IV's reign. On the one hand, the statute did not lie entirely unused. In 1476 or thereabouts Henry, lord Grey of Codnor, was indicted for retaining.[62] The case was heard before the king's council where lord Grey pleaded guilty and took an oath not to retain illegally. On the other hand, retaining continued, even on the part of lord Grey of Codnor.[63] The most well-documented case is, of course, that of William, lord Hastings. Professor Dunham has suggested that Hastings's indentures actually reflected the effects of the statute, because those who drafted them took pains to use phraseology that stressed the lawfulness of the services Hastings was requiring from his retainers.[64] But this is an interpretation that overlooks the total proscription of retaining by the statute.[65] In reality, Edward IV must have turned a blind eye to the prevalence of retaining after his restoration to the throne in 1471. His regime remained under the shadow of a renewal of the war with France; and, even though his invasion of 1475 aborted and he became a pensionary of the

French king, the situation remained one of truce and at his death in 1483 the likelihood of renewed war was strong. In these circumstances he must always have had to bear in mind that his leading subjects might have to raise men on his behalf; and the continuance of some retaining in time of peace would provide a base on which military resources could be built in time of war. From the king's standpoint the success of such an attitude depended on two circumstances. First, the extent of peacetime retaining must not be excessive. And, second, every effort should be made to ensure that lords did not engage in grants of livery. It is impossible to document the existence of these concerns on the part of Edward IV and his advisers. But the assumption that policy was conceived in these terms does explain both the apparent discrepancy between the literal terms of the statute of 1468 and particular circumstances. The substantial retaining on the part of William, lord Hastings, would not concern the king. Hastings was one of the peers of the realm closest to him and, indeed, he owed his territorial wealth and power to royal patronage since 1461. In fact, there is good reason to believe that Hastings's retaining was indirectly an instrument of royal authority since through the followers of the king's most trusted supporter it helped to spread the tentacles of royal power and influence through the Midlands, a region dominated until 1471 by the earl of Warwick and then, until 1478, by the treachery-prone duke of Clarence.[66] The contrast provided by the treatment of Henry, lord Grey of Codnor, is instructive. What must have given offence to the king and led to the proceedings against him was the fact that a mere baron who was not part of the inner circles of power had retained two hundred men. Moreover, when retaining on this scale took place on the part of a baron or member of the gentry, the limits of his landed income meant that he could only afford to recruit men outside the ranks of landed society, including even peasants and tradesmen. It was precisely at this level that lords were prone to make grants of livery. It is reasonable to assume that these elements in the situation were well known to Edward IV. Henry V had taken action to discourage livery at this social level; and, the case of lord Grey of Codnor apart, there is evidence that Edward IV did so also.[67]

In a sense, therefore, just as the appearance of the statute of 1468 in the summer of that year must be explained as a threat directed at the earl of Warwick and those contemplating joining his retinue, it remained a warning to any others of Edward IV's subjects who might be planning to amass power and influence in the form of retainers. It is unwise to approach the study of the statute's effects simply in terms of a literal reading of its clauses or the absence of much in the way of prosecutions under it or the language of lord Hastings's indentures. In comparison with previous monarchs, Edward IV was in a stronger position to enforce his will after 1471, since he had recovered his throne and destroyed the power of the Nevilles, greatly increased as this had been by royal patronage after the Yorkist *coup* of 1461. To be sure, the royal will had still in considerable measure to be enforced in the localities through loyal magnates, chief of whom was William, lord Hastings. But, if some acceptance of retaining was part of such arrangements, it is still possible to detect an erosion of older attitudes. There was emerging a stronger sense of a concept of 'lawful service' to the king at levels directly below the ranks of the leading subjects who directly served him;[68] and it is quite conceivable that this is what is reflected in the indentures of William, lord Hastings.

The full effects of these changes were to be seen by the end of the reign of the first Tudor, Henry VII. Legislation on the scale of that of 1468 did not occur until 1504, almost twenty years after his seizure of the throne. Even so, during these years policies were followed which both maintained the traditions of Edward IV and also created new controls. In the new king's first parliament in 1485 all the temporal lords and the knights present there took an oath that they would not retain illegally.[69] In the same month a commission was appointed to administer an oath of allegiance to the knights, squires and 'commonalty' of the northern counties.[70] The oath concluded with the clause, 'Ye shall make no retainder otherwise than the law will, by oath, indenture or promise to no manner [of] person contrary to king's laws.' The language clearly borrowed from the statute of 1468. On 4 January 1486 another commission was empowered to call upon all knights, squires, gentlemen, yeomen and other men giving liveries and retainder to make oath before the commissioners promising not to retain or give aid and comfort to any man knowing him to be a misdoer, felon or outlaw.[71] These terms reveal an awareness that retaining had spread below the ranks of the gentry. Recent research has demonstrated that from the early years of Henry VII's reign existing legislation, including the statute of 1468, was enforced whenever circumstances made this desirable in the interests of royal authority.[72] A lord who maintained a retinue outside his household without involving himself or it in local disputes which came to the attention of the king or his councillors might well avoid prosecution.[73] But there is plenty of evidence of indictments; and in many cases the Crown was not content with the penalties enjoined by statute or the purchase of a pardon but also imposed a recognizance for future good behaviour, the amount forfeited in the event of misbehaviour being very high.

Henry VII's policy, more demonstrably than that of Edward IV, was one of control rather than the detection and prosecution of offences. What made this approach effective was a policy analogous to that of Henry V.[74] From almost the beginning of his reign Henry VII insisted that those who held offices by his gift or appointment or those who were tenants of the Crown should be retained by no one except the king. An act of 1487 laid down that no one was to retain the king's tenants 'contrary to the statutes'. Tenants of the king were to serve him alone. Tighter language was employed to circumvent any attempts to claim to act in the king's name: the king's tenants could only be summoned at his command and 'always in the king's livery or sign, with a cognizance of him that so conveys them by the king's commandment'.[75] There is evidence that this statute was enforced throughout the reign. In 1498 the council of the duchy of Lancaster treated it as part and parcel of the body of legislation against liveries and retaining when they required the authorities of the borough of Leicester to enforce the statute and, in particular, ensure that the inhabitants were not retained 'except only with us to do us service when they thereunto shall be required, in the retinue of our stewards there'.[76] In 1505 the king wrote to the stewards of several of his lordships within the duchy of Lancaster requiring them to take an oath fom the tenants, 'that they will not be retained by oath, promise, or otherwise to any person, or wear any livery or cognizance, but only our badge of the red rose, and to be wholly retained with us to do unto us service under your rule and leading'. Refusal to take this oath was to be met with imprisonment at the king's pleasure.[77]

This measure of 1505 suggests that constant vigilance was required to enforce this policy. But certainly, whatever difficulties were encountered at the local level and in areas distant from Westminster, our information reveals an organised and articulate effort at enforcement. From the beginning of his reign, Henry VII and his advisers saw that the territorial resources he enjoyed as a beneficiary of the absorption of the inheritances of Lancaster, York and Neville within the estates of the Crown provided him with resources, denied on such a scale to previous monarchs, which could be used to put down liveries and retaining on the part of his subjects. Patronage in the form of offices on royal estates or annuities from their revenues could increase the size of the king's own following among the lords and gentry. Moreover, local offices could be given to gentry from other shires, thus breaking the traditional hold of local families on office. For example, quite early in the reign all the king's revenues from the Marcher lordship of Denbigh, once part of the Yorkist inheritance, were paid out in the form of annuities to eighteen persons most of whom came from outside Wales.[78] Equally important was the fact that the officials who administered the estates in royal hands could be employed as instruments of royal authority, thus supplementing the justices of the peace and the officials of shire administration. But Henry VII was also quick to see at the beginning of his reign that the tenants of his estates were sources of military power as well as revenues and that they could be organised for this purpose through the stewards and other offices of estate administration. In this respect he was simply building on the custom that had for centuries enjoined on tenants the duty to serve their lord in war.[79] But Henry VII did more than act as the greatest lord in the kingdom. Custom was converted into royal law in two special ways. First, the statute of 1487 placed the rule that the king had the sole right to the services of his tenants side by side with the prohibition that no one else should retain the king's tenants or give liveries to them. Second, in 1495 the special duty of those who held offices or annuities fees, was emphasised. A statute of that year,[80] stated that 'every subject, by the duty of his allegiance is bounden to serve and assist his prince and sovereign lord at all seasons when need shall require . . . and most especially such persons has have by him promotion or advancement, as grants and gifts of offices, fees and annuities'. Accordingly, if the holders did not attend the king in his wars when summoned, their grants were forfeited. The king was now quite deliberately employing for the enhancement of royal power and authority those very resources of lordship that had been the cause of royal weakness because of the exploitation of them by the leading subjects of his predecessors.

The culmination of these policies was seen in the parliament of 1504 when Henry VII promulgated a statute that, in effect, refurbished that of 1468. The preceding twenty years had been marked by much vigilance and some legislative efforts. But by 1504 it was desirable to legislate in terms that were both firm and coherent. Henry VII's political situation had precluded such an effort at an earlier date. Even at the time the king's last parliament had been held – January 1497 – the pretender Perkin Warbeck was still at large and Henry VII had to exercise some caution. By 1504 his throne was secure. At the same time other circumstances had developed to expose weaknesses in current royal policy towards liveries and retaining. One element in the political situation that had assisted the working of royal policies in this area for the first decade or so of the reign had been the inability of the two most powerful families in the kingdom to provide any focus for resistance to the king. When Henry VII conquered the throne the Stafford duke of Buckingham was a boy of seven who did not enter into his inheritance until 1498. The Percy earl of Northumberland was removed from the scene by death in 1489, leaving a boy of eleven as his heir who also took over his inheritance in 1498. Both the duke and the earl held the greater part of their lands in areas distant from Westminster; and both, as the wealthiest nobles in the kingdom, had financial resources that enabled them to take maximum advantage of that exception in the law that permitted a lord to grant annuities for past and future services. When parliament was summoned in 1504, recent events had driven home the dangers implicit in Stafford and Percy power through the activities of another peer – George Neville, lord Burgavenny. He had both greatly expanded his retinue and included in it undesirable persons whom he made insufficient efforts to control. In Trinity Term 1503 a series of indictments came into the King's Bench which exposed the dangers of lord Burgavenny's feud with a rival family in Kent and the subornation of a jury through retaining. The details also underlined the potential for lawlessness when retaining spread below the ranks of the gentry into the ranks of the peasantry.[81]

In basic terms the statute of 1504 was a re-enactment of that of 1468. But Henry VII did much more than remind his subjects through the medium of parliament of existing legislation, since his statute contained novel features. Two of these were especially important. One lay in the way in which the prohibition of liveries and retaining was formulated:

> no person, of what estate or degree or condition he be . . . privily or openly give any livery or sign or retain any person, other than such as he giveth household wages unto without fraud or colour, or that he be his menial servant or his officer or man learned in the one law or the other, by any writing, oath, promise, livery, sign, badge, token, or in any other manner wise unlawfully retain.

While the language is distinctly reminiscent of the statute of 1468, this prohibition introduces the words 'or in any other manner wise unlawfully retain', thus implying that some retaining could be lawful. It is, in fact, in this statute, not that of 1468, that we see the firm acceptance of the concept of 'lawful service'. The purpose of the statute's approach can only be understood in the light of another feature – the total omission of any exception in favour of annuities for past and future servies.[82] Some historians have speculated whether this omission was deliberate or not. But, in view of the quality of the legal talent available to Henry VII and the care such ministers took in the prosecution of royal rights, it is impossible to believe that the omission was not deliberate. In fact, it must be explained in terms of the language used in the central clause of the statute. Those who drafted it were well aware that the exception in favour of annuities in the statute of 1468 substantially weakened its power. What they did was decide to omit it and at the same time use the words 'unlawfully retain' in the core of their draft. In these circumstances it would be open to the Crown to indict a person who had given annuities. The onus would then be on the accused to argue, if he wished, that he had not engaged in retaining *per se* and to prove that the services were lawful. To be sure, there is no known instance in which an accused attempted to defend himself by drawing a distinction between retaining and the granting of annuities. But it must be argued that the words 'or in any manner wise unlawfully retain' had to be construed to include annuities and, more important, the stress of the statute's approach was on unlawful intent behind the actions of the lord. Nor is it likely, in view of the means of enforcement set out in the statute, that such legal technicalities would have bulked large in the thinking of those who heard or saw its words or pondered its effects. While, like its predecessor of 1468, the statute employed the resources of the common law, for the discovery of offences, ultimately it relied upon the royal council for its enforcements:

> And the said Chancellor or keeper of the seal, the King in his Bench, or the said Council to have power to examine all persons defendants and every of them, as well by oath as otherwise, and to adjudge him or them to convict or attaint, as well by such examination as otherwise, in such penalties as is aforesaid as the case shall require.

In the last resort the interpretation of the statute as well as its enforcement depended on royal prerogative.

The other main novel feature of the statute of 1504 lies in the way its took account of circumstances in which retaining could be of benefit to king and kingdom – the need for men for the king's wars. It did so my providing that,

> this act extend not to the punishment of any person or persons the which by the virtue of the King's placard or writing signed with his hand and sealed with his privy seal or signet, shall take, appoint, or indent with any person to do and to be in a readiness to do the King service in war, or otherwise at his commandment, so that they shall have such placard or writing for their part use not by that retainer, service, attendance, or any other wise the person or persons that they shall take, appoint or indent with, nor the persons that so do indent to do the King service use not themselves for their part in doing service or giving attendance to them that shall have authority by reason of the King's writing to take, appoint or indent with them, in any thing concerning the said act otherwise than shall be comprised in the same the King's placard or writing, and that placard or writing to endure during the King's pleasure and no longer.

The language implied that the king was already following the practice of granting licences to retain. In this matter, in fact, the statute was doing no more than recognising this; and, since the royal right to give such licences was part of the king's prerogative, it is at first puzzling that an explicit statement on this point was thought necessary. One reason may have been the desire to state in clear and explicit terms that such licences were intended solely for the purposes explained in them and could not be exploited to provide the retaining lord with a following that he could treat as his own. Another explanation may lie in the growth of a conception of royal authority that can be seen in other statutes and activities of Henry VII, undoubtedly strengthened by the existence of a reservoir of military power in the form of the tenants on the royal estates. In his statute of 1495 the king had laid explicit claim to the services of all his subjects. Two years before the statute of 1504, in 1502, a proclamation against liveries and retaining, addressed to the sheriffs of Kent and Sussex and the cities or Rochester and Canterbury, undoubtedly issued in response to the activites of lord Burgavenny, proclaimed that the king had 'reserved from the beginning of his reign the retainder to himself of all his subjects'.[83] The way in which the statute of 1504 states the royal authority to licence the retaining makes the principles involved very clear. For this reason it may well be that the use of a proviso to deal with the royal licencing power gives a misleading impression of its importance in the production of the statute and a firm statement of royal authority in this matter was as important as a more stringent proscription of retaining.[84] At any rate, at least some of the indictments against retaining over the next few years stressed that they were not licensed by the Crown.[85]

One feature of this statute cannot be explained in terms of the traditions of royal policies towards liveries and retaining. It was not to extend beyond the life of Henry VII.[86] Because of this its terms were short-lived, since Henry VII died in April 1509, the statute thus being in effect for slightly under five years. It is difficult to understand why the king and his advisers would have wanted to limit the life of so important a piece of legislation.[87] It is more reasonable to suppose that its terms aroused opposition among the Lords or the Commons. If resentment occurred and was expressed, it is most likely that it fastened on the more rigorous language used in the proscription of retaining, especially since it put the Crown in a more advantageous position; and, if so, concerns in this area could only have been aggravated by the creation of conciliar procedures for dealing with offences under the statute. The Lords may well have had some sympathy with lord Burgavenny, the more so since his retaining was of long standing,[88] and the Crown had taken no action until recently. The available evidence indicates that Henry VII did not treat the licencing system as a means of reconciling the reality of retaining with the claims of his prerogative. Rather, rigorous inquiries about the intended retinue were made before the licence was issued and its terms were confined to a retinue of carefully defined and listed membership.[89] For those who sat in the Lords all the signs pointed to a more repressive royal attitude towards retaining at a time when many who sat there lived in the shadow of recognisances with heavy financial penalties.[90] How far such fear infected the gentry in the Commons it is impossible to say. But it is worth noting that the parliament of 1504 was marked by resistance to the king's financial demands.[91] There is thus good reason to believe Henry VII encountered opposition in parliament and compromised by agreeing to limit the legislation to his own lifetime.

This history of the policies pursued by successive kings and their parliaments toward liveries and retaining is thus one of growing rigour, moving from the proscription of livery outside the household to efforts to bring indentured retaining itself under royal control. It was only in the reign of Henry VII that the Crown dealt effectively with the need to maintain a balance between the maintenance of the military resources of the kingdom and the dangers inherent in uncontrolled retaining. Some awareness of this problem can be discerned in the legislation of Henry IV; and Henry V was the first king to see the potential of royal patronage as a weapon in this situation. Understanding of the issues weakened during the next reign, even before the outbreak of civil war; and Edward IV, at least until 1471, lacked the political security that was essential if radical solutions were to be achieved. Even Henry VII, despite his readiness to use the resources of royal patronage from the beginning of his reign, had to wait twenty years before he could make a clear and final statement of the authority of his Crown.

In one sense the development of the Crown's policies and the grievances expressed by the commons in parliament in the late fourteenth century mirrored the realities of lordship in this period. From the standpoint of the Crown and the interests of most gentry, livery had to be the first target of legislation. It was the most visible of the weapons employed by those who wished to dominate local society and manipulate the organs of justice; and it was also the instrument of lordship that imposed least strain on the resources of those who had such ambitions. In fact, indentured retaining and the granting of annuities for past and future services had controls built

into them, because the scale of the expenditure they involved was governed
by the extent of a lord's financial resources. This no doubt explains two
phenomena that appeared by the fifteenth century – a tendency to recruit
by means of oaths and promises and a readiness to recruit below the level
of the gentry class, both of these requiring expenditure below the level of
the fees and annuities paid to knights and squires.

In the last resort legislation and constant vigilance by royal government
could not solve all the problems inherent in retaining. By 1504 a coherent
programme and the mechanism for its application had emerged. Over the
next century or so two influences reinforced the efforts of successive Tudor
monarchs. One was the restructuring of the territorial basis of lordship
throughout the kingdom. Retaining had never been simply a matter of giving out liveries, fees or annuities. Such practices by a lord were generally
rooted in the traditional links between his family and the gentry who
dwelled in the neighbourhood of his esates. The political vicissitudes of
mid-fifteenth century England left Henry VII in 1485 in control of the territories held over the previous century by the houses of Lancaster and York
and the main branch of Nevilles. Two families remained whose territorial
strength lay in areas remote from Westminster – the Staffords and the Percies. But the power of the former was broken with the execution and forfeiture of Edward, duke of Buckingham in 1521;[92] and a decade later there
began the pressures engineered by the Crown that ended in 1537 with the
final breakup of the Percy inheritance, the bulk of it falling into royal
hands.[93] Other families were certainly to move up the ranks of great territorial wealth, especially as a result of royal patronage following the dissolution of the monasteries. But it would have taken generations for them to
build up the traditions of loyalty and the connections that were the foun-
dation of the power of the great families of late medieval England. Meanwhile
the second influence – inflation – had intervened. During the sixteenth and
early seventeenth centuries it led to an erosion of real income and then,
even when more effective estate management led to recovery in real terms,
served to discourage substantial expenditure on a following. Indeed, it led
to a reduction in the size of households, the one area of lordship which
had remained untouched by legislation against livery and retaining.

Notes

1 In what follows my indebtedness to two important articles – Storey, 'Liveries and commissions of the peace' and Cameron, 'Livery and retaining' – will be obvious.
2 Statute of Westminster, I, cc. 25, 28.
3 I Ed. III, st. 2, c. 16.
4 *Rot. Parl.*, ii. 62–3.
5 4 Ed. III, c. 11.
6 See B. H. Putnam, 'The transformation of the keepers of the peace into the justices of the peace, 1327–80', *TRHS*, 4th Ser., xii (1929), 19–48.
7 For the most recent contribution see Saul, *Gloucestershire Gentry*, pp. 164–7.
8 *Rot. Parl.*, iii, 23.
9 *Westm. Chron.* p. 83.
10 *Ibid.*, pp. 355–7.
11 Storey, 'Livery and Commissions of the Peace', p. 133.
12 *Ibid.*, pp. 134–5. One of his followers was pardoned while parliament was sitting. In the case of the leader, John Pelham, this was at the instance of the earl of Derby in 1389. Despite his later rise in Derby's favour when he became king it is not possible to be certain about his relationship with the earl at his time. He was not knighted until the eve of Henry IV's coronation in 1399; but he then became a 'bachelor' (*Hatton's Book of Seals*, p. 340, no. 492). In 1389 he was probably a squire of the earl's household. For a summary of Pelham's career see J. S. Roskell, *The Commons in the Parliament of 1422* (Manchester, 1954), pp. 208–11).
13 Storey, 'Liveries and Commissions of the Peace', p. 135, based on *Westm. Chron.*, pp. 355–7.
14 Thomas Walsingham, *Historia Anglicana* (ed. H. T. Riley, Rolls Ser., 2 vols., London, 1863–4), ii, pp. 195–6.
15 *Rot. Parl.*, iii, 265.
16 Storey, 'Liveries and Commissions of the Peace', p. 144.
17 *Ibid.*, pp. 144–6.
18 The text is conveniently consulted in *Selectd Documents of English Constitutional History, 1307–1485,* ed. S. B. Chrimes and A. L. Brown (London, 1961), pp. 157–8.
19 The term 'bachelor' was also used, presumably to differentiate the ordinary knight from a banneret.
20 See the references collected in Storey, 'Livery and Commissions of Peace', p. 131.
21 *Rot. Parl.*, iii, 307
22 Storey, 'Liveries and Commissions of the Peace', p. 147. Strictly speaking, however, this complaint was not part of Haxey's petition which dealt only with the royal household.
23 *Ibid,* p. 147, n. 54, with references to PRO, KB27.
24 16 Ric. II, c. 4; 20 Ric. II, c. 2.
25 See R. R. Davies, 'Richard II and the Principality of Chester, 1397–9', in *The Reign of Richard II. Essays in Honour of May McKisack* (London, 1971), pp. 267–9.
26 See above, pp. 238–40 and App. III.

27 *Westm., Chron.*, pp. 82–3.
28 *Rot. Parl.*, iii, 428; I Hen. IV, c. 7. For an effort at enforcement of this statute only a few months after its promulgation, see *Cal. Inq. Misc.*, vii (1399–1422), no. 88. It concerned a squire of the earl of Huntingdon who wore his lord's livery about his neck. Since he answered requests for removal by stating that he would continue to wear it while his lord was alive, the episode must have occurred before news arrived of the earl's rebellion and death on 9/10 January 1400.
29 *CCR, 1399–1402*, p. 182.
30 *Ibid., 1402–5*, p. 377.
31 2 Hen. IV, c. 21.
32 7 Hen. IV, c. 14.
33 *CCR, 1413–9*, p. 51.
34 PRO, KB 27/613 *Rex*, rot. 36.
35 *Ibid.*, rot. 20.
36 *Ibid.*, rot. 30. The facts and the background are usefully summarised in *Comp. Peer.*, v, 317.
37 These were three drapers, two vintners, a tiler, a saddler, a tinner and a plumber. Of the five liveries given by John Wele (one of those indicted but not prosecuted) one was to a barber and one to a mercer.
38 *CPR, 1416–22*, pp. 316–7.
39 *Rot. Parl.*, iv, 40, 96.
40 E.g., *CPR, 1452–61*, pp. 111, 353, 478, 625, 628–9, 633.
41 It is worth noting that *ibid.*, p. 123 refers to liveries of badges, gowns and caps.
42 PRO, KB9/148–9.
43 *CCR, 1454–61*, p. 205. The livery of Edward, prince of Wales was excluded, as well as the king's.
44 *CPR, 1413–16*, and *ibid., 1416–22, passim.*
45 *Ibid., 1396–99*, pp. 534–71. Attention was dawn to these confirmations in Tout, *Chapters*, iv, 53, n. 2. For details of the retainers see App. III and Lewis, 'Gaunt indentures', pp. 90–112. Out of seven confirmations given to knights retained by John of Gaunt five imposed this condition: in the case of squires the equivalent figure was ten. The same condition was also imposed in the case of the confirmations of annuities. I hope to discuss other aspects of the matter on another occasion.
46 See, e.g., PRO, Ches. 2/71.
47 *Proceedings and Ordinances of the Privy Council of England*, ed. Sir Harris Nicolas (London, 1834–37), vi. 209.
48 Fortescue, *Governance*, p. 153.
49 *Rot. Parl.*, v, 487–8.
50 *Ibid.*, v, 633; 8 Ed. IV, c. 2.
51 Dunham, *Hastings' Retainers*, pp. 91–2.
52 *Rot. Parl.* vi, 157; 13 Ed. IV, c. 4. The arguments in Dunham, *Hastings' Retainers*, p. 75, n. 17 are strained. The text contains nothing to support the suggestion that the reason for this statute was 'to designate those persons to whom the (the prince) would give livery rather than to enable him to retain lawfully'. No names are mentioned.
53 Dunham, *Hastings' Retainers*, pp. 78–9.

54 *Ibid.*, p. 79.
55 *Ibid.*, p. 82.
56 See above, pp. 105–7, 109–12. The absence of such language in the case of Richard, duke of Gloucester, deserves emphasis.
57 J. G. Bellamy, 'Justice under the Yorkist kings', *American Journal of Legal History*, 9 (1965), 151–4.
58 *Ibid.*, p. 153.
59 Warkworth, *Chronicle*, pp. 3–4.
60 *Calendar of Letter-Books preserved among the Archives of the Corporation of the City of London at the Guildhall. Letter-Book L (temp. Edward IV–Henry VII)*, ed. R. R. Sharpe (London, 1912), p. 73.
61 *The Great Chronicle of London*, ed. A. H. Thomas and I. D. Thomley (London, 1938), p. 207: 'the which earl was ever had in great favour of the commons of his land, by reason of the exceeding household which he daily kept in all countries wherever he sojourned or lay, and when he came to London he held such a house that six oxen were eaten at a breakfast, and every tavern was full of his meat, for who that had any acquaintance in that house, he should have had as much and roast as he might carry upon a long dagger'.
62 Cameron, 'Livery and retaining', p. 20, n. 4.
63 *Ibid.*
64 Dunham, *Hastings' Retainers*, p. 76.
65 Cf. *ibid.*, pp. 80–2.
66 Cameron, 'Livery and retaining', p. 20.
67 Dunham, *Hastings' Retainers*, pp. 83–4.
68 The term 'lawful' in the statute of 1468 indicates that concepts of 'lawful service' were already present; and the continued existence of the statute and its enforcement would certainly have strengthened its acceptance.
69 *Rot. Parl.*, vi, 287–8.
70 *CPR, 1485–94*, p. 40. The counties involved were all those north of the Trent, with the exception of Lancashire and Cheshire. The commission's appointment referred to a threatened invasion of the Scots.
71 *Ibid.*, p. 71.
72 Cameron, 'Livery and retaining', pp. 25–6.
73 A recent discussion suggests that the story of the prosecution of the earl of Oxford for retaining which followed the hospitality he gave the king on a visit to East Anglia may not deserve its apocryphal reputation. See R. Virgoe, 'The recovery of the Howards in East Anglia, 1485 to 1529', in *Wealth and Power in Tudor England*, ed. E. W. Ives, R. H. Knecht, J. J. Scarisbrick (London, 1978), p. 10.
74 There was a Yorkist precedent. Richard III had ordered that the tenants of the honour of Tutbury take on oath promising that they would be retained by no one except the king (Dunham, *Hastings' Retainers*, p. 94).
75 3 Hen, VII, c. 15. For the importance of this statute through the Tudor period see Cooper, *Land, Men and Beliefs*, pp. 78, 81.
76 Dunham, *Hastings' Retainers*, p. 94, n. 11.
77 *HMC, Sixth Report*, Part I (1877), p. 444.
78 *Fifteenth–century England*, p. 114.
79 See above, pp. 180–2.
80 11 Hen. VII, c. 18.

81   19 Hen. VII, c. 14. The major portions of the text may be conveniently consulted in G. R. Elton, *The Tudor Constitution* (2nd edn., Cambridge, 1982), pp.
34–7. The comments on pp. 31–2 are less than adequate, ignoring Cameron, 'Livery
and retaining'.
82   Cf. R. L. Storey, *The Reign of Henry VII* (London, 1968), pp. 155–6; S. B.
Chrimes, *Henry VII* (London and Berkeley/Los Angeles, 1972), p. 189.
83   *CPR, 1494–1509*, pp. 286–7.
84   Cameron, 'Livery and retaining', p. 25.
85   *Ibid.*, p. 25.
86   Cf. Chrimes, *Henry VII*, p. 190.
87   The point is not addressed in Cameron, 'Livery and retaining', where, however,
evidence of royal licensing of retinues after 1509 is given (pp. 21–3).
88   *Ibid.*
89   *Ibid.*, pp. 33–4.
90   See J. R. Lander, *Crown and Nobility, 1450–1509* (London and Montreal,
1976), pp. 267–300.
91   Chrimes, *Henry VII*, pp. 200–1.
92   On this see the comment of Rawcliffe, *Staffords*, p. 186, on the 'lack of positive
reaction' to Buckingham's fall.
93   Bean, *Percy Estates*, pp. 144–57.

CONCLUSIONS
AND PERSPECTIVES

The concept of 'bastard feudalism' is a compound of two main assumptions. One is the view that feudalism was an institution, instead of an example of the historian's tendencey to use a word or phrase to cover a variety of social forms which display apparent similarities. The other is the sense that the heart of what is defined as 'feudalism' – the personal performance of military service in return for the holding of land – presents a stark contrast with the provision of military service in return for pay. In essence this attitude is anchored in an older assumption that the whole social and economic history of the middle ages could be construed as the decline of a natural economy, payment in kind gradually giving way to the use of money. To be sure, it had never been possible to interpret the Mediterranean world in this way; and in the study of medieval English society it had become difficult to maintain this view even before the traditional interpretation of the introduction of 'feudalism' by William the Conqueror had achieved its final statement at the hands of Sir Frank Stenton and his generation. Even so, assumptions about some form of natural economy, at least in the earlier centuries of the middle ages, for a long time stood in the way of a more objective assessment of the evidence for the existence of feudal institutions in Europe in general, and in England in particular.

In the light of the preceding chapters it is difficult to see how 'bastard feudalism' deserves to survive as a term intended to delineate the forms of relationship between lord and man in late medieval England. It is impossible to argue in the case of indentures of retinue, the form of relationship which has received most attention from historians, that these arose out of a desire or need to raise men for foreign wars by means of financial contracts, since their beginnings go back well before the wars of aggression of the reign of Edward I. Nor is it possible to accept the notion that lies at the heart of the concept of 'bastard feudalism' – the view that its relation-ships hinged on the payment of money by a lord to his man in return for service. In the surviving indentures of the late thirteenth and fourteenth centuries benefits in kind within the household bulk large, occasionally more than the payment of an annual money fee. There are even some inden-tures that confer only household benefits in time of peace. These facts, in the light of evidence that indentures of retinue were developing before the middle of the thirteenth century, lead to a new understanding of this form of relationship. Circumstantial though the evidence may be, there is every reason to believe that the roots of the indenture of retinue lay in the lord's household. Because of changing political, social and legal conditions in the thirteenth century, coming to a head in its last years, retaining was in some measure transferred outside the household; but, because of the continuance of household benefits, it never left it completely and, until the fifteenth century it continued to be sustained by values that had been nurtured in the household in peace as well as war in the preceding centuries.

The practice of livery constitutes a separate proof of the household origins of so-called 'bastard feudalism', since it began as a means of dis-tinguishing lords' household followings from those of others. *Mutatis mutandis* this is also true of the granting of annuities. One of the purposes of the present study has been to place this form of relationship in its proper perspective. At first sight it would appear to be a totally different type of practice from the indenture of retinue or from livery, since the grant of an annuity did not contain any household benefits. But an examination of its origins shows that the mechanism of payment for an annuity often lay within the household in the thirteenth century.

Nor is there any justification for a tendency to equate 'bastard feudalism' with the resources of power available to the magnates of late medieval Engand. Even if we lump annuities with indentures of retinue, the resulting expenditure was not a major drain on the financial resources of the majority of magnates. To be sure, it is true that the practice of recruit-ing retainers by indenture or granting annuities flourished between the late thirteenth century and the close of the fifteenth, to an extent that was a source of concern to the Crown and a reason for legislation in parliament. But even in this aspect of the subject the role of the household bulks large. What concerned the Crown and the Commons in Parliament from the beginning of the reign of Edward III through the fifteenth century was the problem of controlling the granting of liveries, the loosest of the several forms of lordship and the one most prone to increase in times of weak government and political crisis. To be sure, from 1468 onwards legislation went beyond this; but neither parliamentary statute nor efforts at enforcement destroyed a lord's capacity to create a following within the confines of his household. Indeed, all the legislation directed at the evils inherent in lordship contained explicit exceptions in favour of the wearing of livery by the members of the household.

It is impossible to argue successfully that all these phenomena, together with their antecedents, can be subsumed under the label of 'bastard feudalism'. It is true that, if we construe 'feudalism' in Engand as a body of relationships between lord and man that was based on the tenure of land, the characteristics of late medieval lordship are distinctly different. Even so, to view them as constituting a body of relationships based upon a cash nexus is to base our overall interpretation on one element without taking others into account and at the same time to ignore the evidence relating to origins.

These conclusions have implications for our understanding of the relationships that historians have called 'feudalism', even if we confine this term to its limited sense – the tenure of land in return for military service. Historians have studied the history of medieval England, like that of other areas of Western Europe, as if 'feudalism' embraced the middle of the medieval period, coinciding with the 'high' or 'central' middle ages. It has been depicted as growing out of the Dark Ages and declining with the onset of the late middle ages. It is essential that any study of lordship in any of these periods free itself of such assumptions. The experience of each region of Western Europe in the developments that led to the forms of lordship labelled as 'feudalism' varied. In the case of England the body of relationships so described arose, whatever the tendencies towards it in the late Anglo-Saxon period, from the tenurial upheaval wreaked by the Norman Conquest and the means by which William the Conqueror and his sons imposed a new ruling class on the kingdom, together with a body of rights that defined their authority over it. No other series of events in English history has produced an almost total change in landowning outside the Church and led to a hierarchical system of tenure. What occurred was the destruction of the warrior aristocracy of late Anglo-Saxon England and, the church's holdings apart, the substitution for it of a new landowning group. The new Norman rulers' need to define their authority over the followers they rewarded with land led to the formation of the body of rights and tenures that have been labelled 'feudalism'. There was no such tenurial revolution again in England until the dissolution of the monasteries; and that involved no more than a quarter or so of the land that changed hands as a result of the Norman Conquest.

These considerations explain why the changes brought by the Norman Conquest have bulked so large in the thinking of historians of medieval England and why they have been so prone to accept the inevitability of attaching the label 'feudalism' to them. To be sure, the enormous scale of these changes, as distinct from their definition, cannot be a matter of dispute. But this fact alone serves to throw doubt on the wisdom of placing the 'bastard feudalism' of the late middle ages in contrast with the 'feudalism' of the late eleventh and twelfth centuries. The forms of lordship that gave rise to the former term – the indenture of retinue, the annuity for past and future services and the granting of livery – were never so widely disseminated or planted so deep in the ranks of landowning society as the obligations involved in feudal tenure.

It may be appropriate to employ the term 'feudal' to describe a system of landholding outside and above the level of peasant manorial landholding, together with the body of rights and obligations attached to it (including military service). But there was lordship in England before the exceptional series of events that led to the creation of a system of feudal tenure; and lordship continued to exist after military service on this basis had ceased to be a reality. Indeed, in the form of a body of relationship organised within the lord's household it had continued to exist, side by side with feudal tenures, through the two centuries following the Norman Conquest. It had been a source of the manpower that lay behind William the Conqueror's successful invasion; and it was in considerable measure the desire to reward household followings that led to the creation of feudal tenures. While both terms embrace elements that deserve careful attention from historians, the concepts of 'feudalism' and 'bastard feudalism' are encumbrances that stand in the way of a sound understanding of the nature of power in medieval England. Rather, the key to this lies in an awareness of the continuity of lordship. Its forms necessarily changed over a period of thousand years. And the historian's primary obligation is to depict and analyse the nature and the impact of these forms. This task can only be accomplished if research and writing are free of simplistic terminology that is fraught with assumptions that bear no relation to the realities of the evidence.

Throughout all the phases of lordship men joined the service of lords in the hope of reward. In terms of the motives that influenced both lords and men there is nothing fundamental to distinguish those who followed Beowulf from those who flocked to the standard of duke William of Normandy or from those who entered the service of John of Gaunt. To be sure, the hope of gaining land was in the minds of the warriors of early

Anglo-Saxon England and was even stronger in the case of the followers of duke William simply because his intention was to win a kingdom. In contrast, the retainers of John of Gaunt lived in a different society in which lords were not in a position to endow their followers with lands. Even so, such thinking was not entirely absent from the minds of the retainers of the late fourteenth century. They did know, however, that only the most fortunate among them could gain land through service and in the case of these it would be achieved, not by means of direct grants of inheritances from the lord, but as the result of the investment of the financial profits they made in his service or through his influence with the Crown.

It is precisely this contrast that provides the key to the understanding of the great sea-change that occurred in the evolution of lordship in medieval England. The desire to gain land at the hands of the lord naturally begat the urge to hand it down to one's issue. For this reason the tendency to convert *laenland* into bookland can be observed through Anglo-Saxon history; and tenants-in-chief and mesne tenants by the end of the century or so following the Norman Conquest had largely succeeded in making 'fee simple' equate with inheritance. This process inevitably weakened the bonds of contemporary lordship. But the need for a great landowner to exercise power over his neighbours and serve his king in war meant not only that lordship endured but also that efforts had to be made to maintain it. The mechanisms of lordship had always had to be adjusted as a result of the special circumstances of war, conquest or leadership at any given time. What occurred in late medieval England was a process of adjustment to the changed environment created through the emergence of landed inheritance. It was a process that was bound to hinge on the lord's household arrangements; and it is there that we must search for the forces that produced new forms of lordship. All this means that we should not lose sight of the fact that the lord's household had always been present. The warband of Beowulf appears in obvious respects different from the household of the late medieval magnate, but both were nurtured by the mutual obligations of loyalty and reward that were always part and parcel of the exercise of lordship. There were, indeed, contrasts between late medieval England and the two centuries that had preceded it. But this does not make the earlier 'feudal' and the later 'bastard'.

If we seek to delineate a trend that ran through the evolution of lordship from the beginnings of Anglo-Saxon England into the modern period, it makes more sense to think in terms of the title of the present study: *From Lord to Patron*. This is a phrase that encapsulates the constant tendency of lordship to adjust to its environment and the fundamental tensions that were created by the process of adjustment in the context of medieval England. Once lords sought to recruit as retainers those who held land in inheritance or who had hopes of one day doing so, they had to turn to usages that had for centuries been anchored in their households. They had to do this, however, in an environment that was the product of forces created by royal authority in the form of a bureaucracy and a kingdom-wide system of justice. A retainer who joined the service of a lord would hope for tangible benefits in the form of, for example, money payments or perquisites through membership of his lord's household; but he would also expect to enjoy his lord's favour in a less tangible way – for example, support and influence in the courts of law or assistance in securing offices from the Crown. It is these elements that explain a perceptible weakening of the role of the household if we examine the evolution of indentures of retinue, especially in the fifteenth century.

The role of the patronage of the Crown became much more pronounced from the middle of the sixteenth century onwards. The great landed inheritances that had so often dominated the politics of late medieval England had been shattered. And those who strove to create great inheritances in the Tudor and early Stuart periods had to construct bonds of lordship at a time when the effects of inflation made the careful husbanding of their financial resources a matter of increasing urgency and, in particular, the maintenance of a large household a policy of dangerous extravagance. The Crown's role as a source of patronage even for the mightiest in the land had been present as a source of power and additional wealth from Anglo-Saxon times. But the situation of royal authority in sixteenth and seventeenth century England and the economic changes that affected its subjects' exploitation of their revenues from land made a share of the fruits of royal patronage even more attractive for the nobility and gentry of England. In effect, from the beginning of the sixteenth century onwards the role of the great lord as a conduit to favours at the hands of the Crown became more important than benefits gained directly at his hands through membership of his household or wider affinity.

Elements of this situation had always been present. The difference between lordship and patronage is not a total one. The term 'lordship' involves a situation in which the relationships between a lord and his follower depend on the lord's use of wealth which is his own. A patron, on the other hand, while he may use his own resources, will also assist his man in a looser way that involves, not his tangible assets, but the influence he wields. The meaning of the word 'lordship' goes back to primitive times, when political relationships were essentially those of the warband. Patronage, in contrast, belongs to an environment of settled government, when influence and connexion in time of peace were more important than success in war.

In fact, lordship and patronage so defined prove the chronological beginning and end of the development of lordship in medieval England. In the Anglo-Saxon and Norman periods it retained the characteristics of its primitive period, the lord rewarding his followers for their services with shares of the winnings of war and, in the case of the most deserving of them, grants of land. But from the early twelfth century onwards lordship had to be exercised in a rapidly changing context, in the shadow of a royal authority that more and more transcended that of any lord within the kingdom. In particular, the potential benefits of office, both central and local, under the Crown were bound to affect the calculations both of the kingdom's great lords and of their followers. Elements of the older lordship remained powerful, the mutual obligations of both lord and man being nurtured through membership of the household. This was the repository of values that were now being extended by means of retaining practices into a wider affinity that lay outside its confines. And in this situation what brought men into the service of lords was not merely the financial benefits they thus obtained but also the promise of the lord's influence being exercised on their behalf in their dealings with royal authority, including the courts of law. After the close of the medieval period it was the functions of influence and favour that became dominant, the older lordship being transformed into modern patronage.

Any study of relationships of lord and man in late medieval England must emphasise, on the one hand, the continuity of the basic elements of lordship through the whole of the medieval period. But, on the other hand, it must also take into account the ways in which lordship adjusted to the changes in its environment that began to appear a century or so after the Norman Conquest. Lords had to maintain a balance between basic ties between them and their men that went back for centuries, and new forces unleashed by the growth of royal power and wars of aggression outside the kingdom. The result was the forms of relationship that historians have wrongly labelled 'bastard feudalism'.

APPENDIX I

The division of the spoils of war

For lord, knight and squire and for their followings in late medieval England war was both a major source of wealth and an avenue of advancement. Apart from the rewards that a grateful king or magnate might bestow in the form of grants of land, revenues or offices, the warrior at every level could gain profits from prisoners' ransoms and booty. This was part of his way of life that went back through the unrecorded past. But although there is evidence that lords in the society delineated by *Beowulf* divided profits among their followers, mentions of such practices before the fourteenth century throw no light on the precise methods of division. However, the formalisation of the bonds of lordship that then occurred in the form of indentures of retinue does provide some solid information about the division of the spoils of war.

This topic has been investigated by Professor Denys Hay in a well-known article.[1] His analysis of the indentures made by Edward III, the Black Prince, John of Gaunt and other lords led him to conclude that

> there is every appearance of a variety of usages prevailing in the disposal of booty and ransoms of prisoners not claimed by crown, superior lord or captain in the first decades of Edward III's reign. The references we find to royal practice suggest that the third was of old standing in the royal household; yet the persistence of the half in the following of a royal duke and prince precludes any certainty that in general the larger fraction was exceptional. There does, however, seem to be every likelihood that the royal system of taking only a third was gradually adopted during the period after the Peace of Brétigny, and was pretty universal by the last decade of the reign. The reason for this lies doubtless on the growth of the indentured army . . . As the tradition of separate feudal contingents declined, uniformity spread in all military relationships.[2]

This interpretation presents a disarming neatness which has to give way to doubts once it is set against the background of the surviving indentures of the fourteenth century and the forces that led to their appearance. Professor Hay's view is, of course, rooted in assumptions about the chronology of the appearance of indentures of retinue that the past thirty years of scholarship have dissipated. *A priori*, it is odd that a kingdom-wide custom took so long to emerge within the fourteenth century itself, since the Hundred Years' War had started in 1337 after forty years of intermittent war against the Scots. In fact, the actual period in which it is claimed that a final method of division was achieved was one in which the chances of the profits of war for English nobles and gentry must have been less than in the preceding generation. It is worth noting that a study of the organisation of the war effort under Edward III was noticeably cautious about the method of division of the spoils of war.[3] Above all, the remarkable feature of the surviving life-indentures for the period before 1399 is that only a minority of them contain any mention of the method of division, whether 'halves' or 'thirds'. The best illustration is to be found in those of John of Gaunt since they nearly all belong to the years in which, according to Professor Hay, the practice of taking 'thirds' was adopted kingdom-wide and then universally followed. Out of his surviving indentures – fifty-six for knights and one hundred and two for squires – only three knights'[4] and nine squires' mention the practice of taking 'thirds'.[5] Instead, the spoils of war were subsumed with other aspects of the lord's treatment of his retainer within a general formula in which the lord undertook to treat the knight or squire on the same basis as others of his condition. It must, however, be said that the formula of the 'thirds and thirds of thirds' – that is, the arrangement under which the king and all lords below him took a third of their men's winnings – is much more frequently encountered in the fifteenth century. It is, for example, invariably inserted in the life-indentures made by the Nevilles – Richard, earl of Westmorland, his son the earl of Salisbury and the latter's son, the earl of Warwick, as well as those of Humphrey, earl, then duke, of Buckingham.[6]

Even so, it is in the fifteenth century that we encounter a piece of evidence that both undercuts the interpretation of Professor Hay and leads to another explanation of the phenomenon he sought to explain. This is an indenture, in print for a century and a half, made between Sir Robert Plumpton and eight archers on 12 October 1420 which reads at one point that 'they that are at the horsing of the aforsaid Robert truly to pay unto him half the goods that they win by war; and they that are at their own horsing, truly to pay him the third part that they win by war.[7]

Is it, therefore, possible that the references to 'thirds' and 'halves' examined by Professor Hay were in fact the result of the application of the rule set out in the Plumpton indenture? In other words, was there a practice whereby a retainer paid over a third of his winnings to his lord if he provided his own horse but gave up a half if his horse was provided by his lord?[8] There is certainly some apparent support for this interpretation in the extent to which indentures, even when 'thirds' or 'halves' are not mentioned, give attention to the lord's obligation to replace horses lost on his service, these being valued when his retinue mustered for a campaign.

An indenture made by John of Gaunt with Nicholas Atherton on 24 March 1370 gives explicit support to this view.

> And his horses of war will be valued, and if any of them are lost in the service of the said duke, compensation (*restor*) will be made to him as reason requires, and then the said duke will have the half of the prisoners and gains of war taken and gained by the said Nicholas. And if any of the horses of the aforesaid Nicholas are not valued, then the aforesaid duke will have accordingly the third part of the profits of war thus gained by the said Nicholas.[9]

But an indenture made a few years later (27 February 1373) between the duke and Sir William Beauchamp, second son of the earl of Warwick, contains details that do not fit this interpretation.

> And for war the said Sir William will be bound to serve the said lord with one squire as man of arms and will take such wages for himself and his said squire as other 'bachelors' of his condition shall take, and also livery or wages for ten horses, in the same manner as other 'bachelors' of his estate; and his war-horses shall be reasonably valued, and according to the said valuation compensation will be paid to him if any of them are lost in the service of our said lord; and then our said lord will have half of the profits of war taken or won by the said Sir William, his squire or his chamberlain, and from all other men who are at the wages of our said lord the third part if none of their horses are lost.[10]

These clauses do not spell out all aspects of the relationship between Gaunt and Beauchamp in this areas. But their language implies the existence of a hierarchy in the division of the profits of war won by this retainer and his contingent. A distinction appears to be made between 'horses of war' – that is, those of men-at-arms – and those of other soldiers; and an explicit commitment is made only for the valuation of the former. In the event of the loss of any of them on the duke's service, the 'half' rule would apply to the winnings of Sir William himself, his squire and his chamberlain, this implying that any of his contingent riding the other war-horses – presumably seven – would not be so treated. The language employed regarding the other soldiers and their horses mentions a 'third' rule only. This suggests either than they would be responsible for their own losses or that their expectations in such circumstance would depend on negotiation. It would, however, be unwise to assume that this indenture was typical of Gaunt's policies regarding his retainers' profits of war. Beauchamp was an important 'bachelor', the son of an earl who might even one day succeed to an earldom. Moreover, the size of the annual fee in peace and war promised him by the indentures – one hundred marks – and the comparatively lavish benefits in kind he received suggest that there might have been some special adjustments over the profits of war made by him and his own retinue.

The picture that emerges from what evidence we have for Gaunt's practices does indicate the existence of a body of rules on this matter within his household, even though we have no information about many aspects of it. The fact that the majority of his surviving indentures contain no explicit mention of this matter suggests that there were practices which he, and his knights and squires, took for granted. But the rules were not inflexible: the case of Beauchamp shows that adjustments could occur as a result of bargaining with individuals. What indications we have for other lords' practices in the fourteenth and fifteenth centuries contain nothing that conflicts with the application of this conclusion to them also. Exceptions could occur because of the element of personal bargaining that was an inevitable part of the relationship between lord and man. But there was a custom that in general led to the lord extracting a half of his man's winnings when he provided a horse but a third when this was furnished by the retainer. The conclusion that this was a custom subject to negotiation in particular cases is confirmed by a small group of six indentures,[11] made by a Northumbrian knight, Sir John de le Strother, when recruiting his company in September 1374 for service under the earl of March in the Brittany campaign of 1375. Sir John was to receive 'the third part of what [the man-at-arms and his retainer, or other followers] gain by way of war for his lord the earl. And the said Sir John will have of the other two parts of all their winnings the fourth part to his own profit.' The man-at-arms and their men were responsible for their own losses and arms, but there was no mention of replacement of the former if lost.

In one sense this is an unsatisfactory conclusion because it leaves in the shadows that lay beyond the terms of surviving indentures many important issues in the purely business aspects of the relationship between lord and man. This, however, is an inevitable consequence of the development of the indenture of retinue. As a result of pressures that emerged in the late thirteenth century and then grew apace centuries old relationships between lord and man were formalised in indentures of retinue. But the study of this form of contract has shown that there were pronounced variations in the forms of indentures both within particular periods and over the whole span of the fourteenth and fifteenth centuries. It is not surprising, therefore, that variations occurred in the treatment of the profits of war, lords relying in varying degrees in the last resort on the time-old practices of their households. For example, not every indenture made explicit reference to the rule that the king had a right in war, subject to reasonable reward, to captives of royal blood and leading commanders. If this could be omitted, it is hardly remarkable that there were sometimes ambiguities or obscurities in the treatment of the profits of war and even omissions of these altogether.

It is in this light that we must assess some aspects of Professor Hay's discussion of this matter. On the one hand, what he has to say about the emergence of the 'third' in place of the 'half' rests, the surviving indentures of John of Gaunt and the Black Prince apart, on remarkably few documents. We cannot, therefore, exclude the possibility that such references as he cites to the practice of requiring a 'half' arose from quite exceptional bargains between lord and man.[12] There is thus good reason to believe that in the division of the spoils of war there was a general expectation that the lord would secure one-third of his man's winnings if the man provided his own mount. There is nothing to indicate that this was not the situation well before the appearance of our earliest information regarding this practice. On the other hand, Professor Hay is undoubtedly right in delineating a growing concern with the insertion of the 'thirds' rule in indentures of retinue. In the late fourteenth century this was especially marked in the case of indentures made for single campaigns or short periods.[13] And, the Plumpton indenture apart, in the surviving indentures of the fifteenth century there appears an underlying assumption that a clause relating to the sharing of the profits of war should be inserted and that this would invariably state that the lord's share was one-third of the retainer's winnings.[14]

Nor is this surprising. The contract system under which indentures of retinue were employed was intended to delegate from the king downwards all the burdens of recruitment. In other words, at the level of each contract that was made the lord concerned sought to pass on the burdens of securing men and equipment. Apart from the total armour of leading commanders, the most expensive single piece of equipment was the horse. As the need to put large armies in the field overseas became recurrent, the periods of service involved sometimes being substantial, it made sense to ensure that the retainer, not the lord, was responsible for the production of his horse. The Plumpton indenture indicates the rule that the lord took a share of the man's winnings when the latter was provided with his horse had not disappeared in the closing years of the reign of Henry V; but the logistics of maintaining large armies overseas must have meant that it was rarely encountered in indentures of retinue.[15]

This discussion does not exhaust all the issues involved in the division of the profits of war in late medieval England.[16] Above all, there are many issues arising out of those practices that can be defined which cannot be elucidated. This is because indentures of retinue arose from efforts to adapt the age-old relationships between lord and man to the changing circumstances of politics and war. By its very nature the process of adaptation was uneven; and in defining the relationships between individual lords and their retainers it involved the assumption that these would in the last resort be governed by the age-old sense of mutual loyalty and obligation nurtured in the household.

Notes

1 D. Hay, 'The Division of the Spoils of War in Fourteenth-century England, *TRHS*, 5th Ser., iv (1954).
2 *Ibid.*, pp. 105–6.
3 Hewitt, *Organization of War*, pp. 107–9.
4 *JGRA*, i, 293 (no. 782); *ibid.*, i. 298–9 (no. 788); *ibid.*, i, 330–2 (no. 832).
5 *Ibid.*, i, 299–300 (no. 789); *JGRB*, i, 21–2 (no. 45); Lewis, 'Gaunt Indentures', pp. 88, 96–7 (nos. 2, 10–14).
6 See above, pp. 97–9, 104–5.
7 *Plumpton Corr.*, Introd., pp. xlviii–ix.
8 This was stated as long ago as 1888, though no evidence was cited (Denton, *England in the Fifteenth Century*, p. 290).
9 Lewis, 'Gaunt Indentures', p. 88 (no. 2).
10 *JGRA*, i, 331 (no. 832).
11 Northumb. RO, ZSW 4/43–4, 46, 48, 50.
12 For example, in an indenture between William, earl of Salisbury and a squire, Geoffrey Walsh (12 July 1347), the lord was given his 'half', despite the fact that the retainer provided his own mount and that this was to be valued and compensation was to be provided in the case of loss on service. But the scale of benefits in kind, food in hall being extended to the retainer's chamberlain and groom as well as himself, suggests that the 'half' may have resulted from special circumstances (PRO, E101/68/3/68). In the case of two indentures made in 1347 the Black Prince required a half of the ransom of any prisoner, although the knights concerned and their retinues brought their own mounts and provision was made for losses of these on service. But the benefits were substantial: the annual fees were 100 and forty marks respectively, the status of 'bachelor' on campaign was given and *bouche de court* secured for the knight himself, his companion and two squires. No other profits of were mentioned apart from ransoms. (*BPR*, i, 128–9; PRO, E 36/144/116d–7).
13 These remarks are based on the collection of indentures in *ibid.*, E101/68/3–9.

It is especially interesting to note the invariable insertion of a clause relating to 'third' in two series of indentures made by leading commanders for the duration of campaigns for which they had themselves contracted with the crown – Sir Thomas Felton in 1380 (*ibid.*, 8/195–6 and 9/197–212) and Thomas, duke of Gloucester in 1392 (*ibid.*, 74/1–52).

14 Even so, variations could occur. Of the four surviving life-indentures made by Ralph Neville, earl of Salisbury, (see above, pp. 104–5) two (with Ralph, lord Grays-toke and Sir Thomas Strickland) follow the 'thirds and thirds of thirds' practice. But the other two (with Sir Thomas Dacre and Sir James Strangeways) assign the earl 'the third of winnings of war gotten by the said Sir Thomas/James or by any of his said men which he shall have at wages or cost of the said earl'. An indenture of the earl's for half a year's service made in April 1431 applies the same rule as for Greystoke (*Trans. Cumb. Westm.* AAS, New Ser., ix (1909), 284).

15 This explains why the royal ordinances for the conduct of armies in France under Henry V take the 'third' rule for granted (Nicolas, *Agincourt*, App., p. 34). The same assumption was also made in the case of Richard II's Scottish campaign of 1385 (*Black Book of the Admiralty* [(ed. Travers Twiss, 4 vols., Rolls Ser., London 1871–6), i, p. 45; Cf. Hay, *art cit.*, p. 96, n. 1]. The 'third' rule was also employed by Sir Hugh Hastings in indentures he made in 1379–80 to recruit men for one year's service on a campaign in 1380 (Norfolk RO, MR 314 [242×5]).

APPENDIX II

The growth and size of the indentured retinue of John of Gaunt

John of Gaunt is the sole[1] magnate of medieval England whose surviving archives contain a list of his retainers.[2] It was entered towards the beginning of the register of his chancery that covers the years 1379 to 1383, immediately preceding copies of indentures of retinue made in the regnal years covered by the register. It is placed under the heading *Nomina militum et scutiferorum. Retinencia diversorum militum et scutiferorum.* It begins with two earls – the earl of Derby, Gaunt's son and heir, and the earl of Nottingham – and continues with three barons – Roos, Neville, and Dacre. It then provides the names of a total of ninety-six knights and 126 squires.

This list, however, cannot be accepted as it stands, since it was altered and enlarged after its original compilation. Ten names of knights were marked as 'cancelled' in the margin, three being described as dead.[3] Similar alterations were made in the case of the squires, eighteen being cancelled in some way or other.[4] Of these, six had apparently been promoted to knighthood. A total of thirty names at the end of the list is in a different hand from the single one of those preceding them. The list includes the names of knights and squires whose indentures were copied into the register of 1372–76. But, despite this fact and the insertion of the list at the beginning of that portion of the register of 1379–83 which contains the indentures of retinue, it is impossible to conclude that it was completed in the course of those years and then entered in the register, since it includes the names of three knights – Sir Thomas Wennesley, Sir Ralph Bracebridge and Sir Thomas Beek – whose indentures were respectively dated 10 December 1384, 4 April 1385 and 1 December 1386. It is also important to note that the names of knights and squires are not entered according to either the dates

of their indentures or the order in which they appear in the surviving register.[5] The most likely explanation is that the list was compiled in the course
of the years 1379–86 in order to provide a record of the duke's halves of
indentures of retinue that were kept in his chancery. It was then inserted
in the register of 1379–83 when it was bound, or rebound, in 1386 or
shortly after.

As it stands, the list suggests that by the end of 1386 John of Gaunt
had a retinue of approximately eighty-four knights and eighty-five squires.
But the difficulty in using this conclusion is that it relates to a point little
more than halfway through John of Gaunt's tenure of his duchy of Lancaster,[6] so that the list throws no light on the size of his retinue either before
1379 or after 1386.

The most sensible way to approach the problem of charting the growth
of Gaunt's retinue over the whole period of his tenure of the duchy is to
start with the evidence of the valors compiled by his auditors and stewards.[7]
These do not provide details of indentures of retinue as such or the names
of individuals described as retainers. Instead, they summarise the amounts
spent by Gaunt's receivers on fees and annuities that were not connected
with the administration of the estates. The collection of these documents
that has survived relates to the decade or so preceding Gaunt's death in
1399, beginning almost a decade after the list of 1379. Their evidence is
summarised in Table 1.[8]

Table 1 *Valors covering the decade or so preceding 1399, summarising
amounts spent by Gaunt's receivers on fees and annuities not connected
with the administration of the estates*

Date	'North parts'		'South parts'[11]	
	Net value[9]	Annuities[10]	Net value	Annuities
1387–88	4185.2.10[12]	1227.19.2		
1388–89			3402.13.2	955.2.11
1389–90	4671.3.11	1312.11.2		
1390–91			3710.12.9	1455.6.11
1391–92	4579.4.8	1349.18.7		
1392–93			3747.3.4	1546.4.3
1393–94	?[13]	1482.8.0		

There are difficulties in using this information for an assessment of the scale of Gaunt's expenditure on indentured knights and squires. First, the 'valors' do not in any of these years include any material from the accounts of the duke's receiver-general. Second, there are no valors after Michaelmas 1394. Third, and most important, the totals do not distinguish between the fees and annuities of indentured retainers and those annuities granted by the duke for past and future services. The first and second of these difficulties, however, do not present insoluble problems. Accounts of the receiver-general have survived for 1392–93 and 1396–97.[14] Their information does not suggest that many fees and annuities were the responsibility of this official. If we exclude payments to family members, annuities total-led £259 3s 4d in 1392–93 but only £119 3s 4d in 1396–97. Nor is this surprising. It was in the interest of grantees to have payment from manorial issues or a receivership in their neighbourhood, so that even during their own absence from the locality or even out of the kingdom on a war campaign their attornies could collect. In the case of the situation after 1394 enough information exists to indicate that the duke continued to recruit indentured retainers. The confirmations made by Richard II and Henry IV after Gaunt's death indicate that he made indentures with at least three knights,[15] and with twenty-three squires[16] after Michaelmas 1394, the last such contract being dated within a few weeks of his death. The total of the peacetime fees involved in these indentures amounted to £201 13s 4d a year.[17]

An attempt to distinguish between the payments to indentured retainers, on the one hand and, on the other hand, annuities for past and future services is much more difficult. Any results are bound to be impressionistic and can only be based on the two registers that survive which cover only nine years of the thirty-seven during which Gaunt held the duchy of Lan-caster. Table 2 summarises the number of indentures of retinue and grants of annuities in the complete years covered by the registers[18] and also the totals of expenditure involved (peacetime fees in the case of the inden-tures).

On the basis of this evidence it is fair to assume that a substantial pro-porton of the total expenditure on annuities in the 1380s and 1390s went on annuities in the strict sense of the term. In the years covered by this table the average ratio between expenditure on indentured retainers and annuitants was 23:10. If we assume that this ratio was maintained after 1383, the total of £3,028 12s 3d spent on annuitants in the 'North Parts' in 1393–94 and in the 'South Parts' in 1392–93 can be made to yield a rough total of £2,110 from all the estates spent in these years on indentured

*Table 2   Numbers of indentures of retinue and grants of annuities,
and totals of expenditure covered by Gaunt registers
in the years 1372–1382*[18]

| Year | Indentures of Retinue | | | | | | | | | Annuities | |
| | Knights | | | Squires | | | Totals | | | Total | Total |
	Total	Total without peace-time fees	Total expenditure £ s d	Total	Total without peace-time fees	Total expenditure £ s d	No.	Without peace-time fees	Expenditure £ s d	No.	Expenditure £ s d
1372	11	2	280.0.0	22	2	225.0.0	33	4	505.0.0	30	94.10.0
1373	14	1	620.0.0	10	2	86.13.4	24	3	706.13.4	13	69.3.9
1374	4	0	213.6.8	3	1	13.6.8	7	1	226.13.4	18	86.17.6
1375	0	0	0	0	0	0	0	0	0	19	112.10.0
1380	3	2	20.0.0	3	3	0	6	5	20.0.0	1	5.0.0
1381	5	0	113.6.8	7	6	10.0.0	12	6	123.6.8	6	329.3.4
1382	3	1	30.0.0	3	3	0	6	4	30.0.0	5	10.13.4

retainers. It is possible to convert this figure into approximate totals of
knights and squires. The details of the surviving indentures that were made
after 1379 suggest average fees of £20 a year for a knight,[19] and £10 a
year for a squire.[20] These provide a reasonable basis for calculations. We
can also make the assumption that the retinue at this time contained knights
and squires in roughly equal proportions.[21] Such calculations produce a
total of seventy knights and seventy squires. But these figures must be
revised upwards. A few retainers were paid from Welsh revenues which
are not included in the 'valors'. More important, it is clear that some
knights and a high proportion of squires received no fee in time of peace.
We must also take into account the fact that Gaunt continued to recruit
retainers after Michaelmas 1394. Moreover, the details in Appendix III
suggest that most squires in these years may have receive ten marks, not
£10, a year. In the light of all these considerations we would not be far
wrong if we concluded that at the time of his death in February 1399 Gaunt
possessed a retinue totalling at least 200, perhaps 220, probably divided
in roughly equal proportions between knights and squires.[22]

The growth of this retinue is extremely difficult to chart, since, apart
from three indentures,[23] we have no evidence at all before 1371 and there
is a gap in our knowledge between the end of the register of 1372–76 and

the beginning of that of 1379–83. And the indentures that have survived through the confirmations made by Richard II and Henry IV represent only a portion of those made between 1383 and 1399. Even so, rough conclusions are possible. There are strong indications that the number of knights and squires retained by the duke for life before 1371 was well below the total during the next decade or so. In the course of 1372 and 1373 he recruited twenty-five knights and thirty-three squires, spending a total of £1,211 13s 4d in peacetime fees. Comparison of these figures with those in the valors of the late 80s and 90s and the conclusions derived from these documents suggests that 1372 and 1373 saw a deliberate effort to increase the size of the retinue, presumably in preparation for the great campaign in France of the latter year. This conclusion is supported by the extraordinarily high fees paid to some of the knights with whom indentures were made,[24] which suggest that the duke was making a special effort to attract knights of known judgement and leadership. A list[25] of those paid war fees in the early months of 1372 consists of twenty knights and fifty-five squires.[26] Even if not all those in the retinue early in 1372 are not included in this, these figures certainly indicate a total well below that achieved by the end of 1373, let alone the last years of John of Gaunt.

The information we possess from the register of 1379–83 suggests that these years did not see recruitment on the scale of 1372–73. At the same time the totals of annuities we can derive from the 'valors' of the 1390s suggest that the indenturing of knights and squires in that decade and the preceding one was by no means a replacement of services ended through death or other causes. It is unfortunate that the incidence of survival of receivers' accounts, 'valors' and copies of indentures in the mid-1380s is so sparse and sporadic as to preclude any effort at an assessment of the effects the duke's decision to prosecute on the battlefield his claim to the throne of Castile had on the recruitment of his retinue. But the evidence of some of the 'valors' does indicate that his ambitions in Gascony in the 1390s led to further efforts at recruitment. At any rate, there are strong indications that the total of knights and squires in his indentured retinue increased by a quarter or so between 1386 and 1399.

Notes

1   Neither the list of the retainers of the earl of Gloucester in 1267 (see above, p. 22) nor the livery roll of the earl of Devon in 1384–85 (see above, p. 19) is comparable. The former is not necessarily complete, while a high proportion of those listed in the latter did not consist of indentured retainers.

2   *JGRB*, i, 6–13.

3 Two are cancelled with a cross in the margin and one simply has a cross beside it.

4 None of these was described as dead. One had only a cross in the margin.

5 App. III(a), nos. 46–8.

6 It is the source of the list printed by S. Armitage-Smith, *John of Gaunt* (London, 1904), pp. 440–6. It is not necessary to suppose that it was compiled in connection with a particular campaign (*Cf*. Maddicott, *Thomas of Lancaster*, p. 44, n. 1).

7 PRO, DL 29/728/11980–6.

8 The valor for the 'North parts' for 1399–1400 (*ibid*., 11987) is not included because it contains grants made by Gaunt's son and heir as duke in August–September 1399 and during the first year of his reign as Henry IV.

9 The 'net values' have been calculated by deducting from the totals of rents and farms and all other revenues 'decayed' rents and all administrative costs and allowances, including fees and wages and repairs to local castles. The latter are the main explanation for the marked fluctuations in the 'net values'.

10 This is the term used in the valors: it includes both fees and annuities in the technical senses of these terms.

11 The 'South parts' does not include the duke's Welsh estates.

12 The totals in this and the following years include the entries provided at the end of each valor for manors and lands in the hands of individuals, except some worth £125 and £210 respectively in the hands of the earl of Derby and the duke of Gloucester. These have been excluded because they obviously relate to family settlements; but they did, of course, reduce net disposable income still further.

13 The receipts section for the Halton (Cheshire) receivership is damaged.

14 DL 28/3/2, 5.

15 App. III (a), nos. 54–6.

16 *Ibid*., (b), nos. 80–102.

17 The evidence of the surviving receivers' accounts is less reliable, since they often do not indicate whether a particular fee or annuity was being paid to an indentured retainer. But there are indications of an expansion in the expenditure on fees and annuities.

18 Figures are not provided for 1371 or 1379 because it is uncertain whether the respective registers cover the whole of these calendar years.

19 App.III (a), nos. 35–56.

20 *Ibid*., (b), nos. 46–102.

21 This is certainly supported by the list of 1379–86, if we deduct the thirty written in later hands.

22 McFarlane (*Nobility*, p. 102) stated that 'there were something like two hundred at a time on the duke's books', referring to the whole body of retainers. The figure of 200 in Maddicott, *Thomas of Lancaster*, p. 44, n. 4., attributed to McFarlane, wrongly mentions only knights.

23 App. III(a), nos. 1–3.

24 E.g., App. III(a), nos. 16, 18, 19, 20, 22, 25, 30.

25 *JGRA*, ii, 47–50 (no. 969).

26 Those who were obviously administrative officials or household officers are not included. It is assumed that the designation *dominus* means a knight and that the rest were squires (apart from a few whose status was obviously lower).

APPENDIX III

The surviving indentures of John Gaunt, duke of Lancaster, 1361–99

(a) Knights

Key to symbols:

B   mention as a 'bachelor' in the category of benefits indicated
D   with power of distraint
s preceded by a numeral   the number of squires sharing benefits in this category
c preceded by a numeral   the number of chamberlains sharing benefits in this category
WWB   wages of war or wages and food and drink (*autielx gages de guerre ou autrement autielx gages et bouche de court* as other knights, or 'bachelors', of his condition).

	Name	Date	In Time of Peace			In Time of War		
			Fee	Food and drink	Wages	Fee	Food and drink	Wages
1	Sir Hugh Hastings	16 May 1366	£20 D	x 2s 1c	x	166.13.4	–	x
2	Sir John d'Ipre the elder	8 Dec. 1367	20.0.0. D	–	–	20.0.0. D	–	–
3	Sir Gerard Useflete	1 Apr. 1370	20.0.0.	x B 1s 1c	x B 1s 1c	40.0.0.	x B 2s	–

	Name	Date	In Time of Peace			In Time of War		
			Fee	Food and drink	Wages	Fee	Food and drink	Wages
4	John, lord Neville of Raby	10 Nov. 1370	33.6.8.	x	–	333.6.8.	–	x as paid by king
5	Sir Walter Penhergard	10 Aug. 1371	–	–	–	26.13.4	–	x
6	Sir Richard Whitfield	3 Jan. 1372	–	x B 1s	x	20.0.0	–	x
7	John, lord Welles	12 Feb. 1372	20.0.0.	x B 1s 1c	x	30.0.0 1s	x B 1s	x
8	Sir Thomas Southward	1 May 1372	13.6.8.	–	x	20.0.0	–	x
9	Sir Thomas Dale	9 June 1372	20.0.0.	x 1s 1c	–	33.6.8	x 1s	x 1s
10	Sir Nicholas Longford	12 June 1372	40.0.0. D	–	–	40.0.0	–	x 1s
11	Sir Richard Northland	28 June 1372	20.0.0.	–	–	as other knights of his condition	.	x
12	Sir Thomas Ilderton	9 July 1372	20.0.0.	–	x 1s	33.6.8	–	x 1s
13	Sir William Cantelo	1 Aug. 1372	20.0.0.	–	–	40.0.0	–	x 2s
14	Sir Edmund Frithby	13 Aug. 1372	–	x	x B	20.0.0	–	x
15	Sir John Marmion	27 Aug. 1372	26.13.4. D	x B 1s 1c	–	26.13.4	x	x B 1 knight 2s

	Name	Date	In Time of Peace			In Time of War		
			Fee	Food and drink	Wages	Fee	Food and drink	Wages
16	Sir Walter Urswick	28 Aug. 1372	100.0.0.	–	–	100.0.0.	–	–
17	Sir Thomas Travers	20 Feb. 1373	20.0.0. D	–	x	26.13.4. D	–	x
18	Sir William Beauchamp	27 Feb. 1373	66. 13. 4. D	x 1s 1c	x	66.13.4.	–	x 1s
19	Sir Richard Burley	1 Mar. 1373	66.13.4.	–	x B	66.13.4.	–	x B
20	Sir Thomas FitzSimon	15 Mar. 1373	66.13.4 D	–	x 1s	66.13.4	–	x 1s
21	Sir Thomas Fichet	24 Mar. 1373	40.0.0 D	x 1s	–	40.0.0 D	–	x 1s
22	Sir Thomas Fog	24 Mar. 1373	66.13.4 D	–	x	66.13.4 D	–	x
23	Sir Roger Trumpington	24 Mar. 1373	20.0.0	–	x 1s	26.13.4	–	x 1s
24	Sir Roger Curzon	26 Mar. 1373	20.0.0	–	x 1s	26.13.4	–	x 1s
25	Sir John de Liniers	29 Apr. 1373	133.6.8	–	x	133.6.8	–	x
26	Sir Robert Clifton	9 May 1373	20.0.0	x	x	20.0.0	x	x
27	Sir Walter Blount	18 May 1373	33.6.8 D	–	x B	33.6.8 D	–	x B
28	Sir Thomas Dale	7 July 1373	20.0.0	x 1s 1c	x	20.0.0	x 1s	x
29	Sir Philip Denis	13 Nov. 1373	–	x	x	20.0.0	–	x

No	Name	Date	In Time of Peace			In Time of War		
			Fee	Food and drink	Wages	Fee	Food and drink	Wages
30	Sir Thomas Banastre	1373	46.13.4 D and lands	–	x B	46.13.4 D and lands	–	x B
31	Sir John Swinton	3 May 1374	40.0.0	x	x	40.0.0	–	x
32	Sir John Doddingsells	24 May 1374	40.0.0	x	x	40.0.0	–	x
33	Sir Otto Grandison	5 Aug. 1374	66.13.4	x 1s	x	66.13.4	x 1s	x
34	Sir John Gruer	5 Aug. 1374	66.13.4	x 1s	–	66.13.4	–	x
35	Sir William Hawley	1 Nov. 1379	13.6.8	x 1s	x	13.6.8	–	x B 1s
36	Sir John Thornbury	29 Nov. 1380	–	x	x	–	–	x B as paid by the king of England
37	Sir Thomas Erpingham	1380	20.0.0	x 1s	x	33.6.8		WWB
38	Sir Richard Balderston	1 Feb. 1381	13.6.8	x	x	6.13.4		WWB
39	Sir John Dabridgecourt	1 Aug. 1381	20.0.0	x 1s	x 1s	20.0.0		WWB
40	Sir Geoffrey Workesleigh	1 Aug. 1381	20.0.0	x 1s	x 1s	20.0.0		WWB

No	Name	Date	In Time of Peace			In Time of War		
			Fee	Food and drink	Wages	Fee	Food and drink	Wages
41	Sir William Frank	6 Sept. 1381	40.0.0	x B	x B	40.0.0	x	x as from the king of England
42	Sir William Lussy	8 Nov. 1381	20.0.0	x 1s	x 1s	20.0.0	WWB B	
43	Sir Baldwin Berford the son	5 Feb. 1382	20.0.0	x B	x B	20.0.0	WWB B	1s
44	Sir John d'Ipre the son	16 Feb. 1382	10.0.0	x B	x B	20.0.0	WWB B	
45	Sir Robert Charles	26 Oct. 1382	–	x	x	as from the king of England	–	B as taken from the king of England
46	Sir Thomas Wennesley	10 Dec. 1384	13.6.8	x	x	20.0.0	–	x B
47	Sir Ralph Brascebridge	4 Apr. 1385	–	x	x 1s	–	fees & wages 1sB	–
48	Sir Thomas Beek	2 Dec. 1386	20.0.0	x	x	20.0.0	WWB	
49	Sir Henry Green	6 Mar. 1391	33.6.8	x B	x B	33.6.8	x B	x B
50	Sir Nicholas Dabridgecourt	31 Aug. 1391	20.0.0	x	x	20.0.0	WWB B	
51	Sir Maurice Berkeley	2 Nov. 1391	20.0.0	x B 1s	x B	20.0.0	WWB B	

	Name	Date	In Time of Peace			In Time of War		
			Fee	Food and drink	Wages	Fee	Food and drink	Wages
52	Sir John Dabridgecourt (in replacement No. 40)	20 Apr. 1392	33.6.8 D	x B	x B	33.6.8	x B 1s	x B 1s
53	Sir Henry Houghton	6 Feb. 1393	20.0.0	x B	x B	20.0.0	x	x B
54	Sir Hugh Huse, 'bachelor'	7 Aug. 1397	20.0.0	x B	x B	20.0.0	x B	x B
55	Sir John Botiller, 'bachelor'	7 Aug. 1397	20.0.0	x B	x B	20.0.0	x B	x B
56	Sir Thomas Fleming	14 July 1398	13.6.8	x B	x B	13.6.8	x B	x B

(b) **Squires**

Key to symbols:
- — no benefits in category
- x benefits in category
- K the indenture includes arrangements that are to take effect if the squire is made a knight.

WWB wages of war or wages and food and drink (*autielx gages de guerre ou autrement autielx gages et bouche de court* as other squires of his condition).

	Name	Date	In Time of Peace			In Time of War		
			Fee	Food and drink	Wages	Fee	Food and drink	Wages
1	Nicholas Atherton	24 Mar. 1370	10.0.0	x	x	10.0.0	–	x
2	Stephen Pulham	6 Apr. 1371	–	x	x	13.6.8	–	x
3	Thomas Masterton	10 Aug. 1371	–	x	x	13.6.8	–	x
4	Richard Massy	10 Aug. 1371	10.0.0	–	–	10.0.0	–	x
5	Robert Standish	23 Jan. 1372	10.0.0	–	x	13.6.8	–	x
6	William Bradshaw K	28 Jan. 1372	10.0.0	–	–	13.6.8	–	x
7	John Swinton	29 Jan. 1372	20.0.0	x 1c	x 7 ½d.	20.0.0	–	x
8	Louis Reconches de Luce	31 Jan. 1372	10.0.0	–	–	10.0.0	–	–
9	Robert Beyville	3 Feb. 1372	–	x	x	13.6.8	–	x
10	Henry Ward	3 Feb. 1372	–	x	–	13.6.8	–	x
11	Robert Pilkington	10 Feb. 1372	13.6.8	–	x	13.6.8	–	x
12	Thomas Bradley	1 Mar. 1372	10.0.0	–	–	13.6.8	–	x
13	William Stanes	1 Mar. 1372	10.0.0	–	x	13.6.8	–	x
14	John Reynold	2 Mar. 1372	20.0.0	–	x	20.0.0	–	x

| Name | Date | In Time of Peace | | | In Time of War | | |
		Fee	Food and drink	Wages	Fee	Food and drink	Wages
15 John Talbot K	2 Mar. 1372	10.0.0	x	x	20.0.0	x	x
16 William Chetwynd K	10 May 1372	6.13.4	–	–	13.6.8	–	–
17 William Haybere	13 May 1372	10.0.0	x	x	13.6.8	–	x
18 Edward Beauchamp	26 June 1372	10.0.0	–	x	13.6.8	–	x
19 Richard Hoo	29 June 1372	10.0.0	–	x	13.6.8	–	x
20 John Sotherton	6 Jul 1372	6.13.4	–	x	13.6.8	–	x
21 John Holm	14 Jul. 1372	–	x	–	13.6.8	–	x
22 Raulyn d'Ipre	16 Jul. 1372	11.13.4 D	x	–	20.0.0 D	–	x
23 William Notton K	22 Jul. 1372	6.13.4	–	x	10.0.0	–	x
24 Richard Wirley	14 Aug. 1372	13.6.8	–	x	20.0.0	–	x
25 Thomas Goys	19 Aug. 1372	16.13.4	–	x	16.13.4	–	x
26 Robert Cansfield	30 Aug. 1372	10.0.0	–	x	10.0.0	–	x
27 John Colpepper	7 Dec. 1372	16.13.4	–	x	16.13.4	–	x
28 Adam Newsom	?? 1373	6.13.4	x	x	13.6.8	x	x

	Name	Date	In Time of Peace			In Time of War		
			Fee	Food and drink	Wages	Fee	Food and drink	Wages
29	Robert Hatfield	16 Mar. 1373	6.13.4	x	x	13.6.8	x	x
30	Edward Gerberge	18 Mar. 1373	13.6.8	–	x	13.6.8	–	x
31	Robert FitzRalph	19 Mar. 1373	20.0.0	–	x	20.0.0	–	x
32	Thomas Tutbury	12 Apr. 1373	13.6.8	x	x	13.6.8	x	x
33	William Chetwynd K	30 Apr. 1373	6.13.4	–	–	6.13.4	–	6.13.4
34	John Strange	13 May 1373	13.6.8	x	–	13.6.8	–	x
35	Madoc Fernyll	12 Jun. 1373	–	x	–	20.0.0	x	–
36	William Sudbury	27 Jun. 1373	–	x	–	13.6.8	x	x
37	Walter Oliver	9 Dec. 1373	6.13.4	x	x	6.13.4	x	x
38	Simkin Molyneux	15 Feb. 1374	6.13.4	x	x	10.0.0	x	x
39	Roger Pyrton	10 May 1374	6.13.4	x	x	10.0.0	x	x
40	Ellis Thursby	9 Jul. 1374	–	x	x	13.6.8	–	x
41	William Chetwynd	1 Apr. 1376	10.0.0	–	x	13.6.8	–	x
42	Peter Melbourne	24 Nov. 1376	10.0.0	x	–	10.0.0	x	x

	Name	Date	In Time of Peace			In Time of War		
			Fee	Food and drink	Wages	Fee	Food and drink	Wages
43	Thomas Eland	24 Feb. 1379	10.0.0	–	–	10.0.0	WWB	
44	Robert Rokeleigh	28 Oct. 1379	10.0.0	–	–	13.6.8	–	x
45	Thomas Bradley	1379	13.6.8	x	x	13.6.8	either food or wages as paid by king of England	
46	Ralph Radcliffe	20 Mar. 1380	–	x	x	13.6.8	–	x
47	Thomas Driffield	23 Jun. 1380	–	x	x	13.6.8	x	–
48	John Scargill K	23 Jun. 1380	–	x	x	13.6.8	x	–
49	William Gascrick	25 Sept. 1380	–	x	x	13.6.8	x	–
50	William Hervy	11 Feb. 1381	–	x	x	–	–	x
51	Thomas Berkeley	5 May 1381	–	x	x	–	wages or food	
52	John Gifford	5 May 1381	–	x	x	–	wages or food	
53	William Tunstall	24 Jul. 1381	–	x	x	–	–	x
54	Jenkin Pole	25 Sept. 1381	10.0.0	x	x	10.0.0	–	x
55	Richard Holland	21 Nov. 1381	–	x	x	fees, wages and food as the duke takes from the king of England		

	Name	Date	In Time of Peace			In Time of War		
			Fee	Food and drink	Wages	Fee	Food and drink	Wages
56	Thomas Trewennok	1 Dec. 1381	–	x	x	fees, wages and food as the duke takes from the king of England		
57	Peter Roos	16 Feb. 1382	–	x	x	–	food or wages as other squires	
58	Hugh Heywood	26 Oct. 1382	–	x	x	–	fees and wages or food as duke takes from the king of England	
59	Roger Perwich	29 Oct. 1382	–	x	x	–	fees and wages or food as duke takes from the king of England	
60	William Barwell	13 Apr. 1383	–	x	x	–	–	–
61	William Seymour	13 Jun. 1383	–	x	x	fees, wages and food as from the king of England		
62	William Newport	4 Dec. 1386	13.6.8	x	x	13.6.8	wages or food as other squires	
63	Thomas Popham	22 Jan. 1387	6.13.4	x	x	13.6.8	fees and wages of war and wages or food as other squires	
64	John Massey	22 Jul. 1387	6.13.4	x	x	6.13.4	wages of war or food *dedeins court* or wages *for de court*	
65	Richard Eton	26 Jul. 1387	6.13.4	x	x	6.13.4	wages of war or food *dedeins court* or wages *for de court*	

	Name	Date	In Time of Peace			In Time of War		
			Fee	Food and drink	Wages	Fee	Food and drink	Wages
66	John Cauncefield	1 Aug. 1387	6.13.4	x	x	6.13.4	wages of war or food *dedeins court* or wages *for de court*	
67	Robert Sherwin	1 Aug. 1387	–	x	x	6.13.4	wages of war or food *dedeins court* or wages *for de court*	
68	Nicholas Talbot	1 Sept. 1387	10.0.0	x	x	10.0.0	wages of war *dedeins court* or wages *for de court*	
69	John Hull	22 Nov. 1387	6.13.4	x	x	6.13.4	wages or food as other squires	
70	Richard Boyton	26 Mar. 1389	6.13.4	x	x	6.13.4	WWB	
71	Thomas Chaucer	26 Mar. 1389	6.13.4	x	x	6.13.4	WWB	
72	Thomas Dale	22 Sept. 1389	10.0.0	x	x	10.0.0	WWB	
73	John Swell	1 Jan. 1390	13.6.8	x	x	13.6.8	WWB	
74	John Rixton	10 Mar. 1390	10.0.0	x	x		WWB	
75	Robert Simeon	24 May 1390	13.6.8	x	x		WWB	

	Name	Date	In Time of Peace			In Time of War		
			Fee	Food and drink	Wages	Fee	Food and drink	Wages
76	Arnold Buade	6 Feb. 1391	10.0.0	x	x	10.0.0	x	x
77	Robert Urswick	20 Mar. 1391	10.0.0	x	x	10.0.0	WWB	
78	Thomas Gloucester	12 Nov. 1391	6.13.4	x	x	6.13.4	x	–
79	Robert Boleran	8 Jan. 1393	10.0.0	x	x	10.0.0	WWB	
80	John Corne-waille of Kilvert	12 Mar. 1395	13.6.8	x	x	13.6.8	x	x
81	John Chetwynd	24 Apr. 1395	6.13.4	x	x	6.13.4	WWB	
82	William Isnell	24 Apr. 1395	6.13.4	x	x	6.13.4	WWB	
83	John Merbury	20 Oct. 1395	6.13.4	x	x	6.13.4	WWB	
84	Eamon Yshel	7 Jan. 1396	10.0.0	x	x	10.0.0	x	x
85	Richard Clitheroe	13 Jan. 1396	6.13.4	x	x	6.13.4	WWB	
86	Richard Altrincham	19 May 1396	6.13.4	x	x	6.13.4	x	–
87	Edmund Barry	25 Dec. 1396	10.0.0	x	x	10.0.0	WWB	
88	Ivo Wyram	10 June 139	6.13.4	x	x	6.13.4	x	x
89	Nicholas Atherton	30 Sept. 1397	6.13.4	x	x	6.13.4	WWB	

	Name	Date	In Time of Peace			In Time of War		
			Fee	Food and drink	Wages	Fee	Food and drink	Wages
90	Matthew Cauncefield	1 Oct. 1397	6.13.4	x	x	6.13.4		WWB
91	William Hulme	2 Oct. 1397	6.13.4	x	x	6.13.4		WWB
92	Richard Newton	3 Oct. 1397	6.13.4	x	x	6.13.4		WWB
93	Thomas Holand	24 Feb. 1398	10.0.0.	x	x	10.0.0		WWB
94	Edmund Granchester	22 Mar. 1398	6.13.4	x	x	6.13.4		WWB
95	John Tybenham	10 Apr. 1398	5.0.0	x	x	5.0.0		WWB
96	Edmund Whitmore	5 May 1398	6.13.4	x	x	6.13.4		WWB
97	Robert Radcliffe	24 May 1398	missing	x	x	missing		WWB
98	John Broxtow	4 Jul. 1398	–	x	x	– –		WWB with fees
99	Walter son of Roger Corwan	17 Jul. 1398	6.13.4	x	x	6.13.4		WWB
100	Richard del Croke	29 Aug. 1398	6.13.4	x	x	6.13.4		WWB
101	Thomas Lucy	28 Dec. 1398	6.13.4	x	x	6.13.4		WWB
102	John Burford	2 Jan. 1399	6.13.4	x	x	6.13.4		WWB

Notes

(a)

1 Norfolk RO, MR 314/241/5.
2 Lewis, 'Gaunt indentures', p. 87, no. 1.
3 PRO, DL 42/15, f. 53.
4 Lewis, 'Gaunt indentures', pp. 88–90, no. 3.
5 *JGRA*, i, 294–5 (no. 784).
6 *Ibid.*, i, 293 (no. 782).
7 *Ibid.*, i, 298–9 (no. 788).
8 *Ibid.*, i, 311–2 (no. 805).
9 *Ibid.*, i, 310–1 (no. 804).
10 *Ibid.*, i, 310 (no. 803).
11 *Ibid.*, i, 312–3 (no. 806).
12 *Ibid.*, i, 313–4 (no. 807).
13 *Ibid.*, i, 332–3 (no. 833).
14 *Ibid.*, i, 324–5 (no. 822).
15 *Ibid.*, i, 322–3 (no. 819).
16 *Ibid.*, i, 325 (no. 823).
17 *Ibid.*, i, 333–4 (no. 834).
18 *Ibid.*, i, 330–2 (no. 832).
19 *Ibid.*, i, 334 (no. 835).
20 *Ibid.*, i, 336–7 (no. 838).
21 *Ibid.*, i, 340–1 (no. 845)
22 *Ibid.*, i, 309 (no. 802).
23 *Ibid.*, i, 342 (no. 848).
24 *Ibid,.*ii, 290 (no.775).
25 *Ibid.*, i, 337–8 (no. 841).
26 *Ibid.*, i, 2 (no. 863).
27 *Ibid.*, i, 347–8 (no. 855).
28 *Ibid.*, i, 349 (no. 857).
29 *Ibid.*, i, 328 (no. 829).
30 *Ibid.*, i, 342–3 (no. 849).
31 *Ibid.*, ii, 5–6 (no. 868). For the indenture he made as a squire, see below (b), no. 7.
32 *Ibid.*, ii, 6–7 (no. 869).
33 *Ibid.*, ii, 4 (no. 866).
34 *Ibid.*, ii, 4–5 (no. 867).
35 *JGRB*, i, 14–15 (no. 24).
36 *Ibid.*, i, 18 (no. 31).
37 *Ibid.*, i, 17–18 (no. 29).
38 *Ibid.*, i, 18 (no. 32).
39 *Ibid.*, i, 20 (no. 39).
40 *Ibid.*, i, 19–20 (no. 38).
41 *Ibid.*, i, 20 (no. 40).
42 *Ibid.*, i, 20–1 (no. 41).
43 *Ibid.*, i, 22–3 (no. 46).

44   *Ibid.*, i, 24 (no. 49).
45   *Ibid.*, i, 24 (no. 50).
46   Lewis, 'Gaunt indentures', pp. 92–3 (no. 6).
47   Nottingham UL, Mi 10, calendared in *HMC* (Middleton), lxix. 99.
48   Lewis, 'Gaunt indentures', pp. 93–4 (no. 7).
49   *Ibid.*, pp. 102–3 (no. 23).
50   PRO, DL 42/15, f. 41.
51   Lewis, 'Gaunt indentures', p. 103 (no. 24).
52   *Ibid.*, pp. 104–5 (no. 25).
53   *Ibid.*, p. 105 (no. 26).
54   *Ibid.*, pp. 105–6 (no. 27).
55   *Ibid.*, pp. 108–9 (no. 34).
56   *Ibid.*, p. 111 (no. 38).

(b)

1   *Ibid.*, pp. 87–8 (no. 2).
2   *JGRA* i, 290–1 (no. 777).
3   *Ibid.*, i, 292 (no. 779).
4   *Ibid.*, i, 291–2 (no. 778).
5   *Ibid.*, i, 297–8 (no. 787).
6   *Ibid.*, i, 302–3 (no. 793).
7   *Ibid.*, i, 299–300 (no. 789).
8   *Ibid.*, i, 302 (no. 792).
9   *Ibid.*, i, 318–19 (no. 813).
10   *Ibid.*, i, 304 (no. 795).
11   *Ibid.*, i, 303 (no. 794).
12   *Ibid.*, i, 304–5 (no. 796).
13   *Ibid.*, i, 307 (no. 799).
14   *Ibid.*, i, 305–6 (no. 797).
15   *Ibid.*, i, 307–8 (no. 800).
16   *Ibid.*, i, 315–6 (no. 809).
17   *Ibid.*, i, 317–8 (no. 812).
18   *Ibid.*, i, 319–20 (no. 815).
19   *Ibid.*, i, 316–7 (no. 811).
20   *Ibid.*, i, 316 (no. 810); PRO, DL 42/15, f, 53v.
21   *JGRA* i, 319 (no. 814).
22   *Ibid.*, i, 314–5 (no. 808).
23   *Ibid.*, i, 320–1 (no. 816).
24   *Ibid.*, i, 323–4 (no. 820).
25   *Ibid.*, i, 301 (no. 791).
26   *Ibid.*, i, 326 (no. 825).
27   *Ibid.*, i, 328–9 (no. 830).
28   *Ibid.*, i, 344–5 (no. 851). The dating clause is missing from the Register's copy. He was, however, already retained for life by 28 January 1372 (*ibid.*, ii. 23–4 [no. 916]). Since the latter document was a warrant directing payment of his annual fee, it has been assumed that the indenture was made in the course of that month.

29 *Ibid.*, i, 335 (no. 837).
30 *Ibid.*, i, 339 (no. 843).
31 *Ibid.*, i, 340 (no. 844).
32 *Ibid.*, i, 345–6 (no. 852).
33 *Ibid.*, i, 344 (no. 850) This took the place of an earlier indenture (no. 16 above). the new indenture added wages of ten marks in time of war and also provided increased benefits in the event that Chetwynd became a knight.
34 *Ibid.*, i, 346 (no. 853).
35 *Ibid.*, i, 338–9 (no. 842).
36 *Ibid.*, i, 348–9 (no. 856).
37 *Ibid.*, i, 349–50 (no. 858).
38 *Ibid.*, ii, 2–3 (no. 864).
39 *Ibid.*, ii, 7 (no. 870).
40 *Ibid.*, ii, 3–4 (no. 865).
41 Lewis, 'Gaunt indentures', pp. 90–1 (no. 4). This indenture took the place of a predecessor (no. 33 above) which Chetwynd had lost. It was, however, also stated that the duke wished to increase his benefits.
42 Lewis, 'Gaunt indentures', p. 91 (no. 50); PRO, DL 42/15, f. Iv.
43 PRO, DL 42/15, f. 45.
44 *JGRB*, i, 13–14 (no. 23).
45 *Ibid.*, i, 16 (no. 26).
46 *Ibid.*, i, 18–19 (no. 34).
47 *Ibid.*, i, 17 (no. 28).
48 *Ibid.*, i, 16–17 (no. 27).
49 *Ibid.*, i, 18 (no. 30).
50 *Ibid.*, i, 18 (no. 33).
51 *Ibid.*, i, 19 (no. 35).
52 *Ibid.*, i, 19 (no. 36).
53 *Ibid.*, i, 19 (no. 37).
54 *Ibid.*, i, 21–2 (no. 45).
55 *Ibid.*, i, 21 (no. 42).
56 *Ibid.*, i, 21 (no. 43).
57 *Ibid.*, i, 23 (no. 47).
58 *Ibid.*, i, 24 (no. 51).
59 *Ibid.*, i, 24–5 (no. 52).
60 *Ibid.*, i, 25 (no. 54).
61 *Ibid.*, i, 21 (no. 44).
62 Lewis, 'Gaunt indentures', p. 94 (no. 8).
63 *Ibid.*, p. 95 (no. 9).
64 *Ibid.*, pp. 95–6 (no. 10).
65 *Ibid.*, p. 96 (no. 11).
66 *Ibid.*, p. 96 (no. 12).
67 *Ibid.*, p. 96 (no. 13).
68 *Ibid.*, p. 97 (no. 14).
69 *Ibid.*, p. 97 (no. 15).
70 *Ibid.*, pp. 97–8 (no. 16).
71 *Ibid.*, p. 98 (no. 17).
72 *Ibid.*, pp. 98–9 (no. 18).

73 *Ibid.*, pp. 99–100 (no. 19).
74 *Ibid.*, p. 100 (no. 20).
75 *Ibid.*, o, 101 (no. 21).
76 *Ibid.*, pp. 101–2 (no. 22).
77 *Ibid.*, p. 106 (no. 28).
78 PRO, DL 42/15, f. 45v.
79 *Ibid.*, f. 60.
80 *Ibid.*, f. 44v.
81 Lewis, 'Gaunt indentures', pp. 106–7 (no. 29).
82 *Ibid.*, p. 107 (no. 30); PRO, DL 42/15, f. 47v.
83 *Ibid.*, f. 46v.
84 *Ibid.*, f. 40v.
85 *Ibid.*, f. 47.
86 *Ibid.*, f. 43v.
87 Lewis, 'Gaunt indentures', p. 107 (no. 31).
88 *Ibid.*, p. 108 (no. 32).
89 *Ibid.*, p. 109 (no. 34).
90 *Ibid.*, p. 110 (no. 35).
91 *Ibid.*, p. 110 (no. 36).
92 PRO DL 42/15, f. 58v.
93 *Ibid.*, f. 58.
94 *Ibid.*, f. 59v.
95 Lewis, 'Gaunt indentures', p. 110 (no. 37).
96 PRO, DL 42/15, f. 48.
97 *Ibid.*, f. 46.
98 Nottingham University Library, Middleton MSS, Mi. f 10.
99 Lewis, 'Gaunt indentures', p. 111 (no. 39).
100 *Ibid.*, p. 111 (no. 40).
101 *Ibid.*, p. 111 (no. 41).
102 *Ibid.*, p. 111 (no. 42).

INDEX OF NAMES AND PLACES

INDEX OF SUBJECTS